D0948457

Events on the battlefields of the Pacific War were not only out-growths of technology and tactical doctrine, but also the products of cultural myth and imagination. A neglected aspect of the history of Marine Corps operations against Imperial Japan has been any close study of how the marines themselves shaped the landscape of the battlefields on which they created new institutional legends. Marines projected ideas and assumptions about themselves and their enemy onto people, situations, and events throughout the war, and thereby gave life to formerly abstract ideas and molded their behavior to expectations.

Focusing specifically on the First Marine Division, this study draws on a broad range of approaches to its subject. The book begins with a look at the legacy of the Marine Corps on the eve of Pearl Harbor, and then turns to gender studies to shed light on the methods of "making" marines. At the heart of the book are close examinations of how three broad categories of myth and imagination directly affected the First Division's campaigns on Guadalcanal, Peleliu, and Okinawa. The study concludes by considering what happened to the myths and images of the Pacific War in the Korean War, and how they have been preserved in American society up to the present.

AMERICAN SAMURAI

AMERICAN SAMURAI

*MYTH, IMAGINATION, AND THE CONDUCT OF BATTLE
IN THE FIRST MARINE DIVISION, 1941–1951*

CRAIG M. CAMERON
Old Dominion University

CAMBRIDGE
UNIVERSITY PRESS

Published by the Press Syndicate of the University of Cambridge
The Pitt Building, Trumpington Street, Cambridge CB2 1RP
40 West 20th Street, New York, NY 10011–4211, USA
10 Stamford Road, Oakleigh, Melbourne 3166, Australia

© Cambridge University Press 1994

First published 1994

Printed in the United States of America

Library of Congress Cataloging-in-Publication Data
Cameron, Craig M., 1958–
American samurai : myth, imagination, and the conduct of battle in
the First Marine Division, 1941–1951 / Craig M. Cameron.
p.   cm.
Based on the author's thesis (Ph.D.)–University of Chicago,
1990.
Includes bibliographical references.
ISBN 0-521-44168-4
1. United States. Marine Corps. Division. 1st. 2. War–
Psychological aspects. 3. War–Mythology. I. Title.
VE23.22 1stC36   1994
359.9'6'09048–dc20   93-10530

A catalog record for this book is available from the British Library.

ISBN 0–521–44168–4 hardback

To My Parents,
Betty and Dean Cameron

CONTENTS

ILLUSTRATIONS AND TABLES

ILLUSTRATIONS AND TABLES

Tables

PREFACE

The combination of myth and imagination on the one hand and the conduct of ground warfare on the other is not the most natural in traditional Western thought. In writing about their interrelationships and discussing them with other scholars and students, I have often been left with the impression that such a study tends to slip between the cracks of various subspecialties within the historical discipline. I offer a brief note of clarification here in order to avoid misplaced expectations of what follows and to clarify the nature of the book. As a piece of military history, this book does not conform to conventional narrative forms centered on a particular unit, service, campaign, or even a single war. It is not a social history "from the ground up" or an operational history except in the indirect sense of relating myths and imaginary constructions of the battlefield to actual events and decisions. This book is not about the First Marine Division per se: it is about myth and imagination within the First Marine Division. The categories into which these myths and images can be placed are nearly universally shared and are what give the "American samurai" some occasionally close similarities to their Japanese counterparts. Parallels present themselves in many places, with the experiences of the French colonial light infantry and repeatedly with the language and images mobilized by the Germans on the Eastern Front. What sets the marines apart from those cases are the differences in specific context and the cultural responses to the perceived threats. Strong traditionalists among military historians may find the scope of this project too broad and amorphous. Those with a special fondness for an instrumental approach have been disconcerted that definitions are often imprecise and that so many arguments cannot be sustained by definitive, incontrovertible proof of the kind that underpins other types of military history. Such evidential difficulties are an inherent drawback in dealing with cultural and social myth and imagination, and in places argument by inference is necessarily the only recourse.

In contrast to the miltary historians, social historians and cultural

xi

anthropologists may find the scope of this work too narrow. Rather than using the First Marine Division as a case study, some have advocated expanding it to cover the entire Marine Corps experience in the Pacific War, or even including the Army as well. Unfortunately, it is exactly this sort of broad homogenization that dilutes and devalues most cultural and social histories related to military topics. Specific contexts are crucial in establishing bridges between cultural imagination and actual battlefield behavior. Generalizations destroy such connections. All historians establish artificial barriers, and I am as vulnerable to charges of intellectual gerrymandering as anyone, but to stray too far from the experiences of the First Marine Division would undermine the particularistic imaginary constructions that are my subject. With these points understood at the outset, perhaps some of the old debates can be shifted to new ground.

It is a pleasant obligation to acknowledge here those individuals and organizations that have helped me in formulating and revising my ideas and conducting my research. Old Dominion University awarded me a Summer Research Fellowship Grant and a yearlong release to take a postdoctoral fellowship and complete my work. The Department of History provided both collegial support as well as support for some of the production costs. As a 1991–1992 John M. Olin Postdoctoral Fellow at Yale University, I was freed from all teaching responsibilities and able to devote a full year to finishing revisions of the manuscript. To that end, the scholarly atmosphere in the International Security Programs, the outstanding libraries, and generous research funds were important and greatly appreciated. The Marine Corps Historical Foundation provided substantial funding through their dissertation fellowship program and then extended to me a second research grant so I could follow through on my revisions.

Many archivists, curators, and librarians have helped me along the way. The entire staff at the Marine Corps Historical Center, Washington Navy Yard, were very kind and professional in their assistance and made the center a most congenial and fruitful place to conduct research. In particular, before their departures, Joyce E. Bonnett, as head of the archives section, and J. Michael Miller, curator of the personal papers collection, repeatedly demonstrated their intimate knowledge of their respective holdings and helped greatly with their suggestions for finding the materials I sought. Head Librarian Evelyn A. Englander and Jack Dyer, curator of the Marine Corps Art Collection, were also friendly and went out of their way to help. The staff in the archives section at the U.S. Army

Military History Institute, Carlisle Barracks, enabled me to make the most of the short time I was able to spend there. John Barnett, curator of the Naval Art Collection, U.S. Naval Historical Center, Ron Lunn of the Marine Corps Association, and Verne E. Schwartz of the Army Art Activity, U.S. Army Center for Military History, all helped me to assemble useful graphic materials. Deborah L. Miller and Susan T. Cooke of the Graphic Arts Department at Old Dominion University demonstrated great patience and skill in reworking the maps into their present form.

Among individuals inside the academy I owe special thanks to my dissertation director, Michael Geyer, whose conceptual insights and questions helped me give form to this book. Omer Bartov, Bruce Cumings, Akira Iriye, Michael Sherry, and John Shy all toiled through the complete manuscript in one or another of its various stages and contributed their own insights and often highly detailed suggestions. Carl Boyd, my colleague at Old Dominion, offered a broad range of material and moral support and never failed to provide sound advice.

I am indebted to Frank Smith, Russell Hahn, and Pamela J. Bruton for their meticulous attention to the editing and production of the book. Personal notes of thanks are due to Maxine Pilkington and to Becky and Arthur Amiot. And finally, I am most grateful to my wife, Lynn, who accepted uncomplainingly burdens far more onerous than mine during my extended absences and long preoccupation with this project.

AMERICAN SAMURAI

INTRODUCTION
IMAGERY AND INSTRUMENTALITY IN WAR

"The sincere admiration of the entire Third Fleet is yours for the hill[-]blasting, cave[-]smashing extermination of 11,000 slant-eyed gophers. It has been a tough job extremely well done." So read Admiral William F. Halsey's congratulatory message to the troops who had seized the island of Peleliu in October 1944. Coming from one of the most outspokenly racist officers in the Navy, Halsey's epithet might be dismissed as nothing more, perhaps, than an example of typical wartime hyperbole and personal bombast except for the apparent coincidence that the language and imagery used by Halsey find echoes throughout the ranks of the American military services among those who contributed directly to the barbarization of the Pacific War. Ernie Pyle, unofficial voice of the common GIs in the European theater of operations, recorded his impressions after he traveled to the Pacific in early 1945 and spoke at length with soldiers, sailors, marines, and airmen about the enemy: "In Europe we felt our enemies, horrible and deadly as they were, were still people. But out here I gathered that the Japanese were looked upon as something subhuman and repulsive; the way some people feel about cockroaches or mice." Simply seeing a group of prisoners, Pyle wrote, "gave me the creeps, and I wanted to take a mental bath after looking at them."[1]

Whether a fleet admiral in command of devastating fast carrier raids on the Japanese home islands or a common rifleman personally confronting "slant-eyed gophers" on Peleliu and elsewhere, what these Americans thought about the enemy, themselves, and the world around them shaped the character of the Pacific War. Combat between the Americans and Japanese was conducted with tremendous intensity and frequently punctuated by acts of savage barbarism, whether measured on the grand scale, like the Bataan

---

1 Halsey message is quoted in letter dated 14 May 1947 from Paul J. Mueller to Admiral William F. Halsey; Paul J. Mueller Papers, U.S. Army Military History Institute, Carlisle Barracks. Ernie Pyle, *Last Chapter* (New York: Henry Holt, 1945), 5. Having survived some of the worst fighting in Europe, Pyle's death on Ie Shima seemed to confirm the images he used here to describe the Japanese.

1

death march and the bombing of Hiroshima, or on the level of the individual who collected bones or ears as trophies from the enemy dead.[2] What is left inadequately explored – indeed, often unquestioned – is how the barbarization of the war related to the often abstract images men carried onto its battlefields. Myth and imagination preceded and gave form to action by shaping expectations, and when combatants projected their assumptions onto people, events, and situations, they molded the landscape of their battlefields. The reification of abstract images gave them a historical identity and deadly role of their own. Any attempt to address the subject of the barbarization of the war requires closer consideration than hitherto given to the precise relationship among the acts themselves, the operative instrumentalities of war – those elements governed by putatively rational rules included under the general rubric of "doctrine" – and the underlying images and myths that determined the development and employment of the instrumentalities themselves.[3]

More than a century before the "Fat Boy" culminated the slaughter of the Pacific War in a blinding flash of light, the Prussian military theorist Carl von Clausewitz wrestled with ideas about the nature of war and violence that defied exact or reassuring combination. How, he asked himself, do you define war, "a true chameleon" that changes color to match its changing background. In partial answer, he listed the composite characteristics that make war distinct from any other human endeavor:

> As a total phenomenon, its dominant tendencies always make war a paradoxical trinity – composed of primordial violence, hatred, and enmity, which are to be regarded as a blind natural force; of the play of chance and probability within which the creative spirit is free to roam; and of its elements of subordination, as an instrument of policy, which makes it subject to reason alone.[4]

2 James J. Weingartner, "Trophies of War: U.S. Troops and the Mutilation of Japanese War Dead, 1941–1945," *Pacific Historical Review* 61 (February 1992): 53–67.
3 John Dower's study *War without Mercy* (New York: Pantheon, 1986) examines graphic and verbal images in both Japan and the United States to demonstrate "how stereotyped and often blatantly racist thinking contributed to poor military intelligence and planning, atrocious behavior, and the adoption of exterminationist policies" (x). The scope of Dower's study, however, does not include linking clearly the images he discusses, which were intended primarily for the consumption of civilians and raw recruits, to military doctrine and day-to-day behavior on the battlefield.
4 Carl von Clausewitz, *On War*, edited and translated by Michael Howard and Peter Paret (Princeton: Princeton University Press, 1984), 89.

Nobody who had fought across the hellish landscape of Iwo Jima, watched kamikaze aircraft run the gauntlet of fire to hurtle into American warships, or witnessed from the ground the immolation of tens of thousands of civilians in mass incendiary raids would question the elemental power of Clausewitz's first characteristic. Clausewitz himself, however, by dismissing wartime hatred as a "natural force," effectively placed it beyond human control. He thereby dismembered his trinity and created a bipolar framework – the more familiar war as an art and a science – upon which he then erected his theory. Yet the Pacific War witnessed the mobilization of ideas and images for the express purpose of stirring up the elemental force of wartime hatred and harnessing it to military policy. Whether in the context of the Pacific War or some other specific case, one challenge for military thinkers and historians today is to examine more closely the point at which all three elements of Clausewitz's trinity meet.

Historical tradition, like Clausewitz's theory, has kept the individual elements artificially separate and compartmentalized. It would be unfair to hold Clausewitz responsible for this shortcoming, because he was understandably constrained by his interest in explicating a theory of broad applicability. Nevertheless, he represents better than anyone else the process by which this occurred. Giving careful consideration to the distinctions between art and science as applied to war, Clausewitz vaguely defined the object of art as "creative ability" and that of science as "pure knowledge." In the best Hegelian dialectic, he then concluded that war was neither art nor science but a synthesis of the two and distinct from both. From the nagging question of how the elements actually combined, he sought refuge in two ways: first, he united the art and science of war in special individuals possessed of military genius; and second, he swept the messier aspects under the accommodating rug he labeled "moral factors." Clausewitz plainly recognized that the towering majority of soldiers are not possessed of Napoleonic genius and that "moral factors" defied neat categorization or thorough treatment, but he had to settle for frequent, often pithy, admonitions not to ignore such intangibles while concentrating on the scientific principles.[5] For Americans in general,

5 The elements recur throughout Clausewitz's work, but he most clearly states his arguments in Book 1, Chapter 1, "What Is War?"; Chapter 3, "On Military Genius"; Book 2, Chapter 3, "Art of War or Science of War"; and Book 3, Chapters 3–5, on moral factors. He warns against overemphasizing military genius, "which is above all rules; which amounts to admitting that rules are not only made for idiots, but are idiotic in themselves" (184). He likewise writes that probing the moral factors "like a diligent professor" "all too easily leads to plat-

as for Clausewitz in particular, reliance on a dualistic universe of art and science, mental and material, good and evil, has given rise to some very problematic historical thinking that has frequently spilled over into events.

According to one Clausewitzian dictum, whether on a grand strategic scale or at the level of battle, the selection of political goals or military objectives dictates the level of force used to attain them. To explain events on the Pacific battlefields, however, requires looking beyond the objectives enunciated in abstract, rational plans to grasp as well the unofficial goals or objectives pursued by the men charged with performing the missions. The latter virtually always had an agenda that diverged radically from the Clausewitzian ideal, with profound ramifications on the conduct of battle. Or as Clausewitz wrote in a typical corrective against leaping to easy generalizations, "we must face the fact that war and its forms result from ideas, emotions, and conditions prevailing at the time."[6]

In the course of the Pacific War, Americans, like the Japanese, violated many traditionally accepted limits on the exercise of force such as sparing enemy wounded or prisoners and distinguishing between uniformed combatants and civilian noncombatants.[7] Refusals to take prisoners might be dismissed as isolated acts of barbarity arising from the "passions of battle," but the decisions to employ unrestricted submarine warfare and indiscriminate strategic bombing by means of mass incendiary raids were systematized, approved policies that carried beyond former limits placed on the use of violence. Did these policies represent a temporary expansion of such boundaries or their breakdown altogether?

How this question has been answered illustrates an important problem that has plagued military historiography. The complex relationship among historical acts, instrumentality, and underlying purposiveness has become fragmented in contemporary histories. Consider those histories that focus on aspects of war supposedly governed by "rational" rules and conforming to Clausewitz's dis-

itudes," and "unwittingly we find ourselves proclaiming what everybody knows" (185).
6 Ibid., 580. A slightly different translation of this passage (Anatol Rapoport, ed., Penguin, 1968) reads: "we shall have to grasp that the idea of War, and the form which we give it, proceeds from ideas, feelings, and circumstances which dominate for the moment" (369–70).
7 Primarily in the Anglo–German context, Geoffrey Best discusses traditions and precedents concerning the subjects of "soldiers and civilians," "sea war and the civilian," and "aerial bombardment" in *Humanity in Warfare* (New York: Columbia University Press, 1980), 217–24, 240–41, 261–85.

tinction of the "scientific" side of military thought, to which I will hereafter refer as instrumental histories. Uniformed writers and official historians are quintessential "instrumentalists." They invariably direct their attention to such issues as the organization, equipment, and the doctrinal foundations of armies for the purpose of instituting reforms based on their historical studies or publicizing the accomplishments of the services. Since source materials on these topics are usually ample given the profusion of documents militaries manufacture, especially in this century, staff histories may appear, if not convincingly "objective,"[8] at least "scientific."[9] The conventional instrumentalist argument maintains that unrestricted submarine warfare and strategic bombing were rational policies arising simply from the concatenation of technological innovation and grand strategic aims. Likewise, the hill-blasting and cave-smashing side of the Peleliu battle is easily explained in most American histories of the subject by focusing on the weapons, tactics, organization, and logistics – the instrumentalities that enabled the soldiers and marines literally to burn and blast the island landscape, along with those who happened to occupy it.[10] But how were these instrumental or technocratic choices made? Assumptions made, for instance, about how long the Japanese would resist profoundly affected the Peleliu campaign; as did the interservice rivalry between the Marine Corps and Army, fueled by pride and resentment – themselves the products of myths and images.

If instrumental history, representing the "science" of war, often falls short in explaining the forms of combat and battlefield behavior, simple battle narrative, more appropriately exploring the realm of war as art, seldom does much better. Relating the contributions of chance, spirit, military genius, and moral virtue, tra-

8 The problems of objectivity and thoroughness among staff historians associated with specific institutional factions go beyond the scope of my discussion here but are introduced well in Michael Howard, "The Use and Abuse of Military History," *Royal United Service Institute Journal* 107 (February 1962): 4–8.
9 Just as theorists like Clausewitz and Jomini were the products of the Age of Reason, so too did the mantle of scientific rationality surrounding the Rankian school transform military history in the late nineteenth century from a hobby of dilettantes into an instrument of policy that remains with us, in different form, to this day. See Gordon A. Craig, "Delbrück: The Military Historian," in Peter Paret, ed., *Makers of Modern Strategy* (Princeton: Princeton University Press, 1986), 326–53.
10 Representative of these conventional histories are Samuel Eliot Morison, *Two Ocean War* (Boston: Houghton Mifflin, 1963), 493–512; United States Air Force, Historical Division, *The Army Air Forces in World War II*, edited by Wesley Frank Craven and James Lea Cate, vol. 5, *The Pacific: Matterhorn to Nagasaki* (Chicago: University of Chicago Press, 1953), 608–27; and Frank O. Hough, *The Island War* (Philadelphia: J. B. Lippincott, 1947), 291–313.

ditional narrative sounds the vicarious call to arms with riveting and colorful accounts, just as staff histories, neatly dissecting plans and movements, emerge from the smoke and bedlam of the battlefield to bring order. Both historical methods clearly lay the groundwork for further scholarly development, but too often the best books inspire derivative reprises of the same stories without any new insights. John Keegan details well the deficiencies that have plagued what he labels "battle pieces." Military historians have long employed euphemism, unstudied misrepresentation, and calculated omission to hide or skirt around disagreeable, unattractive, or complex aspects of combat.[11] Identifying the shortcomings of traditional approaches, however, has proved easier than redressing them.

As Keegan observes, the real dilemma plaguing military historiography does not lie exclusively with an incomplete and antiseptic view of the battlefield itself; it arises also from historians' neglect of internalized ideas and values and the myths and images to which they give rise.[12] Myths as well as machine guns can be highly effective weapons on the battlefield, but the former, being intangibles, are difficult to work with and by definition highly subjective. For these reasons ideas and images are grossly oversimplified or shunned altogether by uniformed and official historians.[13] A balanced interpretation and analysis of any military subject require understanding that seemingly scientific or rational decisions are the product of, and in turn affect, myth and imagination. The trinity Clausewitz identifies is interactive and integrative.

11 John Keegan, *The Face of Battle* (New York: Viking Press, 1976). The historiographical first chapter remains among the best essays on the subject of writing operational military history.
12 Keegan does an excellent job of weaving a vast amount of detail into an interesting and enjoyable narrative, setting a new standard of technical accuracy and directness in the writing of operational history. But although he carries the "battle piece" to new heights of descriptive detail, he concentrates on the empirical aspects of his subject without developing the more problematic conceptual aspect he identifies. For examples see his brief references to British and Commonwealth troops' refusals to take prisoners or his abbreviated treatment of the social origins, recruitment, and training of the Pals battalions (ibid., 48–51, 215–25).
13 Machine guns are the subject of a fascinating history that blends the mythic and instrumental aspects of war to explain why there was so much opposition to their development. Although it was a fabulously useful technological innovation, the machine gun aroused great and lasting opposition for "dehumanizing" combat and robbing it of its moral character. But chivalric or heroic images did not disappear with widespread use of the machine gun in the Great War; instead, praise was frequently heaped upon the enemy's machine gunners for their courage and coolness, as if to attribute the terrific carnage to human, morally responsible agents rather than the machines they served. John Ellis, *The Social History of the Machine Gun* (New York: Arno Press, 1981).

The organization of mass violence in war revolves simultaneously around both personal and collective experience. Campaign histories can be misleading when they reduce individuals
who plan and conduct battle to their institutional and group
identities to the exclusion of their personal attitudes. At the same
time, even soldiers who view their enemies as subhumans act
within the framework of an organized military service. The reification of myth and imagination, however unrealistic they may
be, often explains events, as Clausewitz suggested, that are in-
comprehensible according to any military logic. In contrast to the
logic imparted to events in instrumental histories, impressionistic,
anecdotal recollections, as compiled in Studs Terkel's Pulitzer
Prize–winning oral history, "The Good War," offer vivid vignettes,
but they seldom establish a context in which to interpret events.[14]
Synthesizing the two extremes reveals the extent to which the
rationalized and systematized management of war arose in reaction to a mythic understanding of events.

The best history to date to provide such a detailed synthesis
linking American mythology and imagination with the development of strategic thought and operational decision making is Michael Sherry's *The Rise of American Air Power*. Sherry argues
convincingly that the origins of air power are to be found in the
American collective imagination: "The bomber was the product of
extravagant dreams and dark forebodings about the role it might
play in war and peace." Significantly, what Sherry labels the "creation of Armageddon" reached its destructive apotheosis against
Japan: not in the atomic bombings of August 1945 but in the mass
incendiary raids that began in March. Military leaders, politicians,
and the American public all contributed to the devastation visited
on Japanese society. The use of the atomic bombs, like the history
of strategic bombing, "resulted from choices but not from a moment of choice. Both were the products of a slow accretion of large
fears, thoughtless assumptions, and incremental decisions." The
same arguments apply to the marines' role in the ground war. To
paraphrase Sherry, histories of the marines have been written from
other perspectives – tactics, technologies, organizations, and campaigns – and these elements must be accounted for, but practical
developments were usually secondary to imagination in shaping
ground combat.[15]

The trick for historians is to identify the vast array of ideas
and images that may have influenced operations in such unpre-

14 Studs Terkel, *"The Good War"* (New York: Pantheon, 1984).
15 Michael S. Sherry, *The Rise of American Air Power* (New Haven: Yale University
    Press, 1987), x–xi, 363.

dictable ways. Given the scope and elusive nature of the problem, there can be no definitive, comprehensive solutions; instead, clues to what ideas lay behind various policies and actions are often hidden after the manner of Poe's purloined letter. Language, such as that contained in Halsey's message, was a powerful tool for generating and reshaping images. Moreover, such images could directly alter perceptions and behavior, a fact certainly not lost on the Japanese, who very carefully intertwined linguistics with traditional myth to produce imagery supporting the prosecution of the war.[16] The links between images, ideology, and history are inseparable, or as one scholar of the subject, W. J. T. Mitchell, writes,

> Images are not just a particular kind of sign, but something like an actor on the historical stage, a presence or character endowed with legendary status, a history that parallels and participates in the stories we tell ourselves about our own evolution from creatures "made in the image" of a creator, to creatures who make themselves and their world in their own image.[17]

Although images should not be elevated to the status of autonomous "actors" removed from human control, they might accurately be described as props or costumes for the historical players. Imaginary constructs were key throughout the Pacific War: in precipitating it, in shaping the way it was fought on the battlefield, and in restoring a new equilibrium once peace returned.

Imaginary constructions – groups of images, often of more than one type – varied in form and content and derived from several sources. Mitchell separates images into rough categories, including graphic representations (pictures, photographs), perceptual (appearances, sense data), mental (dreams, memories, ideas), and verbal (metaphors, descriptions). Paralleling the duality between "objective" and "subjective" in military histories, the first two are, arguably, the more "objective" or at least publicly shared images, and, in contrast, the last two are obviously solely creations of the individual mind.[18] All images, however, are perceived and interpreted differently, depending on the background and experiences of the observer and on the specific circumstances under which the images are encountered. The contextual element is particularly

16 For a specific example see Dower's discussion of the so-called Kyoto School of ideologues (*War without Mercy*, 226–28). A more general polemic on the subject is Saburō Ienaga, *The Pacific War, 1931–1945* (New York: Pantheon, 1978).
17 W. J. T. Mitchell, *Iconology* (Chicago: University of Chicago Press, 1986), 9.
18 Ibid., 10–13.

important for historians who explore the influence of images on behavior.

An excellent contribution to the subject of soldiers' imaginary construction and ordering of their world is Eric J. Leed's book *No Man's Land: Combat and Identity in the First World War*. Far from obscuring the true nature of war, Leed maintains, myth and imagination often serve to amplify it:

> [I]t is arguable that, in general, the myths and fantasies of war cannot be regarded as false imprints of phenomenal realities. They were the necessary articulation of the combatant's experience of realities.... The technological actualities [of the front] ... eviscerated previous conceptions of war and the warrior. The myths and fantasies of war attempt to revive these conceptions in a new landscape. They attempt to close the gap between the surprising realities of life and initial expectations.[19]

Myth shaped expectations going into battle the first time, the actual experiences of battle, and the ways those experiences were remembered and given meaning afterward. Paradoxically, for example, some Germans found liberation in images of the "machine," whereas British memoirists tended to see the machine as their downfall.[20] Given the imperfections of human perception, the limits of the combatants' horizons, and the inadequacies of words to give expression and meaning to actual experiences, myth is, Leed argues, an essential outgrowth of war. Although it is not Leed's purpose to go into operational details or explore in great depth how myth and imagination were manipulated to mold battle itself, he establishes a synthesis of myth and instrumentality that could significantly expand upon the traditional accounts.

Within the context of the entire Pacific War it would be difficult to examine the influence of imaginary constructs – that is, groupings of images that define a "reality" – divorced from the objects or attitudes that gave rise to them. Aside from the sheer scope of such a project, the precise nature of this influence and its evolution over time and with experience differ drastically depending on where the focus lies. Policy and doctrine governing air or naval warfare, for

19 Eric J. Leed, *No Man's Land* (New York: Cambridge University Press, 1979), 116.
20 Comparing European memoirs of the First World War to American memoirs of the Second, British works, like Edmund Blunden's *Undertones of War* and Robert Graves's *Goodbye to All That*, are closer in tone to those of American citizen-soldiers, like J. Glenn Gray's *The Warriors* (New York: Harper and Row, 1970), whereas the tone of German books, like Ernst Jünger's *Im Stahlgewittern* and *Feuer und Blut* reflects more closely the warrior mentality and celebration of martial ability often present in the Marine memoirs to come out of the Pacific.

instance, were largely the products of abstract conceptualization. The sites of decision making were much farther removed both spatially and emotionally from the scene of battle than was possible in the ground war. In addition, the informal, grass roots interaction and adaptation that characterized land battle resulted in myths different from those of the naval and air wars because there was no dominant technology or machine that mediated between men and events. The attitudes, images, and myths of the infantrymen who fought the Japanese at close quarters carried greater resonance on the battlefield and, however indirectly, within the planning agencies of ground commands than did those of the submarine captains or bomber pilots inside COMSUBPAC or SAC.

An iconographic study of America in the Pacific War reveals many of the inconsistencies, ironies, and paradoxes in our conception of those events that left a swath of destruction extending from Pearl Harbor to Nagasaki. Ideas expressed through visual images were powerful and lasting, and none remains more famous in the American iconography of the war than Joseph Rosenthal's Pulitzer Prize–winning photograph of the flag being raised on Mount Suribachi. But contrast the image conveyed by the Marine Corps War Memorial with those contained in the scrapbook of a common marine. As a young Marine corporal in the 3d Armored Amphibian Battalion (which was attached to the First Marine Division on Peleliu and Okinawa), Werner Claussen assembled a photo album that captured not only scenes he wanted to remember but ideas and feelings of the time. Rosenthal's picture reflected a heroic and stirring reality of the Pacific War on one level, but just as surely, Claussen's pictures of young American men grinning self-consciously at the camera, bare-breasted Polynesian women provocatively posed, and badly disfigured Japanese corpses all captured realities of the war on other levels.[21] With the years of reassessment that followed the events and feelings captured in these pictures, the inter-relationships between these realities have been simplified and compartmentalized to the point that Rosenthal's and Claussen's photographs appear virtually unrelated. This process is in itself important for deciphering the meaning of events and as a mechanism for individual and collective healing.

---

21 Werner Claussen Papers, Personal Papers Collection (PPC), Marine Corps Historical Center (MCHC). Claussen's pictures show slightly more variety than those in most of the other scrapbooks, but in terms of the general iconographic categories represented, his collection is quite typical. For insights into the shifting meanings ascribed to the Rosenthal picture see Karal Ann Marling and John Wetenhall, *Iwo Jima: Monuments, Memories, and the American Hero* (Cambridge: Harvard University Press, 1991).

Joe Rosenthal's photograph of the Mount Suribachi flag raising is the most enduring American icon of the Second World War. (*Joe Rosenthal and AP/ Wide World Photos*)

For Claussen and his comrades – and ironically for the men pictured in Rosenthal's photograph as well[22] – the heroic image conveyed in the Suribachi flag raising was an essentially mythic reality that arose later, after the fighting. The subjects of Claussen's scrapbook were the reality with which they were concerned at the time: camaraderie and belonging, sexual fantasy and role playing, killing and death. Circumstances did not allow the luxury of a dispassionate or "objective" view of their actions. The emotional, psychic distancing from the events of battle could come only after the physical separation from the scene of action.

If photographs provide one set of insights into the imagery of

22 Only three of the six men pictured survived the war. Ira Hayes, one of the survivors of the flag raising, was unable to reconcile the mythic reality surrounding that moment on Mount Suribachi and the celebrity that attended it with the realities of life on an Indian reservation after the war, where he died, a confused and tragic alcoholic. The irony of his story was also recognized by Hollywood in a movie about Hayes appropriately called *The Outsider*. Histories of him include William Bradford Huie, *The Hero of Iwo Jima and Other Stories* (New York: Signet, 1962), and Albert Hemingway, *Ira Hayes: Pima Marine* (Lanham, Md.: University Press of America, 1988). For the best brief overview see Marling and Wetenhall, *Iwo Jima*, 170–94.

Werner Claussen's scrapbook captured both images and feelings of the war that he wanted to preserve: the camaraderie and belonging; sexual fantasy and role playing; killing and death. *(Personal Papers Collection, Marine Corps Historical Center)*

battle, language offers another. Visual images tend to provoke immediate, often heightened emotional responses, whereas verbal images go through an interpretive process in an individual's mind that may be just as evocative as a visual image, but more muted. Consider the gulf between the events as experienced by the individual riflemen and the same events as described in the carefully clipped language of a battalion logbook. On 20 May 1945, the 2d Battalion, 1st Marine Regiment,[23] attacked Japanese positions around Wana Draw on Okinawa. Among the attackers, marines of G Company ran into heavy fire from Japanese cave positions almost as soon as they rose up to advance. Several were killed in the first few minutes, and others were wounded and had to be carried back to the battalion aid station. Pinned down by the enemy fire, the company commander called on battalion headquarters for support to suppress the Japanese positions, in particular a group of caves on his left flank. In response, the battalion commander released a gun tank and two flamethrower tanks to come forward and saturate the area with high explosives and streams of napalm. While this was happening, however, the marines remained under concentrated fire and several more men were hit. The situation deteriorated further when the tankers, whose vision was limited to the small periscopes inside the vehicles, became confused as to the precise location of the Japanese positions and began firing into the marines' positions. At the same time as men scrambled for cover from this "friendly fire," the company commander became a casualty (whether the result of American or Japanese fire is not clear), and the executive officer had to take charge and attempt to sort out the chaos. Here are the same events exactly as recorded in the battalion message log:

Time	To	From	Message
1105	Vulcan Sk Bay	Vulcan George	Need Stretcherbearers
1145	Vulcan George	Vulcan 3 [battalion operations officer]	A regular beetle and two zippoes are coming around your right flank to work over your left.

---

23 In accordance with conventional usage, the three regiments of infantry and one of artillery in the First Marine Division will generally be referred to as the 1st, 5th, 7th, and 11th Marines, respectively. The three component battalions in each infantry regiment will be given in shorthand, battalion number/regiment, e.g., 1/1, 2/1, 3/1 or 1/5, 2/5, 3/5. To avoid confusion, the division will always be spelled out, either the First Marine Division or First Division, and the regiment will be labeled simply the 1st Marines.

1150	Vulcan George 6 [company commander]	Vulcan 3	It won't be long until beetles clear out the area on your left front. The beetles and zippoes are working there now[;] as soon as you can take the beetles that are there now and move out.
1153	Vulcan	Vulcan George	More stretcherbearers
1230	Vulcan 3	Vulcan George 5 [co. executive officer]	Our own tanks are firing into our own left flank platoon... Vulcan George 6 has just been hit

The log continues, bearing messages from other companies, from adjacent units, and providing many details of a costly, partially successful assault, another day of combat in a long, draining campaign.[24]

Logs such as this are history of a special sort. They were a starting point for instrumental reforms: staff officers read these messages and concluded that extra men would have to be detailed as stretcher-bearers and better measures established for the infantry to identify targets for the tanks. These logs were major source documents for the official Marine Corps histories of military operations in the Pacific. How events on the ground were described also serves to record the desensitization and reordering of brutal, terrifying, nonrational moments in hundreds of men's lives. Keegan describes the value of this process in the training and indoctrination of Sandhurst cadets:

> [B]y teaching the young officer to organize his intake of sensations, to reduce the events of combat to as few and as easily recognizable a set of elements as possible, to categorize... the noise, blast, passage of missiles and confusion of human movement... as 'incoming fire', 'outgoing fire', 'airstrike', 'company-strength attack', one is helping [the future officer] to avert the onset of fear or, worse, of panic and to perceive a face of battle which, if not familiar, and certainly not friendly, need not, in the event, prove wholly petrifying.[25]

---

24 2d Battalion, 1st Marine Regiment, Log Journal Sheet for 20 May 1945, Record Group (RG) 127/65A-5188/Box 23/file A39-2. This is not a complete copy of the message traffic monitored by the battalion headquarters.
25 Keegan, *The Face of Battle*, 22.

In other words, by trying to teach soldiers to substitute common verbal images for the perceptual images encountered in battle, military services are attempting to convert images into instrumentalities themselves. To be sure, the effort is seldom wholly successful or especially thorough, but it serves as an acknowledgment of sorts that although the language of the message logs describes the same things as Rosenthal's and Claussen's photographs, it does so on an intellectual level that is separate and distinct from the graphic sensory reality.

Taking as its premise that Clausewitz's "paradoxical trinity" of war ultimately converges in the individual combatants, this book explores how myth and imagination exercised a formative influence on military operations within a specific study group: men who fought in the First Marine Division between 1941 and 1951. In discussing precise ways in which instrumentalities were reconciled with imaginary constructs on the battlefield, context and background are critically important. Establishing this context requires going beyond the events surrounding the campaigns to consider the derivation of such myths and constructs, how they were adapted to the needs of newly trained marines, and what happened to their form and content after the men experienced combat and subsequently returned to civilian life. At each step of the way, the men were bombarded with graphic, perceptual, and verbal images that shaped their development and their later recollection and interpretation of their experiences. Some elements in these transitions were deliberate and carefully controlled by the Marine Corps, whereas others were the unforeseen consequences of policy and the products of chance or individual peculiarities. This approach poses several problems: as Leed observes, "The evanescent bonds and self-images formed in wars, revolutions, riots, carnivals, and New Year's parties are often historically invisible. They slip through the web of methods fashioned to describe the development of stable social and psychic entities."[26] Trails nevertheless exist that indicate how some men interpreted and reacted to the bewildering variety of images that they encountered and how they incorporated them into patterns of conduct of which they were largely unconscious.

The study is confined to a single division for purposes of scope and continuity. Differences in experience, indoctrination, and perspective make it difficult to compare in sufficient detail wartime experiences across combat roles (pilots versus sailors versus infantrymen) or across service lines (Army riflemen versus Marine ri-

26 Leed, *No Man's Land*, 5.

flemen). Even within the Marine Corps it is equally problematic to ignore men's identification with a particular division. Each division had a perceived "personality" or reputation based on its leaders and the campaigns in which it had served. The division also represents the lowest level at which operational planning and policies were set and was, in turn, most affected by and receptive to the attitudes and behavior of the men in the lines.

The selection of the First Marine Division over the other five Marine divisions or over the many Army divisions that fought in the Pacific is a practical matter. Exploring informal attitudes and abstract, often unarticulated images requires unofficial materials that are unavailable in equal quantity or quality for any other American division in the Pacific. For example, every well-known marine memoir written from an infantryman's perspective by either an enlisted man or junior-grade officer, with the exception of William Manchester's, was written by a veteran of the First Division. Additionally, correspondents Richard Tregaskis, John Hersey, and Ira Wolfert provided striking coverage of the marines during the Guadalcanal campaign that was to be matched later only by Robert Sherrod at Tarawa and Saipan. And while personal papers collections offer cross sections more representative of the whole Marine Corps than is the case with published materials, more of the collections come from members of the First Division than from any of its five counterparts. Even the official records, at least those from Guadalcanal, provided a richer, less sanitized picture of operations and the Japanese than available elsewhere. Besides being better documented than others, the First Division is also the most historically useful example of any American division because it played a central role in both the first and the last campaigns of the war, four in all, was subsequently sent to North China at the time when the Nationalists and Communists were fighting for control of the country, and a few years later was the sole Marine division dispatched to Korea. The First Division spans a broader spectrum chronologically and experientially than any other (see Map 1).

Exploring images over a ten-year period even within a single division requires simplifications and generalizations. Thus I focused exclusively on ground combat, primarily from the perspective of the infantry. Ideas and images were frequently borrowed from artillerists, tankers, even pilots, but I discuss them only as they relate to the nature of the fighting in the front lines. It is not my purpose here to give an evenly balanced view of the contribution made by various supporting arms or other services, nor are those issues surrounding strategic and operational planning covered in any great detail. Not only have these topics been treated thoroughly in official and quasi-official histories, but to the extent that these omissions mirror perceptions of the Marine infantrymen at the time, they support this approach. There is likewise no concerted effort to provide a balanced view from the other side of no-man's-land. Aside from practical considerations, the emphasis, again, is to explore the enemy's perceptions only to the extent that they were actually known by and influenced the marines. As a final caveat it should be remembered that the opinions and images culled from the available materials were never intended to be, and are not presented here as, representative of all marines or the entire division, nor do they describe an exclusively "little man's" view of the war; they serve only to illustrate certain relationships between specific ideas and specific events. The purpose here is to get below the universals and generalities to explore particular cases.

As a history of Pacific War myth and imagination, the book is structured in three broad parts corresponding loosely to "before," "during," and "after" the 1941–45 war. It begins more than twenty years before the First Division was created, considering, among other things, the conflicting legacies of the Great War and the so-called banana wars. The other chapter in this section concerns how civilian recruits were socialized and consciously "made" into marines. Three central chapters examine in greater detail three broad categories of imaginary constructions in the Pacific War, each within the specific context of a First Division campaign: images of the Japanese "Other" shaped the Guadalcanal campaign and contributed to the increasing barbarization of all subsequent campaigns; images of the "Self," and in particular the influence of interservice rivalry, significantly affected the Peleliu operation by polarizing and radicalizing the behavior demanded of the marines; and what Sherry labels the "triumph of technological fanaticism"[27] has its counterpart with the ground fighting in the final months of the war where technology bridged the gap between the marines' exterminationist warrior ethos and the means to realize it. The study of Pacific War myth and imagination carries beyond 1945 to provide perspective on its importance. The sixth chapter considers how the Pacific War images lost their practical value within the institution in 1951 when the marines were no longer able to apply them to operations in the context of the "limited" war in Korea.

27 Sherry defines the expression as "a pursuit of destructive ends expressed, sanctioned, and disguised by the organization and application of technological means"; in other words, American military leaders did not pursue the destruction of the enemy as a clear means of achieving the country's political ends but, in part, because technology enabled them to do so. *The Rise of American Air Power*, 251–52.

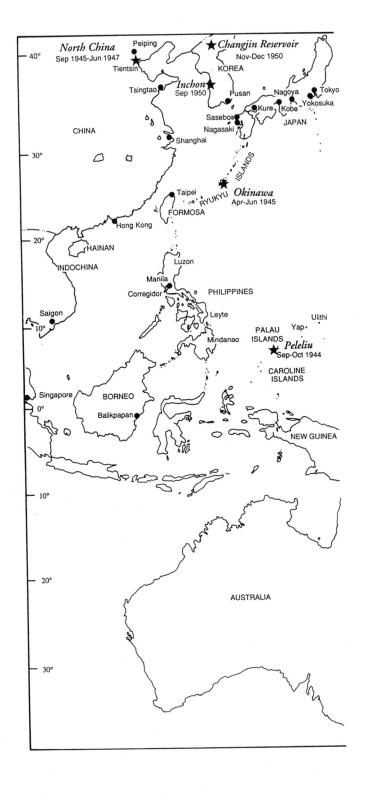

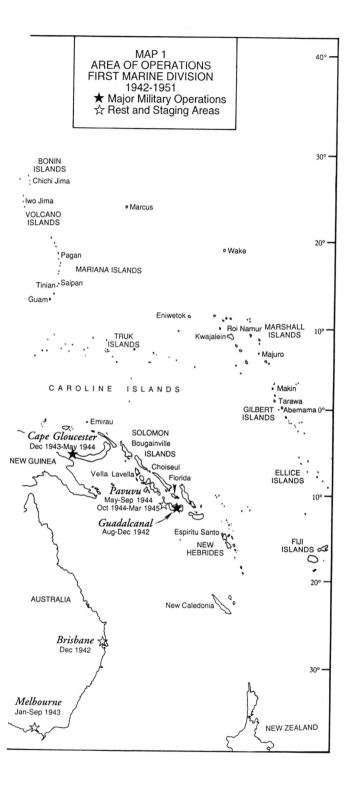

MAP 1
AREA OF OPERATIONS
FIRST MARINE DIVISION
1942-1951
★ Major Military Operations
☆ Rest and Staging Areas

40°

BONIN
ISLANDS
Chichi Jima

30°

Iwo Jima
Marcus
VOLCANO
ISLANDS

Pagan
MARIANA ISLANDS

Wake

20°

Tinian Saipan

Guam

Eniwetok
Roi Namur MARSHALL
Kwajalein ISLANDS
Majuro

10°

TRUK
ISLANDS

CAROLINE ISLANDS

Makin
Tarawa
GILBERT Abemama 0°
ISLANDS

Emirau
SOLOMON
Cape Gloucester
Dec 1943-May 1944
Bougainville
ISLANDS

NEW GUINEA
Choiseul
Vella Lavella
Florida

ELLICE
ISLANDS

Pavuvu
May-Sep 1944
Oct 1944-Mar 1945

10°

Guadalcanal
Aug-Dec 1942
Espiritu Santo
NEW
HEBRIDES

FIJI
ISLANDS

20°

AUSTRALIA
New Caledonia

Brisbane
Dec 1942

30°

Melbourne
Jan-Sep 1943

NEW ZEALAND

In a larger sense, however, the wartime images took on a life of their own in the unofficial representations of the Pacific War: the myths and images were given lasting, often sanitized form and meaning; combatant and civilian views were reconciled; and the foundation was laid for the assumptions and expectations that shaped the early years of the Vietnam War.

Examining myth and imagination on the battlefield illuminates a distinctly "American way of war." Russell F. Weigley, in his book of that title, argues that there is, indeed, a uniquely American approach to the conduct of war, at least at the levels of strategic and grand strategic policy. This level of analysis, however, especially in the twentieth century, can hardly illustrate national differences in war-making that are not better explained by military or power-political considerations that are situationally, not culturally, specific.[28] A more persuasive argument can be found at the operational level, where social or cultural attributes reveal themselves in different forms. The precise images that influenced the nature of Marine ground combat in the Pacific War were products peculiar to American society, culture, and this particular military institution at that moment in time. Unlike "rational" theories of strategic thought, imaginary constructions emerged from no general body of knowledge but from characteristically American perceptions and interpretations of the world. Parallels with other countries abound, but for all their similarities, the marines were not the same as the German military elites on the Eastern Front or the Japanese on the other side of the lines. The American samurai looked to their own distinctive cultural heritage for answers to the questions all soldiers must ask.

28 Russell F. Weigley, *The American Way of War* (Bloomington: Indiana University Press, 1973).

1

MYTHIC IMAGES OF THE MARINES
BEFORE PEARL HARBOR

In light of the power and prestige enjoyed by the Marine Corps at the close of the Second World War, it is sometimes difficult to remember the years of struggle and comparative obscurity that marked its prewar history. The corps's wartime accomplishments have colored most studies of the preceding years, in which every prewar development is viewed with an eye to explaining subsequent events. The exhaustive studies of doctrine, equipment, training, and strategic planning during the 1930s are indispensable to understanding the policies and methods that the Marine Corps articulated prior to the war, but they do not address the myths and images from which such instrumentalities derived.[1] The preparations for war necessarily began as imaginary constructions of the future battlefields. The origins and forms of these constructions arose from many sources, of which four are particularly pertinent. First is the growth of strong public images of the marines as a result of their exploits in the Great War, carefully nurtured by increasingly sophisticated public relations techniques. Emphasizing the corps's selective recruitment and the marines' readiness and physical toughness, such popular images acknowledged the passage of the service into institutional maturity with its own identity separate from the Army and Navy. Second, combat experiences in a series of interventions in Latin America reflected the marines' extensive employment as colonial light infantry and presaged all too accurately many of the physical and psychological characteristics of the war against Japan. Third, the interwar search for a mission that would guarantee institutional survival and some measure of political autonomy within the military establishment led to the develop-

---

1 For instance, Jeter A. Isely and Philip A. Crowl, *The U.S. Marines and Amphibious War* (Princeton: Princeton University Press, 1951), remains the standard secondary reference on the development of amphibious warfare doctrine, a remarkable tribute forty years later, but insofar as the authors' stated purpose is to analyze scientifically the amphibious warfare doctrine "as exemplified and developed in practice" in the Pacific War (v), the book also represents precisely the sort of teleological approach to interwar developments that has characterized much of the historiography.

ment of a detailed amphibious warfare doctrine, considered by some "the blueprint of victory" in the Pacific War. And finally, the literary and artistic revolt of the interwar period recast many of the traditional concepts and symbols that gave meaning to the Marine historical tradition, carrying over into the Second World War and beyond. Collectively, these elements attracted certain types of people to the corps and, more important, influenced the institution's image of the "ideal" marine, which served as an emotional and behavioral template at the recruit depots on the eve of the Pacific War.

Before the First World War the military heritage of the Marine Corps, even generously embellished, consisted of little that was apt to gain much popular attention or stir any great respect or awe among dispassionate observers. By the time the armistice went into effect, however, this had changed dramatically. Upon American entry into the war in 1917, General John J. Pershing had reluctantly included the 5th Marines, hastily assembled from a disparate assortment of prewar units, among the first expeditionary forces dispatched to France, and the Marine Corps collected as quickly as possible enough additional men for shipment to France to form the Fourth Marine Brigade.[2] At the height of the war, the corps had 24,000 men in Europe, or roughly one-third of its total strength, while the rest were occupied with training or other overseas commitments. Of those marines in France, more than half served in noncombat roles ranging from dockside stevedores to train guards - at least until replacements were needed to return the Fourth Brigade to full strength after its frequent battles.

The Fourth Marine Brigade, paired with an Army brigade in the Second Infantry Division, attracted an exceptional amount of attention for its hard-fought battles in France. In a classic demonstration of the vagaries in the enforcement of censorship regulations and the machinations of fate, correspondents were prohibited from identifying units by number but allowed to distinguish Marine from Army units.[3] Since there was only the one Ma-

2 The Army, and Pershing in particular, were reluctant to accept the marines at all, and only a presidential order ended the discussion; Edward M. Coffman, *The War to End All Wars* (Madison: University of Wisconsin Press, 1986), 151–52. The 5th Marines were shipped to France in June attached to the First Division; the arrival of the 6th Marines and the 6th Machine Gun Battalion in February 1918 allowed the establishment of the brigade itself; Allan R. Millett, *Semper Fidelis*, 2d ed. (New York: Macmillan, 1991), 292–94.

3 Correspondent Floyd Gibbons of the Chicago *Tribune* was rumored to have been killed while covering the marines' first battle at Belleau Wood, and as a special gesture his "final story" was passed by the censor uncut. This set a precedent that actually drew extra coverage to the Marine brigade because correspondents liked the easy recognition of their stories. The *Recruiters' Bulletin* printed an account of this episode by Alexander Woolcott in October 1919; cited by Robert

rine brigade at the front, the Marine Corps in this way gained important access to the public at home. The marines skyrocketed to prominence in early June of 1918 during the battle of Belleau Wood. Dramatic utterances filled the newspaper accounts of events in this battle and have since become shibboleths familiar to every marine who has served since: Captain Lloyd Williams's retort to a panicky French officer's advice, "Retreat Hell! We just got here"; and veteran sergeant Dan Daly urging his men forward by yelling, "Come on, you sonsofbitches! Do you want to live forever?"[4] Not surprisingly, the sanitized version of the battle emphasized at the time and taught in classes for recruits on Marine Corps history, customs, and traditions hides some harsh facts.

The reality of Belleau Wood was that the Fourth Brigade suffered appallingly in a battle in which the tactical gains were incommensurate with the costs. In twenty-one days of ferocious fighting, under pressure placed upon them by the brigade commander – an Army cavalryman, not a Marine officer[5] – the marines lost more than 4,700 men, over half of the brigade's strength.[6] General Böhm, commander of the German 28th Division, was impressed by how the marines pressed home their attacks and offered an explanation for their behavior that would be echoed almost exactly by a Japanese general on Guadalcanal twenty-four years later: "it is not a question of the possession or nonpossession of this or that village or woods, insignificant in itself; it is a question whether the Anglo–American claim that the American Army is equal or even the superior of the German Army is to be made good."[7] The notion of battle as a test of cultural mettle and institutional reputation figured prominently and self-consciously in Marine Corps thinking from

Lindsay, *This High Name* (Madison: University of Wisconsin Press, 1956), 32–33. Clyde H. Metcalf, *A History of the United States Marine Corps* (New York: Putnam, 1939), 484–85, offers what was the standard account on the eve of the Second World War. Gibbons's contemporary account concentrates on his wounding; see *"And They Thought We Wouldn't Fight"* (New York: George H. Doran, 1918), 312ff.

4 Logan Feland, "Retreat Hell!" *Marine Corps Gazette* 6 (September 1921): 289–91; Coffman, *The War to End All Wars*, 217.

5 Brigadier General James G. Harbord demonstrated a poor grasp of the tactically and operationally feasible, and little in his control of the battle was to enhance his reputation, although it did not prevent his subsequent promotion to command of the Second Division; Coffman, *The War to End All Wars*, 220. It is interesting to note that Holland M. Smith, who would command the Tarawa, Saipan, and Iwo Jima campaigns in the Pacific War, wrote that he "always took Harbord as a model"; Norman V. Cooper, *A Fighting General* (Quantico: Marine Corps Association, 1987), 34.

6 Coffman gives the figure 5,200, "more than 50 per cent" (*The War to End All Wars*, 221); the figure here, 112 officers and 4,598 men, comes from Millett, *Semper Fidelis*, 304.

7 General Böhm quoted in Coffman, *The War to End All Wars*, 221–22.

that time forward. This was not a new idea in the annals of military organizations, but it marked for the Marine Corps a rite of passage to maturity. A respected foe[8] had granted recognition of the marines' institutional distinctiveness that perforce made them a representative of the United States, separate from the Army. Never before had the Marine Corps been so clearly set apart from other American soldiers, and to this day, marines take great pride in the sobriquet "devil dogs" (*Teufelhunden*) bestowed on them in their first major battle.

The war brought several more battle streamers for the regimental colors of the 5th and 6th Marines, but at a cost high in human lives and interservice friction. At Soissons, St. Mihiel, Blanc Mont, and in the great Meuse-Argonne offensive, the Fourth Brigade suffered over 6,600 additional battle casualties. Coverage of these battles generated widespread public appreciation of the service and its accomplishments, but in the words of Robert Lindsay, a former marine and author of a 1953 history of Marine Corps public relations, the reputation acquired was "double-barrelled." The "boundless admiration" of the general public was counterbalanced by a belief among many, especially in the Army, that Marine Corps prowess was "an artificial concept – built, cultivated, and ceaselessly propagated by some vague but vast complex of press agentry." The popular notoriety was earned through valorous action and sacrifice, but it was an understandable cause for resentment among Army units that had performed as valorously but without comparable recognition.[9] Many Army officers, including Douglas MacArthur, thought that the Marine Corps had pursued glory at the Army's expense, and their enmity would continue to resurface for years to come. Marine officers, in turn, felt indignant about General Pershing's efforts to absorb the Marines into the Army and were to take offense at the postwar attempts to minimize the importance of the battles in which they had fought.[10]

8 The concept of "worthy foe" is in itself heavily freighted with meaning, as Dower makes clear in his comments about the image of the "good German" in the Second World War (*War without Mercy*, 8). Whatever the atrocities laid at the door of the Kaiser's armies in Belgium or the U-boats at sea, Germans were still perceived most often as versions of "us" gone astray rather than something inherently malevolent; besides, enemy soldiers must be respected as warriors if our own warriors are to accept the sacrifices required to achieve victory. For a general discussion of the ambivalence in images of the enemy as worthy opponent, see Sam Keen, *Faces of the Enemy* (San Francisco: Harper and Row, 1986), 66–72.

9 Lindsay, *This High Name*, 23. Lindsay's work is quite useful, but aside from his unabashed partisanship, it is also colored by the aftershocks of the unification controversy and the Korean War.

10 Ironically, Pershing tried unsuccessfully to do to the Marine Corps exactly what

Whatever the harsh realities of the fighting or future harvest of interservice conflict, the Marine Corps emerged from the war to embody in the public eye qualities of elitism, voluntarism, readiness, and martial virtue. Behind the slogan "First to Fight," recruiters of 1917–18 stressed the marines' readiness for immediate deployment and combat. Their claim of elitism was bolstered when the corps exercised the unusual wartime luxury of rejecting almost three-quarters of the applicants screened. Accepting only 60,189 men from 239,274 applicants, the Marine Corps wielded a degree of selectivity the Army and Navy could not match.[11] Moreover, because the number of applicants for enlistment far exceeded the Marine Corps quota when selective service was introduced in 1917, the service escaped the provisions of the draft until all voluntary enlistments were halted in August 1918. Recruiters naturally capitalized on their status as an all-volunteer force, which in turn became an important element of the marines' conception of themselves.[12]

Even before the war had opened new opportunities to capture the attention of American society, the Marine Corps had experimented with an innovative public relations program to increase its name recognition and bolster recruitment. In 1907 recruiters in the Chicago office established a publicity bureau to help their local efforts, and four years later the commandant of the Marine Corps formally established a servicewide Recruiting Publicity Bureau. The bureau published an internal newsletter called the *Recruiters' Bulletin*, which offered advice on how recruiters could more effectively "market" the Marine Corps to the American people. By establishing good relations with the press, learning what sorts of stories appealed most to the public, and taking a more active role in local affairs, Marine recruiters helped lower the barriers that traditionally separated the military and civilian communities. They also fostered an almost mystical image of the service and harnessed it to specific institutional needs. The bureau was so successful in winning support from business concerns, patriotic organizations, and pri-

the French and British wanted to do to the American Expeditionary Forces – that is, break it up and feed it into existing frontline organizations piecemeal; Coffman, *The War to End All Wars*, 9–11, 48–49; Millett, *Semper Fidelis*, 293, 318.

11 Millett, *Semper Fidelis*, 289.

12 Seven thousand draftees were finally accepted before the end of the war, but they reached France after the armistice was signed, and their existence has since been minimized and almost forgotten in the histories of the Marine Corps; Lindsay, *This High Name*, 24. The importance of the all-volunteer force self-image is reflected in John W. Thomason, Jr., *Fix Bayonets!* (New York: Charles Scribner's Sons, 1926), x–xiv; and it was picked up again after Pearl Harbor in Gordon F. Ogilvie, "Draftee vs. Volunteer: Serious Problem," *Marine Recruiter* 2 (January 1942): 6.

vate individuals prior to the U.S. entry, that once war was declared recruiters were forced to turn away volunteers, who inundated their offices seeking enlistment. The images used to attract enlistees served to sharpen the service's distinctiveness and laid the basis for a more expansive public relations program that extended its primary mission of promoting recruitment.[13]

The slogans, recruiting posters, and ad campaigns used to draw men into the service created an archetypal public image of the marines that has persisted in modified form to this day. Like George Creel's Committee on Public Information (CPI), the Marine Corps turned to professional civilian advertisers and artists like Charles Phelps Cushing, Edward B. Waterworth, and Paul Woyshner to bring their expertise to the public relations mission. Some, like Cushing, were given reserve commissions to lend institutional support and legitimacy to their activities.[14] A host of artists painted recruiting posters that portrayed very different aspects of the Marine Corps. Joe Leyendecker created stiff, formalized pictures of spit-and-polish marines in dress blues that one critic described as "Teutonic toy soldiers." Howard Chandler Christy's posters for the Marine Corps and Navy typically exploited veiled sexual appeals. John A. Coughlin and Charles Buckles Falls emphasized the first-to-fight theme of the marines in 1917 and their commitment in action. James Montgomery Flagg painted his "Tell That to the Marines" poster in front of a large crowd on the steps of the New York Public Library.[15] "America," one scholar perceptively writes, "went to war in 1917 surrounded by mirrors."[16] The images of the recruiting posters offered flattering reflections for potential recruits to which they tried to conform.

According to their own publicists, the Marine Corps managed to attract "a particularly virile strain of young American manhood." Lindsay calls upon a long string of witnesses to validate this contention with statements that the marines of 1917–18 were "the cream and flower of American manhood," "the adventurous, the patriotic and the brave," and "some of the best blood in the land."[17]

13 Lindsay, *This High Name*, 9–15, 23–25, 28.
14 Ibid., 25–26.
15 Clay Barrow, "Marine Mystique," *United States Naval Institute Naval History* 3 (Fall 1989): 37–43; James Montgomery Flagg, *Roses and Buckshot* (New York: G. P. Putnam's Sons, 1946), 158–59; Libby Chenault, *Battlelines* (Chapel Hill: Rare Book Collection, Wilson Library, University of North Carolina Press, 1988), 132–33; Walton Rawls, *Wake Up, America!* (New York: Abbeville Press, 1988), 166, 249.
16 Thomas C. Leonard, *Above the Battle* (New York: Oxford University Press, 1978), 161.
17 Lindsay, *This High Name*, 26–28. Those quoted here are John A. Lejeune, A. S.

Although blatantly subjective and self-serving, such encomiums, which could be produced by all the services, were largely accepted by the public during and after the war. The suspension of public credulity associated with the dismaying intemperance of the CPI during the war and the reactionary excesses of 1919 served the goals of the Marine Corps beyond all expectations.[18] The public image of the marines interacted with their self-image and affected the selection process before the war and behavioral standards during the war. Nor did the Marine Corps allow this success to fade after the armistice.

After the war Marine public relations received a tremendous boost from John A. Lejeune, commandant from 1920 to 1929. In addition to instituting educational and organizational reforms, he also emphasized the need to "seek good publicity": "The future success of the Marine Corps depends on two factors: First, an efficient performance of all the duties to which . . . assigned; second, promptly bringing this efficiency to the attention of the proper officials of the Government and the American people."[19] He helped organize the Marine Corps League in 1923, a veterans association that maintained a separate institutional identity from other, larger veterans organizations. In addition, with little prodding from Lejeune, Smedley D. Butler, the colorful, outspoken commanding general at Quantico from 1920 to 1924, staged an uninterrupted string of public events that attracted support from key politicians and kept the service in the news. Butler used the newly renamed East Coast Expeditionary Force to make Quantico the military showplace for Washington politics. War games and Civil War reenactments staged in surrounding states regularly drew crowds of 100,000–150,000, including presidents, cabinet members, influential congressional leaders, and senior officers of the Army and Navy. Butler sponsored football games against nearby college teams, successfully exploiting the sport as a metaphor for Marine prowess. Other attractions included Marine-sponsored summer camps, reunions, and parades. In an age of barnstorming and flamboyant showmanship, Butler also capitalized on any publicity gimmick that would serve his goal of promoting support for the corps. One example was his introduction of the first official bulldog mascot to embody the "devil dog" heritage from the trenches and

McLemore, Albertus W. Catlin, and William Almon Wolff; the first three were marines.

18 David M. Kennedy, *Over Here* (New York: Oxford University Press, 1980), 60–63, 73–75.

19 Headquarters Memorandum dated 21 September 1925, quoted in Lindsay, *This High Name*, 38.

give the marines "both a convincing public image and a credible warrior ideal to suit contemporary notions of manliness."[20]

As publicity was integrated as a tool of Marine Corps policy, the importance of what Lindsay labels "internal public relations" grew correspondingly. Marine indoctrination became more pervasive and carefully controlled. In the smaller and less sophisticated "old corps" antedating the Great War, recruits were trained at Marine barracks scattered around the country without any standardized curriculum. But this individualized, patchwork approach and the anti-intellectualism that had pervaded it for so long were unable to keep pace with changing conditions. The growing complexities of Marine duties, the experience with a formalized boot camp beginning in 1915, and the corps's need to strengthen its own identity after emerging from the trenches with national recognition of its institutional independence, all pointed to the need for new, more refined methods. Among the traditions created, one example that Lindsay personally found especially compelling was the annual Marine Corps birthday message, which began under Lejeune in 1921. Invoking past glories, the message, which appears in the *United States Marine Corps Manual*, appeals to a mystical belief in the Marine Corps. With honors and distinction won on every battlefield, "the term Marine" was said "to signify all that is highest in military efficiency and soldierly virtue." The message continues, having received from their predecessors "this high name" of "Marine,"

> we also receive from them the eternal spirit which has animated our corps from generation to generation.... So long as that spirit continues to flourish marines will be found equal to every emergency in the future as they have in the past, and the men of our Nation will regard us as worthy successors to the long line of illustrious men who have served...[21]

For those who truly believe, this message promises marines immortality for their warrior spirit and assures them that the men of the nation will hold a high regard for their masculine virtues. Conversely, disregarding this spirit or allowing it to lapse opens the door to the possibility of failure and the shame and ignominy that go with it. The entire birthday ceremony is carefully staged, height-

---

20 Hans Schmidt, *Maverick Marine* (Lexington: University of Kentucky Press, 1987), 129–30, 136, 143. Schmidt argues plausibly that Butler's Quantico circus "perhaps saved the day" for the Marine Corps in the early 1920s. The ramifications of show over substance for the service remain to be considered. On Lejeune's role as commandant see Merrill L. Bartlett, *Lejeune* (Columbia: University of South Carolina Press, 1991), 146–68, 191–93.
21 From Lejeune's first birthday message, now printed in the *Marine Corps Manual*, quoted in Lindsay, *This High Name*, 90.

ening the emotional atmosphere in which this message is read. One
of the other passages most frequently quoted at the annual ball has
always been King Henry's "band of brothers" speech to his troops
from Shakespeare's *Henry V*. Such ritual often proved to be a particularly effective means of indoctrinating young men, frequently
still in their teens or early twenties.

Lejeune's birthday message comes as close as any single document
to a formal enunciation of a Marine warrior code. As a statement
of martial and institutional values it is even distantly related to the
Japanese bushido and some of the Imperial Rescripts carried by
the troops in their packs. For Lindsay himself, who closely associated with his Marine experiences, such indoctrination was the
epiphany. It transcended even the rational and historically communicable:

> It is this "high name" which motivates the individual Marine;
> the Marine Corps has had to do little more than remind its
> members of it. Rooted deeply in a solid bedrock of deeds, the
> Marine Corps' internal public relations is as simple as it is
> effective. One word must be added, however: no historical
> study, no matter how painstakingly thorough, could possibly
> convey the spirit of this public relations policy – for that, at
> heart, is what it is – of the Marine Corps.[22]

Once integrated into training, doctrinal innovation, and operational decision making, such belief constituted one of the corps's
greatest strengths and, ultimately, one of its greatest vulnerabili-
ties.[23]

The Marine Corps of the interwar period came to represent in
its own eyes and those of the public a special military group within
the democratic, freedom-loving nation. Accepting public pronouncements at face value, the marines' service in East Asia, Latin
America, and Europe between 1900 and 1941 could take on the

22 Ibid.
23 The chapter entitled "The Invention of Tradition" in Douglas Porch, *The French
Foreign Legion* (New York: HarperCollins, 1991), offers a strong parallel between
Lejeune's efforts with the Marine Corps in the interwar period and those of
Paul Rollet, the "Father of the Legion," in the 1930s. For a variety of reasons,
the Legion set about to create a vast, codified "tradition" to underpin it. Porch
writes, "Rollet's purpose was to teach a new generation of legionnaires to speak
in a common idiom, to create an image borrowed from myth to design a collective
mentality, to formulate a common view of reality" (414). The only point that I
would rephrase in applying this statement to the Marine Corps is that Lejeune
and Butler did not use tradition to provide a "view of reality" (implying something external, separate, or distinct from "reality"); their manipulation of custom
and tradition, for many men besides Lindsay, was reality itself. In both cases
the costs and benefits were quite similar (439–40).

appearance of guardianship over democracy. The visions of adventure and heroism surrounding popularized views of the marines in the Great War resulted in a self-selecting process that was given reinforcement through the service's recruitment policies and its indoctrination of new recruits. Against Japan, this image would shift further, along the lines of Böhm's comment, to the point that the marines regarded themselves as warrior representatives of their country, a kind of American samurai class.

In addition to service in the Great War, the Marine Corps in 1941 drew heavily upon its more established heritage as colonial light infantry and experiences of intermittent warfare in Latin America over the interwar years. Since the turn of the century, marines had become increasingly active in what they derisively dubbed "banana wars." Whether taking part in the punitive Boxer Expedition in 1900, the Cuban occupation, the two-year war in Nicaragua, or the occupation of Veracruz, the marines were a reliable tool of American foreign policy before the Great War, and such duty remained a mainstay of the service until the mid-1930s. Even while committed to the fighting in Europe, the Marines preserved their ongoing role as agents of American gunboat diplomacy, and especially their duties as hemispheric policemen. As diplomats descended on Versailles, the primary overseas mission of the corps reverted to the Caribbean interventions and occupations, which had an enormous influence on many men who were to play prominent roles in the years ahead. As legation guards, on ships' detachments, posted to naval shore installations, and organized in special expeditionary units, the Marine Corps remained actively employed.

The nature of their duties in Hispaniola provides insights into the marines' attitudes and methods of the Pacific War that their service in Europe does not. Active American military intervention on the island in 1915 led to a nineteen-year occupation in which the marines played a central role as organizers of American-led native constabularies and as the backbone of antiguerrilla operations. In 1918, at the same time as marines were fighting a "worthy" enemy in Europe, they were also killing "grasping niggers" and "savage monkeys" in the remote hills and jungles of Haiti and the Dominican Republic.[24] The Germans fought ferociously, but they were seen as generally abiding by the same rules of conduct understood and accepted by the marines. The *cacos* (Haitian "bandits") and Dominican rebels were seen in familiar racist stereotypes that

24 Cited in Schmidt, *Maverick Marine*, 84, 86.

viciously or paternalistically dehumanized them and fostered a war with few rules or boundaries.[25]

Herman Hanneken, a future battalion commander on Guadalcanal, became a hero in October 1919 and thereby helped set the tone for this type of warfare. In the midst of a violent uprising, Hanneken, a Marine sergeant with a captain's commission in the Gendarmerie, made elaborate plans to lure into a trap the rebels' putative leader, Charlemagne Péralte. The action culminated with Hanneken infiltrating a patrol consisting of himself, a Marine corporal (with a lieutenant's commission in the Gendarmerie), and sixteen Haitian gendarmes, all disguised as *cacos*, into Péralte's camp, where the *caco* leader was shot and his body brought back for public display.[26] Hanneken earned the Medal of Honor and a regular Marine commission for this performance, but such methods, although very effective against guerrillas, hardly fitted any lingering nineteenth-century romantic views of war or the honorable warrior image cultivated in battle against the Germans. The European and colonial war experiences fostered conflicting images of marines both in and outside the service. Representatives of corps and country at Belleau Wood, marines did not harbor images of the Germans as polarized as those of the *cacos*; against enemies perceived as beneath "warrior" status, marines proved savagely utilitarian and even treacherous.

The parallels between behavior cultivated among the marines serving on Hispaniola and those who would fight on Guadalcanal are often striking. American brutality during 1917–18 has sometimes been attributed to the siphoning off of many of the best officers and noncommissioned officers from the Caribbean occupation forces to serve in France. Although stripping commands for

25 In the correspondence of Smedley D. Butler and especially Louisianan Littleton W. T. Waller, there are also familiar throwbacks to the plantation images of the slaves; ibid., 84, 87–89, 94–95. In addition to images of the "worthy foe," Keen also discusses categories more directly applied to Latin American wars, especially "enemy as criminal" and, to a lesser extent, "enemy as beast, reptile, insect, germ" (*Faces of the Enemy*, 50–54, 60–64).

26 For details of the trap and the overall mission see Herman Hanneken, interviewed by Benis M. Frank, 21 January 1981, 31–34, Oral History Collection (OHC), MCHC; R. H. Greenhouse, "King of the Banana Wars," *Marine Corps Gazette* 44 (June 1960): 29–33; Ivan Musicant, *The Banana Wars* (New York: Macmillan, 1990), 215–18. On the issue of images, the Americans badly mishandled the Péralte case. Hanneken had Péralte's body brought back to the town of Grande Rivière, where it was tied to a door and photographed, with the pictures distributed to prove he had been killed; but "[d]espite the evidence of an autopsy verifying that Péralte had died of a bullet wound, Haitians persisted in believing the whites had crucified the *caco* leader on a door"; Lester D. Langley, *The Banana Wars* (Lexington: University of Kentucky Press, 1983), 162.

32   AMERICAN SAMURAI

men certainly fostered much resentment among those who remained, the evidence does not support the contention. One case
in particular is usually cited to illustrate its baneful effects. Charles
Merkel, the notorious "Tiger of Seibo," a province in the Dominican
Republic, was promoted from the ranks to captain because of the
shortage of officers on the island during the war. After numerous
charges of torture and wanton cruelty, Merkel was arrested in
September 1918, but he shot himself before being brought to trial.[27]
Notwithstanding the Merkel case, however, barbarous marine behavior was not solely the result of lower quality personnel, as evi-
denced by the conduct of marines shipped back to Hispaniola from
Europe in 1919. One colonel who arrived in Haiti from France saw
too many "fleeing prisoners" shot down. Lieutenant Louis Cukela,
who had won the Medal of Honor and his commission in the
trenches, killed a group of prisoners in the middle of a Marine
camp. Many atrocities had nothing to do with the marines' mission
against the *cacos* and stemmed instead from enlisted men seeking
alcohol or women as an escape from the dismal reality of their
duty.[28] Aside from simple racism and environmental factors, such
conduct was also driven by rumors that the Haitians mutilated and
cannibalized Marine captives – exactly the type of rumor that would
circulate about the Japanese.[29]

Another explanation for the barbarous conduct of the marines
was the failure of the senior leadership to exercise effectively existing formal and informal legal and institutional controls. At least
until reforms in the early 1920s, most atrocities went unpunished,
partly on account of officers' reluctance to prosecute such crimes
and also because witnesses seldom came forward to testify against
the offenders. Cukela, for instance, instead of being court-
martialed was transferred to the Dominican Republic, where he
led a group disguised as bandits that terrorized Seibo Province.[30]
Major Clarke Wells, also accused of murdering prisoners, was likewise transferred and the charges were dropped. Some marines were
simply hospitalized and their actions attributed to isolated instances

27 On the attractions of European service, see Langley, *Banana Wars*, 152–53, and
    Schmidt, *Maverick Marine*, 96–97. On Merkel see Langley, *Banana Wars*, 152.
    Officially, Merkel was credited with concealing the suicide weapon in his cell; a
    different and more revealing version maintains that two Marine officers left
    him the weapon with a single bullet.
28 Millett, *Semper Fidelis*, 199–200.
29 The most widely circulated atrocity story surrounded the death of Sergeant
    Lawrence Muth in a Haitian ambush: in addition to being decapitated and his
    heart hacked out, according to later confessions the heart had been cannibalized.
    Subsequent fighting in May of 1920 was the most brutal of all the Caribbean
    interventions. See Langley, *Banana Wars*, 162; Musicant, *Banana Wars*, 222–23.
30 Millett, *Semper Fidelis*, 200.

of insanity. In September 1919 the most sensational court-martial that came to trial led the commandant of the Marine Corps, George Barnett, to conclude in a letter dated 2 October 1919 "that practically indiscriminate killing of natives has gone on for some time." The subsequent uproar prompted the secretary of the Navy to order an investigation. The results cleared the Marine Corps of any genocidal practices and rebuked Barnett for his unguarded comments, but the public outcry had tarnished the Marine image. The failure of the institutional controls to contain the problem had seriously undermined the corps's credibility.[31] Lejeune's emphasis on more positive public relations and the search for a different mission plainly came at least in part in response to this crisis and sought to restore pride and confidence in the corps, inside the service and out.

The last large-scale combat experience for the marines prior to 1941 came during their occupation of Nicaragua between 1926 and 1933. By the spring of 1928, the elusiveness of Augusto C. Sandino began to threaten the marines' military prestige, and the chase to capture the charismatic nationalist leader became almost obsessive.[32] The resulting years of patrolling, ambushes, and jungle fighting against the Sandinistas resembled the fighting on Guadalcanal in some ways, and many officers, such as Merritt Edson, Lewis B. Puller, and Wilburt S. Brown, gained valuable leadership and tactical experience that they carried into the Pacific War. In conventional Marine Corps histories, the Nicaraguan war is treated as a catalyst for the development of doctrine and training in the 1930s, but it also revealed a troubling antagonism that influenced Marine attitudes and methods after 1941.[33] The growing antipathy of American public opinion and government leaders toward military interventions in the Caribbean, coupled with the efficacy of the enemy's guerrilla tactics, thwarted the marines' efforts to develop the technological and doctrinal means to achieve the ends dictated

31 Captain Becker and Sergeant Louis Brokaw were placed in asylums for their actions in Haiti (Musicant, *Banana Wars*, 224–25). For details about the court-martial and the resulting public backlash, see ibid., 226 (portion quoted), 227–29; and Millett, *Semper Fidelis*, 202–3.
32 Langley, *Banana Wars*, 201.
33 Best known of the tactical innovations were experiments by Marine aviators with dive-bombing and other close air support and resupply techniques, Isely and Crowl, *Amphibious War*, 6; Vernon Magee, "The Genesis of Air Support in Guerrilla Operations," *United States Naval Institute Proceedings* 91 (June 1965): 49–57; Musicant, *Banana Wars*, 316. For examples of the experiences of the Marine officers see Jon T. Hoffman, "Edson's 'First Raiders,' " *United States Naval Institute Naval History* 5 (Fall 1991): 20–25; Burke Davis, *Marine!* (Boston: Little, Brown and Company, 1962), 56–66; and Wilburt S. Brown, interviewed by Benis M. Frank, 22–24 August 1967, OHC, MCHC.

by government policy and their own military indoctrination. The frustration and impotence resulting from the gap between capabilities and goals are reflected in the recollections of the Marine officers of this period who retired in the 1950s and 1960s. The old war-horses ignored the political and cultural failures of American interventions and instead nostalgically recalled only a rich store of anecdotes about various personalities, policies, and militarily successful operations. Goals, means, and indoctrination coalesced in the world wars, but they did not in the colonial wars. As a result, historical memory focused on events that these officers had stripped of larger meaning, thereby preserving their own self-images and burying the evidence of the marines' failure. This also thrust them into the role of institutional guardians.[34]

Although Americans, since venturing overseas around the turn of the century, had self-righteously abjured the kind of colonial warfare witnessed among the European powers, the military simultaneously sought recourse to precisely those methods that the public found most morally repugnant. In many instances, the marines had been preferred over Army troops because, as Henry L. Stimson suggested to President Taft during the Nicaragua fighting in 1912, the marines were equated with transient gunboat diplomacy, and their employment often escaped international characterization as outright invasion and conquest.[35] Service as colonial infantry attracted much favorable publicity for the marines in the first fifteen years of the century, and figures like Smedley D. Butler were constantly grabbing headlines and providing colorful stories to keep the corps in the public eye, but not without cost. As early as the Philippine War of 1899–1902 a Marine officer had very nearly been made a scapegoat for the excesses committed by Americans in both the Army and the Marine Corps, and even though exonerated, Major Littleton W. T. Waller found his career permanently tainted.[36] The marines in Haiti, the Dominican Republic,

34 Langley, *Banana Wars*, 220–21.
35 Schmidt, *Maverick Marine*, 44–45.
36 In the most serious instance of Army–Marine Corps political conflict before the Second World War, the court-martial of Waller for the murder of several Filipino prisoners in 1901 was designed to shift the spotlight on American atrocities away from the Army and onto the Marines. It almost backfired when Waller in effect implicated the entire Army chain of command extending back to the military governor, Major General Adna R. Chaffee. Formal punishments of Waller and his immediate superior, Army Brigadier General Bell, for their excessive zeal were mild and the incident quietly subsided, but with residual bitterness among the principals. Waller had been a likely candidate for commandant, but even though acquitted, the court-martial overshadowed the rest of his career and helped block his final promotion. U.S. Congress, Senate, *Affairs in the Philippines, Hearings before the Committee on the Philippines of the United States*

and Nicaragua, like those in earlier overseas expeditions, demonstrated a contempt for their mission, their environment, and the people around them in ways that have been repeated throughout the history of troops on colonial duty.[37]

The actual images fostered by the marines' overseas occupation duties depended largely on the predisposition of the observer. Some viewed the Marine Corps as a tool of the State Department and the big corporations with overseas investments: to these people the marines were rapacious, undisciplined thugs for the imperialists. From retirement two-time Medal of Honor winner Smedley Butler denounced the mission of the marines in Central America as one of safeguarding American corporate investments at the inhabitants' expense.[38] The preferred view within the Marine Corps was that they had served as honorably and capably as circumstances allowed to protect American lives and property and serve their nation's foreign policy.[39] In practice, the two views were not necessarily mutually exclusive.

Although created by an act of Congress over a century and a half earlier, at the time of the attack on Pearl Harbor the Marine Corps had still not won full acceptance in the defense establishment. Ostensibly a fully autonomous service within the Department of the Navy, in reality the corps had always lived in the shadow of its larger cohort, dependent upon the Navy for missions that would ensure its continued viability. Fulfilling no prominent military role obviously distinct from the Army or Navy, the Marines continually suffered from legislative parsimony, which in turn made it difficult for the corps to carve out a larger niche for itself. As a consequence, the Marine self-image remained veiled by a sense of beleaguerment.

Senate, 3 pts., 57th Cong., 1st sess., 1902, S. Doc. 331; *Charges of Cruelty, Et., to Natives of the Philippines*, 57th Cong., 1st sess., 1902, S. Doc. 205; [Mansfield Storey], *Secretary Root's Record, "Marked Severities" in Philippine Warfare* (Boston: George W. Ellis, 1902); Richard E. Welch, Jr., "American Atrocities in the Philippines: The Indictment and the Response," *Pacific Historical Review* 43 (1974): 233–53.

37 Douglas Porch, in *The Conquest of Morocco* (New York: Alfred A. Knopf, 1983) and *The Conquest of the Sahara* (New York: Alfred A. Knopf, 1984), for example, 241–47, explores the institutional and behavioral effects of colonial service on the soldiers who served overseas, with indications that the French experience has some important parallels with that of the Marine Corps at this time. Also pertinent in this respect is his *French Foreign Legion*.

38 Butler's famous "I was a racketeer for capitalism" epigram surfaced in many of his speeches throughout the 1930s; Schmidt, *Maverick Marine*, 231–32.

39 Major Earl H. Ellis acknowledged that the marines killed many people in the Latin American wars but insisted that "the Marines are only doing their job as ordered by the people of the United States." See E. H. Ellis, "Bush Brigades," *Marine Corps Gazette* 6 (March 1921): 1–15.

This feeling served as a beneficial spur to planners searching in the interwar years for an essential mission that would ensure the service's survival. The perceived threat to a Marine identity also resulted in the effort to imprint the stamp of radicalization on every man who wore the uniform. Members of the corps were taught, explicitly and implicitly, to perform to some abstract standard of behavior, a standard so high that it was intended to compensate for the marines' sense of inferiority. This standard pervaded every level of the Marine Corps and affected the way troops were employed and performed in combat with mixed results. At times the marines lived up to this amorphous institutional self-image without suffering inordinate casualties, but on other occasions the Marine doctrine and standards of comportment conflicted with more rational, commonly accepted military practices, and at these times the marines paid a price in blood incommensurate with their accomplishments.

The history of the Marine Corps, especially in the 1920s and 1930s, is reflected in its search for a single, great mission. Because the Navy was the senior service around which Marine Corps functions were tailored, its duties since inception had consisted of little more than providing ships' detachments and guards for shore installations. Around the turn of the century, when the United States acquired overseas possessions for its coal-fired navy, the Marines finally found an expanded role for themselves in the defense of the more far-flung bases and coaling stations. These advanced-base forces became the nucleus of the Fourth Marine Brigade, which fought so well in Europe, as well as other expeditionary units employed in the Caribbean. While Marine participation in the European war was a public relations boon, on an institutional level, where survival was predicated on possessing an important mission distinct from the other services, it was dangerous. The Marines had been, after all, no more than a tiny adjunct to the American Expeditionary Forces (AEF).

To avoid any appearance of redundancy with the Army, some staff officers began to devote serious thought to the use of advanced-base troops in a role both necessary and unique to the national defense. Eventually, after the war, these troops evolved into the Fleet Marine Force and during the interwar period became an integral part of a fledgling amphibious warfare doctrine.[40] These developments were certainly not solely the product of bureaucratic politics between the services, but they did serve that end as well.

40 For a good brief overview of this period see Millett, *Semper Fidelis*, Chapter 12, especially 324–29, 331–33.

The bloody fiasco of the British and ANZAC forces at Gallipoli in 1915 had made clear the lesson that large amphibious operations could not be cobbled together on an ad hoc basis; careful planning and close liaison between naval and ground commanders were essential if potential disasters were to be avoided.[41] The study of the tactical and logistical problems associated with an amphibious assault came to dominate staff schools by the mid-1930s, but as with the armor enthusiasts in the United States and Europe during the interwar period, Marine thinkers had to overcome the indifference and hostility of the other services, internal opposition, and limited resources to test their ideas.

As it evolved, the amphibious warfare mission was exactly what the Marine Corps had always sought. First, it was of great value to the national defense. By the late 1920s and early 1930s the architects of Plan Orange, the blueprint for a possible war with Japan, recognized that the defeat of Japan would likely require the seizure of enemy bases before the Navy could administer the coup de grâce in a great Jutland-style battle.[42] To the extent that the Marine Corps could dominate the study of the strategic and tactical problems involved in amphibious operations and lay the necessary groundwork, it would dramatically increase its role in the defense establishment relative to the other services. Second, after early interest by the Army, this mission became the sole domain of the Marine Corps. Confronting the constraints of postwar demobilization, drastic budget cuts, and its own institutional inertia, the Army relinquished virtually any role in formulating an amphibious war doctrine.[43] Third, this mission fitted exactly the image the Marine Corps wanted for itself and in the eyes of the public.

The amphibious warfare mission embodied in the *Tentative Manual for Landing Operations* as it evolved in the 1930s provided justification for Marine self-images that had been fabricated and disseminated over two decades earlier. For much the same reason

41 R. H. Dunlap, "Lessons for Marines from the Gallipoli Campaign," *Marine Corps Gazette* 6 (September 1921): 237–52.
42 Ronald H. Spector, *Eagle against the Sun* (New York: Free Press, 1985), 54–69; Weigley, *The American Way of War*, 254–55.
43 The military services enjoyed larger budgets during the interwar period than before the Great War, but they were also more thinly stretched: the Army budget had to accommodate the extremely costly development of the Army Air Corps, as well as experiments with armor and airborne tactics; and until open Japanese abrogation of the naval arms limitation treaties in 1936 freed money for extensive new ship construction, the Navy was still expected to meet its widely flung strategic commitments with the limited and often outmoded resources then at hand; Ronald Spector, "The Military Effectiveness of the U.S. Armed Forces, 1919–1939," in Allan R. Millett and Williamson Murray, eds., *Military Effectiveness*, vol. 2, *The Interwar Period* (Boston: Allen and Unwin, 1988), 70–72, 78–80.

that airborne units became an elite within the Army, so amphibious assault made a sort of elite of the entire Marine Corps. Both missions envisioned troops being thrust into unknown, highly dangerous situations, lightly armed, perhaps largely unsupported, and with no means of evasion or escape for the individual soldiers once committed to combat. These missions required – in the new parlance of the Great War – storm troops. Whether the marines might usefully be classified as a military elite is of secondary importance to the belief they held in their own unique status. Every military institution builds upon the notion of its own distinctiveness as a means of developing esprit de corps and cohesiveness, but the means by which the Marine Corps managed this process were in some ways unique in the American experience.[44]

Public images of the Marine Corps must be considered within the context of the social and intellectual turmoil that followed the First World War. New images and assumptions about war arose that differed markedly from those carried to France by the doughboys. Demographic shifts, expanding roles for women, and increased federal intervention at all levels of society proved to be more than transient effects of wartime mobilization. Changing social conditions, accelerated during the war, fostered questions about values that seemed to apply to a bygone era. One of the more vivid forms of this clash was the literary revolt of the 1920s. The results, however, were far from clear or definitive. In the midst of the general societal upheaval and long-delayed reaction to the effects of industrialization and technological change, the writers of the younger generation developed a peculiarly bifurcated view of war that retained many romantic and fantastic images side by side with recognition of its realistic and ironic elements. Much of the old symbolism was appropriated for new uses, with the result that Americans entering the Second World War were not so idealistically self-assured as their forebears had been in 1917.[45]

44 Dennis Showalter discusses at length the concept of hereditary, functional, and warrior elites and concludes that the Marine Corps developed into a mixed functional/warrior elite; *Marine Corps Gazette* 63 (November 1979): 44–54. For a more general discussion, see Anthony Kellett, *Combat Motivation* (Boston: Kluwer-Nijhoff, 1982), 112–16.

45 My discussion of the American literature of the Great War benefits from several insightful commentaries, including Kennedy, *Over Here*, 205–30; Leonard, *Above the Battle*, 130–98; Jane Marcus, "Corpus/Corps/Corpse: Writing the Body in/at War," and Sharon O'Brien, "Combat Envy and Survivor Guilt: Willa Cather's 'Manly Battle Yarn,'" both in Helen M. Cooper et al., eds., *Arms and the Woman* (Chapel Hill: University of North Carolina Press, 1989), 124–67, 184–204; and Sandra M. Gilbert, "Soldier's Heart: Literary Men, Literary Women, and the Great War," in Margaret Randolph Higonnet et al., eds., *Behind the Lines* (New Haven: Yale University Press, 1987), 197–226.

American understanding of the Great War was shaped by romantic traditions dating back to the Civil War. Woodrow Wilson and his Progressive supporters clung to the Civil War heritage, in which the healing of American society and the restoration of the Union justified the war's terrible destructiveness. Images of just cause, virtue, sacrifice, and progress were part of a unified world view in which distinctions were, if not always absolute, at least unambiguous. The pain and sorrow of war were subsumed into its cathartic, rejuvenating effects on the individual and society. Individuals could be judged by their values, and these values were clearly visible for others to see.[46] Authors like Willa Cather and Edith Wharton could unselfconsciously portray fields of battle they never saw because they were interested primarily in how war affected the moral lives of individuals. For such insulated idealists, this "was a war without hatred of the enemy or guilt about the bloodshed – a war that could only be described in the language of dreams."[47]

As with past crusaders, patriotic Americans brandished their intolerance like the sign of the cross. Rescuing the world from European decadence, preserving Christian virtues, or supporting the one righteous political system, Americans seemed uniformly unquestioning of their assumptions, even when these conflicted among themselves. The single-minded idealism that Wilson promoted was easily co-opted by those with other political and moral agendas who exploited wartime passions for their own dubious causes. Americans fought against all enemies of order: "the Hun," perpetrators of atrocities and instruments of evil; Haitian *cacos*, atheistic, subhuman savages; as well as socialists, labor unions, and hyphenated Americans, who would steal the fruits of war and corrupt society in a vulnerable moment. That the old "order" was defined in distinctly male-oriented terms by an exclusive element of white society served to heighten the impact of the discord that followed the failed peace.[48]

46 For a useful overview of the romantic tradition as it influenced American literature see Charles V. Genthe, *American War Narratives, 1917–1918* (New York: David Lewis, 1969), 106–9.

47 Leonard, *Above the Battle*, 163. For more detailed discussions of these two authors and their literary agendas see the two chapters "Angel of Devastation: Edith Wharton on the Arts of the Enslaved" and "Lighting out for the Territories: Willa Cather's Lost Horizons" in Sandra M. Gilbert and Susan Gubar, *No Man's Land*, vol. 2, *Sex Changes* (New Haven: Yale University Press, 1989), 123–68, 169–212

48 Kennedy, *Over Here*, 84–92, 233–34; Margaret R. Higonnet and Patrice L.-R. Higonnet, "The Double Helix," in *Behind the Lines*, 31–47. The image of the war as a crusade was graphically presented in the official CPI poster entitled "Pershing's Crusaders," reproduced in Chenault, *Battlelines*, 56.

American volunteers who served with the European armies before U.S. entry wrote extensively of their experiences and preserved the romantic images of war intact. Men like Alan Seeger and Guy Empey provided occasionally vivid descriptions of the mud, suffering, death, and even atrocities, but the trenches remained abstractions whose remoteness produced sanitized descriptions of the battlefield.[49] Even when the AEF arrived in force in 1918, however, firsthand experience of combat tended to reinforce further the romanticist images, not transform them. The saccharine language of *The Stars and Stripes*, Y(MCA)-men, and other observers "assured readers that it had been a war without drawbacks: soldiers had learned discipline and piety as they passed from innocent camp amusements to duty in comfortable trenches and battles without terror."[50] The views of those who dissented were generally discredited because they did not fit the natural order of things; the harshness with which they were often silenced was as unnecessary as it was unjustified.

Several young writers emerged to challenge the fundamental assumptions of the romanticists. None truly shared the bitter, deep-seated disillusionment of their European counterparts; they were instead, in the words of Malcolm Cowley, "*rebels* in art and life." They spearheaded what was essentially an aesthetic and generational revolt and treated the war as "a fabulously useful, if expensively purchased, metaphor for the corruption of the culture they had under siege."[51] Ernest Hemingway so objected to the form and complacency of the romantic ethos typified by Willa Cather's *One of Ours*, that he inverted the meanings of all her images in *A Farewell to Arms*. The war was something ugly and profane from which the central character escapes only upon reverting to the sort of domesticity that Cather abjured. For others, like William Faulkner, e e cummings, and F. Scott Fitzgerald, the war served primarily as a backdrop and a metaphor for the destructive changes introduced into modern society.[52] Finally, there existed a small group of authors who more closely imitated the images and ideas of the

---

49 Alan Seeger, *Poems* (New York: Charles Scribner's Sons, 1917); Arthur Guy Empey, *"Over the Top" by an American Soldier Who Went* (New York: G. P. Putnam and Sons, 1917). Leonard (*Above the Battle*, 135–39) discusses the disillusionment of American participants before 1917 and the books that were widely available, such as *A Book of Verse of the Great War* put out by Yale University Press and the allegedly subversive book by Ellen N. LaMotte, *The Backwash of War: The Human Wreckage of the Battlefield as Witnessed by an American Hospital Nurse* (1916), which was banned in Britain, France, and the United States after 1917.
50 Leonard, *Above the Battle*, 165.
51 Cited in Kennedy, *Over Here*, 222, 227.
52 Leonard, *Above the Battle*, 178–80, 190–94.

famous European memoirists like Henri Barbusse, Erich Maria Remarque, and Edmund Blunden. These writers sought to portray the war in starkly realistic and harshly ironic terms that denied all remnants of romanticism. The Americans were not necessarily reflecting psychic wounds left by the war itself but rather commenting on the world at the time of their coming of age.[53]

To this group of authors the war was dirty, impersonal, mechanistic, and utterly futile. Man's individuality counted for nothing in his struggle against the forces of industrialization, where the machinelike quality of society was mirrored in the Army itself and the way it fought. John Dos Passos, in his novel *One Man's Initiation*, highlights the wastefulness and pain of the war: "God, if there were somewhere nowadays where you could flee from all this stupidity, from all this cant of governments, and this hideous reiteration of hatred, this strangling hatred . . ."[54] In his later novel *Three Soldiers*, Dos Passos compares the mechanical "production" of soldiers to the nature of war and American society as a whole. He traces individuals' evolution from recruit training and shipment to France ("Making the Mold" and "The Metal Cools"), to their combat experiences ("Machines"), and finally to the soldiers' – and, by implication, society's – ultimate dissolution ("Rust"). Dos Passos dwelt upon the unromantic side of soldiering, life in squalid garrisons and the oppressive, petty authoritarianism exercised over the common men. Traditional heroic figures are mocked: officers are incompetent, the hated "Y-men" venal, and the ranks brutish. The war and the corruption of the Old World have contaminated the once-innocent Americans and warped their values, an idea repeated by many authors of the period.[55]

From a fairly limited field of works written after the war depicting frontline life and values, a disproportionate number dealt in particular with the Marines rather than the Army. The three most prominent were the novels *Through the Wheat* and *Company K* and the play *What Price Glory*. Each conveyed images of the enemy, the Marine Corps, and the individual that were remarkably analogous to those in the memoirs and letters of Pacific War veterans. These images were self-conscious and occasionally heavy-handed efforts to deny the romantic standards that emphasized the purity and righteousness of Americans, assured the triumph of their cause,

53 Ibid., 177–95; Paul Fussell, *The Great War and Modern Memory* (New York: Oxford University Press, 1975), 160–61, 220–21.
54 John Dos Passos, *One Man's Initiation: 1917* (Ithaca: Cornell University Press, 1969), 81.
55 John Dos Passos, *Three Soldiers* (Boston: Houghton Mifflin, 1921); Leonard, *Above the Battle*, 180–84.

and legitimated all their sacrifices. Instead they showed the squalor of the lines and the human qualities of the marines, including their physical weaknesses and ethical failings.

The first of the three to come out was *Through the Wheat* in 1923. Author Thomas Boyd, a former marine, gave a view of Marine Corps life through the central character, Hicks, that normally remains invisible. Stuck doing stevedore duties with "evil-odored blacks" for nine months, Hicks finds life at the front, when he finally reaches it, to be far from what he imagined. Instead of great bravery and meaningful deaths he sees suicides, self-inflicted wounds, recklessness, callousness, and butchery. But Boyd expresses a deep ambivalence about the war when, from the senselessness and cowardice he depicts, bravery and victory arise. Hicks becomes oblivious of the fire and numb to his fear and ends by inadvertently leading a successful attack. Boyd sees the marines largely as victims of the war whose natural state is one of miserable and uncomprehending passivity. Individuals can exercise a limited degree of autonomy, but fate and circumstances beyond anyone's control may at any time render human action purposeless. In this way Boyd displaces the causes and effects of battlefield events onto abstract, impersonal forces.[56]

When it was first staged in 1924, the popular play *What Price Glory* shocked audiences with its profanity. Generally associated with the movement toward greater realism and more natural use of the vernacular in American theater, *What Price Glory* also offered a portrait of the Marine Corps that, if not entirely complimentary, at least appealed to audiences as an apparently authentic and darkly attractive picture of the marines at war. Playwrights Laurence Stallings, who as a Marine officer lost a leg in the war, and Maxwell Anderson did not intend their portrayal as an indictment against the Marine Corps but as a description of the character type drawn to the service. The cynicism and turpitude of Captain Flagg and First Sergeant Quirt in dealing with the French girl Charmaine went against the accepted romantic images of Americans' chivalry, but the two men showed a loyalty to the corps and their profession that would only be equaled by John Wayne in the movie *Sands of Iwo Jima*. In combat these salty old-timers were without peer. They did not perform superhumanly – indeed, Quirt exposes his leg to enemy fire so he can return to the rear ahead of Flagg – but they were tough, professional, and knowledgeable about combat and human nature. Quirt's action, for instance, comes only at the end of the company's tour in the front lines and after several harrowing

---

56 Thomas Boyd, *Through the Wheat* (New York: Charles Scribner's Sons, 1923).

trips to keep the marines supplied. Acting according to their own moral code, Flagg and Quirt provided the discipline and inspiration necessary to mold recruits and newly commissioned officers into useful combatants. The realities of the front lines were graphically staged: the filth, the blood, and the language with which all the men armored themselves against the strain. The popular success of the play, which was also made into a silent movie directed by Raoul Walsh, attracted more attention for the Marine Corps than it had ever known in peacetime America.[57]

If the risqué dialogue in *What Price Glory* was intended to capture realistically the language and attitudes of the old-time marines in France, the events described in *Company K* represented an effort to invert virtually every traditional romantic image of war. Utilizing vignettes of 113 marines in a fictional Company K, the author, another former marine, exposes the seamy underside of overseas service and wartime hatreds. All morals and scruples disappear: the marines steal from impoverished French peasants, get drunk, commit rape, and contract venereal diseases from the whores they visit; they are victimized by the Red Cross and YMCA men; and they suffer at the hands of their own stupid officers. The men demonstrate barbarity of the kind attributed in the wartime propaganda to the "Huns" in Belgium. The justice of the trenches, official and unofficial, is harsh and swift, whether in the execution of a man for cowardice or in the case of a private who takes matters into his own hands and bayonets his lieutenant in the trenches. One man suggests attending a general court-martial as a corrective to all that talk about the "nobility and comradeship of war." These men appear to have lost all ability to discern right and wrong or act according to anything but the basest morality. As a counterpoint to romantic tradition, the book cuts straight to the core.[58]

The relationship between combatants in *Company K* might be describing Guadalcanal in 1942 instead of Europe in 1918. Americans and Germans behave with equal bestiality toward each other. A helpless marine, blinded in a gas attack, is brutally clubbed and bayoneted in the act of surrender during a German night raid. A terrified German asks to be killed because he has heard of American atrocities against prisoners. "Well, the dirty louse," responds a marine, "to say a thing like that when everybody knows it's the *Germans*, and not ourselves who do those things." When a German prisoner kills one of his captors with a concealed knife, the marine's avenging

57 Maxwell Anderson and Laurence Stallings, *What Price Glory* in *Three American Plays*, edited by Kenneth MacGowan (New York: Harcourt, Brace, 1926).
58 William Edward March [Campbell], *Company K* (1933; reprint, New York: Sagamore Press, 1957), 45–141 passim.

friend savagely knifes and clubs the German, afterward noting, "It all goes to show that you can't trust a German. I know I never gave one an even break after that." The central episode of the book is the cold-blooded execution of twenty-two German prisoners on the blatantly illegal orders of the company commander while they were held safely under guard behind the lines. Virtually all of these characterizations recur in marine images of the Japanese nine years later. The only difference is that the Germans and Americans depicted in the book are essentially alike, whereas the Japanese would be seen as a species apart and unrelated.[59]

An unusual aspect of *Company K* compared to other American literature covering the war are the glimpses given of the marines' homecoming. In keeping with the rest of the book and with the time it was published – 1933, shortly after the breakup of the Bonus Army[60] – the marines find no peace or escape from the war. Returning with physical and emotional wounds, the marines are treated with pity, revulsion, or ignored altogether. Wives cannot stand the sight of disfiguring scars or have been unfaithful; the men have lost their jobs, and nightmares drive others to suicide. Although exaggerated, everything portrayed in the book is based on real events, emotions, and behavior generated by the Marine Corps, by the war hatreds and dehumanizing conditions at the front, and by the attitudes of the people at home. Although its popular success never fully matched its critical acclaim, *Company K* provided insights into the war not equaled elsewhere in American literature of the period.

Aside from the notoriety gained from the literary revolt of the 1920s, the Marines reached a larger and more diverse audience through a new ally, the Hollywood filmmakers. The Marine Corps could not have chosen a better public relations partner, and with the First World War a close liaison began that has lasted up to the present. "Of all the armed forces," writes one film critic, "the Marine Corps has been the one branch that over the years best publicized its role in the nation's martial history."[61] By providing actual

59 Ibid., 46, 48, 50, 79–90.
60. The onset of the Great Depression had pushed many veterans to the point of desperation, and with no programs in operation to assist them, the Bonus Army, numbering more than 40,000 men, had descended on Washington to press for the immediate payment of a cash bonus. In mid-1932 the Republican administration and the press saw the convergence of the destitute veterans on the capital as a threat of either communist revolution or rampant fascism. The chief of staff at the time, Douglas MacArthur, ordered mounted cavalry and infantrymen using fixed bayonets and tear gas to disperse the marchers and run them and their families out of the District. See D. Clayton James, *The Years of MacArthur* (Boston: Houghton Mifflin, 1970), 1:382–414.
61. Lawrence H. Suid, *Guts and Glory* (Reading, Mass.: Addison-Wesley, 1978), 92.

marines as extras, access to bases and training facilities, and technical advisors, the Marine Corps helped ensure that in movies like *Star Spangled Banner* (1917) and *The Unbeliever* (1918), the service was depicted as an elite organization, combat-ready and professional. Lon Chaney, in the role of a tough drill instructor in *Tell It to the Marines*, served as a prototype illustrating how the Marines turned raw recruit-boys into mature, courageous men. Other typical film titles of the period include *Let It Rain, Flight, The Leatherneck, The Cockeyed World, Leathernecking, Come on Marines, Moran of the Marines, Devil Dogs of the Air*, and *The Marines Are Coming*. Except for the movie version of *What Price Glory*, most films about the Marines in the interwar period dealt with their roles in China and the Caribbean. Such films emphasized the romantic allure of these distant stations and helped give the prospect of Marine service an exotic flavor.[62] As cinematic art there was little to recommend these pictures, but as vehicles for expounding and perpetuating the mythic dimensions of the Marine Corps they were excellent.

Although little of the interwar literature or film received lasting acclaim, many of the images they presented recur throughout the Second World War and into the post-1945 period. Foremost is an image of toughness, more or less brutal, like the old frontiersmen of American myth. Partly the product of the environment they have chosen, partly a measure of their distance, physical and psychological, from society, the marines, like backwoodsmen, could not be harnessed by society or, as in the case of Captain Flagg, even by their superiors. By personal outlook, behavior, and their own code of honor they appeared best suited for work on the periphery, whether in the trenches of France, the jungles of Central America, or the ports of China and the Philippines. Yet the marines were not untrammeled individualists; they showed strong discipline and loyalty, but only according to their own internal standards. These myths were not simply a reflection of an existing reality; they were a source and a condition of that reality. Myths served to harness past experiences together with expectations for the future and create the volatile universe in which the marines would see themselves moving on the eve of going into battle.

The difficulty of measuring the impact of the literary and iconographic conflict after the First World War on attitudes in 1941 is compounded by the way their apparently irreconcilable images coexisted with each other. Few American soldiers entering the

---

62. These misleading images became so pervasive at one point that Headquarters Marine Corps issued a warning that overseas service in these places was "devoid of the thrills and glory of actual combat" (Millett, *Semper Fidelis*, 262).

service after Pearl Harbor had illusions about the awfulness of combat or exaggerated ideas of the war's abstract meaning, but they still found meaning in the war, if only later.[63] The great irony in comparing the First and Second World Wars is that the negative, horrifying aspects of war became themselves the source of romanticization. The goal of war became cynically, if understandably, foreshortened by 1945 to one of survival. Grand political motives, as embodied in Roosevelt's Four Freedoms, were never as important for the soldiers' consumption as for the civilians back home. The measure of success for most GIs was to have served and endured the threats of physical annihilation at the hands of the enemy.[64]

The key to this paradoxical shift was the change in focus between different levels of perception and understanding. Many "romanticists" in 1918 tried to find transcendent meaning in war as an earlier generation did in 1865, but the conditions had changed dramatically: "Silent men have again come home from war, just as they had after Appomattox. But this time the veterans are mute because they are half-dead and cut off from the society that sent them to fight, not because they guard the treasured memory of an inexpressible ordeal." It was not from lack of firsthand experience of war's horrors that men like Oliver Wendell Holmes and Floyd Gibbons wrote as they did; rather they hoped that romanticism would provide a bridge between the experiences of soldiers and noncombatants; it would provide a medium by which the war's meaning could be expressed in terms comprehensible to civilians. This was possible under the conditions of the Civil War, but "[c]oming to terms with war" in 1918 meant "coming to terms with yourself, with the men who fought at your side, and with the citizens

63. Samuel A. Stouffer et al., *The American Soldier*, vol. 1, *Adjustment during Army Life* (Princeton: Princeton University Press, 1949), 437–42. A methodological caution and explanation are in order here since Stouffer et al. deal exclusively with the Army. These particular conclusions, and others that will be cited later, were drawn from men immediately after induction, before they had received the institutional imprint of Army ideas (i.e., before recruit training) as distinct from the Marine Corps indoctrination, and thus they apply with equal validity (within the parameters of statistical error established by the authors) to all inductees drawn from this society. Various memoirists such as Russell Davis and Eugene Sledge individually support Stouffer's position, and I have found no Marine accounts that directly contradict it. I have avoided using other data from this study that were collected at later stages of individuals' military service and thus less easily applied to the Marine case.
64. American soldiers in 1917 had little or no understanding of or interest in the ideals for which they were depicted as fighting; Leonard, *Above the Battle*, 167. In the Second World War American soldiers are portrayed as pragmatists and realists completely lacking any crusading spirit; Peter Aichinger, *The American Soldier in Fiction, 1880–1963* (Ames: Iowa State University Press, 1975), 34, 37.

who sent you to fight."[65] This overtaxed the power of romanticism, but it was still the language that was best understood. David Kennedy writes of the First World War that

> at the level of popular culture, there remained a residue, if not of the older values about war, at least of their rhetorical forms. For the former doughboys who clung to those forms, the literature of disillusionment was not only obscure and mystifying, but seemed to deny the very authenticity of their perceptions of their experience in France.[66]

What Eric J. Leed has labeled the "liberal" and "conservative" experiences of war co-existed side by side.[67] And indeed those rhetorical forms upon which the realists, or "writers of disillusionment," depended necessarily drew to a great extent on that romantic tradition, further confusing the distinction.

This overlapping of traditional rhetorical forms and images continued through the Second World War as well. Memoirists attempting to manipulate the conventions with the intention of ascribing new meanings to old symbols and metaphors often discovered that their audiences had so poor a conception of the actual realities of war and being under fire that they could not recognize the new distinctions intended by the authors. Nor could uninitiated readers fill in gaps left in the narratives. Russell Davis spoke respectfully of a friend's "intelligent cruelty" that effectively quelled his sense of panic in his first battle, but the creeping hysteria that Davis felt and the combination of affection and true, institutionally sanctioned cruelty behind the friend's actions remain at best only partially articulated.[68] Likewise the euphemistic, sanitized, highly selective stories covering battles and service life written by correspondents and official service reporters produced a language of war-for-public-consumption that remained virtually unexamined and unchallenged. Heightened public sensitivity to propaganda created the irony of readers making allowance for exaggeration or omission before blithely accepting such descriptions or pronouncements without discrimination. Partial truth became widely accepted, and deeper meaning was seldom sought.[69]

65. Leonard, *Above the Battle*, 194.
66. Kennedy, *Over Here*, 229.
67. In simplified terms, the liberal experience emphasized "loss of youth, the death, horror and pollution of war"; the conservative "centered upon the experience of comradeship and community" (Leed, *No Man's Land*, 25).
68. Russell Davis, *Marine at War* (Boston: Little, Brown and Company, 1961), 82.
69. Paul Fussell, *Wartime* (New York: Oxford University Press, 1989). Fussell's central purpose is to illustrate how the war damaged "intellect, discrimination, honesty, individuality, complexity, ambiguity, and irony, not to mention privacy

When war came at the end of 1941, the Marine Corps again appeared ready to be the first into action. The young men who flooded Marine recruiting offices in the weeks after Pearl Harbor were looking to join the service of Captain Flagg and the old "Horse Marines" of Peiping. They assumed it would be "tough" but that the Marines would be in action first and get the job done faster.[70] The Marines had two divisions formed, at least on paper, and had been planning for such an opportunity for the previous ten years. The men who sailed for Guadalcanal in the summer of 1942 possessed a strongly self-conscious image of themselves as marines that was in part based on the interwar myths that had grown up around the corps. They also had an identity that was the product of their initial training and their first taste of actual life in the service that even the most realistic books and movies never reveal in full.

To emphasize the power and extent of these institutional and public images is not to argue for any systemic explanation of events. The historical actors were not mere puppets of forces they did not understand and could not escape, but the images created and disseminated by recruiters, public relations men, and correspondents, while serving the institutional needs of the Marine Corps by bolstering recruitment and individual standards, also took on a life of their own, establishing standards and expectations inside and out of the service that affected all that followed. The amphibious warfare expertise developed in the 1920s and 1930s defined the institution's goals and prescribed the means for achieving them; the public images shaped goals and methods on a personal level. The creation of an ideal marine was thus the product of direct institutional action, but not wholly under its control. These images were lenses through which the marines viewed their world. To the extent that these lenses contained distortions or colorings, they help to explain the reasons for the marines' behavior in the Pacific War.

and wit" (ix). This is a long casualty list indeed. See also Fussell's comments on the language listed in his brief glossary of adopted "feudal" terms in *The Great War and Modern Memory*, 21–22.

70. This attitude is almost universally expressed in every memoir that mentions motivations for enlisting. For examples see Davis, *Marine at War*; Robert Leckie, *Helmet for My Pillow* (New York: Random House, 1957); and typewritten manuscript, Nolan V. Marbrey Papers, PPC, MCHC.

2

CREATING MARINES – AND A
MASCULINE IDEAL

In one sense, the measure of the marines' wartime success is the degree to which their behavior matched the hypermasculine ideals they extolled. At the heart of the process of institutionalized pro-creation – of consciously "making" marines – was the manipulation of gender roles to both define and instill those ideals. Gender-specific archetypes served two militarily useful functions: first, by fostering the emotional separation of marines from civilian society, they created a strong corporate identity with its own rules and values; and second, they generated highly polarized boundaries that reduced any "outsiders" – broadly defined – into potential objects for violent overthrow. Socialization began at the time of induction and continued until a man was no longer a contributing member of the corps as a result of discharge, crippling wounds, or debilitating illness.

The masculine ideal consciously fostered in Marine training encouraged misogyny as a means of learning a process of objectification that could then be transferred to the Pacific battlefields and the brutal conquest of the Japanese. The same phenomenon occurred in the radical process of "reconstructing bodies" as practiced among German fascists. The military training environment, what Klaus Theweleit labels the "drill-machine," produced particularly masculine soldiers by freeing them of civilian values and sensibilities, and this led to the creation of a larger, collective "troop-machine." This troop-machine became self-sustaining, replicating itself through a specific ideological imperative that expressed consciously masculine traits of "determination, strength, precision," and "the strict order of straight lines and rectangles," which were then tied to other male constructs "such as the 'nation.' " The some-times pathological fear and loathing that many of Theweleit's *Frei-korps* subjects felt for everything female was easily channeled into similar reactions to the Bolshevik/Asiatic "floods" in the East.[1] The

---

1 Klaus Theweleit, *Male Fantasies*, vol. 2, *Male Bodies: Psychoanalyzing the White Terror* (Minneapolis: University of Minnesota Press, 1989), 155, 160.

Marine Corps achieved a transformation among its recruits that
was comparable in substance if not form. The institutional programs of indoctrination and training represented a mechanism to
sustain perpetual war, driven by an escalatory cycle of self-defined
military necessity. To the extent that the Marines achieved a generally higher degree of homogeneity among their members than
did either the Army or the Navy, and perhaps a deeper commitment to the institution's ideals, the results were the product of
deliberate policies and historical conditions, not any inherent superiority suggested in myth.[2]

Although some histories of the Marine Corps in the Pacific War
emphasize the importance of recruit training in preparing men for
battle, among First Division memoirists the subject receives little
comment.[3] From the notes and letters that have survived this stage
of the marines' experience, the world into which the individual was
thrust at the time of recruit training made a profound first impression. But with subsequent assignments to provide additional perspective, the sense of disjunction fostered by the boot camp
environment often receded and appeared commonplace or even
quaint when juxtaposed to the liminality of battle. In one notable
exception, Eugene Sledge attributed his survival on Peleliu to his
senior drill instructor, "a strict disciplinarian, a total realist about
our future, and an absolute perfectionist dedicated to excellence."
Sledge's example makes plain the importance of the twin functions performed by this initial training and indoctrination: as a
bridge from civilian to military society and as a template for subsequent attitudes and behavior.[4] J. Glenn Gray, a draftee soldier-

2 Written at the height of American discontent with the Vietnam War, William
  Mares's *The Marine Machine* (Garden City: Doubleday, 1971) was intended as an
  indictment of Marine training methods by one who had experienced them firsthand. If the title suggests some parallel to Theweleit's model, Mares's description
  of what he considers a dehumanizing process bears even more striking parallels
  to the methods successfully utilized by Theweleit's proto-Nazis to create ideologically committed soldiers. A more superficial but contemporary example is the
  chapter on making marines in Keith Ayling, *Semper Fidelis* (Boston: Houghton
  Mifflin, 1943), 13–33.
3 Not surprisingly, the numerous quasi-official and unofficial wartime histories of
  the corps and anecdotal or pictorial collections also downplay this side of the
  Marine Corps experience. See Rolfe Boswell, *Leatherneck* (New York: Thomas Y.
  Crowell, 1943); Aimée Crane, *Marines at War* (New York: Hyperion Press, 1943);
  James D. Horan and Gerold Frank, *Out in the Boondocks* (New York: Putnam,
  1943); William P. McCahill, *First to Fight* (Philadelphia: McKay, 1943); Clyde H.
  Metcalf, *The Marine Corps Reader* (New York: Putnam, 1944); and Ted Shane,
  Heroes of the Pacific (New York: Messner, 1944).
4 E. B. Sledge, *With the Old Breed* (Novato: Presidio Press, 1981), 158. In his intro-
  duction to Mares's book, David M. Shoup, former commandant of the Marine
  Corps, writes tellingly that a crucial function of boot camp is to teach recruits to

philosopher who fought in Europe, saw two distinct identities
brought out by military service that "could succeed each other with
lightning rapidity": as human beings, soldiers were capable of kind-
ness, gentleness, and honesty; as military functionaries, they "could
be brutal beyond measure."[5] These twin personalities were fostered
and brought into uneasy coexistence by basic training. Eric J. Leed
suggests that the pervasive sense of estrangement felt by soldiers
of the First World War was the direct result "of being 'made'
strange."[6]

In granting license to kill, American society was supposedly sending conflicting messages that were difficult for common soldiers to
sort out. An oft-quoted passage from S. L. A. Marshall expresses
the basic dilemma that the Army and, by extension, the Marine
Corps had to confront in trying to superimpose their institutional
values atop those supposedly ingrained among civilians:

> The Army cannot unmake him. It must reckon with the fact
> that he comes from a civilization in which aggression, con-
> nected with the taking of life, is prohibited and unacceptable.
> The teaching and the ideals of that civilization are against
> killing, against taking advantage. The fear of aggression has
> been expressed to him so strongly and absorbed by him so
> deeply and pervadingly – practically with his mother's milk –
> that it is part of the normal man's emotional make-up.[7]

Marshall overstates his case as part of an elaborate societal myth
intended to camouflage a more unpleasant truth. The idea of citizens being "remade" as killers, of adopting a new persona in uniform, is widely expressed by memoirists, but it is a specious
argument to assuage moral sensibilities among civilians. As Gray
suggests, the killer exists in men all along and has simply to be
brought out and encouraged. Americans proved as adept and ruthless in the exercise of violence as their totalitarian enemies: the
targets and the forms of violence were different, but the specific

---

live with each other and instill "a deep understanding of interdependence" among
marines.
5 Gray's draft notice and doctorate in philosophy from Columbia University arrived
in the same mail (Gray, *The Warriors*, 8–9).
6 Leed, *No Man's Land*, 4.
7 S. L. A. Marshall, *Men against Fire* (1947; reprint, New York: William Morrow,
1964), 78. Marshall saw this point as the core issue regarding the abilities and
limitations of "the American fighting man." Moving beyond a superficial validity,
this argument has serious problems: foremost is the monolithic image Marshall
suggests both as related to how all American soldiers feel and regarding the
cultural heritage used as a measure; for more general discussions regarding social
inhibitions on the taking of human life see also Kellett, *Combat Motivation*, 294–
95; and Richard Holmes, *Acts of War* (New York: Free Press, 1985), 376–93.

language of justification, making allowances for cultural differences, was strikingly similar.[8]

To the extent that they succeeded in producing men who outwardly conformed to their ideal, the Marines greatly enhanced their
carefully cultivated reputation as a select group of warriors. Concrete circumstances were far more important for their success than
reliance on their often mystical explanations, but it is in itself significant that the line between the two sometimes becomes blurred.
Because they were the smallest of the Depression-starved services,
the Marines were able, in the late 1930s as in the First World War,
to exercise an exceptional degree of selectivity in recruitment. Out
of approximately 205,000 applications for first-time enlistment in
the three fiscal years preceding the war, only 38,080 were accepted.[9]
They developed among their new recruits and officer candidates
a dedication to the institution's ideals that was often regarded by
critical outsiders as antithetical to America's liberal, democratic traditions, ideals whose imagery seems disquietingly suggestive of contemporary fascist spectacles. A young, middle-class midwesterner
found the institutional purposiveness and methods largely unchanged when he went through Officer Candidate School (OCS)
almost twenty years after Pearl Harbor. After noting how appropriate the "monastic isolation" of the training camp was for the
purpose, he observed, "It was a society unto itself, demanding total
commitment to its doctrines and values, rather like one of those
quasi-religious military orders of ancient times, the Teutonic
Knights or the Theban Band."[10] The outward circumstances of this
training were not much different from those of the Army, but the
new marines, at least at the start of the war, were treated more as
initiates than simple inductees, and their drill instructors claimed
for themselves a larger role as proselytizers and not mere teachers.
After 1943, with the forced presence of draftees and the experiences of actual fighting in the Pacific, the emphasis on indoctrination shifted increasingly toward training in technical skills and
more realistic exercises. The inculcation of special attitudes among
marines during and immediately after boot camp or OCS did not,

8 Richard Drinnon makes this case forcefully in *Facing West* (New York: New
   American Library, 1980). Even in the process of destroying entire cultures they
   regarded as inferior – or simply nonexistent – Americans maintained the same
   argument Marshall makes.
9 United States Marine Corps, *Annual Report of the Major General Commandant of
   the United States Marine Corps to the Secretary of the Navy for the Fiscal Year 1939*,
   4 (hereafter cited as *Annual Report*, FY [year]); *Annual Report*, FY 1940, 9; *Annual
   Report*, FY 1941, 14.
10 Philip Caputo, *A Rumor of War* (New York: Holt, Rinehart and Winston,
   1977), 8.

however, mark the end, or even the culmination, of military socialization.

This process evolved throughout a marine's service. However strong and vibrant the attitudes of a new marine private or second lieutenant, these changed upon the individual's assignment to a line unit, his movement to the theater of operations, his first and subsequent experiences under fire, shipment back to the United States, and his eventual separation from the service. This was the long road to what James Jones labeled "the final EVOLUTION OF A SOLDIER."[11] To maintain units at full strength, recent recruits were constantly being mixed in with veterans, and in this process each group influenced the attitudes of the other. These transfusions of "new blood," combined with the unit history and reputation, created and re-created the quality and character of every combat formation. The continuous interplay between the "old corps" and new men affected how informal standards of conduct were established at the time of Guadalcanal and influenced the directions in which they shifted as the war continued.

Although available statistics and explicit policies cannot unravel the complex dynamics of military indoctrination and socialization, they provide a logical starting point to separate official from unofficial practices and attitudes. The Marines were able to cobble together a division for an overseas campaign nine months after Pearl Harbor only because the possibility had long been foreseen that the United States would eventually enter the war. During the "short-of-war" period, which had started with the proclamation of a national emergency on 8 September 1939, the United States had taken several measures to enhance military preparedness. Of particular importance were the call for general mobilization, including the activation of the Reserves, in the fall of 1940, and the implementation of the nation's first peacetime draft in the spring of 1941, from which the Navy and Marine Corps were initially exempt. Despite these efforts, however, the steps actually taken fell short of those required for full mobilization. Pearl Harbor precipitated an instant manpower crisis among the military services. The problems of recruiting, classifying, and training the necessary military manpower have been best explored in the case of the Army, but the Marine Corps, on a smaller scale, shared these same difficulties.[12]

11 On the "evolution of a soldier," see James Jones, *WWII* (New York: Grosset and Dunlap, 1975), 16, 25, 30–31, 54–55, 196–201, 255–56.
12 See especially Russell F. Weigley, *History of the United States Army* (Bloomington: Indiana University Press, 1984); United States Army, Office of Military History, *United States Army in World War II*, vol. 1, *The Army Ground Forces*, pt. 1, *The*

Although modest if measured by subsequent wartime programs, the steps taken during the short-of-war period were nonetheless significant. Appropriations and authorized manning levels were adjusted upward by Congress in steady increments. Two months before the German invasion of Poland the Marine Corps carried 18,013 enlisted men on their rolls. One year later this number had risen to 26,369, and by 30 November 1941 the total strength of the corps, officer and enlisted, had expanded to 65,881.[13] Of this additional manpower, a large percentage went into the Fleet Marine Force (FMF), the Marine ground and aviation expeditionary units. The FMF grew from a minuscule 4,840 in mid-1939 to 9,749 in August 1940, and then more than tripled to 29,532 by 30 November 1941.[14] This expansion of the FMF allowed the Marines to raise the First and Second Divisions in February 1941, the first division-sized units in their history.

One reason for this swift expansion of the Marine Corps was the order for general mobilization issued on 15 October 1940 that called up the reserve forces. In mid-1940, to complement the 26,000 enlisted regulars, a further 14,976 men were in the Reserves. With the call-up in October, 232 officers and over 5,000 enlisted men came onto active duty immediately, with other cases reviewed by Headquarters Marine Corps for further disposition; by June 1941, 9,468 reservists had come on active duty.[15] These men were integrated with the regulars in existing units rather than being maintained in separate reserve formations. Although primarily a matter of expediency in a service as small as the Marine Corps, this policy also served to erase outward distinctions between regulars and reservists that for a time plagued the Army's original tripartite system structured around separate divisions raised from regulars, the National Guard, and selective service conscripts.[16]

Despite these additions to their rolls, however, Marine resources

Organization of Ground Combat Troops, by Kent Roberts Greenfield, Robert R. Palmer, and Bell I. Wiley, and pt. 2, *The Procurement and Training of Ground Combat Troops*, by Robert R. Palmer, Bell I. Wiley, and William R. Keast (Washington: Historical Division, Department of the Army, 1947–48).

13 *Annual Reports*, FY 1939, 9; FY 1940, 9; FY 1941, 14; and United States Marine Corps, *History of U.S. Marine Corps Operations in World War II*, 5 vols. (Washington: Historical Branch, G-3, HQMC, 1958–71) (hereafter cited as Official History), vol. 1, *Pearl Harbor to Guadalcanal*, by Frank O. Hough, Verle E. Ludwig, and Henry I. Shaw, Jr. (1958), 48.

14 Official History, 1:47–48.

15 *Annual Report*, FY 1941, 14, 46. Of those called in October, 1,183 enlisted reservists, or 19%, were granted delays, discharges, or a new duty status; United States Marine Corps, Division of the Reserve, *The Marine Corps Reserve: A History* (Washington: Division of the Reserve, HQMC, 1966), 59.

16 Weigley, *History of the Army*, 427–36.

remained seriously overstretched. Although thousands of new men came in, a large number had to be diverted to nonoperational duties like providing guards for the growing number of naval installations, and others were urgently needed to help garrison outposts like Wake and Midway.[17] Neither division was at more than 50 percent of its established strength when war broke out. Typical of the disorder during this period, the First Division was without the entire 1st Marine Regiment, which had been deactivated in the summer of 1941 because of manpower shortages. Even before Pearl Harbor the First Marine Division was made up mostly of new, inexperienced men, but the flood of wartime volunteers further diluted its small core of experienced veterans. First-time enlistments in the Marine Corps for fiscal year 1939 numbered only 5,861, but in 1940 this figure rose to 11,059, and for the fiscal year ending 30 June 1941 there were 19,084 new enlistments, men upon whom both divisions drew heavily.[18]

In accordance with accepted military practice, the First Division relied on the use of cadres to build new units – that is, drawing off experienced officers and NCOs from existing battalions to train the men in newly activated units. In one more extreme case, virtually all of 1st Battalion, 5th Marines was used to form the 1st Raider Battalion – a unit outside the division's control – and had to be rebuilt by drawing down the strength of the other battalions.[19] The recently fleshed-out units in turn often had to provide similar cadres for yet other units. This spread the experienced men very thin, and as a result, many NCOs were promoted who had little more experience than the troops they were to lead.

Immediate operational commitments compounded the divisions' difficulties by drawing off their more seasoned men. The Second Division detached almost half its existing strength in mid-1941 for guard duties on Iceland and in January 1942 for defense of American Samoa. Likewise, in March 1942 the First Division detached the 7th Marines for duties in Samoa. Many of the division's most experienced men were transferred into the regiment in expectation that they would be in combat before the bulk of the division.[20] As it turned out, the division fought for over a month on Guadalcanal

17 Official History, 1:50.
18 Annual Reports, FY 1939, 9; FY 1940, 9; FY 1941, 14.
19 According to Gerald C. Thomas, the division was "robbed" to make up this unit that some felt to be superfluous in "an outfit as good as the Marine Corps"; Gerald C. Thomas, interview by Benis M. Frank, September–November 1966, 230, 235, OHC, MCHC.
20 George McMillan, The Old Breed (Washington: Infantry Journal Press, 1949), 12.

before the 7th Marines were able to rejoin it and see their first combat.

Because of the turmoil caused by the constant assimilation and redistribution of men within the First Division, training was severely constrained. The men who fought on Guadalcanal were proficient in the use of individual weapons, and because these were often the only types of training available under the existing circumstances, they were also relatively well trained in individual field skills and squad- or platoon-level tactics. Company commanders, however, often had difficulty simply keeping track of the new faces moving into their units and had limited opportunities to conduct field exercises. The situation was even worse for battalion and regimental commanders and their staffs, most of whom had to learn the complexities of their jobs in combat because neither the time nor the facilities existed to run thorough exercises at these levels. This was just one of the unintended and potentially disastrous by-products of the hurried, improvisational expansion. Another was that in an effort to bolster the FMF units, experienced officers and NCOs were sometimes stripped from the training establishments, making the task of the latter even more difficult.[21]

Although the Marine Corps expanded neither as rapidly nor, relatively speaking, as extensively as the Army or Navy (see Table 1), the pace of expansion nevertheless outstripped the ability of its training establishment to keep up. There were two recruit depots in the Marine Corps: Parris Island, South Carolina, trained most of the men recruited east of the Mississippi and supported the First Division, stationed at New River, North Carolina, and the depot at San Diego – the "Hollywood marines" – quickly supplemented with nearby Camp Elliott, trained those men recruited from the western half of the country and supported the Second Division at Camp Pendleton. In the aftermath of Pearl Harbor, the Marines were inundated with men who required training and organizing in a hurry. Whereas the number of men inducted in November 1941 had been 1,978, in December this number shot up to 10,224, and in January 1942 it soared further to 22,686 (see Table 2). Large

21 Many of the basic skills that would later be taught in boot camp and the replacement centers had to be taught by the divisions in 1941. To compound their difficulties, the division had to construct its own base and training facilities in the newly acquired North Carolina scrub around New River. For different high-level perspectives on the nature and difficulties of training during this period see A. A. Vandegrift and Robert B. Asprey, *Once a Marine* (New York: Norton, 1964), 98–105; and Thomas interview, 226–42; on a more personal, anecdotal level see Lester W. Clark, *An Unlikely Arena* (New York: Vantage, 1989), 10–12; and Francis Fox Parry, *Three-War Marine* (Pacifica: Pacifica Press, 1987), 35–39, 41–51.

Table 1. *Relative growth of the armed forces, 1940–1945:*
male personnel strength, by service

Date	Army	Navy	Marine Corps	Total
30 June 1940	100	100	100	100
31 Dec. 1941	630	240	270	470
31 Dec. 1942	2,010	780	850	1,500
31 Dec. 1943	2,700	1,450	1,410	2,220
31 Dec. 1944	2,970	1,930	1,630	2,520
30 June 1945	3,040	2,040	1,640	2,600

Index: 30 June 1940 = 100.

Source: Eli Ginzberg, James K. Anderson, Sol W. Ginsburg, and John L. Herma, *The Ineffective Soldier*, vol. 1, *The Lost Divisions* (New York: Columbia University Press, 1959), 18.

tent cities grew up overnight to accommodate the new recruits, but the fourfold increase in the monthly average of recruits trained, from 1,600 to 6,800, created additional problems.[22]

Aside from shortages of equipment and facilities, the biggest problem affecting the training establishment throughout the war was obtaining qualified instructors. There were not enough existing drill instructor (DI) teams to cope with the influx of new recruits in early 1942. Even after grabbing those enlisted men awaiting Officer Candidate Class and, over the strident protests of the staff, temporarily assigning 121 NCOs from the First Division, Parris Island still had to resort to the expedient of holding on to recently graduated recruits for this duty. The use of privates first class with only two or three months in service as assistant DIs to train and indoctrinate the new recruits was far from ideal, and the quality of recruit training suffered because of their inexperience. A DI school was eventually established at Parris Island, but there were no uniform or servicewide guidelines for a DI's duties and responsibilities. Nor were there provisions to monitor how closely or precisely a single platoon or series followed the training schedule, which was itself subject to frequent change and without clearly established, servicewide standards.[23]

Rapid expansion threatened the sense of professionalism that

22 United States Marine Corps, "Marine Corps Ground Training in World War II," by Kenneth W. Condit, Gerald Diamond, and Edwin T. Turnbladh (Washington: Historical Branch, G-3, HQMC, 1956, Typed manuscript), 158–59 (hereafter cited as "Ground Training").
23 Ibid., 160, 173.

Table 2. *Monthly inductions into the Marine Corps, volunteer and selective service, February 1941–July 1945*

Month	1941	1942	1943			1944			1945		
	Volunteers	Volunteers	Volunteers	Sel. Serv.	% Sel. Serv.	Volunteers	Sel. Serv.	% Sel. Serv.	Volunteers	Sel. Serv.	% Sel. Serv.
January		22,686	3,463	6,111	63.8	2,584	7,855	75.2	1,429	3,333	70.0
February	963	12,037	3,485	9,349	72.8	1,446	5,678	79.7	1,223	2,156	63.8
March	1,883	7,913	2,575	10,639	80.5	3,584	14,305	80.0	1,749	1,768	50.3
April	1,360	7,405	1,215	10,911	90.0	3,725	13,126	77.9	2,134	3,624	62.9
May	1,297	9,357	1,866	8,518	82.0	1,136	11,056	90.7	1,822	3,417	65.2
June	2,704	10,721	3,777	8,711	69.8	728	11,756	94.2	3,739	1,871	33.4
July	2,449	14,029	1,909	8,614	81.9	1,191	5,003	80.8	4,214	5,506	56.6
August	2,649	15,569	2,949	11,153	79.1	1,010	2,117	67.7			
September	2,416	18,592	2,809	9,957	78.0	1,123	1,138	50.3			
October	2,116	16,240	2,273	12,084	84.2	1,055	922	46.6			
November	1,978	15,107	2,998	12,759	81.0	1,476	799	35.1			
December	10,224	18,083	2,191	11,253	83.7	1,623	1,569	49.1			
Aggregate by year	30,039	167,739	31,520	120,059	79.2	20,681	75,324	78.4	16,310	21,675	57.0

Source: U.S. Marine Corps, "Marine Corps Administrative History" (Washington: Marine Corps Historical Division, 1946, Typed manuscript), 15–17.

had been carefully nurtured during the interwar period. High recruitment standards during the 1930s had "created something of an institutional memory of a 'golden age' " that many prewar marines had in mind when they argued that standards would slip quickly unless harsher training and discipline were imposed on the newcomers. Typical of such men was one lieutenant colonel who warned of the chronic decline of military discipline and absolute obedience in an article entitled "The Secret Weapon That We Do Not Possess."[24] He argued for better leadership, more carefully directed training, and draconian enforcement to solve the problem. The distinction between discipline and hazing, especially inside the training commands, became blurred.

Hazing came as a response to a personnel crisis that the training command was not equipped to handle. Recruits before the war had been regarded as men, not boys, and although discipline was strict, it seldom took the form of regular corporal punishment. With wartime mobilization, however, many young and inexperienced DIs found it difficult to assert their authority over men their own age without disparaging them as children or boys and without relying "upon their fists and heavy doses of profanity to gain ascendancy over recruits who could not hit back." The inexperience or acquiescence of supervisory officers and NCOs allowed abuses to spread, and so some untrained DIs spent more time hazing their recruits than in productive training.[25] Significantly, as Eugene Sledge recalls, hazing tended to diminish significantly during marksmanship training: "the harassment that had been our daily diet gave way to deadly serious, businesslike instruction in marksmanship." Range personnel were usually of the highest quality and took great professional pride in teaching a skill that even the greenest, most insecure DIs respected.[26] The wartime generation of marines accepted whatever treatment they received at boot camp with little demur for many reasons: because the hierarchical and coercive system allowed few alternatives but acceptance; out of patriotism and the desire to serve; and as a natural outgrowth of the corps's reputation for toughness.[27] Sixty-eight percent of all

24 Lt. Col. John S. Letcher, "The Secret Weapon That We Do Not Possess," *Marine Corps Gazette* 28 (January 1944): 47–50.
25 Keith Fleming, *The U.S. Marine Corps in Crisis* (Columbia: University of South Carolina Press, 1990), 12–16.
26 Sledge, *With the Old Breed*, 12–14.
27 *Marine Corps Reserve*, 96–97. Fleming suggests that hard times suffered in the Depression also made toleration of abuses easier (*Marine Corps in Crisis*, 16). Some recruits accepted physical abuse as natural or even welcomed it as an element of discipline; William Manchester, *Goodbye, Darkness* (Boston: Little, Brown, 1979), 120–22.

Marine Corps personnel during the war were reservists on active duty only "for the duration," and the sense of urgency that brought the reservists onto active duty also helped to push into the background the difficulties endemic in the problem.[28]

In an effort to get the most men into combat units as quickly as possible, Headquarters Marine Corps reduced the period of training from seven to six weeks immediately after Pearl Harbor, and down to only five weeks in January 1942 before restoring it to seven weeks in March. Changes were necessary in the types of subjects taught and the number of hours devoted to them. The five-week schedule devoted 96 hours of instruction to weapons training, 56 to garrison duties, 32 to field subjects, and a mere 4 hours to physical training. The first seven-week schedule called for 138 hours on weapons training, 62 on garrison duties, 57 on field subjects, and 14 on physical training. Curiously, the two recruit depots functioned independently, and because the details were left up to the two commands, the precise course of training was never the same in both places until a master training schedule was finally issued in February 1944.[29]

There was, from 1943 onward, a drive toward more technically oriented training in response to actual battlefield experience. The change was most readily apparent in the numbers of hours spent on related areas of training. Immediately before the master schedule was issued, the San Diego and Parris Island recruit depots devoted twenty-four and forty-five hours, respectively, to physical training, a dramatic increase over the hurried training of early 1942. Moreover, this conditioning moved away from simple calisthenics to more useful exercises, including swimming and physical contact sports like boxing, wrestling, and judo. Similarly, much more time was spent on weapons training and "field subjects" relative to "garrison-type" subjects.[30] Despite these efforts, however, complaints grew louder from organizations receiving incompletely trained men. Recruit training was supposed to produce basically trained riflemen; from the depot individuals would be sent on to

28 *Marine Corps Reserve*, 59.
29 "Ground Training," 159, 161–62, 170–72. It would be difficult to measure accurately any possible effect this may have had on the men in combat, nor has the reason for the absence of central control up to this time been clearly explained.
30 Ibid., 161, 164–65, 167. The eight-week master schedule called for 195 hours on weapons training, 98 on field subjects, 89 on garrison duties, and 39 on physical training. Except for the amount of time devoted to field subjects, the percentage of training time devoted to each area in the master schedule, 46%, 23%, 22%, and 9%, respectively, was relatively consistent throughout the war (172).

another school to receive extra training in their assigned specialty. The problem was that the Replacement Training Centers had to spend 25–50 percent of their time teaching fundamentals that should have been thoroughly learned at boot camp.

Given all the different organizations crying for manpower from a limited pool, the only surprise about selective service catching up with the Marine Corps was that it took fourteen months after the war started. Despite the early boom of enlistments following Pearl Harbor, by the end of 1942 Marine recruiters had trouble filling quotas as rapidly as Congress increased authorized manning levels, even after entrance requirements were lowered. In order to ensure that all the services met their personnel needs in the most equitable manner, the Marine Corps was placed under selective service guidelines before the war was a year old. The first Marine draftees received their induction notices in November 1942 and reported to boot camp in February 1943. To protect their elitist image, the Marines found it essential to maintain some semblance of voluntarism. One largely cosmetic device, pushed by Marine recruiters, was to discharge willing inductees and allow them to enlist in the regulars or Reserves, thus dropping the damning "SS" (selective service) designation after their names.[31] To obtain true volunteers, however, the Marines had to look outside the eighteen to thirty-six age group covered by selective service. The most profitable program drew almost 60,000 seventeen-year-olds into the Marine Corps Reserve between 1943 and 1945, calling them to active duty as they turned eighteen.[32] Despite their efforts at concealment, the Marine Corps depended heavily on the draft. Almost 80 percent of those who came into the Marine Corps in 1943 did so through the selective service, whether "volunteering" for the Marines at the induction centers or not (see Table 2), and without the men brought in by selective service, the Marines could not have recruited enough volunteers to make up the difference.[33]

It is difficult to gauge precisely what impact the appearance of draftees had in the ranks of combat units. One reason for the increased hazing in recruit training was the desire to compensate for the presence of presumably unmotivated draftees, and they were often singled out for attention. In the First Marine Division,

31 United States Navy Department, *Administration of the Navy Department in World War II*, by Julius Furer (Washington: Government Printing Office, 1959), 567 (hereafter cited as Navy, *Administration*). On the need to "sell" these voluntary inductions, see Farmer Seale, "Salesmanship Still Important," *Marine Recruiter* 3 (February 1943): 4–5.
32 Navy, *Administration*, 567–68.
33 United States Marine Corps, "Marine Corps Administrative History" (Washington: Marine Corps Historical Division, 1946, Typed manuscript), 15–17.

draftees began to filter in as replacements before the Peleliu campaign. Among four rifle companies for which records exist, over one-quarter of the men were draftees.[34] It came as a mild shock among the older volunteers when these men first appeared in their midst, but as long as the draftees did not complain about being victims of a coercive system there was little friction.[35] Ironically, the Marine Corps found the draft useful, not only to provide recruits but also as a means, through their institutional histories, to emphasize the importance of the part played by volunteers. Selective service was depicted as a system forced upon the Marines, not – according to most histories – because of any inherent institutional problems, but to democratize and rationalize the process on a national level. Even among draftees, they maintain, the spirit of voluntarism remained strong.[36]

A conventional overview of personnel policies illustrates only a single dimension of a complex and important process that also built on unspoken assumptions and attitudes. Although not entirely haphazard, Marine Corps training procedures lacked the institutionalized structure that characterized most military training programs. This was not simply the result of disorganization arising from hectic wartime mobilization but rather was a product of years-long practices that did not begin to break down until 1944. The long absence of servicewide training schedules, close, uniform supervision of instruction, and explicit codification of general training principles made the Marines unique. As with virtually every military institution, there was a tension underlying the training program that, on the one hand, stressed the thorough teaching of rudimentary military skills and, on the other, emphasized those intangible qualities that constituted the core of its institutional identity. The latter was used to justify increased harshness in basic training. Neither of these two competing philosophies dominated to the complete exclusion of the other, and, indeed, every good marine had to have a mix of both. But the real history of this subject must go beyond issues like the number of hours spent in a particular type of instruction or the number of draftees inducted versus volunteers. To

34 Embarkation Rosters, RG 127/65A-5188/Box 40/file B17-1. Of 890 men listed in A Company, 1/7, and I, K, and L Companies, 3/7, 239 were selective service.
35 Leckie, *Helmet for My Pillow*, 281; Sledge, *With the Old Breed*, 171–72. Selectees found "voluntary" inductions attractive as a way to avoid the stigma attached to draftees.
36 One official history published during the early buildup in Vietnam makes this argument explicitly and minimizes the influence of draftees by providing the (uncited) figure of only 75,000 inductees total over the course of the entire war; *Marine Corps Reserve*, 63.

be of any use on the Pacific battlefields, every man had to internalize an identity distinct from what he knew as a civilian. Understanding how the Marines created their own traditions, defined a "Marine" identity, and conveyed them to new recruits is necessary for any interpretation of subsequent events.[37]

Claiming for themselves an institutional "imprint" unique and distinct from any other service, the Marines, like every military organization, imposed it on their initiates as a rite of separation from civilian social experience.[38] For DIs, the creation and inculcation of this identity seemed to depend on an intuitive understanding and acceptance of a remote and abstract ideal of what the term "marine" should embody. Without this ideal the depots would not have been able to utilize privates first class for DI duty no matter how outwardly zealous or capable. Attempting to articulate this nebulous ideal, the product of film and fiction, "old corps" myth and wartime legend, seemed for some marines to strip it of symbolic value. Lindsay felt as both a marine and a historian that it was inexpressible. Another marine, a "mustang" (an officer commissioned from the ranks), expressed his understanding of that ideal:

To the Marine, the *Corps* is his religion, his reason for being. He cannot be committed up to a point. For him, involvement is total. He savors the traditions of his Corps and doubts not the veracity of them. He believes implicitly that he must live up to those epics of physical and moral courage established by those who preceded him. He believes that the Corps is truly unique – that it is the most elite military organization ever devised and that he, as an integral part of that organization, must never bring disgrace or dishonor upon it.[39]

Allowing for no deviation, this is not an elucidation of values but a definition of a monolithic military identity. Since the identity was the product of "traditions," however, it could be molded to serve shifting goals. Like most military institutions, the Marine Corps carefully choreographed key ceremonies to introduce members

37 The success of the Marine Corps at creating an institutional tradition is in one sense measured by how many Marine authors cited below and elsewhere can offer no definition of a Marine identity but simply assert it as a natural and unconscious fact of their existence. This point is brought up by Eric Hobsbawm, "Introduction: Inventing Traditions," in Eric Hobsbawm and Terence Ranger, eds., *The Invention of Tradition* (New York: Cambridge University Press, 1983), 1–14.
38 Commenting upon the idea of using rites of "initiation" Leed writes, "What is most often revealed in traditional rites is the sacred underpinnings of the group; what was revealed in war was not 'sacred,' even though it seemed to acquire a demonic force" (*No Man's Land*, 29).
39 Gerald P. Averill, *Mustang* (Novato: Presidio Press, 1987), 3.

into the secrets and the central tenets of the organization.[40] The pervasiveness and the degree to which corps values were internalized were central in defining how the marines fought in the Pacific and will be considered further in connection with the Peleliu campaign. The means by which the identity was spread and so deeply instilled was through the manipulation and fabrication of gender roles.

By both design and circumstance the Marine Corps was an all-male world, effectively unpopulated by women, in which the influence of gender roles was constantly at play, even among combat troops. The sense of male identity was integral to unit cohesion and effectiveness and necessarily coexisted with a sense of what constituted female attributes and boundaries.[41] For many men, women occupied traditional roles and were symbols of home, fidelity, and peace, objects of longing, and hopelessly romanticized and idealized by lonely, homesick boys. This was the view taken in American propaganda, and at least some marines went to their graves sincerely believing in the romantic ideal. Shortly before he died of wounds received on Guadalcanal Harry G. Findlay wrote to his son, "[T]he true love of a woman is the most beautiful thing in the world. Value it beyond all else. Do nothing that will tarnish your memory in relationship to womanhood."[42] For others, women were simply sexual objects: much of one marine's memoir, written over forty years after the events it chronicles, is devoted to recounting his sexual conquests and their often bizarre circumstances.[43] At an unspoken extreme, women could become objects of hatred, symbols of everything obscene that engulfed men in combat and the embodiment of all the indignities and injustices they had to suffer.[44] The precise forms of this objectification varied a great

40 The parallels with Theweleit's account mentioned at the beginning of the chapter apply here as well: compare *Male Fantasies*, 2:143–53 with Lindsay, *This High Name*, 89–90. The British army and their regimental system, the SS and Blackshirts with their quasi-religious military rituals in Germany and Italy, the commissar system in the Red Army, and the Imperial Japanese Army's stress on the bushido and the emperor all offer, to varying degrees, similarities in the close control and manipulation of mythic images in the process of training and indoctrination.

41 Although the Marine Corps accepted women, it was the most reluctant of the services to do so, and there remained throughout the enlisted ranks of the corps, as with all the services, tremendous antipathy toward women in uniform; D'Ann Campbell, *Women at War with America* (Cambridge: Harvard University Press, 1984), 39–42.

42 Diary entry dated 6 August 1942, Harry G. Findlay Papers, PPC, MCHC.

43 Typewritten manuscript, passim, Nolan V. Marbrey Papers, PPC, MCHC.

44 The theme of women as victimizers is powerfully conveyed in British literature of the Great War; the examples of Siegfried Sassoon's "Glory of Women" and

deal, and none of them could be regarded as universal, but they nevertheless represented a tool by which men were manipulated *by whom?* to do battle.

The Marines did not undertake the process of redefining social conventions and gender roles on their own; they exploited existing divisions and tensions. American propaganda supported familiar, dichotomous tropes: women as nurturers, healers, and victims; men as noble soldiers and protectors – traditional categories one author labels "Beautiful Souls" and "Just Warriors."[45] Commercial advertising as well as poster art supporting everything from war bond drives to recruitment or industrial productivity tended to objectify or trivialize women's roles in society.[46] American society as a whole became the major "theater of operations" in what some literary women perceived as an ongoing "war of the sexes."[47] For example, the stories of Kay Boyle suggest, in the words of one scholar, "that what women face in wartime is not only the unleashed violence of sex-starved men but also the elaborate images such men construct as a compensation for and a retaliation against the sex they are presumably fighting to preserve." Marines harnessed and appropriated the divisions arising out of the war of the sexes as a mechanism to prepare men for battle against the Japanese. At the same time, fighting in the Pacific added another arrow to the quiver from which men drew in this domestic struggle.[48]

To delineate their break from female domination of their en-

Wilfred Owen's "Greater Love" are discussed in Gilbert and Gubar, *No Man's Land*, 2:260–62.

45 Jean Bethke Elshtain, *Women and War* (New York: Basic Books, 1987), 3–13.

46 Susan M. Hartman, *The Home Front and Beyond* (Boston: Twayne, 1982), 41. See also Leila J. Rupp, *Mobilizing Women for War* (Princeton: Princeton University Press, 1978), 137–66; and Maureen Honey, *Creating Rosie the Riveter* (Amherst: University of Massachusetts Press, 1984).

47 This is the general theme in Gilbert and Gubar, *No Man's Land*. It is stated explicitly in the first chapter, "The Battle of the Sexes: The Men's Case," of vol. 1, *The War of the Words* (1988). In one example from around the turn of the century that is particularly apposite of Marine attitudes in the Pacific War, at the beginning of the chapter entitled "Fighting for Life" the authors quote George Egerton: "It seems almost congenital with some women to have deeply rooted in their innermost nature a smoldering enmity, ay, sometimes a physical disgust to men, it is a kind of kin-feeling to the race-dislike of white men to black [or 'yellow']" (1:65).

48 Susan Gubar, " 'This Is My Rifle, This Is My Gun': World War II and the Blitz on Women," in Higonnet et al., *Behind the Lines*, 257. The title of this marvelous essay comes from the famous Marine rhyme referred to by Sledge (*With the Old Breed*, 10), Clark (*Unlikely Arena*, 10), and Leon Uris's *Battle Cry* ([New York: Bantam, 1953], 53) that distinguishes between the military weapon (rifle) and the sexual weapon (gun [penis]): "This is my rifle, / This is my gun, / This is for fighting, / This is for fun."

vironment, the marines reordered their world and reassembled it in a form that made greater sense to them, a world in which masculine virtues represented the highest standards of conduct and order. The process began in earnest with the arrival of new recruits at boot camp. The exaggeratedly all-male atmosphere of recruit training was part of what Theweleit labels the "crucial transformation" of eros.[49] As psychogenic fantasy, this transformation created an antagonistic view across the gender line not unlike the race line that separated Americans from Japanese. The transformation of eros fostered the objectification of women. Signs of weakness, failure, and denigration were often labeled in female terms, whereas strength, success, and praise emphasized an individual's masculinity. In the atmosphere of the camps maternalistic or nurturing traits generally associated with women were inverted and became threatening, and individuals prided themselves on the extent to which they could remain untouched by such influences. Women also became objects of danger and disgrace in classes on sex hygiene. Marines were taught that syphilis was an invisible danger lurking everywhere, not just with prostitutes but even with a sweetheart back home. Under these circumstances, any sexual relations posed a potential threat of infection that might result in a man's separation from his buddies or even the service.[50] Once begun, this indoctrination continued until either the man received his discharge from the Marine Corps and returned to civilian life or he suffered serious injury or sickness that at least temporarily stripped him of his self-sufficiency and isolated him from the male group.

Recognizing, at least subconsciously, that the processes by which inductees were socialized and indoctrinated were in some ways highly misogynistic, the Marine Corps carefully cultivated a public image intended to reassure the civilian community that the changes being effected on its husbands, sons, or brothers were not as profound or fundamental as they eventually proved to be. Through several official books and pamphlets published on recruit training,

49 Theweleit, *Male Fantasies*, 2:170.
50 Men with an active venereal disease were not allowed to ship overseas. One Army inspector general found that some malingerers would pay men with open venereal sores for pus or semen with which to infect themselves in order to avoid shipment to North Africa; Elliot D. Cooke, *All but Thee and Me* (Washington: Infantry Journal Press, 1946), 92. For more on official policy and education, see United States Army, Medical Department, *Preventive Medicine in World War II*, vol. 5, *Communicable Diseases, Transmitted through Contact or by Unknown Means*, edited by Ebbe Curtis Hoff (Washington: Office of the Surgeon General, 1960).

and with the help of a few quasi-official books written by marines, the Marine Corps drew attention away from the earnestness with which DIs and recruits approached training and instead emphasized the superficial aspects of the training program and trivialized the efforts aimed at redefining moral and behavioral standards.[51] With traces of juvenile excitement, for instance, as at the initiation into the secrets of a new club, virtually every account mentions the new vocabulary learned at boot camp, often including a glossary of terms. Families could expect their men to return on leave speaking an esoteric language spiced with nautical terms like "deck," "head," and "scuttlebutt." Of course omitted from mention were expressions familiar to any recruit like "shitbird" (his new nom de guerre), "donkey dick" (for a variety of meats served in the mess halls), or "fuckin' A" (for emphatic affirmation). Almost with a sense of wonder, recruits in these books discover how well their platoons can drill together by the end of training, and all express personal pride in successfully emulating the bearing and spotless appearance of the ideal Marine – their senior DI. Yet training with the bayonet or in hand-to-hand combat only hinted at what lay ahead. Hidden from the recruits' vision was the knowledge that these episodes were not ends in themselves; the Marine Corps did not expect the new recruits to be able to hold their own as a result of a few drills run against bayonet dummies. These authors were describing, with heavy-handed efforts at humor, the process of being set apart from mainstream civilian life, "being 'made' strange."[52]

The inculcation of discipline in all its many forms was only a means to an end. To the recollection of Robert Leckie, every action taken in recruit training focused on discipline:

> There was absolutely no talk of the war; we heard no fiery lectures about killing Japs, such as we were to hear later on. ... Everything but discipline, Marine Corps discipline, was steadfastly mocked and ridiculed, be it holiness or high finance. These drill instructors were dedicated martinets. Like the sensualist who feels that if a thing cannot be eaten, drunk or taken

51 The more significant examples of these generally uninspiring books are Gilbert P. Bailey, *Boot* (New York: Macmillan, 1944); Jim Lucas, *Combat Correspondent* (New York: Reynal and Hitchcock, 1944); Rowland Vance, *They Made Me a Leatherneck* (New York: W. W. Norton, 1943); and Martin L. Myers, *Yardbird Myers* (Philadelphia: Dorrance, 1944).
52 Myers, for example, writes, "Now that we have gotten a little accustomed to military life, we don't quite know how to act when thrown in with civilians again" (*Yardbird Myers*, 220). Similarly innocent reactions also appear in Jack Colegrove's correspondence with his mother (Jack Colegrove Papers, PPC, MCHC) and in the Robert Graff Papers (PPC, MCHC).

to bed, it does not exist, so were these martinets in their outlook. All was discipline.[53]

With each move from boot camp to regular garrison and finally
into combat, the discipline described by Marine memoirists weakened. The real purpose behind what they describe was subtler,
more insidious, and largely beyond the conscious control of the
DIs or their charges. Separating men from civilian sensibilities
created a common perspective and shared pattern of thought. The
institutional shaping of thought made allowances for individuality,
within certain limits; it did not matter if a man was religiously
devout, introverted, or so on. What counted in this process was
that certain ideas were superimposed on all of the variegated personalities assembled in the Marine Corps, not to the exclusion
of the underlying personalities, but with sufficient intensity to
weld them into militarily useful men. In 1942 these fundamental ideas revolved around an almost tangible self-consciousness, an
awareness of past traditions juxtaposed to the historical moment,
when the war seemed still to hang in the balance. By 1945, these
shared ideas had shifted away from a remote imagination toward
a pragmatism and technocratic expertise linked directly to the
harsh realities of the front lines. In both cases, however, they
provided the common ground between men of highly disparate
backgrounds and attitudes. Discipline and comportment were easily sloughed off in combat, but the underlying ideas often remained.

From the perspective of a seventeen- or eighteen-year-old recruit, gender issues did not involve an abstract appreciation for
the battle of the sexes. A book published in 1943 entitled *When
Your Son Goes to War* serves as an example of where and how the
line separating the boy-recruit from the man-marine was drawn.
As a military wife and mother of a draft-age son, the author,
Clella Reeves Collins, accepts as her due male expressions of
sympathy: " '[W]e feel sorry for you mothers. We know eighteen
seems awfully young, and you're full of fears for what may happen
to Johnny when he gets where you can't remind him to put on
his overshoes, drink his milk, and get in early!' " To Reeves the
snatching of a generation of sons, however just and necessary, is
"a clarion challenge" to all women to defend their civilization:

53 Leckie, *Helmet for My Pillow*, 10–11. Manchester "yearned for stern discipline"
to find legitimation of his manliness (*Goodbye, Darkness*, 123). Sledge makes clear
that his DI was "neither cruel nor sadistic." As a disciplinarian he toughened
Sledge for the ordeal he would face in combat (*With the Old Breed*, 158).

"The mother instinct for preservation of the race is being evoked as never before in the history of humanity."[54] The Marine Corps promised not just an escape from cloying maternal instincts and reminders to drink milk; it provided an alternative model of civilization to that the crusading "mother instinct" envisioned. It was also a celebration of release and exaltation of an abstract masculine ideal.

The image of war as an escape from female-dominated society, common among the eighteen- and nineteen-year-old marines who made up the bulk of the line companies, has many parallels. It is a recurrent theme in American literature, whether with Huck Finn wanting to "light out for the Territory" or Willa Cather's Claude Wheeler fleeing domestic stagnation to the trenches of France. In attracting men who sought adventure and escape, the Marine Corps, like the French Foreign Legion, preferred men who were somewhat "dysfunctional" or at least unsatisfied with civilian society.[55] The oft-mentioned influence of the Eton playing fields on the battle of Waterloo also had parallels for the marines during the Second World War: the camaraderie, the competition, the role playing that many boys had experienced on the high school football fields – often only a few weeks before arriving at training – were. not simply mirrored but magnified upon initiation into the mysteries of the Marine Corps. Social group pressures, often distinctly adolescent, exerted a strong influence on marines thrust into unfamiliar and frequently dangerous situations.

In every marine memoir there is at least one great celebration, typically tinged with juvenile exuberance, of release from societal strictures. For Robert Leckie, this began as he and his new acquaintances started to "revel in the hardship of the train ride" down to Parris Island. He ascribes this to the "intangible mystique" of the Marines, but a subsequent observation, reminiscent of Theodore Roosevelt, is more revealing: "We were having it rough, which is exactly what we expected and what we signed up for.... The man who has had it roughest is the man to be most admired. Conversely, he who has had it the easiest is the least praiseworthy."[56] Russell Davis remembered ten days spent on "anti-submarine watch" as the most idyllic of the war. On a remote "island paradise" with his immediate friends, all that was unpleasant – and often

---

54 Clella Reeves Collins, *When Your Son Goes to War* (New York: Harper and Brothers, 1943), xvi–xvii.
55 Porch, *Foreign Legion*, 426.
56 Leckie, *Helmet for My Pillow*, 6. His comment also bears upon the earlier discussion regarding men's acceptance of growing abuses in recruit training.

associated with women – diminished to the point of leaving these men blissfully oblivious of the war and its vileness, allowing them to act out what was, in essence, a boyhood fantasy.[57]

The celebration of manhood had many elements entwined with the notion that the war was an adventure. For many, the war represented the first time they had left the narrow social and geographical boundaries of their childhood that were linked to nurturing, clinging, puritanical, or indifferent women. It became both a literal and a symbolic journey into adulthood. One obvious aspect of this journey for many of these young men was their sexual initiation. Given the pressures of training and the relative scarcity of available women in the presence of so many servicemen, the nature of this initiation often contributed significantly to the objectification of women.[58] For others, the war allowed them to act out male fantasies. The military in general attracted a variety of "swashbucklers" and "gunslingers," men who dressed and swaggered about like movie-house renegades, carrying knives or pistols, and posturing at least as much for their own benefit as for those around them.[59] The war seemed to offer these men a return to the American frontier days; it created new opportunities to prove one's worth, demonstrate self-reliance, and restore a "proper" balance between the sexes.[60]

By the time a marine had embarked for his overseas adventure, women had in one sense become little more than part of the scenic backdrop to war. The tropical islands were at first evocative of a Dorothy Lamour movie for many. After taking a stroll into the jungle on Pavuvu, Second Lieutenant Richard C. Kennard described the scene in a letter home: "The noises of the birds and parrots in the high trees filled with vines made the whole place remind me of the Tarzan jungle pictures."[61] Even the less innocent

57 Davis, *Marine at War*, 134–49.
58 In Tijuana, while his friend and a girl went behind a curtain, Marbrey, for a dollar, had intercourse with the girl's mother on the floor (Nolan V. Marbrey, PPC, MCHC). Manchester wrote (*Goodbye, Darkness*, 146), "I wanted to be a man, and an essential step in the process ... was the forfeiture of my own virginity." The next twelve pages, tracing Manchester's two failed efforts to achieve his goal in wartime San Diego, fully support Cynthia Enloe's conclusions concerning the militarization of women as sexual objects in *Does Khaki Become You?* (Boston: Pandora Press, 1983).
59 James Jones, *The Thin Red Line* (New York: Charles Scribner's Sons, 1962), 6–22. A recurring theme throughout the novel is the notion of men seeking, in essence, an external symbol of manhood, and Jones takes sixteen pages at the beginning of the book to describe one "gunslinger" pfc's successful effort to steal a pistol for this purpose.
60 This was an attitude actively exploited by the Marine leadership; see below, 117–18.
61 Kennard, letter dated 31 May 1944, Richard C. Kennard Papers, PPC, MCHC.

observations and comparisons contained an almost equally naïve quality. Upon his arrival in Samoa a few months before the Guadalcanal landings, a lieutenant in the 7th Marines confided in his diary, "I must, in all fairness, mention the local breasts. They are, true to narrative, wondrous to behold in their unrestrained nearly natural state. They would, aside from their color, make many American women green with envy."[62] Noting how marines eagerly approached native "maidens," who, "though dark brown, were comely and friendly," one chaplain worried about fighting "some pitched battles with the devil" to protect their pure white souls. Yet he need not have worried so much; the marines' encounters with native women seldom received much more attention than the coconut trees and simply added to the already exotic allure of overseas service. These bare-breasted women, like those captured in the photographs of various marines' scrapbooks, were not regarded with obsessive prurient interest by the young men headed into battle for the first time; they were a curiosity, intriguing and even attractive, but virtually part of the island scenery.[63] On Samoa this tropical landscape was relatively benign, but on Guadalcanal and in subsequent campaigns, where the island scenery took on more sinister and hostile meanings, associations with women became likewise more ugly and threatening.

In their descriptions of the jungles on Guadalcanal and New Britain, marines used metaphors that explicitly identified them with women. The tremendous fecundity of the jungle shocked the Americans. Observing the "black, circling funnels" of flies that swarmed out of several Japanese corpses, Leckie noted with horror and disgust that "the tropics had won; her minions were everywhere...."[64] T. Grady Gallant echoed this revulsion: the "savagery of Nature" in disposing of the dead was represented by the armies of huge ants sent "to penetrate the liquefying mass and disappear on a mission that revolted the imagination."[65] The stench of rotting

This was also Sledge's short-lived first impression of Pavuvu as viewed from the ship's rail (*With the Old Breed*, 34).
62 Joseph H. Griffith, diary entry, dated 6 June 1942, Joseph H. Griffith Papers, PPC, MCHC.
63 This was also the result in part of quick preventive measures taken by chaplains, the provost, and the Samoans to ensure the marines did not get out of control. Quoted observations from H. H. Tower, *Fighting the Devil with the Marines* (Philadelphia: Dorrance, 1945), 123; he also insisted that the "boys" wanted only companionship rather than sex (150). Such specific issues are never broached directly in the official history; United States Navy Department, Bureau of Naval Personnel, *The History of the Chaplain Corps, United States Navy*, 2 vols. (Washington: GPO, n.d.).
64 Leckie, *Helmet for My Pillow*, 88.
65 T. Grady Gallant, *On Valor's Side* (Garden City: Doubleday, 1963), 316.

In the Kerr Eby sketch *Marksman*, the gloomy New Britain jungle threatens
to engulf a First Division marine and consume him, as it has already begun
to swallow the dead Japanese soldier at his feet. (*Courtesy of Naval Art
Collection, U.S. Naval Historical Center*)

vegetation, often mixed with that of decaying flesh, and the very
textures of the jungle and mud seemed – at least to two American
novelists of the Pacific War – symbolic of womanhood and men-
struation.[66] The incessant breeding of flies and mosquitoes, aside
from rapidly spreading disease across every battlefield the marines
ever occupied, was a reminder to them of how the reproductive
cycle dominated in nature. Corpses were reduced to nothing more
than Nature's breeding grounds. The accompanying decay that
engulfed the marines took many forms, assaulting their senses and
their sensibilities and blurring lines between the living and dead
wherever they might go and without cease.[67]

The language and imagery used in these and other examples

---

66 Norman Mailer, *The Naked and the Dead* (1948; reprint, New York: Henry Holt,
    1976), 133, 456–58; and Jones, *Thin Red Line*.
67 On the subject of decay and dissolution, the experiences described by Sledge,
    Leckie, and others have close parallels to the Great War. Leed describes how a
    young officer became incurably shell-shocked after falling atop the decomposing
    corpse of a German soldier and choking on a mouthful of its entrails: "It would
    be difficult to find a more complete violation of the distinctions which separate
    the dead from the living, friend from enemy, rotten from edible, than this
    experience which left a lasting mark of pollution upon the young officer" (*No
    Man's Land*, 19). Cf. Gilbert and Gubar, *No Man's Land*, 2:265–69.

reinforced polarized gender identities. "Mother" Nature was the source of corruption and decay, and "her minions" – arguably males "penetrating" the object – carried forward this process. Carried to its extreme, women in general could be viewed as somehow to blame for the war itself, and the soldiers and marines sent to fight and die in the fetid jungles of the Pacific were simply the "minions" of some other natural order, preserving a world governed, or more accurately, domesticated, by female sexuality and sensibilities. Eugene Sledge recalled a jarring image from Half Moon Hill on Okinawa:

> The scene was so unreal I could hardly believe it: two tired, frightened young men sitting in a hole beside a machine gun in the rain on a ridge, surrounded with mud – nothing but stinking mud, with so much decaying human flesh half buried in it that there were big patches of wriggling fat maggots marking the spots where Japanese corpses lay – looking at the picture of a beautiful seminude girl.[68]

On the verge of mental breakdown, the picture shocked Sledge with the dawning realization that the only world that existed for him was full of explosions, blood, and decay. The liminality that Leed suggests is inherent in all war was heightened when juxtaposed to examples of "civilization" represented by photographs of voluptuous, half-naked women. Distanced from that "other" world, the marines created new boundaries and bonds among themselves.[69]

To the extent that the passions of love and erotic sexuality could be channeled into combat, they proved valuable, if unacknowledgeable, allies to the military institution. Pondering the relationship between love and war as he noted it from his experiences with the Army in Europe, J. Glenn Gray differentiated between three forms of love: "erotic love between the sexes, preservative love, which is independent of sex distinctions, and the love called friendship."[70] The dominance of the superficial and animalistic aspects of erotic love sometimes was related to the strength of the individual and group warrior identity.[71] The pervasiveness of this overworked,

68 Sledge, *With the Old Breed*, 256. As an added irony, one of the men's relationship with the woman in the picture was adulterous, and he was expressing ambivalent feelings of guilt and pride to his buddy.
69 Leed, *No Man's Land*, 13–17.
70 Gray, *The Warriors*, 64.
71 Porch quotes a French Legionnaire who might easily have been speaking for the marines: "although legionnaires constantly talked of women, they were only an abstraction: 'The real woman does not exist. The Foreign Legion is a unit without women. For starters it is too virile for them.... Outside the barracks, it

74   AMERICAN SAMURAI

even obsessive concern was beyond doubt, and the impromptu discussions overheard by Gray might have been identical to those circumspectly remarked upon by correspondents in the Pacific.[72] The language used to discuss erotic love linked sexual performance to the conduct of war:

> [S]exual passion and war have been married from the beginning. . . . To be sure, the sexual partner is not actually destroyed in the encounter, merely overthrown. And the psychological aftereffects of sexual lust are different from those of battle lusts. These differences, however, do not alter the fact that the passions have a common source and affect their victims in the same way while they are in their grip. . . . Both reveal man as a berserker, outside of his humanity, a dangerous beast of prey.[73]

Gray's second category of love, preservative love, was a meliorative emotion in war, but it carried little of the resonance in the Pacific that it had for GIs in Italy or Germany. A closer sense of kinship between the Americans and their European antagonists occasionally reduced some of the wanton destructiveness and cruelty in ways seldom duplicated with the Japanese.

Men interpreted their introductions to war and to sexual intimacy as distinct rituals of passage. In both cases the experience produced a sharp sense of irreversible separation, from civilian/recruit to warrior/veteran on the one hand and from boy/virgin to man/sexually experienced on the other:

> The knowledge gained in war was rarely regarded as something alienable, something that could be taught, a tool or a method. Rather, it was most often described as something that was part of the combatant's body, like a chemical substance in the veins, a mark, a scar, a set of reflexes, a part of the individual's very potency. The best analogy to the knowledge acquired in war is perhaps to sexual knowledge, a knowledge that transforms the character and condition of the knower from that of an innocent to that of a bearer and administrator of potent wisdom.[74]

is physical sexuality, mechanical, in pleasure spots. Inside, the woman remains in the idealized imagination' " (Foreign Legion, 426).
72 Richard Tregaskis, Guadalcanal Diary (New York: Random House, 1943), and John Hersey, Into the Valley (New York: Alfred A. Knopf, 1943), both allude to such conversations among the marines.
73 Gray, The Warriors, 68.
74 Leed, No Man's Land, 74.

Some young men seemed to hope that sexual initiation would open to them some secret of manhood that they could draw upon in combat.

Although the explicit eroticism of some marines' scrapbook pictures and of the images of a tropical paradise on Samoa and elsewhere were not unusual, there were few readily available outlets for their sexual lusts. Whatever the fantasies that grew out of the all-male society of overseas military service, the realities were often reduced to the hunt for sexual conquests. Out of the forty months that the First Marine Division spent overseas before the Japanese surrender, only eight months were spent near a source of widely available female companionship, during rehabilitation outside Melbourne. Once the marines left Australia the range of alternatives was distinctly limited. The division history warns its readers against believing "the outlandish tales of adventures with native girls": such fiction was "monstrously and unfairly exceptional as fact, distorting beyond repair the essential truth that unrelieved frustration was one of the important psychological facts about the out-of-battle Pacific environment."[75] Not only were native women rarely encountered, but because of race, typical appearance, and operational imperatives, those whom the marines did run across were rarely regarded in sexual terms. Even the pictures of attractive Polynesian women in Werner Claussen's scrapbook were unlikely to have been taken by him; indeed, he probably never set eyes on these women. Like many of the combat shots found in marine scrapbooks, Claussen's tawny beauties were photographed on Samoa or elsewhere and copies made available for wider distribution.

Take away the attractive myths surrounding the conquest of tropical women and few alternatives remained as an outlet for sexual frustration. It was white women about whom the marines fantasized,[76] and many a B-movie watched by marines rebuilding on Pavuvu found some pretext for putting them in close, available proximity to the commissioned combatants – usually as nurses. The actual options were so limited under conditions of heterosexual privation that to feel the prickling of arousal was in some circumstances virtually a betrayal of the group, undermining the camaraderie, shared hardship, and all-male sanctity of the division. To be treated by a female nurse might be interpreted as a sign of regression to the soft, civilian, nurturing influences that had been stripped away in boot camp.

75 McMillan, *Old Breed*, 229.
76 For a sanitized example, see David Tucker Brown, Jr., letter dated 28 November 1944, in *Marine from Virginia* (Chapel Hill: University of North Carolina Press, 1947), 72.

These two photographs were labeled simply "What We Expected" and "What We Found." *(Kenneth Bogard Papers, Personal Papers Collection, MCHC)*

White women crossed the path of the marines in three different but equally remote guises. In a tactful letter written shortly before loading ship for Peleliu, Richard Kennard describes the scene when a USO show finally reached the division on Pavuvu:

> When this little dance[r] came out with bare legs and little else covering her figure the men yelled and screamed. Some haven't seen a white woman in 10 months. The show sure built up our morale, but it also made us all realize more vividly just what we were missing back home. You get what I mean.[77]

Patti Thomas, the woman Kennard describes, was less important to the men as an individual than as the embodiment of several remote, overlapping, and often conflicting ideals. In Kennard's passing reference she evokes the traditional image of a wife or girlfriend back home, but she is also an object of imagined sexual conquest and a symbol of a lighthearted world and culture remote and unconnected with their lives at the moment. For many men in

77 Kennard, letter to fiancée, dated 8 August 1944, Kennard Papers, PPC, MCHC.

the audience, this untouchable, taunting figure was the last woman they ever saw.

Returning from Peleliu, a campaign that had pushed many far beyond the limits of past, expressible experience, some marines were stunned to encounter upon disembarking on Pavuvu six young women in Red Cross uniforms serving canned grapefruit juice in paper cups. While most of his companions looked sullenly on these women from a distance, one marine joined some others, accepting the proffered cup in some confusion: "My mind was so benumbed by the shock and violence of Peleliu that the presence of an American girl on Pavuvu seemed totally out of context. I was bewildered. 'What the hell is she doing here?' I thought.... As we filed past to board trucks, I resented her deeply."[78] Nor was he alone in his resentment. As the division history accurately points out, the impossibility of the Red Cross mission is revealed in a simple equation: six women and fifteen thousand marines. The Red Cross club itself was generally avoided, but the mere presence of these women was immediately noticeable in the prohibition against nude swimming, the sheets of burlap hung over the "heads," and, more ominously, the high, floodlit barbed-wire fence that surrounded

78 Sledge, *With the Old Breed*, 164.

On the eve of the Peleliu campaign, Patti Thomas's USO performance on Pavuvu before an audience of First Division marines prompted a young artillery officer to comment that it "sure built up our morale, but it also made us all realize more vividly just what we were missing back home." *(USMC, National Archives)*

the plantation house in which the women lived and the war dog patrols that watched over them.[79] Here were restrictions imposed on the men, a regression toward the female-centered society of the civilian world left behind, arising simply because a half dozen women had invaded their sanctuary.

At the naval base hospital and depot on the neighboring island of Banika such "invaders" had landed in greater force and reintroduced the poison of their influence. Sent to the hospital from Pavuvu, Robert Leckie described the female nurse he found "in a glass-enclosed cubicle" as remote and cold. Not of the same species as an enlisted marine, she robbed him of his masculinity, refusing even to "lift a finger to nurse a man. The corpsmen would do the nursing." These nurses, "far from being angels of mercy in the Pacific," instead generated tremendous resentment and hostility.[80] Unlike the Red Cross women, the nurses were officers; unap-

79 McMillan, *Old Breed*, 344–45, 348–49.
80 Leckie, *Helmet for My Pillow*, 270.

proachable to the enlisted men, their sex and grade combined to emphasize the inequities of the military rank structure; and the contempt they showed to the men transformed them, in the eyes of some marines, into symbols of castration. The nurses also generated hostility among the corpsmen alongside whom they worked. One corpsman nostalgically recalled the time before the nurses' arrival, when the doctors had shared their liquor rations with the enlisted men and everything " 'was like one big happy family.' " He lamented: " 'Then the nurses came and everything changed overnight. We weren't good enough any more. No more liquor, no more top chow, no more friendliness. The nurses talked only to doctors and the doctors talked only to God.' "[81] The presence of women fostered competitiveness among men that destroyed the bonds of comradeship and shared loyalties crucial to unit effectiveness. They also left the quest for sexual gratification poignantly unfulfilled.

With female companionship effectively out of reach after departing Melbourne, the marines had to find some other outlet for their needs. The most obvious way to relieve sexual tensions was through masturbation, which appears to have been common.[82] The other readily available source of physical gratification was through some form of homosexuality. Despite efforts to screen them out through psychological testing, gay men served in the armed forces, including the Marine Corps, in large numbers. Estimates of the number of gay men who served in the military, based on approximate numbers in the civilian population, range from 650,000 to 1.6 million.[83] The Marines actually attracted men of ambivalent or avowedly homosexual orientation because of their reputation for "making men." For recruits like Ted Allenby, who found little but intolerance and oppression for his feelings and sensibilities, the Marine Corps was a source of masculine legitimation.[84] Military

---

81 Ibid., 275. Obviously not all nurses reflected these attitudes or generated such hostility, but the men of the First Division have little good to say of the nurses on Banika.

82 The fictional accounts of Mailer and Jones are full of such references; other accounts are more circumspect, for example, McMillan, *Old Breed*, 231.

83 Allan Bérubé, *Coming out under Fire* (New York: Free Press, 1990), 3. One of the difficulties about even raising the issue of gays in the service is the absence of both hard statistical data and a broad range of anecdotal evidence to support definitive arguments. Although my conclusions must be speculative, it is important to broaden the scope of discussion and add a dimension usually missing from military histories.

84 Allenby perceived the label of "homosexual" as a skull and crossbones: "It's bad, it's a disease, it's a poison. This is my dirty little secret." After the war, where he served as a machine gunner on Iwo Jima, Allenby earned his credentials to serve as a Navy chaplain assigned to marines. At the recruit depot men came

service also provided a means for gays to meet each other, and gay men and lesbians emerged from the war for the first time as a social group with a sense of community within American society.[85]

A wide range of homosexual practices were accepted in the Marine Corps given broader wartime definitions of deviant behavior and greater permissiveness. Among gay men, marines acquired a reputation for being difficult to pick up but amenable if approached properly: " 'The idea was that all marines were available, but they never wanted to talk about it and would hit you in the nose if you brought it up. . . . There were lots of obviously gay men during the war.' " Like men in other services who felt their masculinity threatened by gays, marines also tended to exhibit some of the most brutal reactions to overt homosexuality, especially as brig guards.[86] Among most memoirists the subject of homosexuality is muted, hidden behind the more socially accepted images of wartime camaraderie.[87] The line between the two is difficult to identify with precision, and the "situational" aspects were clearly present, whether in the joking and teasing that went on in the communal showers at boot camp, the cramped conditions on the troop transports, or nude bathing behind the lines. Even military clinicians admitted that there was much "experimentation" that did not represent serious "pathological illness."[88] Gay marines earned the acceptance of others for risking their lives in combat and sharing all the hardships of active campaigning.[89]

to him who "had joined the marines for the same reason I did: It'll make a man of me. I'll show 'em how tough I am" (Terkel, *The Good War*, 176, 181).

85 This is the basic argument in Chapter 2, "Forging a Group Identity: World War II and the Emergence of an Urban Gay Subculture," of John D'Emilio, *Sexual Politics, Sexual Communities* (Chicago: University of Chicago Press, 1983), 23–39.

86 Bérubé, *Coming out under Fire*, 111, 191, 220–21.

87 One exception is Manchester's commentary about a colonel whose fame from Guadalcanal helped him escape prosecution after being caught performing anal sex and a sergeant major who boasted of promiscuous oral sex (*Goodbye, Darkness*, 99–103, 107–8). Fiction remains the best source of nuanced discussions of homosexuality in the services. In the fictionalized account of his experiences with the 25th Infantry Division on Guadalcanal, for example, James Jones describes different manifestations of homosexuality in one rifle company, ranging from tacit understandings to overt sexual acts (*Thin Red Line*, 119–20, 463–65). Novelists like Norman Mailer, Gore Vidal, Loren Wahl, and James Barr made the issue of homosexuality an important secondary theme or, in the case of the last two, the primary focus of their work (Bérubé, *Coming out under Fire*, 272–73).

88 Bérubé, *Coming out under Fire*, 39–41, 191–94. United States Army, Medical Department, *Neuropsychiatry in World War II*, edited by Albert J. Glass, 2 vols. (Washington: Office of the Surgeon General, 1973), 2:636–37.

89 Bérubé's chapter "Comrades in Arms" (175–200) is the best discussion of the subjects of situational homosexuality, adjustment, and acceptance at the front; John Costello has a chapter of the same title that has a wider focus, mixing British and some other examples with American, in his *Love Sex and War* (London: Collins, 1985).

In the absence of acceptable human outlets for gratification, the only remaining possibility lay in combat itself. Jones's novel *The Thin Red Line* is full of allusions to the intense sexual tension that seemed to fill the battlefield for many men. In one scene, he describes the sensations felt by a group of men who discover an American soldier's shirt, torn and bloody where a bullet hit his chest:

> There was a peculiar tone of sexual excitement, sexual morbidity, in all the voices – almost as if they were voyeurs behind a mirror watching a man in the act of coitus; as though in looking openly at the evidence of this unknown man's pain and fear they were unwillingly perhaps but nonetheless incontrollably seducing him.

For many of the men in the novel, the experience of being under enemy fire has sexual overtones. One man, to the immense amusement of his comrades, is discovered to have an erection while under fire, and after the initial fear, the reaction of many other men to the dangers of combat became more intense and exhilarating than anything experienced before. "Could it be," Jones asks through one character, "that *all* war was basically sexual? Not just in psych theory, but in fact, actually and emotionally? A sort of sexual perversion? Or a complex of sexual perversions?"[90] Given the strong sexual tensions underlying marines' contacts with women outside the normal social boundaries that separated the military and civilian worlds, it is possible that at least some found the outlet on the battlefield the most satisfying.[91]

Many marines ultimately reached a point when the male-ordered world of the corps broke down. For Russell Davis, lightly wounded on Okinawa and later chronically sick, a nurse he met in an Army hospital, clean and sweet-smelling, represented safety and comfort.[92] His physical and emotional well-being had been so reduced in the grinding routine of the front lines that he had to seek solace and respite outside the bounds of the idealized Marine environment. Gray more fully describes the same phenomenon in different terms:

> [S]oldiers long for the gentleness and affection that only women can bring into the very male character of martial ex-

90 Jones, *Thin Red Line*, 64, 147, 200, 277, 309.
91 Theweleit sees this expressed explicitly in the German memoirs on combat. See, for instance, his discussion of images involving soldiers as human bullets penetrating the enemy (*Male Fantasies*, 2:179–82).
92 Davis, *Marine at War*, 233.

istence. . . . A soldier who feels this may not know what it is that
stirs him so profoundly about a girl's presence, but he surmises
that it is her presence itself and not merely her body that moves
him. It is the feminine quality of being that he unconsciously
wants to fulfill him. Physical and spiritual elements are so fused
in his desire that they are indistinguishable.[93]

This was the feeling stirred by Patti Thomas that generated both
longing and unease. Marines who were badly wounded and evacuated could make this transition more quickly and often with less
equivocation than did men who rotated home.

For many marines, the gender identities internalized since boot
camp frequently carried over into civilian life. The anxieties experienced by Marine veterans and the difficulties they had adjusting
after the war frequently arose because the communities to which
they returned were not governed by the gender relationships imagined in the service. Davis, for example, confronted his breaking
point on Okinawa, but returned years later in his memoir, like
many ex-marines, to testify to the value of his indoctrination. The
sense of disjunction also fostered further conflict between the sexes
in postwar America as seen in efforts to create what Betty Friedan
labeled the feminine mystique – an idealization of the imagery that
dominated Marine indoctrination.

Two additional areas of Marine Corps personnel policy that require
special attention are the recruitment and training of officers and
the replacement system. Although the early flood of wartime volunteers and selective service provided the Marine Corps with the
manpower to fill the enlisted ranks throughout the war, obtaining
high-quality officers to lead these men defied any easy solution.
The Marines tried to recruit most of their officers from among
college graduates, but competition among all three services at the
outbreak of the war quickly exhausted the available pool of candidates. Over a span of thirty weeks, college graduates could complete Officer Candidate Class (OCC), receive their commissions,
finish the Reserve Officers' Course (ROC), and be in a position to
join a unit in the FMF. This was the major source of new officers
immediately prior to Pearl Harbor: two-thirds of the 560 officers
commissioned in fiscal year 1941 were reserve officers who went
through this program. As had been the case with recruit training,
in an effort to turn out more officers after the start of the war the
period of training was sharply curtailed and a new class started

93 Gray, *The Warriors*, 71.

every five weeks. The reduction of the training schedule from thirty weeks down to twenty in April 1942 produced extra men quickly, but the quality of the officers suffered as a result.[94]

When the Marines failed to attract enough college graduates to meet their need for new officers in the first year of the war, they relied to an unusual degree on direct commissions and selection of promising enlisted men for OCC. Of 4,210 general duty commissions granted in 1942, an astonishing 1,236 were field promotions. At the same time, large numbers of enlisted men were selected to attend training. Few of these men had much, if any, college education, but they did have basic military training and often some field experience. Such reliance on culling the enlisted ranks for officers was the product of wartime pressures, and although it democratized the service to some degree, the results were uneven and the cause of much complaint by division commanders in 1943.[95]

By 1943 the selection and training of officers had settled down into a workable form. Adopting the Navy's V-12 program, the Marine Corps recruited undergraduates still in school to supply a steady stream of new material and paid selected enlisted men to attend college before going to OCC. All officer candidates had to attend boot camp for eight weeks, OCC for eight weeks, and then, if they received their commissions, ROC for twelve weeks. This gave all candidates a common background and basic military knowledge as well as a firsthand knowledge of what their men went through. In late 1944 each division was allowed to nominate up to ten enlisted men for direct commissioning each month, and NCOs could be selected for OCS on the basis of 1 percent of the officer strength for the preceding month.[96]

In addition to line officers, the Marine Corps also had to attract a large number of officer specialists. Language officers were needed who could speak Japanese and later Chinese; so too were technical experts needed, particularly in aviation, and a variety of limited duty officers, who filled roles from newspaper editors to personally selected interservice liaison officers. Although the primary criterion for selection of these officers was their facility in a particular skill, most of them nevertheless went through all the standard training prescribed for line officers and frequently more specialized instruction, often at schools run by the other services. Language officers, for example, had to learn interrogation techniques and intelligence

94 "Ground Training," 225–29. See also *Marine Corps Reserve*, 64–69.
95 "Ground Training," 230–33.
96 Ibid., 237; "Marine Corps Administrative History," 386.

procedures to operate effectively at the division level. The success of the Marine Corps in attracting these specialists filled important gaps within the separate divisions.

In the first months of 1942 Headquarters Marine Corps was so preoccupied with the job of expanding the officer corps, enlarging the training system to accommodate new men, filling out existing units, and creating new formations that it came almost as an afterthought when consideration was given to the area of manpower policy crucial to maintaining units in combat: replacement. Staff planners were surprised to discover how high the turnover in combat units proved to be, due not just to battle losses but to sickness, rotation, and expansion as well.[97] Armies of all nations tried approaches to the problem that reflected their efficiency and assumptions about unit effectiveness. The Imperial Japanese Army, for instance, during the Okinawa campaign in 1945, maintained the strength of their badly depleted line units by assigning to them men from service support organizations. Combat efficiency naturally suffered since these men were untrained in infantry tactics, but it served as a de facto cadre system that fulfilled its purpose.[98] In Germany, replacements were drawn from the same regions as the divisions to which they were to be assigned. These men were integrated into their new units by veterans assigned from the divisions to provide their training, and every effort was made to ensure that men separated from their original unit for whatever reason were returned to that unit later. One historian even goes so far as to argue that this close, personalized system was the basis for what he sees as the overwhelming tactical superiority of the German army over its enemies.[99]

In contrast to the German system, the U.S. Army viewed the problem of replacements as one of labor management whose solution might be copied from American industrial practices. Unlike Japan or Germany, there was no regional organization of recruitment. National Guard divisions started out associated with individual states or regions, but draftees and volunteers, even some

97 Sledge's company, K/3/5, landed on Okinawa with 235 officers and men; it absorbed 250 replacements during the campaign and ended with 50 (*With the Old Breed*, 268). Within the First Division on Guadalcanal in November 1942, 16% were ineffective: 4% from wounds and 12% from disease, mostly malaria. For all Marine enlisted men in 1943, the rate of noneffectives ran at over 50 per 1,000, almost twice the rate among Navy enlisted; United States Navy Department, *The History of the Medical Department of the United States Navy in World War II*, 3 vols. (Washington: Bureau of Medicine and Surgery, 1953), 1:163, 3:11.
98 First Marine Division, Special Action Report, Okinawa, dated 10 July 1945, Chapter 8, Intelligence, pp. 35–36, RG 127/65A-5188/file A28-1.
99 Martin Van Creveld, *Fighting Power* (Westport: Greenwood Press, 1982), 75–76.

regulars, were thrown together to bring them up to full strength without regard for their geographic origins. Basic training was conducted in numerous nearby camps, but only as a convenience before shipping the men off to further schooling. Even when assigned to a particular division, there was no effort made to ensure that a soldier, if once separated from his original unit, would ever return to it. Almost as an offshoot of Taylorism, the Army relied on a system of classification to match men to the jobs for which they were best suited. It was assumed that a qualified man could do his job as well with one unit as another and, correspondingly, that the unit would not lose efficiency simply as a result of personnel changes. In practice, neither the classification system nor its underlying assumptions worked as expected. Because it was geared more toward mobilization than combat replacement, the classification system produced too many specialists while certain other types of replacements, particularly trained infantrymen, came up short in both numbers and preparation. In addition, policies of rotation and reassignment often had adverse effects on unit morale and effectiveness. Replacements were handled by an impersonal system that added to the difficulties of fitting in to new units, and the veterans came to expect that they would remain in their units until either killed, evacuated for wounds or sickness, or the enemy surrendered.[100]

The Marine Corps replacement system came virtually as an afterthought to personnel planners and accordingly suffered throughout the war from a number of shortcomings. The insatiable need for manpower among newly forming Marine line units in the early months completely eclipsed the question of maintaining these units in combat. New and existing formations were being raised and filled out so quickly after the start of the war that the decision to divert men for replacements was made only belatedly and grudgingly on 22 May 1942. Training of the first infantry replacements, which were organized into replacement drafts for shipment overseas, began on 1 September at Camp Elliott, one month ahead of schedule, but the training consisted of only two weeks of physical conditioning.[101] Training for subsequent drafts was organized around an eight-week schedule, but predictably it was hampered by a shortage of skilled instructors.

Although some reforms of the replacement system were made, mirroring those of recruit training itself in stressing greater realism,

100 *Army in World War II*, vol. 1, pt. 2:175–79; Samuel A. Stouffer et al., *The American Soldier*, vol. 2, *Combat and Its Aftermath* (Princeton: Princeton University Press, 1949), 456–72; Holmes, *Acts of War*, 261–62.
101 "Ground Training," 177.

its fundamental structural flaws remained untouched. Not until
July 1944, with the end of the Saipan campaign, was the training
schedule finally expanded from eight to twelve weeks. Training
overall was made more realistic and tailored to specific needs: time
spent on small-arms training went from 409 hours to 720, and
jungle warfare training was dropped in favor of tactics instruction
on the reduction of bunkers and fortified areas. One of the basic
problems that remained, however, as with the Army replacement
system, was the inherent impersonality and remoteness of the system itself. Major General Oscar R. Cauldwell, commanding general
of the Replacement Training Command, Camp Pendleton, recognized the replacements' situation:

> They were no longer recruits looking forward with pride to
> becoming Marines, nor did they belong to any organization.
> They were individual students in a vast school system. . . . Men
> in newly-formed combat units automatically adopt . . . team-
> work. . . . Such a desire was superficial among replacements be-
> cause they knew they would finally be members of a different
> organization in combat.

Another shortcoming was that the system had not been designed
"to train a man so thoroughly that he could step directly from the
training center into a strange infantry unit in combat." Planners
had always envisioned Marine operations as short and hard and
followed by a period of rehabilitation during which replacements
would be assimilated. When later campaigns did not conform to
this preconception, however, replacements and line units suffered.[102]

Starting with the Peleliu campaign, operational planners provided for replacements to accompany the division in its assault.
Two provisional companies were to serve with the beach party
unloading supplies until needed in line units.[103] Unfortunately,
losses among frontline units far surpassed the number of replacements available; in fact, "infantillery" units, composed of nones-
sential personnel from the supporting artillery battalions, and ad
hoc formations from the pioneers, military police, and other rear-
area units had to be pressed into service to maintain a continuous
line around the Japanese strongholds.[104] It marked the greatest
failure of the system up to that time when sufficient replacements
were unavailable to sustain the battered 1st Marines and the reg-

102 Ibid., 179, 189–94.
103 "Marine Corps Administrative History," 374.
104 R. A. Evans, " 'Infantillery' on Peleliu," *Marine Corps Gazette* 29 (January 1945):
       50–55.

iment had to be withdrawn to the rear in order to rebuild after only one week in combat.

Although the campaigns on Iwo Jima and Okinawa saw improvements to the system, it still remained flawed. Drafts were standardized at 125 officers and 2,500 men each, and more realistic assessments of possible casualties ensured that more adequate numbers were immediately available. On the other hand, in anticipation of heavy losses on Iwo Jima, additional drafts had to be rushed forward so quickly that several received grossly inadequate training.[105] Even when attached to a division long before a campaign, there were no provisions to have the replacements train with the units to which they would eventually be assigned. Attempts to incorporate replacements while the units were still up on the line during the long, attritional fighting on Okinawa were unsuccessful, and many of them were killed or wounded before they could be logged into their new company or even introduced to their squad leader.[106] Two historians attached to the First Division conveyed the impression of the system as viewed from the lines:

In spite of the Marine Corps pride in itself as infantry "specialists," its replacement system was, to put it moderately, "lousy" and haphazard. Indeed it stank.... We knew hundreds of men who had had no training beyond boot-camp, who were sent into the lines oblivious of the rudiments.... There were those who did not even know that the pin should be removed from grenades before throwing.

We can't help but wonder whether several of our friends mightn't have been alive today, if they had been given half a break....[107]

Despite much unnecessary "wastage" and needless effort, the two marine divisions on Okinawa were kept effectively in the fighting for the duration of the campaign, if at reduced strength. In general, each division was able to rotate one infantry regiment out of the

105 "Ground Training," 194. The 27th Replacement Draft received eight to ten weeks' training instead of the prescribed twelve; the 31st received five to six weeks' training; and the 34th only four weeks' training.
106 5th Marines, Special Action Report, Okinawa, n. d.; RG 127/65A-5188/Box 23/file A43-1; "Casualty compilation" for Official History, vol. 5, *Victory and Occupation*, by Benis M. Frank and Henry I. Shaw, Jr. (1968), in RG 127/14051/ Box 7; Sledge, *With the Old Breed*, 268.
107 Troop observations on the Okinawa campaign by First Marine Division historians, Sergeants Trilling and Schutts, n.d., 8–9, RG 127/65A-5188/Box 36/ unnumbered file. For an account of the replacement process from the perspective of an eighteen-year-old private in D Company, 32d Replacement Draft see diary of George Dunn, George M. Dunn Papers, PPC, MCHC.

lines to rest and give incoming replacements a few days to acclimatize themselves. However imperfectly, the system had worked.

No matter how long or according to what formulas they were trained and indoctrinated, only actual combat could test the efficacy of the marines' preparation. The marines on Wake, Guam, and Corregidor had acquitted themselves well, and, at least in the case of Wake, had added to the mythic record of the corps. But Guadalcanal was to be the first real test. Furthermore, it was to take on the symbolic appearance of a gladiatorial contest between the chosen representatives of the American and Japanese warrior classes: a clash of warring samurai. The marines who filled the ranks of the First Division in mid-1942 were imbued with a solemn awareness of the corps's mythic traditions and their role in adding to them. They were well trained in the tactical fundamentals and knew their weapons thoroughly, but they had not yet proven themselves in combat against the Japanese.

3

IMAGES OF THE JAPANESE "OTHER" DEFINED

GUADALCANAL AND BEYOND

By the time they emerged victorious from the Guadalcanal campaign, the marines of the First Division had confronted the myth of the Japanese as "supermen" and, focusing on specific acts of Japanese cruelty and wantonness to the exclusion of all else, had retired behind a racist ideology that denied their enemies' humanity and reduced them to objects so alien and contemptible as virtually to ensure the increasing barbarization of subsequent battlefields.[1] The eight months that elapsed between the Japanese attack on Pearl Harbor and the Marine landing on Guadalcanal were a dark time for Americans. The seemingly uninterrupted string of military defeats up to the battle of Midway in June 1942 was not only nationally humiliating but also culturally portentous. The rapid collapse of Allied military forces exposed disdainful American assumptions about the Japanese to be wrong, a revelation that few Americans wanted to acknowledge. Japan's miraculous "Hundred Days" rudely shattered Western complacency, which had long been nurtured by presumptions of racial and technological superiority. In December 1941 the pendulum swung from a sense of uneasy security and arrogance to wildly exaggerated fear; one year later it had swung back to a vengeful contempt that could easily accommodate exterminationist policies.

American images of the Japanese drew upon a deeply ingrained racist ideology that has characterized America's expansion since the earliest colonial times.[2] Just as they tended to amalgamate all blacks

---

1 There are a number of very good operational histories on Operation Watchtower, the amphibious attack on the lower British Solomon Islands. The strategic goals and specific conduct of the campaign are beyond the scope of this study but are covered well, from general to specific, in Spector, *Eagle against the Sun*, 184–87, 190–214; Richard B. Frank, *Guadalcanal* (New York: Random House, 1990); and the official histories, especially *Pearl Harbor to Guadalcanal*.

2 Drawing the subtitle of his book from Herman Melville's expression "metaphysics of Indian-hating," Drinnon argues persuasively that "societies are known by their victims," and "wholesale killings and hurtings" reveal "the European-derived subliminal mind" (*Facing West*, xii). The underlying racism that Drinnon discusses in connection with American imperialism in the Philippines at the turn of the

or all American Indians into large, undifferentiated, racially defined categories, so too did white Americans often lump together different Asian peoples. From their first contacts, American images of Asians always contained an element of exotic allure, but this was overshadowed by an abiding fear encapsulated in the vague and ominous "Yellow Peril." Rooted in medieval European experience of invasions from the east and handed down by contemporary chroniclers, the Yellow Peril had three components: first, the fear that Asian invaders could not be militarily defeated; second, that they comprised huge numbers that would flood an area and push out or overwhelm non-Asian peoples; and third, that they were both infidels and barbarians with whom there could be no accommodation.[3]

When driven to act on their ambivalent assumptions, Americans usually favored oppression and intolerance. The first legislative restrictions to immigration, for example, began with the Chinese Exclusion Act of 1882, which eased the way for subsequent restrictions on other nationalities.[4] Increasingly suspicious of Japanese intentions and capabilities after 1905, Americans frequently lashed out at Japanese immigrants in their midst. Montaville Flowers in his 1917 book *The Japanese Conquest of American Opinion* repeated the widely held Social Darwinist argument that introduction of Asian or "mixed" races into the American melting pot would destroy the country.[5] Likewise, efforts to exclude Japanese children

century and in Vietnam decades later applies also to American wartime behavior and attitudes toward the Japanese (ibid., 286–306, 447–67).

3 William F. Wu, *The Yellow Peril* (Hamden: Archon Books, 1982), 10. See also Harold R. Isaacs, *Images of Asia: American Views of China and India* (New York: Harper, 1972). A separate branch of the thirteenth-century Mongol legacy is evident in the striking parallels between American images of the Yellow Peril and those of the "flood" that influenced the rise of fascism and the proto-Nazis of the *Freikorps* in their war against Bolshevism and the "red flood" after 1919; Theweleit, *Male Fantasies*, vol. 1, *Women, Floods, Bodies, History* (1987), 229ff. German officers like Heinz Guderian continued to justify their actions after the Second World War by arguing that Germany was fulfilling its historical and geographical mission of protecting all of central and western Europe from "the Asiatic Bolshevik flood." Cited in Omer Bartov, "Indoctrination and Motivation in the *Wehrmacht*: The Importance of the Unquantifiable," *Journal of Strategic Studies* 9 (March 1986): 18.

4 Wu makes the point that the triple threat described by opponents of Chinese immigration paralleled the traditional threat of the Yellow Peril just described: that Chinese laborers could not be beaten in direct competition; that they would numerically overwhelm the western seaboard; and that they would corrupt American Christian values (*Yellow Peril*, 11).

5 Montaville Flowers, *The Japanese Conquest of American Opinion* (New York: George H. Doran, 1917). Flowers explicitly adheres to the stereotype of Asian patience and incrementalism in conquest: to lose the "battle" for public opinion supporting exclusionary policies would eventually lead to inundation and loss of the whole nation.

from local school systems in the western states were symptomatic of the larger attempt to emplace legally sanctioned bigotry directed against Asians to match the various Jim Crow laws aimed at blacks. The racist fears expressed in the national debate over a Japanese exclusion bill, passed in 1924, were an internationally embarrassing example of American xenophobia guiding policy.[6]

Aside from the manifestations of a wide array of political policies, prejudice toward Asians was also expressed in literature and film that embraced stereotyped figures like the Chinese Fu Manchu and Charlie Chan. English author Sax Rohmer's creation, Fu Manchu, attracted such a large following in the United States that the character became "absorbed into American consciousness as the archetypal Asian villain." Possessed of "a brow like Shakespeare and a face like Satan," Fu Manchu was "the yellow peril incarnate in one man." With "all the cruel cunning of an entire Eastern race" behind him, Fu Manchu served as a representation of the larger threat posed by Asian masses set to overwhelm Europe and North America. In the words of one of Rohmer's narrators, "the swamping of the White world by the Yellow hordes might well be the price of our failure."[7] Charlie Chan, made famous by creator Earl Derr Biggers's six novels and through forty-seven serial and feature films, was an obsequious, nonthreatening counterpoint to the Fu Manchu image, but the character shared identical racist origins:

> The duality represented by Fu Manchu and Charlie Chan in American popular culture is . . . created specifically by certain values and beliefs of white supremacy. These include a belief in the Yellow Peril. Fu Manchu is defined as a villain and the embodiment of the Yellow Peril because he is an Asian whose behavior is uncontrolled by Europeans and white Americans. Charlie Chan is not interpreted as part of the Yellow Peril because his subservient behavior to white Americans indicates he has been, in a sense, domesticated and trained. That Charlie Chan has been tamed, however, implies that he con-

6 Two points are worth noting about such debates: first, Japan offered equally glaring examples of racist intolerance toward outsiders, including similar school "reforms," especially in regard to Korea, which had been annexed in 1910; second, the success of the Exclusion Act was built upon an established alliance of western and southern states and the linkage between Asian immigration and "the Negro problem"; Eleanor Tupper and George E. McReynolds, *Japan in American Public Opinion* (New York: Macmillan, 1937), 95–97, 185–91.

7 Rohmer's thirteen novels, three short stories, and one novella kept Fu Manchu in production from 1913 to 1959 (Wu, *Yellow Peril*, 164–68). As an interesting side note, in Rohmer's 1936 book *President Fu Manchu*, his first novel set in the United States, the key American defender of the "White world" was Mark Hepburn, a Marine captain on special duty.

ceivably could have been wild, or uncontrolled, and so he is a reflection of the Yellow Peril though not part of it.[8]

These images of the Chinese remained a reservoir to be tapped as needed: friends to be assisted after the Japanese invasion in 1937, they reverted to the Yellow Peril upon the triumph of the Chinese Communists in 1949 and especially after intervention in the Korean War the following year.

With the exception of Mr. Moto, figures of specifically Japanese descent in literature and film of the 1930s tended to perform background roles, usually as villains. First appearing in John Marquand's 1935 *Saturday Evening Post* serial *No Hero*, the character of Mr. Moto was actually a man of charm, loyalty, and patriotism. The five novels written between 1935 and 1942 are free of overt racial hostility, and the only slur of the series, a reference to Mr. Moto as a "little yellow bastard," appears in the sixth and final novel, published in 1957. A secret agent who "plays the game" according to the commonly shared unwritten rules, Mr. Moto is himself an acceptable or even likable figure, but the country he serves is depicted as culturally twisted, obsessively suspicious, and "an arrogant nation" that understands only force.[9] More frequently, Japanese figures appeared as stock villains in the pulps that proliferated at this time. The Japanese were portrayed as an alien, implacable, and vicious enemy.[10]

In addition to images conveyed in popular cultural media like the movies and pulps, American attitudes toward the Japanese gained expression through "informed" public debate. The authors of a 1937 study drawn from newspaper editorials, congressional debates, and publications of special-interest groups identified several swings in American public opinion toward Japan that relied upon a variety of racist stereotypes to explain events. A good example was when public opinion turned sharply against the Japanese after the 1932 attack on Shanghai. Comments in the press foreshadowed many of the same views that resurfaced in 1941. Some papers ascribed Japanese aggression to national insanity, "Japanese military efficiency gone mad." Others took the paternalistic view that Japan was a child after the pattern of the United States, but gone astray: "We raised our Japanese boy to be a soldier, a fierce

8 Tupper and McReynolds, *Japan in American Public Opinion*, 182.

9 Richard Wires, *John P. Marquand and Mr. Moto* (Muncie: Ball State University, 1990), 74. It is worth noting that Mr. Moto was a product of such abstract imagination that Marquand was unaware that "Moto" was only a suffix rather than a proper name.

10 Tony Goodstone, ed., *The Pulps: Fifty Years of American Pop Culture* (New York: Chelsea House, 1976).

patriot, a clever and shifty trader, an irresponsible imperialist, and a grim diplomatic realist." Many drew on the Yellow Peril imagery to depict the Japanese as inherently arrogant and ruthless: "Humble and conciliatory when the bayonet is at his own belly, this yellow dwarf, pretending recognition of civilized usages, gives no quarter and shows no mercy in a contrary situation."[11]

Yet, for all the malevolent imagery attached to the Japanese, they were not perceived as a threat sufficient to rouse the United States from its isolationist torpor. Condemnation of growing Japanese nationalism and militarism during the 1930s was not backed up by even the credible threat of intervention because Americans remained confident that they could protect their vital interests in the Pacific from a distance.[12] The most famous apocalyptic vision offered of the Japanese menace was Homer Lea's *Valor of Ignorance*, which was first published in 1909, went out of print after 1922, and was ostentatiously resurrected in early 1942. As historian John W. Dower points out, what was most significant about Lea was his revival as an overlooked prophet: "Had Lea been widely remembered, after all, there would have been less racist complacency about the 'little men' of Japan. What carried through over these prewar decades was not so much a clear sense of a specific threat from the Orient, but a rather vague premonition of future peril."[13] Insulated by self-assurance of national greatness and lulled by racist assumptions about the Japanese, most Americans were not willing to give much credence to a future menace.

In the four years between the Marco Polo Bridge incident and the Pearl Harbor attack, American attitudes toward Japan grew increasingly hostile. Americans abhorred the cold-blooded brutality

11 Citations from San Francisco *Chronicle*, New York *World Telegram*, and New York *Daily Mirror*, all in Tupper and McReynolds, *Japan in American Public Opinion*, 319–27. There were a few contrary voices that ridiculed prophecies of doom, and many comparisons appear between Japanese policies in East Asia and U.S. policies in Central America, but the tone set in the sample given here was most prevalent. As Ernest May points out, American press coverage from Japan was as "superficial, fragmentary, insensitive, and, in the end, misleading" as what Tupper and McReynolds find; Ernest May, "U.S. Press Coverage of Japan, 1931–1941," in Dorothy Borg and Shumpai Okamoto, eds., *Pearl Harbor as History: Japanese-American Relations, 1931–1941* (New York: Columbia University Press, 1973), 511–32.

12 Michael Barnhart, *Japan Prepares for Total War* (Ithaca: Cornell University Press, 1987), 19–21, 176–97; and Akira Iriye, *Power and Culture* (Cambridge: Harvard University Press, 1981), 15–23.

13 Dower, *War without Mercy*, 158. Lea spoke highly of the bushido code and "[m]any Japanese must have felt flattered" that Lea viewed them as a formidable, worthy enemy (102); Shōichi Saeki, "Images of the United States as a Hypothetical Enemy," in Akira Iriye, ed., *Mutual Images* (Cambridge: Harvard University Press, 1975), 100–114.

that the Japanese practiced against the Chinese but simultaneously scorned their inability to bring to a decisive conclusion a years-long war against an unsophisticated non-Western country.[14] Smug overconfidence sprang in part from putatively scientific explanations for Japanese military incapacity. It was widely believed, for instance, that physiological defects of the inner ear and myopia prevented the Japanese from becoming good pilots. Military commentator Fletcher Pratt compiled a list in 1939 as to why the United States had nothing to fear from Japan, which included technical ineptitude, inferior individual ability, an implicitly childlike national temperament, and Japanese awe of American superiority.[15]

The assumptions of Pratt and others were grounded in a second component of American attitudes regarding Japan, which went beyond general racism. Michael Adas convincingly argues that, "Europeans' perceptions of the material superiority of their own cultures, particularly as manifested in scientific thought and technological innovation, shaped their attitudes toward and interaction with peoples they encountered overseas." Twentieth-century Americans carried this measure even further than their early modern European counterparts, and indeed the notion of "Yankee ingenuity" was fundamental to Americans' self-image heading into the war. American attitudes grouped under the rubric of "racism,"

14 This required the Chinese to be endowed with Western sensibilities and shared humanity. The same process of "bleaching" and anglicizing has occurred before, as in the case of the Cubans in 1898, but if the reality obtrudes too much on the image, there tends to be an exaggerated reaction, as happened with the Cubans; Gerald S. Linderman, *Mirror of War* (Ann Arbor: University of Michigan Press, 1974), 127–47. In the case of the Chinese, insiders, like Joseph Stilwell, who formed an almost unbounded contempt for Chiang Kai-shek and the Kuomintang, were largely ignored; Barbara W. Tuchman, *Stilwell and the American Experience in China* (New York: Macmillan, 1971). With the racial element never far below the surface, the popularized images stressed qualities that applied much more to American sensibilities than to the Chinese character. Henry R. Luce did much to popularize Westernized Chinese images in America, featuring Chiang on the cover of *Time* six times and the American-educated Soong Mei-ling, Madame Chiang, three times. Nobel laureate Pearl S. Buck, in her wartime novels, articles, and lectures, did much to build upon the positive prewar images of *The Good Earth* (1932). Edgar Snow stirred great sympathy for Mao Tse-tung and the Communists with *Red Star over China* (1938), as did Theodore White and Annalee Jacoby in *Thunder out of China* (1946). All of these images were easily turned around after 1949 when the Yellow Peril merged with the Red Scare.

15 Dower, *War without Mercy*, 98, 102–5. The British mirrored these American attitudes and assumptions as discussed in connection with the Royal Navy and Imperial Japanese Navy in Arthur Marder, *Old Friends, New Enemies* (New York: Oxford University Press, 1981). For perceptions of the Japanese within the First Marine Division see 1st Marines, " ' – and in this corner, the Jap!!' " n.d., Richard F. Lyons Papers, PPC, MCHC; this intelligence document was intended on the eve of Guadalcanal as a corrective to misleading stereotypes.

which might be more accurately labeled ethnocentrism, cultural chauvinism, or physical narcissism, were outgrowths of many beliefs, including proselytizing Christianity, democratic republicanism, and especially conceptions of progress embodied in American industrial achievements.[16] Since the Meiji Restoration in 1868, Japan had often been seen as a childlike wanderer, picking up scraps of Western scientific thought and technology from Europe and the United States.[17] That Japan might have mastered this knowledge, let alone expanded and improved upon it independently, was beyond reckoning for most Americans. John Hersey reverts to this kind of racist imagery when he describes the mental picture he forms of the Japanese soldiers serving mortars that bombard him on a Guadalcanal patrol. The Japanese are not only technologically backward but actually rise no higher than conditioned, uncomprehending beasts:

A swarm of intelligent little animals would fuss around each tube.... Some of the animals would step back, one or two would put their fingers in their ears. Then one, in the attitude of a small boy setting punk to a giant firecracker, would reach over the mouth of each tube.... At the order to fire, he would drop the [shell].[18]

This pattern of thinking conformed to past assumptions and was reassuring to a country poorly prepared for war in the Pacific. It also gave rise to a haughty overconfidence that, when war came, left Americans vulnerable to doubt about their racial superiority

16 Michael Adas, *Machines as the Measure of Men* (Ithaca: Cornell University Press, 1989), 4, 12, 15–16. Adas applies his argument primarily to the cases of European penetration of sub-Saharan Africa, India, and China between the seventeenth century and 1914, but his epilogue is insightful regarding the American distinctions, especially pp. 406–11.

17 This image was sharpened by sometimes self-effacing Japanese characterizations of themselves as backward. Fukuzawa Yukichi (1834–1901), a leading intellectual of the Restoration period, identified Japan in Social Darwinist terms as semi-developed; to advance it would have to acquire "the spirit of civilization" and "sweep away blind attachment to past [Japanese] custom." Although the cultural imagery used by men like Fukuzawa and other proponents of *bummei kaika* ("civilization and enlightenment") was intended for internal consumption to promote reform or ease the strains of rapid modernization, when taken out of context it also conformed with Western condescension and the cycle of unpleasant surprises as Japan expanded and tested its growing power from the Sino-Japanese War of 1894–95 right through Pearl Harbor and the Hundred Days. See Fukuzawa Yukichi, *An Outline of a Theory of Civilization*, translated by David A. Dillworth and G. Cameron Hurst (Tokyo: Sophia University Press, 1973) (the original, *Bummeiron no gairyaku*, was published in 1875); and Kenneth Pyle, *The New Generation in Meiji Japan* (Stanford: Stanford University Press, 1969).

18 Hersey, *Into the Valley*, 82.

and scientific and technological domination and in turn pushed the possibility of unchecked violence dangerously near the surface.

When their forces collapsed in the spring of 1942, the Western Allies quickly manufactured explanations that maintained their racial separation from the Japanese but otherwise contradicted earlier views. Prior to the surrender of Singapore the British had insisted that the Japanese could not fight at night or in the jungle because they feared ghosts and spirits. Afterward, these same superstitious Japanese peasants and urban laborers were suddenly endowed with an inbred affinity for precisely those skills. From this it was a short step to the widespread simian associations, large and menacing apelike images initially, which gave way to smaller, vicious monkey images.[19] Americans shifted the blame for their defeats onto Japanese treachery and deceit and general American unpreparedness, which could conveniently be laid at the feet of a few senior officers and isolationist politicians. Given the subsequent emphasis placed on America's military weakness and vulnerability and the radical reversal of Japanese images from innocuous villain to venomous fiend, what appears most striking is that Japan's Hundred Days lasted no longer than it did. The material deficiencies, for instance, often cited in explaining the precipitate collapse of the Allies' Pacific outposts, had certainly not been rectified by the time the battle of Midway and the invasion of Guadalcanal cut short Japan's expansionist dreams.[20] The days when swarms of modern aircraft, large, powerful fleets, and heavily armed ground forces would strike almost at will throughout the Japanese Empire still lay over two years in the future. During this period Americans could do little but believe in the courage and skill of the individual soldier, sailor, or marine, show faith in the wisdom and resourcefulness of their leaders up and down the chain of command, and hope that good luck would be on their side.

In the aftermath of Pearl Harbor, as the country began to mobilize, American patriotism and chauvinism interpreted the war as a judgment of the national character.[21] As with any country in

19 Dower, *War without Mercy*, 84–88, 103, 112–13; Keen, *Faces of the Enemy*, 60–64.
20 Material deficiencies are emphasized in Isely and Crowl, *Amphibious War*, 72–79, and the official histories of all the services stress the baneful effects of unpreparedness forced upon them by the government. Spector, *Eagle against the Sun*, and to a lesser extent John Costello, *The Pacific War* (New York: Rawson Wade, 1981), provide much more balanced views that properly acknowledge poor planning and major lapses in judgment among the military and civilian leadership.
21 Americans were particularly anxious to find in the war confirmation of their beliefs and way of life not just as a reaction to the string of military defeats suffered in 1942 but also because of the decade-long social and economic turmoil

similar circumstances, the public view of early events emphasized the moral and spiritual superiority displayed by American service personnel even in defeat. A prominent example was the defense of Wake, which became a rallying point in the early days of the war, freighted with much greater popular significance than purely military considerations could justify. In a hopelessly lopsided struggle against a wide array of problems, the garrison of the small atoll performed remarkably well, sinking two destroyers with all hands during a premature Japanese landing attempt and inflicting heavy casualties on the Japanese assault troops before surrendering on 23 December.[22] Further elevating this small "last-stand" battle to mythic dimensions was Paramount Studio's release of the movie *Wake Island* just nine months after its fall, at the very time that the marines were beating off the early Japanese attacks in the jungles of Guadalcanal. Touted as a real-life adventure film but generously embellished by Hollywood scriptwriters, this film revived and updated the Marine warrior image of the Great War. It laid the blame for defeat squarely on the material imbalance between the two sides, vigorously denied any nagging doubts regarding the Americans' racial assumptions, and easily sidestepped any question regarding how the brave lads were abandoned in such a hopeless position in the first place.[23] In his 1943 book *Last Man Off Wake Island*, Marine aviator Walter L. J. Bayler's description of the Wake defenders helped to define the image of the marines on Guadalcanal: "Nasty jobs are what a marine expects, the kind he takes in stride. They were there to hold the island, and hold it they would, as a matter of routine business, till they were relieved or until Tojo ran out of his slant-eyed cannon fodder."[24] Presaging the words of Emperor Hirohito's Imperial Rescript on Surrender issued forty-two months later, the Wake defenders had to accept a third alternative, enduring the unendurable and suffering what is insufferable – unconditional surrender.

Especially in the first year of war, the realities of battle, whether those of the Wake defenders, the carrier pilots at Midway, or the First Marine Division on Guadalcanal, were so far removed from the American public, both spatially and conceptually, that they remained little more than abstractions. As embodied in columns of print, newsreels, and movie-house fantasies like *Wake Island*, the

suffered in the Depression; John Morton Blum, *V Was for Victory* (New York: Harcourt Brace Jovanovich, 1976), 7, 301.
22 For full details see Official History, 1:95–152.
23 Suid, *Guts and Glory*, 39–40.
24 Walter L. J. Bayler and Cecil Carnes, *Last Man off Wake Island* (New York: Bobbs-Merrill, 1943), 102.

war came to be seen as almost orderly, unfolding according to carefully laid plans, a stage for a huge morality play. Melodrama became the medium by which the first year of war was understood and interpreted, and correspondents like Richard Tregaskis gave the American public all they asked for, describing the marines as no more than "pawns in a battle of the gods."[25] By 1945 the real-life melodrama of the war had long worn away, but in the summer of 1942 there was still excitement and meaning in every skirmish and every fallen pilot or marine, and this affected the attitudes of the marines who landed on Guadalcanal. Conditions on Guadalcanal shaped the mythic meaning ascribed to the campaign, in which a lone division of marines, cut off and outnumbered, struggled against the hostile jungle environment as well as an invisible and implacable enemy. Civilians and untested soldiers easily lost sight of the line between reality and fantasy, and, indeed, merged the two. One officer found he needed time to adjust to the "realities" of active campaigning: "When I was a young boy we always played cowboys and Indians, and when I landed on Guadalcanal that's what I felt like – I was still playing a game, it was not real. Even though I knew it was real, it was still unreal." John Hersey noted ironically that an actual infantry patrol seemed "just a little exaggerated, like something out of an unconvincing movie."[26] Guadalcanal became a real-life theatrical event, a saga in which, like its cinematic counterparts, Americans could find either confirmation of their values and beliefs or simply gripping entertainment.

From the outset, the Guadalcanal operation was cast as an ideological struggle to preserve the American way of life and its underlying assumptions of racial and technological superiority. In part, this cultural mission was thrust upon the marines: by correspondents eager to report their observations and experiences, by a government anxious to sustain public support for the war effort, and by Americans at large who sought confirmation of their values. The books and films that came out after the campaign capitalized on this view explicitly. "Above all," read one publicity notice, Guadalcanal "revealed the character of the men who are fighting this war."[27]

---

25 Tregaskis, *Guadalcanal Diary*, 62.
26 Lewis J. Fields, interviewed by Thomas E. Donnelly, March, June 1971, OHC, MCHC, 75. Hersey, *Into the Valley*, 60.
27 Draft publication announcement for *The Island*, Herbert C. Merillat Papers, PPC, MCHC. As far as films are concerned, in mid-1943 Hollywood produced the movie *Guadalcanal Diary* based on Richard Tregaskis's best-selling book of the same title. This film and *Wake Island* were probably the two best wartime movies about the Marines and created a cinematic stereotype that has endured to this

The marines of the First Division who came ashore at Guadalcanal brought with them attitudes toward the Japanese that shaped the course of the campaign and served as a benchmark for every subsequent campaign of the division. Circumstances conspired to give the marines the chance they sought to prove themselves, and until overshadowed by the November invasion of North Africa, they held center stage in the public eye. The exotic setting of the campaign and the heavy press coverage guaranteed a large and receptive audience, and a string of apparently uninterrupted and lopsided victories on the ground gave both the marines and the Americans back home the theatrical extravaganza for which they hungered.

Guadalcanal was perhaps destined to be described as a military epic, rather than simply a spontaneous response to military events on the island, because so many people wanted and needed a symbolic rallying point, both inside the Marine Corps and out. The symbolic meaning Guadalcanal held for the war effort has indeed so overshadowed its history that over the years the voluminous literature dealing with the campaign has largely failed to separate myth from fact or to challenge seriously the images so sedulously cultivated by the Marine Corps and its partisans.[28] For instance, it

day. Other Guadalcanal movies include *Flying Leathernecks*, loosely modeled on the Cactus Air Force, and *Pride of the Marines*, centered on the story of Al Schmid.

28 Guadalcanal remains one of the most written-about campaigns of the war. There were at least six books related to the campaign to come out within roughly a year: Roger Butterfield, *Al Schmid, Marine* (New York: Norton, 1944); Hersey, *Into the Valley* (1943); Herbert C. Merillat, *The Island* (Boston: Houghton Mifflin, 1944); Tregaskis, *Guadalcanal Diary* (1943); W. Wyeth Willard, *The Leathernecks Come Through* (New York: Fleming H. Revell, 1944); and Ira Wolfert, *Battle for the Solomons* (Boston: Houghton Mifflin, 1943). There are two official Marine Corps histories, the monograph *The Guadalcanal Campaign*, by John L. Zimmerman (Washington: Historical Branch, G-3 Division, Headquarters Marine Corps, 1949), and the first volume of the *History of U.S. Marine Operations* (1958). The other official histories are United States Air Force, Historical Division, *The Army Air Forces in World War II*, vol. 4, *The Pacific: Guadalcanal to Saipan* (Chicago: University of Chicago Press, 1950); United States Army, Office of Military History, *United States Army in World War II*, vol. 2, pt. 2, *Guadalcanal: The First Offensive*, by John Miller, Jr. (1949); and the quasi-official Navy histories, Samuel Eliot Morison, *History of United States Naval Operations in World War Two*, vol. 5, *The Struggle for Guadalcanal*, and vol. 6, *Breaking the Bismarcks Barrier* (Boston: Little, Brown, 1950–51). Among the numerous, sometimes obscure secondary works written over the last five decades that focus specifically on this campaign are Henry H. Adams, *1942: The Year That Doomed the Axis* (New York: McKay, 1967); Frank, *Guadalcanal*; Samuel B. Griffith II, *The Battle for Guadalcanal* (Philadelphia: Lippincott, 1963); Eric Hammel, *Guadalcanal*, 3 vols. (New York: Crown, 1987–88); Kermit Holt, *Guadalcanal, 25 Years Later* (Chicago: Chicago Tribune, 1967); Edwin P. Hoyt, *Guadalcanal* (New York: Stein and Day, 1982); Robert Leckie, *Challenge for the Pacific: Guadalcanal, the Turning Point of the War* (Garden City: Doubleday, 1965); Robert Edward Lee, *Victory at Guadalcanal* (Novato: Presidio Press, 1981); Herbert C. Merillat, *Guadalcanal Remembered*

can in hindsight be argued that Guadalcanal was far more one-sided than is credited in the popularized view of the campaign. There was no guarantee of American victory at the outset, but it became increasingly obvious as the fighting progressed that the Japanese ground forces were overmatched by the Americans. In fact, the tactical ineptitude of the Japanese commanders and the material shortcomings of their forces occasionally gave the ground portion of the campaign more the appearance of a nineteenth-century colonial war than the life-and-death struggle portrayed in print. As a rough draft of the division intelligence report bluntly stated, "One great advantage enjoyed by the troops who landed on Guadalcanal was that they were introduced to the realities of war in so many easy lessons."[29] This opinion, deleted from the final report, reflected reality on a different level than that which was of such consuming interest to war correspondents, the American public, and the marines themselves.

By no means did all the ideological pressure come from outside the Marine Corps. Recognizing that its future viability as an institution was linked to its performance in the Pacific, the service fostered ideological extremism and widely publicized its role in the struggle. Building on their experiences in the Great War, the Marines established a Division of Public Affairs at Headquarters Marine Corps under the command of Brigadier General Robert L. Denig, a retiree brought back to active duty. Denig began a program to create a highly effective group of uniformed combat correspondents, who eventually achieved remarkable results.[30] Captain Herbert C. Merillat, who landed with the First Division as public relations officer, exercised a formative influence on how the Marine Corps role at Guadalcanal was articulated at the time and long

(New York: Dodd, Mead, 1982); Thomas G. Miller, *The Cactus Air Force* (New York: Harper and Row, 1969); and Irving Werstein, *Guadalcanal* (New York: Crowell, 1963).

29 First Marine Division, rough draft of "Division Intelligence Report on the Guadalcanal Operation (Phase II)," n.d., p. 19, RG 127/63A-2534/Box 4/unnumbered file (hereafter cited as Draft Intelligence Report).

30 Benis M. Frank, *Denig's Demons and How They Grew* (Washington: Marine Corps Combat Correspondents and Photographers Association, 1967). Robert L. Denig set the tone for the program with a sign on his wall that read "If the public become apathetic about the Marine Corps, the Marine Corps will cease to exist." Gathering experienced journalists, photographers, and artists, Denig had a flood of material reaching the American public from the front lines that by 1944 amounted to more than three thousand stories a month. As with other facets of the Marine Corps during the Pacific War, the business of publicizing itself grew tremendously in technical and organizational sophistication. Although it had the youngest and smallest of the service public relations outfits, the Marine Corps took the program very seriously; as Frank writes, Denig's Demons "certainly won the public relations war for the Corps."

afterward. His gripping news releases attracted a wide audience at home, and his status as a uniformed insider lent extra credence to his stories that the civilian correspondents could not fully equal.[31] With institutional sanction, in 1943 Merillat and his publishers, Houghton Mifflin, quickly brought to press a quasi-official book on the campaign entitled *The Island*, which did not simply mirror popular opinion in and out of the service but enshrined it. The marketing copy elevated those distant events to the level of national myth:

> Whatever happens in the future, the Guadalcanal campaign will remain a landmark in American history. Here the myth of Japanese invincibility was destroyed. Here, no less than at Gettysburg or Verdun or Stalingrad, the tide turned. Proud and confident after months of unbroken successes in the Pacific, the Jap found that he could not beat well-equipped, well-trained, well-led Americans. To the Marines, Guadalcanal was known simply as "The Island." Its conquest set the pattern for everything that followed. It was our laboratory of jungle warfare.[32]

It was unnecessary to complete the analogy that the Japanese soldiers were the laboratory rats in this jungle experiment. Merillat and his publishers provided exactly what the Marines and the public wanted to hear.

The marines who fought on Guadalcanal required sharply defined images of themselves and their enemy that offered unambiguous distinctions by which their purpose could be defined and sustained.[33] These images so profoundly affected men's behavior that victory or defeat often depended upon them. The Japanese suffered far more seriously on Guadalcanal than did the Americans precisely because they so badly misjudged the marines' abilities and will to fight. The attributes they projected onto the Americans provided the justification for repeatedly hurling troops at strong defensive positions with the goal of overrunning an American garrison that collectively outnumbered the attackers by ratios as high as 13 to 1. Moreover, the underlying patterns of thought were so

31 The men in the lines were sometimes more natural and candid if the journalist was himself a marine, and as censor Merillat ensured that an appropriate tone was maintained – neither too stark nor sugarcoated. For an example of this role, see Merillat, *Guadalcanal Remembered*, 240–41.

32 This draft publication announcement for *The Island* was picked up in the New York *Times* and appeared in modified form on p. vii of the book; Merillat Papers, PPC, MCHC.

33 Keen uses the term *Homo hostilis* as the starting point of creating a polarized imagination (*Faces of the Enemy*, 17–19).

powerful and pervasive that repeated defeats throughout the campaign never significantly altered their manifestations in combat.
Images of the Japanese affected the way Americans fought too.
They were derived from many sources and were often grossly
inaccurate, but in the American case the images and tactics evolved
more readily over time and with experience, and generally the
errors were on the side of overcaution rather than rashness.

Aside from a wide array of cultural stereotypes, one of the most
important sources of information on the Japanese for the marines
headed to Guadalcanal was the First Division intelligence section.
The senior Japanese language officer in the division was a newly
commissioned captain, Sherwood F. Moran, who turned fifty-seven
in October, junior in age only to the commanding general, A. A.
Vandegrift. His expertise was the product of forty years spent in
Japan as a missionary. Intimately familiar with Japanese society
and culture, Moran wanted to correct the more warped racist views
concerning the Japanese and convey some of their deeply human
qualities as well as their potential for brutality.[34] In a widely circulated report dated 4 June 1942, Moran noted the centrality of
myth in Japanese society, especially in connection with the emperor.
He also explained why Japanese soldiers sometimes acted contrary
to accepted American standards of military rationality:

> There is something theatrical about all this; this thinking that
> in the last analysis, even if equipment and numbers are in-
> adequate, the *Japanese spirit* (Nippon seishin) that we are con-
> tinually having dinned in our ears, will be the deciding factor
> and bring triumph to the Emperor's army.[35]

In the Americans' image of themselves, war was defined as an
instrument of rational policy, whereas the Japanese viewed combat

34 Moran expressed this view vividly in a letter to his wife from Sasebo shortly
   after the Japanese surrender: "Just as we were landing [an American soldier]
   spoke to me with deep feeling of the cruelty and beastiality [sic] on the part of
   the Japanese troops in the Philippines. He said to me, 'Moran, I have seen things
   with my own eyes that are unbelievable.' He looked around at the people who
   were passing in the streets, all Japanese, and continued, 'And yet I feel that the
   ordinary Japanese are probably innocent of all this.' Then he added with a voice
   tense with indignation, 'But those *bastards*!' meaning the Japanese in the Philippines he had been talking about, and that type of Japanese in general. I
   thought his attitude was fine – an awareness of the extreme cruelty of many
   Japanese soldiers but not on that account condemning a race or nation wholesale
   without discrimination." Sherwood F. Moran Papers, letter dated 24 October
   1945, PPC, MCHC.
35 Sherwood F. Moran, "The Psychology of the Japanese," dated 4 June 1942, 12.
   On the importance of emperor worship, see 1–7. Professor Roger F. Hackett
   of the University of Michigan, who served as a Japanese language officer with
   the D-2 section later in the war, very kindly provided me with a copy of this
   document.

as a test of spirit, at times to the exclusion of conventional Western rationality. Americans cited Clausewitz while the Japanese quoted such maxims as "War is the art of embellishing death."[36] An official report even ascribed the doggedness of the Japanese in pressing home hopeless attacks to their "fondness for the tactically dramatic 'Bushido.' "[37] Yet the theatricality Moran and the final report associated with the Japanese was closely mirrored on the American side: in the public demand for melodrama, in correspondents' stories, and among marines "acting out" roles in defense of their collective warrior spirit.

The marines soon learned from captured documents just how seriously the Japanese looked upon the campaign as a test of American and Japanese spiritual strength. The address distributed by the commanding general of the Sendai Division on the eve of the October offensive was an effort to translate and reify Japanese army ideology into military action. It is perhaps the best example of such documents and worth quoting at some length:

> The ensuing operation for the capture of Guadalcanal island, engaging the attention of all the world, is the decisive battle between Japan and America that will confer success or failure upon the empire. If we are unsuccessful in its capture not even one man should expect to return alive.
>
> The command together with the attached units, all mindful of the Imperial Army's prestige, undaunted by the mass of the enemy, and without bowing to material substance, will display a combination of fortitude, perseverance, and steadfastness. Pressing on vigorously, they will inflict a terrific blow upon the proud heads of the enemy, what is more, a blow to the point where we can anticipate his inability to rise (again).[38]

By substituting "Marine Corps's" for "Imperial Army's," this address might as accurately have reflected the marines' own resolve. Such determination was not expressed so baldly by the American commanders, but it was nevertheless widely held.[39] Guadalcanal

36 Maxim is in Paul Virilio, *War and Cinema*, translated by Patrick Camiller (New York: Verso, 1989), ix.
37 First Marine Division, "Final Report, Phase III, Guadalcanal," p. 14, RG 127/63A-2534/Box 4/file A7-3 (hereafter cited as Final Report, III).
38 Translation dated 3 November 1942 by D-2 of "Address of Instruction" delivered by Lieutenant General Maruyama Masao on 1 October 1942, RG 127/63A-2534/Box 8/file C15-3.
39 The best statement of such determination was the vow by the division chief of staff that Guadalcanal would not become "another Bataan." The Marines, he said, would continue guerrilla operations from the interior should the division be overrun; Gerald C. Thomas interview, 358, OHC, MCHC.

made manifest two dimensions in the ground war: not only was the campaign a forthright military conflict, to be decided by the most efficient exploitation of the limited means at hand, but it also assumed importance as a spiritual clash between warrior representatives of the two cultures.[40]

Although it is neither surprising nor unique that the Pacific War was highly charged ideologically, the way in which the cultural values of the enemy, so often portrayed as alien to the West, were matched among the marines is striking. Beneath the mythology and blatant racism that characterized American images of the Japanese there was always lurking at least tacit recognition of their positive qualities. After all, against these images were often juxtaposed American self-perceptions, justifications for action, and glorification of the fighting men. The Guadalcanal campaign saw a radical swing in the general image of the Japanese, but this reassessment had still to allow some basis for comparison and final ideological judgment.

On the eve of the Guadalcanal landings the predominant image of the enemy was that of a "superman." Throughout this phase of the war, encompassing the campaigns in the British Solomon Islands, New Guinea, and New Britain, all of the fighting took place in the jungle, an environment thought to be somehow almost native to the Japanese. It had been, after all, in the jungles of Malaya, Burma, and the Philippines that the myth of the Japanese superman was born.[41] John Hersey wrote that on Guadalcanal "open spaces were our natural terrain. They were American; the jungle was Jap." The open spaces were dominated by technological sophistication, power; jungle was the domain of animal cunning, cruelty, ambush.[42] This popular image of the Japanese was the cause of significant worry in some military circles. Most senior Marine officers and NCOs were at least familiar with the jungle environment from service in Central America, but the newer men had received no jungle training. Stories about the "almost superhuman qualities of the Japanese as a jungle warrior and incom-

---

40 The Japanese view of the marines as U.S. warrior representatives was stated bluntly: "American troops on Guadalcanal consist of a main body of Marines, whose superiority in character and equipment is the pride of the American Forces" (Intelligence Center Pacific Ocean Areas [ICPOA] Bulletin 12-43, pt. 1, B, "Japanese Opinions on American Tactics Gained through the Fighting on Guadalcanal up to November 1942," in Eugene P. Boardman Papers, PPC, MCHC).
41 Rapid Japanese conquests against superior numbers over inhospitable terrain spawned the images of the Japanese "superman" that Dower explores in detail (*War without Mercy*, 111–17).
42 Hersey, *Into the Valley*, 49.

parable soldier" were to do "incalculable harm in affecting the mental attitude" of Americans sent out to fight him.[43] Overcoming this problem on Guadalcanal not only solved an important tactical dilemma but provided the marines with a psychological advantage as well. The turnabout was obvious within six months.

A flurry of articles by correspondents and military men appeared in the later stages of Guadalcanal and its aftermath with titles like "Exploding the Japanese 'Superman' Myth" and "Debunking the Jap Soldier."[44] They were explicit efforts to define a less threatening image of the enemy and give American ground forces a psychological boost. One reason for these reappraisals was to establish a background suitable for illuminating American military accomplishments. One correspondent wrote unequivocally that the "Japs are the toughest enemy we have ever had to face," with far more "guts" than the Germans.[45] Army Chief of Staff George C. Marshall, in the foreword to a classified pamphlet, "Fighting on Guadalcanal," expressly linked American glory to overcoming a formidable enemy: "The American Marines and Doughboys show us that the Jap is no superman. He is a tricky, vicious, and fanatical fighter. But they are beating him day after day. Their's [sic] is a priceless record of the gallantry and resourcefulness of the American fighting man at his best."[46] A. A. Vandegrift echoed the thought: Guadalcanal demonstrated "the bogey of Jap invincibility was untrue. 'Our people are as able as they . . . [and] we have something the Jap does not have – native intelligence higher than theirs, the ability to work as an individual.' "[47] Personal correspondence echoed these views. A series of *New York Times* articles on the campaign by Hanson Baldwin elicited a sharp response from Lieutenant William H. Whyte: "he praises the Japs as the 'Best jungle fighters in the world' in one breath, and then tells of the terrific casualties the Japs have had fighting us." Having led intelligence patrols behind Japanese lines, Whyte wanted his father to understand the Japanese soldiers' limitations.[48]

Yet efforts to redefine images of the enemy, by reinforcing old

43 Enclosure entitled "Exploding the Japanese 'Superman' Myth" in letter from Lt. Col. C. P. Van Ness to the commandant, U.S. Marine Corps, dated 2 January 1943, RG 127/63A-2534/Box 8/file C9-1.
44 Ibid.; ICPOA Bulletin 12-43, "Japanese Land Forces," no. 6, pt. I, "Debunking the Jap Soldier," dated 18 February 1943, RG 127/63A-2534/Box 8/file C15-5.
45 Wolfert, *Battle for the Solomons*, 185–87.
46 War Department, General Staff Pamphlet, "Fighting on Guadalcanal," iii.
47 Vandegrift quoted in *Marine Corps Gazette* 27 (March-April 1943): 18.
48 Letter from William H. Whyte to his father and Margaret, dated 14 November 1942, William H. Whyte Papers, PPC, MCHC.

racist stereotypes and emphasizing the physical, social, and moral
differences between the two sides, also laid the ideological foundation for exterminationist behavior. One report describes the Japanese as "short-legged, long-bodied, awkward little [men]," "clever
in some things and very dull in others." It continues,

> The most important thing . . . is that their point of view is based
> on a philosophy absolutely divergent from ours; a set of values
> entirely different from ours; and a way of life that is so much
> different from our way of living, that things that are important
> or basic in our minds are almost totally disregarded by them.[49]

This language parallels almost exactly that of the *Wehrmacht* on the
eve of Barbarossa, which legitimized, and indeed ordered, extraordinary brutality.[50] Few saw any contradiction between the racist,
dehumanizing characterizations of the Japanese and the restoration
of an "appropriate mental attitude" in the soldiers and marines.
These images of the enemy were consciously manipulated to influence marine attitudes, and they provided the basis for informal
guidelines that governed conduct in battle.

   As commonly occurs in war, despite the ideological polarization
or the culturally different backgrounds from which they came,
soldiers on both sides necessarily gained fairly intimate knowledge
of each other. To succeed in their jungle campaign the marines
had to learn Japanese habits in much the same way that a hunter
must know his quarry in order to capitalize on its weaknesses. In
this learning process the functional side of the soldier mingled with
the emotional, reactive side, resulting in a more complete picture
of the Japanese. To be sure, this synthesis retained much of the
racist typecasting as before, but the difference in context, the ability
to link it to specific behavior and events, lifted it to an entirely
distinct plane from the abstractions of the uninitiated civilian or
recruit back home.

   At first, the marines had difficulty reconciling their initial contacts
with the Japanese with their preconceptions of them. The landings
on Guadalcanal were unopposed, and, indeed, the enemy had fled

49 ICPOA Bulletin 12-43, "Japanese Land Forces," no. 6, pt. I, "Debunking
   the Jap Soldier," dated 18 February 1943, p. 1, RG 127/63A-2534/Box 8/file
   C15-5.
50 Omer Bartov, *The Eastern Front, 1941–1945* (New York: St. Martin's Press, 1986),
   106–9, 119–25. In his second book, Bartov carries this argument one step further, saying that the entire machinery for military discipline was set in motion
   to underpin an explicitly exterminationist war. The language of euphemism
   and misdirection that enables this process has American counterparts, but the
   overall directions of policy at this point diverge radically; idem, *Hitler's Army*
   (New York: Oxford University Press, 1991), 69–70.

their camps around the airfield in obvious haste. Expecting a bloody battle with Japanese soldiers on the beach and in the jungles just inshore, marines found not combat troops but instead only uniformed laborers whom the marines derisively labeled "termites." According to the intelligence report, these men were unarmed and untrained for combat: "They differed from our CBs in that they were physically poor specimens and of low civilian attainments, declared unfit for military service and conscripted for manual labor on naval projects." The report concludes, "They led a simple, Spartan, obedient and blinkered, but apparently contented cattle existence."[51]

Notwithstanding the absence of any military training among these "harmless and trustworthy conscript coolies," they initially bore the brunt of the harsh treatment that the marines had reserved for the jungle supermen they had expected to encounter upon landing. Driven into the jungle away from their only stocks of food, these hapless men led a bleak, and often very brief, existence in the jungle fringes. Those "termites" who survived their initial encounter with the marines and were taken prisoner looked to the Americans "like fatalistic and expressionless automatic dolls in their cloth caps and drab uniforms." Others, "less fortunate," were shot as they "scurried through the bushes," evidently mistaken for armed enemy patrols.[52] The first men whom correspondent Richard Tregaskis saw were "a measly lot" with sallow skin and "puny" physiques; having been stripped below the waist in search of concealed weapons, these men must have been a wretched sight.[53]

The marines justified their treatment of the laborers as a measured response in a deadly "game" played by all Japanese. As one marine writing soon after the war expressed it, "What we did not realize at the outset was that we were fighting what was essentially a medieval nation, with the medieval conception of total war, total destruction. . . . once they showed us the way, there was nothing for it but to play the game as they wanted it played."[54] Assumptions of perfidy and the strain of waiting for some climactic confrontation that would finally prove or disprove the myth of Japanese invincibility left little room for distinctions regarding who was wearing the enemy uniforms. The division's final report warned that unarmed laborers must not "be presumed to be useless for fighting purposes." In the heavy fighting for Tulagi and the twin islets of

51 Draft Intelligence Report, 21.
52 Ibid., 7–9.
53 Tregaskis, *Guadalcanal Diary*, 54. This security procedure also served to denigrate and belittle the manhood of the prisoners.
54 Hough, *Island War*, 82.

To Richard Tregaskis, Japanese prisoners looked a "puny," "measly lot";
Ernie Pyle wrote simply that they "gave me the creeps." *(Personal Papers
Collection, MCHC)*

Gavutu and Tanambogo across the channel from Guadalcanal, such
men had assisted the regular troops of the garrisons, displaying
the same "combative spirit" as the regulars.[55] After describing a
typical encounter between marines and a group of "termites," an
intelligence summary offers the commonly heard excuse for such
conduct:

> Contacts with termites were also witnessed, and more of these
> laborers might have been taken alive if eager Marines had not
> shot them as soon as spotted. One group of about 20 were
> seen to be mowed down with M[achine] G[un] and rifle fire as
> they came to cross a stream with the evident intention of sur-
> rendering. But such ruthless precautions were perhaps not
> unwise in view of Japanese tactics met with elsewhere.[56]

Such rationalizations represented nothing less than the legitimation
of murder. Vandegrift and his subordinates explicitly sanctioned

55 First Marine Division, "Final Report, Phase II, Guadalcanal," p. 9, RG 127/63A-
    2534/Box 4/file A7-2.
56 Draft Intelligence Report, 18.

"ruthless precautions" among the marines in order to maintain their aggressive spirit and sustain morale. The resulting cascade effect of this policy led to greater ideological polarization, which in turn further dehumanized the enemy and desensitized the act of killing, as with the "termites," under questionable circumstances.

Although the captured laborers offered very limited information about the enemy's abilities and intentions, the abandoned camps provided intelligence personnel with vivid insights into the psychology and social habits of the Japanese. The precipitate flight of the regular troops and the two labor battalions from their encampments around Lunga Point and Kukum left intact a wealth of personal papers and possessions showing exactly how the enemy had lived and worked. At first glance, everything seemed alien and exotic. Tatami mats, silk handkerchiefs, wooden tablets inscribed with Japanese characters or a Buddha, huge bottles of saki and canned fish heads, all found exactly as they had been left, attracted hordes of curious marines. Many items were pilfered: the mats went to line dugouts on the perimeter; kerchiefs and toilet articles were pocketed and used freely by their new owners. The large stocks of beer and saki and much food were looted and consumed in scores of squad messes before officers were able to reassert order and collect what remained. The religious charms "reminded one of our own St. Christophers and Blessed Virgins and Bleeding Hearts." But despite freely using and assimilating most of what the Japanese left behind, the marines believed that in the hands of the enemy these same objects were contaminated, profaned, or distorted in ways not possible among Americans. Thus were "our little yellow brethren" possessed of "narcissistic cleanliness"; their religion was "perniciously tied up with feudalism, nationalism and militarism"; and the availability of alcohol in large quantities indicated "something of a pukka sahib existence" among the conquerors.[57]

The marines were also provided a closer view of the Japanese through their personal possessions. Postcards, snapshots, and voluminous correspondence graphically demonstrated that the Japanese were as nostalgic and homesick as many marines. Virtually every man also kept a diary in which he traced his activities since leaving home on a daily basis, thereby giving away much valuable military information.[58] Concluding from these that "Tojo's char-

57 Ibid., 22, 24–25.
58 On the common Japanese practice of keeping a diary Moran wrote, "They never *expected* to be captured, or their dead simply abandoned on the field of battle, and their documents and diaries captured and scrutinized." This was another

acter was introspective," translators noted, "He was indeed very human, nor was he lacking betimes in irony, humour and insight. A great deal of soul searching too was evident."[59] For the average marine, however, lacking the translators' ability to read the documents or an appreciation for Japanese culture as reflected in the artifacts, blatant stereotyping provided a means for denying commonality even in the face of abundant evidence to the contrary. The average frontline marine either failed to interpret the signs around him as proof of shared ideas and feelings or consciously ignored them. For instance, snapshots of parents or children found on the bodies of Japanese soldiers were unmistakably akin to those many marines carried, but by focusing on physiognomy and native dress the Americans could deny any similarities and maintain their resolve undiminished.[60]

For the chief division interpreter, Sherwood Moran, none of these conclusions were revelatory. In contrast to some of his more outspoken and racist fellow officers, Moran wrote home, "I have proved to my own satisfaction that one can go to war without hate – without hate against the people of the country you are fighting." He took great pride in making "a distinctly human contribution in my method of approach to prisoners." Unlike most marines, Moran could clearly distinguish between individual soldiers and their ideology:

We have talked by the hour with them about their political philosophy, and I am more than ever convinced that the Emperor-centered nation idea is the devilish cause, the spark plug of most of their blind foolish, futile bravery and their whole outlook. People who say it isn't simply don't know.

But while Moran recognized and capitalized on the warmth and humanity of the Japanese captives he questioned, few of the marines in the line units showed an equally enlightened attitude.[61]

Negative assumptions about Japanese ideas and behavior were often reinforced by events. The extent of Japanese treachery was

example of myth (that of invulnerability) affecting operational events. Moran Papers, letter dated 31 October 1942, PPC, MCHC.
59 Draft Intelligence Report, 27.
60 Ibid., 26. Other photographs incited the marines, particularly those that Japanese troops had obviously looted from the Allied dead and prisoners in the Philippines or Singapore before being shipped to Guadalcanal; Moran Papers, letter dated 31 October 1942, PPC, MCHC.
61 Moran Papers, letters dated 22 September, 31 October, and 28 November 1942, PPC, MCHC. Moran wrote contemptuously of "certain officers" making "unnecessarily scurrilous remarks about the people of a certain country, and what *they* would do to make prisoners talk"; letter dated 10 February 1943.

Having spent forty years of his life in Japan, the chief interrogator/translator in the division, Captain Sherwood F. Moran, recognized and capitalized upon the humanity of the Japanese, but he lamented his failure to instill a similar appreciation among some of his fellow marines. *(USMC, National Archives)*

dramatically proven in the minds of the marines their first week ashore as a result of the Goettge patrol. On the night of 12 August, an ill-conceived patrol of twenty-five men, led by the division intelligence officer, Lieutenant Colonel Frank Goettge, was almost annihilated after it came ashore near the village of Matanikau. The stories carried in the press and circulated inside the division insisted that patrols from the 5th Marines had seen a white flag flying over Matanikau and that a Japanese prisoner had told his interrogators that there were others who also wanted to surrender. After landing, the patrol was fired upon from ambush and eventually overwhelmed. Three men managed to escape by swimming miles – rumor stated – through shark-infested waters to the American perimeter. The final flourish to these stories was the statement of one survivor: " 'The Japs closed in and hacked up our people. I could see swords flashing in the sun.' "[62]

Although the facts were somewhat different, this was the "true" account repeated in hundreds of squad messes and "bull" sessions

62 Tregaskis, *Guadalcanal Diary*, 97.

throughout the First Marine Division. The final report attempted to counteract the "sensational versions of the encounter" that had appeared in the press. The white flag was thought to be a Japanese infantry flag with the red disk in the center used as a signal to their submarines offshore. It was emphasized that "the prisoner was not cooperative in any way and there was nothing to indicate that he was acting in concert with others" and that, furthermore, the prisoner had nothing to do with the planning or conduct of the operation.[63] Yet as they affected the Americans' attitudes, these explanations were irrelevant: the Japanese had deliberately lured the marines to their death under the guise of surrender. "The loss of this patrol," recalled one marine, "and the particularly cruel way in which they had met death, hardened our hearts toward the Japanese. The idea of taking prisoners was swept from our minds. It was too dangerous."[64]

The business of offering or accepting surrenders was indeed a dangerous and very complex issue on Guadalcanal. Physical factors were a major problem. Engagements in the jungle were often limited in range to a few yards. Under conditions where a firefight could flare up instantaneously, with one or both sides surprised, terrified, and reacting instinctively, it was often unreasonable to consider surrender a viable alternative to fighting or flight. Also, the Japanese preference for night operations resulted in many engagements being fought under conditions in which it was impossible for anyone to offer surrender.

The greatest obstacle to the capture of prisoners proved to be the culturally ingrained attitudes of the Japanese and the American reactions to them. Marines found that the Japanese soldiers lived up to their reputation for refusing to surrender. An early intelligence report calculated, in round figures, that of 42,550 Japanese troops sent to Guadalcanal only 500 were captured.[65] Of the prisoners, the vast majority were laborers, not regular combat troops; and of the combat troops, very few surrendered but were instead captured while wounded, stunned, or otherwise incapacitated.[66] A later report estimated that the Japanese suffered approximately

63 Final Report, III:6.
64 Gallant, *On Valor's Side*, 297.
65 Assistant Chief of Staff, G-2, XIV Corps, "Enemy Operations on Guadalcanal, 7 Aug 42–9 Feb 43," dated 24 April 1943, p. 8, RG 127/63A-2534/Box 9/unnumbered file (hereafter cited as XIV Corps Report). Given the Marine figures below, this estimate of captures is low.
66 A D-2 report for the period from 7 August to 10 December gives a breakdown of prisoners, except for an unknown number from Tulagi who were not logged in by the division: 154 soldiers or sailors, 506 laborers, 3 natives, and 1 Javanese for a total of 664 (RG 127/63A-2534/Box 8/file C15-4).

10,000 combat deaths and 22,000 deaths from wounds or disease and that 10,000 men were evacuated.[67] This represents a mortality rate of 75.2 percent, and those captured amounted to only 1.2 percent of the whole force. By American standards such losses were unjustifiable, simply on humanitarian grounds. The garrison on Wake had surrendered at the moment they did in part out of concern for the lives of 1,200 unarmed civilian contractors. It had likewise been to avoid unnecessary suffering and death that the troops at Bataan had surrendered. Certainly the Axis and Anglo–American forces engaged at this time in North Africa never continued fighting to such an extreme on a comparable scale.

As a deliberate signal of Japanese resolve, their determination fostered a corresponding callousness among American troops. Marines quickly learned the risks of trying to take prisoners and understandably sought to minimize them, even if this meant killing men who might honestly have wanted to surrender. A mortarman thought that more prisoners might have been taken in the battle of the Tenaru "if one of their early wounded hadn't used a concealed grenade to kill the American medic treating him."[68] Correspondents frequently recorded sentiments among the men echoing the words of one young marine who told John Hersey, " 'You've probably heard about their using white surrender flags to suck us into traps. We're onto that one now.' "[69] These troops also developed a similar attitude toward surrendering to the Japanese, although not so seriously tested. There are no records of American surrenders on Guadalcanal, but between 7 August and 10 December, 194 soldiers, sailors, and marines were reported missing, of whom an undetermined number fell into Japanese hands.[70] In broad terms, neither side was in any way predisposed to give up the fight through surrender.

Constant military indoctrination and rumor reinforced the cultural prohibition against surrender. For both Americans and Japanese the forms these took were essentially identical. On the one hand, they were taught to fear mistreatment if captured. Americans knew of the Bataan death march and the stories surrounding the Goettge patrol, and there were always rumors of Japanese torture or mistreatment of prisoners, like the confirmed report of two

---

67 Prisoners made up a "statistically insignificant" number in the figures given; "Jap Medical Problems in the South and Southwest Pacific," in pamphlet "Know Your Enemy," dated 25 December 1944, 10–11.
68 Clark, *Unlikely Arena*, 42.
69 Hersey, *Into the Valley*, 20–21.
70 First Marine Division, "Final Report, Phase V, Guadalcanal," Annex X, "Numerical Summary of Casualties in Units of First Marine Division (reinforced)," p. 2; RG 127/63A-2534/Box 4/file A7-5 (hereafter cited as Final Report, V).

American soldiers being beheaded on Guadalcanal.[71] Similarly,
Japanese prisoners confessed that they expected to be executed by
their captors, and this threat had been repeatedly reinforced by
their officers. On the other hand, each side also emphasized the
shame with which each individual and his service would be branded
if he surrendered. Japanese prisoners became outcasts of their
society, and for this reason many begged that their names not be
sent home.[72] The social stigma was not so great in the American
case, but the marines felt strongly that they could not bring discredit
to themselves or the corps. In an ideologically charged war between
warrior representatives, surrender not only brought grave personal
risks but also reflected moral weakness in the warriors themselves
and in the society they represented, regardless of the circumstances
of capture. It was a terrible burden to bear for those who fell into
their enemy's hands.

Besides those already pointed out, another important obstacle
regarding the taking of Japanese prisoners was the growth of a
hunter mentality among the marines. Hunters had little leeway in
granting quarter, as John Hersey learned from his observations:

> Now I comprehend for the first time why the marines had
> been taking so few prisoners. It was not just that the boys were
> trigger-happy, as one had boasted. It was not just brutality,
> not just vindictive remembrance of Pearl Harbor. Here in the
> jungle a marine killed because he must, or be killed. He stalked
> the enemy, and the enemy stalked him. . . .[73]

Heavily influenced by myths of Japanese superiority in the jungle,
some marines initially feared that they would be easy prey for
soldiers hidden in the dense undergrowth. One marine naïvely
wished he were fighting Germans:

71 The beheading of two men from the 127th Infantry Regiment was reported in
    a CMC Memo, dated 25 March 1943, "Summary of Combat Observations in the
    South Pacific," p. 1, RG 127/63A-2534/Box 4/unnumbered file.
72 The response of a grenadier in the Sendai Division was typical of many who
    felt that "nothing can be worse than capture" and that prisoners are "the same
    as non-existent in Japan"; Prisoner Report on Ohira Bungo, dated 29 October
    1942, RG 127/63A-2534/Box 8/file C15-4.
73 Hersey, *Into the Valley*, 55. Hersey also emphasizes that the company commander
    in the valley, Captain Rigaud, was a skilled hunter and trapper in civilian life,
    obviously qualities with practical value and defining personal character (31–33).
    Mailer heavily emphasizes that Sergeant Croft, the iron soldier and quiet killer
    in *The Naked and the Dead*, has a strong hunter background (156–64). As a note
    of contrast, Sledge writes that the realization that the enemy would be trying
    to kill him "was the difference between war and hunting. When I survived the
    former, I gave up the latter" (*With the Old Breed*, 20).

"They are human beings, like us. Fighting against them must be like an athletic performance – matching your skill against someone you know is good. Germans are misled, but at least they react like men. But the Japanese are like animals. Against them you have to learn a whole new set of physical reactions. You have to get used to their animal stubbornness and tenacity. They take to the jungle as if they had been bred there, and like some beasts you never see them until they are dead."[74]

Fortunately for the marines, the first major test of the campaign, the battle of the Tenaru, played into their only real strengths at the time, revealing their defensive tactics to be vastly superior to the offensive tactics of the Japanese.[75] Afterward, the myth of Japanese superiority began to reverse itself, and eventually it became the marines who hunted the Japanese. Marine commanders appropriated images of the hunt and made them into a central component of their operational policy.

The successful defense of Guadalcanal required that marines go out in the jungles and find the enemy rather than passively defending the airfield. To gain information about Japanese intentions and capabilities the marines had to patrol actively. Information was insurance; with the knowledge that came from good patrolling the marines improved both their defensive and their limited offensive capabilities. Patrols also maintained marine aggressiveness, curing them of "barbed wire fever" even though the division remained on the operational defensive.[76] For these reasons patrolling and small-unit actions took on an importance surpassing the numbers involved. This sort of jungle fighting and the hunter mentality that underlay it became one of the hallmarks of the Guadalcanal campaign.

In the early weeks of the campaign, the worst fears of American inferiority seemed borne out as Marine patrol activities frequently failed in their primary mission. The final report pointed out some of the causes. "Priceless experience" from Hispaniola and Nicaragua was lost as the division expanded with mobilization in 1941. After weeks aboard ship the men lacked the physical stamina necessary for grueling patrols over rough terrain in an enervating climate. They were unused to a jungle environment, ignorant of its sights and sounds or how to read them. They overloaded them-

---

74 Hersey, *Into the Valley*, 56.
75 One officer stated that "the 1st Marines had the perfect opportunity at the battle of the Tenaru. The only thing they could have done, these kids, was to fight in place in a defensive battle,... and they did it successfully." Merrill B. Twining interview by Benis M. Frank, 1, 10, 21 February 1967, 203–4, OHC, MCHC.
76 Ibid., 206.

selves with equipment, including mortars and heavy water-cooled machine guns. But the greatest problem, summarized in the final report, was that "inexperienced leaders were either overcautious or bold to the point of rashness. Missions were not always carefully regarded; some leaders always looked for, and usually found, a fight[;] others avoided action."[77] The other problems could be solved fairly quickly and easily as men gained experience and confidence, but the shortcomings among leaders at all levels required immediate and more drastic action.

Although no one had expected complete competence throughout all levels of command in a division entering combat for the first time, the problems proved more extensive than first feared. One sign of this was the blunt advice offered in the final report: "Before entering combat all officers who do not appear to possess the requisite ability should be relieved of command. It is better to enter combat with a limited shortage of officers than to be faced with the necessity of relieving the incapable in the presence of the enemy."[78] As one officer later pointed out, some of the younger, more energetic reserve captains, who went on to become the backbone of the field-grade leadership in the division in subsequent campaigns, would have been preferable to some of the older battalion commanders.[79] On the other hand, many company-grade officers not only performed poorly in combat, as brought out in patrols, but also failed to look after the health of their men. For a brief time a single battalion had 365 men incapacitated for foot and leg ailments, and a senior officer expostulated after the campaign that the "youngsters" in the junior officer grades "had no more idea of how to take care of their men than a rabbit."[80]

An even greater disappointment was the failure of several senior commanders with years of service to meet the challenge of wartime campaigning. In a controversy that continued well after the war, the commanding officer of the 1st Battalion, 5th Marines, Lieutenant Colonel William E. Maxwell, was relieved in the midst of an operation on 28 August: his unit's movement was "incredibly slow" and his leadership "irresolute and faltering."[81] Vandegrift, to his

77 Final Report, V:6–7, 9–10, 20.
78 Ibid., 6. For an example of such a relief in the field see Message 2, 0200 22 November from 2d Raider Battalion, D-3 Journal, RG 127/63A-2534/Box 5/file A7-17.
79 Twining interview, 130.
80 Interview with Vandegrift and Colonel Gerald C. Thomas in Quartermaster's office, 30 January 1943, p. 16, RG 127/63A-2534/Box 9/no file number.
81 First Marine Division, "Final Report, Phase IV, Guadalcanal," p. 5, RG 127/63A-2534/Box 4/file A7-4 (hereafter cited as Final Report, IV). See also Thomas T. Grady, "Operations of the 1st Battalion, 5th Regiment in the Vicinity of

great regret, had to send home his close friend Colonel LeRoy P. Hunt along with several other senior officers.[82] Strong, competent leaders soon replaced many of the older unit commanders, and many new lieutenants, mostly in the infantry, were commissioned from the ranks as they proved themselves. Nor did the division commander hesitate to hold up a commission if he thought a man unfit. In this way a younger and more vigorous leadership gradually took charge and pushed their men to perform closer to expectations.[83]

To help the men better adjust to the demands of patrolling and jungle warfare and to foster a hunter mentality, senior Marine officers looked to the American historical past. Merritt Edson found the fighting on Guadalcanal evocative of the American frontier: "I certainly have learned respect for the Japs. What they have done is to take Indian warfare and apply it to the twentieth century. They use all the Indian tricks to demoralize their enemy."[84] Vandegrift advocated studying the lessons of Rogers' Rangers from the French and Indian War and assigned a skilled hunter and woodsman, Colonel W. J. Whaling, to train a scout-sniper detachment in the tactics and leadership techniques of jungle warfare.[85] Whaling's job was to make the marines masters of the area outside the perimeter, known colloquially as "Indian country." The final report notes how quickly he spread "the gospel of long marches, light equipment and scant rations." The report continues:

The result was an immediate and noticeable improvement in patrols and a desire for patrol duty despite its hazards and hardships. The men soon became confident of their superiority

Kokumbona," n.d. (presented in Army Advanced Infantry Officer Course, 1949), RG 127/63A-2534/Box 6/file A15-1.5. For the executive officer's postwar opinions, see the letter from M. V. O'Connell to CMC, dated 30 January 1949, RG 127/14051/Box 2/Comment File.

82 There was an overage of seven full colonels in the division; thus, the precise reasons for relief could be (intentionally) somewhat hazy. LeRoy P. Hunt's difficulties were recognized by Gerald C. Thomas, who became chief of staff when Colonel William Capers James was included among the colonels sent home, and by Merrill B. Twining, who took over Thomas's position as operations officer. Gerald C. Thomas Papers, typed manuscript, p. 48, PPC, MCHC; Thomas interview, 281, 373–74; Twining interview, 203–4. Colonel Clifton Cates likewise wrote to his wife, *"Just between us,* the ones of this lot being returned are, with some exceptions, not the best" (Clifton B. Cates Papers, letter dated 28 October 1942, PPC, MCHC).

83 Vandegrift Conference with Commandant, 1 February 1943, pp. 30–31, 34, RG 127/63A-2534/Box 9/no file number; letter from Vandegrift to Admiral Turner, dated 24 September 1942, in A. A. Vandegrift Papers, PPC, MCHC; letter from Col. Cates to his wife, dated 24 September 1942, Cates Papers, PPC, MCHC.

84 Quoted in Hersey, *Into the Valley,* 11.

85 "Fighting on Guadalcanal," v.

to the enemy in jungle operations and demonstrated it upon every occasion. Never again were we to lose a patrol by ambush and before the end of our occupation the Japanese were to acquire on their own part a morbid fear of meeting us in the jungle.[86]

In later campaigns marines would have to exhibit little more than raw courage, but on Guadalcanal they had also to demonstrate remarkable independence and resourcefulness. By implicitly linking fighting the Japanese with mythic eighteenth-century frontier traditions of individualism and self-reliance, Vandegrift, Edson, and Whaling were honing important skills among their men through an appeal to images from that other time. The exterminationist practices associated with hunting down Indians were explicitly linked with the Japanese, and both were dismissed as brave but organizationally and technologically backward.[87]

In one sense, Vandegrift, Edson, and Whaling embodied Marine Corps tradition and its self-image. On Guadalcanal – unofficially dubbed Operation Shoestring by some – the marines could never depend on outside help to salvage their situation. There were few available reinforcements or replacements; little of the overstretched U.S. war production was dedicated to the South Pacific theater; and only the barest minimum of food and ammunition could even reach the island. Under these circumstances it is not surprising that the Marine leaders turned to the American frontier heritage. Their power had to come from the skill, cunning, and improvisation of their men, who, in turn, had to be in tune with their environment and the enemy. Although the Army possessed its share of these modern-day backwoodsmen, they seldom had to compensate for numerical or material weaknesses by such methods. Moreover, by the end of the war, it had ceased to be the way of the Marine Corps as well. The topography of later battlefields, the wealth of American logistical support, and tactical refinements all combined to obviate the need for those skills that had been essential in the jungles of Guadalcanal. The myths would still proclaim the special abilities of the marines, but by 1945 the jungle frontier, like that of Rogers' Rangers, had disappeared.

The marines' operational preparations were made according to standard doctrine and based on what they knew or assumed of the

86 Final Report, V:20.
87 As one example, drawing on the expression "the only good Indian is a dead Indian," one marine labeled a scrapbook photograph of several dead Japanese soldiers simply "Good Japs" (Charles A. Linhart Papers, PPC, MCHC).

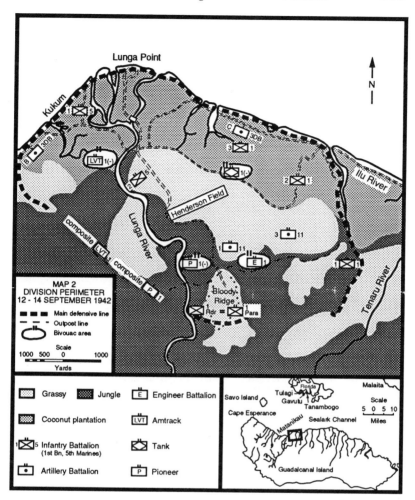

Japanese character. The Japanese had shown in previous campaigns that they were adept at infiltration and preferred night attacks. Since the primary mission of the division was to defend the airfield, Vandegrift attempted to deploy his men in a continuous line around the perimeter rather than in a series of strongpoints (see Map 2). This deployment stretched the manpower available to the division to its limit, but it minimized the threat of the Japanese infiltrating the lines undetected and provided interior lines whereby any threatened sector could be quickly reinforced.[88] As more troops arrived on Guadalcanal – first by bringing across

88 Frank emphasizes well the importance of this rather unconventional adaptation to circumstances (*Guadalcanal*, 261–63, 607–8).

men used on Tulagi and Gavutu-Tanambogo, later by outside reinforcement – not only did the defensive perimeter become more
complete, but limited offensive operations became possible on a
growing scale. These operations were generally in the nature of
raids, providing valuable experience for the units and information
about Japanese intentions and capabilities, and inflicting significant
losses on the enemy. Only after the First Marine Division departed
did the Americans build up sufficient forces to begin the larger,
sustained offensives that actually swept the remaining Japanese off
the island.

The key factor in the outcome of the ground fighting on Guadalcanal was the series of defensive battles fought by the Americans
between August and November. The repeated defeats inflicted on
the Japanese during these months were of such magnitude that
the enemy forces were crippled. Whereas when the Marines attacked, the ratio of Japanese to American casualties was roughly
3:2, on the defense this figure soared to 8 or 9:1.[89] The bulk of
the estimated 10,000 Japanese battlefield deaths was counted after
these defensive battles. Likewise, the majority of nonbattle deaths
probably followed in the wake of these defeats, when falling back
in disarray and without supplies, the Japanese were able to provide
virtually no care for their wounded and sick.[90]

There developed a dualistic understanding of the Japanese that
reflected the instrumental and mythic images of the enemy. The
instrumental aspects, in general, were reflected in the troop commanders and staff officers who studied Japanese tactics and weapons closely. For instance, analyzing the strengths and weaknesses
of the Japanese night attacks, the final report acknowledged the
skill of the Japanese in moving at night and maintaining control
of large units, but it also noted that the Japanese underestimated
"the disadvantages occurring in this type of attack, particularly with
respect to the effectiveness of the prearranged night fires of the
defense."[91] One veteran of Guadalcanal found that the Japanese
had not changed their methods significantly when he described his
experiences as a company commander on Peleliu. The conflicting
images of them as dangerously predatory but witless offer an el-

89 Memorandum for Colonel Riley, from A. A. Vandegrift, dated 5 February 1943,
    RG 127/63A-2534/Box 9/unnumbered file.
90 The horrendous condition of the Japanese medical services on Guadalcanal was
    attested to by many prisoners: XIV Corps Report, 5; also Prisoner Reports,
    passim, RG 127/63A-2534/Box 8/files C15-3, Captured Documents and Material,
    and C15-4.
91 Final Report, V:11.

oquent testimonial to his own ambivalent attitude toward the enemy
and their methods:

> The Jap loves the night, and he loves to sneak. . . . he is dan-
> gerous and clever. But like all animals he succumbs easily to
> the instinct of the mass, and when he attacks in great numbers
> he is blind and stupid and, like a wolf, seeks a crowd and the
> protection of numbers. Then he is easy prey for our weapons.[92]

Marine observers were astonished that these tactics remained essentially unchanged throughout the campaign despite their demonstrated inadequacies. The report of the 1st Marines remarked
that "the Japanese relied on the surprise of quick night attack and
furious assault to win the battle. Thereafter their tactics seemed
for the most part to be charge and charge again."[93] Attacks were
frequently renewed even when the Japanese recognized the obvious
futility of doing so in the face of devastating firepower. With un-
disguised condescension and slight disbelief, the final report noted
that "improvident 'Banzai' charge[s] . . . initiated at long range and
without fire superiority" presented the marines with "gratuitous"
opportunities for "annihilation by fire."[94]

In order to account for what were otherwise inexplicable methods
employed against them, the marines ascribed stereotypical weaknesses to the Japanese that were treated as both congenital and
universal. One senior officer wrote simply that "the Japs are dumb
fighters" whose "headwork" never matched that of the marines.[95]
Moran explicitly linked Japanese military capacity to their ideology:

> Her military totalitarianism is almost unbelievable until you
> talk to Japanese prisoners and learn the philosophy of their
> blind loyalty. Nearly every soldier carries . . . Imperial Re-
> scripts, tracts on patriotism, on warlike traits, etc. It's startling
> and it's pitiful. But it makes them valiant, dogged fighters. But
> it also makes them stupidly foolhardy. Our Marines have noth-
> ing but praise for their do-or-die bravery. But they think very
> little of their accuracy in rifle fire. . . .[96]

A typical comment in the division final report described the Japanese soldiers as suffering from a "lack of intelligence and initiative," continuing that "as individuals, or in groups without formal

92 George P. Hunt, *Coral Comes High* (New York: Harper, 1946), 92.
93 Final Report, IV, Annex G, "History of the First Marine Regiment," 7.
94 Final Report, III:14.
95 Letter from Cates to wife, dated 31 August 1942, Cates Papers, PPC, MCHC.
96 Moran Papers, letter dated 31 October 1942, PPC, MCHC.

leadership the Japanese soldier displayed tenacity and a willingness to die on the spot but no capacity to take independent action to redeem his situation."[97] As they honed their skills at patrolling, marines attributed their successes in numerous small-unit engagements to a general disparity in intelligence and initiative between themselves and the enemy. A patrol to Aola in October reported that the Japanese so neglected basic security precautions "that small detachments of the enemy can be defeated with the utmost ease, as long as they are attacked from an unexpected angle and early in the morning."[98] On 9 October, in the third battle of the Matanikau, the 1st Battalion, 7th Marines, was able to inflict terrible losses on Japanese troops massed in an assembly area. Finding them gathered in a deep ravine poised to counterattack, the marines, rather than descending into the jungle and fighting the Japanese at close quarters, brought down a heavy concentration of artillery and mortar fire on the area. The Japanese broke formation and rushed into the open on a steep slope opposite to escape this fire, whereupon the waiting marines opened with heavy, accurate rifle and machine-gun fire, killing scores and driving the rest back into the jungle below to repeat the winnowing process. As the official history states, "It was a most effective arrangement for methodical extermination."[99]

A critically important dichotomy in marines' images of the enemy was the distinction made between stereotypes purporting to describe the Japanese character and those attempting to categorize Japanese behavior. Blanket characterizations of the Japanese as unimaginative or suicidal purported to represent generalized patterns of behavior. Those who most relied on these sorts of stereotypes were staff officers and correspondents. The former found in them the basis for textbook solutions to tactical and operational problems; the latter, a seemingly inexhaustible subject for speculation to embellish further their already theatrical stories popular among hometown readers. The conclusions arrived at through such stereotyping sometimes seemed to correspond closely to events, and certainly the evolution of Marine tactics owed much to these methods. For the men at the bottom of the ladder, however, those in the foxholes on the line, relying on such stereotypes was perilous. In the words of a regimental intelligence report, "Generalizations are dangerous. We have all heard that 'all Japanese are lacking in

97 Final Report, V:11.
98 Report on Intelligence Patrol to Aola, dated 14 October 1942, RG 127/63A-2534/Box 7/file A41-1.
99 Official History, 1:321. The Japanese lost an estimated 690 killed in this action; Final Report, V:12.

initiative', 'fanatical' 'have very poor eyes'. . . . Yet it takes initiative
to progress from a hermit empire in a feudal state in 1870 to one
of the major world powers in a short 72 years."[100] Infantrymen had
too narrow a horizon to allow for unconditional acceptance of pre-
scriptive stereotypes. They lived in a world where exceptions could
never be discounted. Although not particularly articulate on the
subject, marines saw clearly that they could not rely on the Japanese
always acting in accordance with some obviously shallow formulas.
Only later, when the risks did not involve life or death, could these
stereotypes serve the veterans in explanation of events safely past.

The marines who fought in the lines were quick to see patterns
rather than universals in Japanese behavior. They looked for little
things that might save their lives. These details influenced both the
daily routine and the fighting. Marines quickly learned, for instance, the boundaries of a night battle. The American military in
general thought in linear terms, a holdover from the First World
War, where the continuous lines of trenches had imparted a sense
of well-defined limits, but in the Pacific War Japanese infiltration
skills, real and imagined, changed this thinking. No-man's-land was
now everything outside the individual's foxhole, forward, behind,
or to the sides, and anyone who ventured outside his hole at night
stood a good chance of being mistaken for the enemy and shot.[101]
Men learned quickly that potential danger lay in every direction:
from snipers concealed in the treetops to others lying underfoot
in well-camouflaged "spider-holes," from which they would spring
in ambush as a Marine patrol passed.

The exact forms of various behavior stereotypes differed according to the rank and responsibilities of the observer. The Japanese preference for night operations noted in the final report
carried a specific meaning for the marines in the line: for them
this translated into endless nights trapped in a foxhole, staring into
the inky blackness, and trying to distinguish in the eerie jungle
noises the innocuous from the potentially deadly. The same differences held true in attitudes toward the counterattack launched
east of the Tenaru on 21 August that resulted in the annihilation
of the Ichiki detachment. Senior commanders and staff officers
noted the feeble resistance and the Japanese' complete disregard
for such fundamentals as providing basic flank and rear security,
maintaining a reserve, and remaining flexible in a fluid situation.

100 1st Marines, " ' – and in this corner, the Jap!!' " n.d., Richard F. Lyons Papers,
    PPC, MCHC.
101 Typical of the stories circulated is that of a man shooting his buddy as the
    latter returned from relieving himself, in Mitchell Paige, *A Marine Named Mitch*
    (New York: Vantage Press, 1975), 125. Also Leckie, *Helmet for My Pillow*, 302.

Such observations served as the foundation for subsequent operational plans later in the campaign. The troops, however, paid greater attention to the tricks the Japanese used in placing weapons and deploying troops.[102]

The troops' observations of these tricks gave combat its highly personal nature. As a machine gunner dueled with individual Japanese guns across the Tenaru, he found his decision to remove the tracers from his ammunition belts a wise one when the Japanese concentrated their fire on another gunner who had not done so and killed him.[103] Some marines noticed the Japanese placing machine guns too close together or bunching as many as five men around the base of a single palm tree.[104] Others discovered that blood-smeared Japanese soldiers had hidden themselves among the corpses on the sandspit only after receiving fire from this unexpected source. In later engagements the Japanese sometimes attempted to draw fire by setting off firecrackers or clapping together sticks of bamboo. The Japanese often waited to fire their mortars until the instant after U.S. mortars fired, thereby giving the marines the impression that friendly rounds were falling short.[105] Only by learning these things and a hundred more did the individual marine significantly improve his chances of surviving.

Although the marines never developed much respect for Japanese tactics, they certainly knew what the soldiers endured. They discovered the emaciated victims of starvation. They occasionally brought in wounded men who had been abandoned, their wounds covered by a layer of maggots.[106] They knew the helplessness of being pounded by big naval guns with no means of retaliation, the enormous effort required to hack trails through the jungle, and the debilitating effects of the tropical diseases that swept through both armies without distinction as to race or righteousness of cause.

What is most noteworthy about the marines' knowledge of the enemy's character and recognition of common sufferings is that this understanding provoked no sense of soldierly brotherhood: there was no shared spirit of the front soldier that could occasionally transcend the lines of battle. The race line proved impermeable,

102 Final Report, IV, Annex G, "History of the First Marine Regiment," 5.
103 Leckie, *Helmet for My Pillow*, 81; Clark, *Unlikely Arena*, 38.
104 Final Report, IV, Annex G, 5.
105 Those interviewed gave numerous examples besides these in "Fighting on Guadalcanal," passim.
106 Navy doctors found that they achieved better results when the maggots were left in the wounds, and this became standard practice. It is questionable whether this age-old medical truth would have been rediscovered had the patients been Caucasians (Final Report III, Annex H, Medical, 3). On a more personal and vivid level see Leckie, *Helmet for My Pillow*, 88.

and under the burdens of personal problems and the struggle for survival, thoughts of a common humanity never percolated to the surface. In contrast to the case in Europe, Americans fighting in the Pacific felt no kinship with the enemy that could occasionally temper the ferocity of combat or informally ease the hardships of life in the field.

The durability of this race line was reinforced by sweeping stereotypes of the Japanese character akin to those prevalent in prewar American society as a whole. Although incautious assumptions about behavior were shunned, these other racist images were as basic to most marines as their rifles. First, as conveyed by the correspondents who recorded their comments, the marines considered the Japanese possessed of an almost demoniacal fanaticism. Contrasting them to their own methods, the marines could not understand the suicidal tactics of the Japanese assaults or their last-ditch defenses. Viewing such behavior through the lenses of their own cultural bias, Americans throughout the war attempted to explain such tactics with rumors that the Japanese used liquor or narcotics to steel themselves before battle.[107] Second, the Japanese seemed contemptuous of all life, including their own. Speaking of the monolithic Japanese soldier, one marine wrote, "He did possess at the outset one great advantage: complete lack of inhibiting battle ethics, as defined by modern civilization.... Nothing delighted him more than killing our wounded lying helpless between the lines."[108] There was no sense of shared proportionality with their enemy as was possible with Americans in Europe. The vicious battles of annihilation that took place at close quarters on Tulagi and Gavutu–Tanambogo and the doomed attack at the Tenaru supplied the marines with stark proof of this characteristic. Finally, treachery and cunning made the Japanese dangerous at all times. That this assumption was formed before the marines ever landed on Guadalcanal is demonstrated by the fate that befell the "termites," who suffered far more heavily on Guadalcanal than military necessity dictated. These men were victims of images that were projected onto them and to which they bore only the most superficial resemblance. Filtered through the press, the images conveyed by the marines to those back home derived from convenient racist stereotypes, behind which they could conceal their own fears and weaknesses. Consequently, back in America the public image of the

---

107 Leckie admits to fabricating such rumors himself to humor an audience of sailors (*Helmet for My Pillow*, 128). D-2 never found any evidence of drug use among the Japanese on Guadalcanal, and it was the Americans who consumed the Japanese liquor (Draft Intelligence Report, 25).
108 Hough, *Island War*, 82.

Japanese lacked the leavening of respect and healthy apprehension that the marines had for their enemy.

Intense combat, threats – physical and ideological – that each side saw in the other, and the utter, irreducible polarization created by rampant racism all combined to produce a new reality for the marines. The conventional, socially sanctioned restraints on personal conduct that they had brought ashore with them occasionally broke down, and they seldom looked beyond specific circumstances for justification of their actions. They lost very few men on the sandbar of the Tenaru before they began systematically shooting every body they found in the "brutal but necessary re-butchery of the dead." Tregaskis watched the marines "standing in a shooting-gallery line, thumping bullets into the piles of Jap carcasses." He also recorded the great emotional release felt by the marines as they fired at those Japanese attempting to swim to safety: "Their heads, small black dots amongst the waves, were difficult targets to hit. But our men relished the firing. Whenever we could see the head of a swimming man, a small storm of little waterspouts rose around him as our bullets smacked home."[109] Part of this increasingly unrestrained behavior also involved the looting of the dead. One marine wrote of a friend nicknamed "Souvenirs," who used pliers to extract gold teeth, which he kept in a small bag around his neck – a gruesome tableau common to every subsequent campaign.[110] Most men settled for equipment they could find on the bodies, but whatever form they took, trophies of the fallen enemy were much sought after. In the later stages of the campaign souvenirs even became a form of currency in the bartering that occurred between the marines and shipboard sailors.

The relationship existing between the marines and their enemy was also affected by a form of collective denial on the part of the marines that they shared any of that primal fury seen as commonplace in the Japanese. Because they could not equate the Japanese' ferocious, suicidal tactics with their own views of military rationality, the marines refused to see any parallels between each side's behavior in combat. But whether measured by the souvenir hunting or gleaned from the after-action reports, the marines did exhibit the same savage responses in battle as their enemy. Even a casual perusal of the citations for the five Medals of Honor awarded to men of the division for the campaign serves to illustrate this point. One recipient, a severely wounded officer, "repeatedly led his troops in fierce hand to hand combat for a period of ten hours."

109 Tregaskis, *Guadalcanal Diary*, 145, 147.
110 Leckie, *Helmet for My Pillow*, 86.

Another, a sergeant in charge of a machine-gun section, "continued to direct the fire until all his men were killed or wounded" and later led a counterattack to regain the position.[111] This sergeant subsequently described his actions and feelings during that counterattack:

> I guess I was so wound up that I couldn't stop. . . . I picked up the machine gun, and without noticing the burning hot water jacket, cradled it in my arms. . . . The total weight was about 150 pounds, but the way I felt I could have carried three more without noticing it. . . . the skirmish line came over the nose [of the ridge], whooping like a bunch of wild Indians. We reached the edge of the clearing where the jungle began and there was nothing left to holler at or to shoot at.[112]

This unusual inversion of the Indian imagery was probably as aptly applied to the one side as the other.[113] Did this man appear so different to the Japanese soldiers that night from what the marines saw along the banks of the Tenaru or Matanikau in other battles? Virtually any example of combat on Guadalcanal, as attested to in the correspondents' reports, differed only in degree and detail from these insofar as how men responded to the stresses of being under fire. In this sense, at least, war was a great equalizer.

The men of the First Marine Division, after the fashion of all military units, looked upon their experiences in battle as a rite of passage. By the time the bedraggled ranks boarded transports for Australia in December, their sufferings had imparted to them, at least in their own minds, a unique and indelible status. The American public, based on press releases, came to view the fallen marines, like the Navy pilots at Midway, as martyrs to their cause. Because they had been the first division ashore – and the most widely publicized – this popular image did not extend to other organizations on the island like the soldiers of the Americal Division, or even to the marines of the Second Division. The commanding officer of the 2d Marines attempted to correct this oversight, with little success, by writing letters pointing out that his troops had been the first to land on enemy soil in the campaign and had served longer

111 Medal of Honor citations for Major Kenneth D. Bailey and Platoon Sergeant Mitchell Paige, in McMillan, *Old Breed*, 450, 456.
112 This version comes from McMillan (ibid., 111), presumably from Paige's then-unpublished memoirs, but it is worth noting that for the book *A Marine Named Mitch*, published in 1976, this passage, p. 154, was edited to convey a much less feverish image of the counterattacking marines.
113 In another telling example of this inverted Indian imagery, Sledge writes that souvenir-hunting marines on Peleliu were "like Indian warriors taking scalps" (*With the Old Breed*, 122).

than any unit of the First Marine Division.[114] This imbalance in the shares of public acknowledgment, combined with the attitude of superiority displayed by many men of the First Division, produced a great deal of friction across service lines and between Marine units.

The men who arrived from the "outside" as reinforcements were greeted by the marines with a mix of emotions ranging from relief to overt hostility. The exhausted men holding the perimeter welcomed the new men to the extent that they made their own lives easier, but the First Division marines also envied them for their robust health and despised them for sins not their own. Why could they not have gotten there sooner? Were they trying to upstage the older veterans? The newcomers' attitudes, virtually identical to those of the first marines when they had landed, were now looked at askance: "War was still a lark. Their faces were heavy with flesh, their ribs padded, their eyes innocent. They were older than we ...yet we treated them like children.... they seemed not to show the proper respect for danger."[115] The hostile attitude did not seem to bother the new men, who looked in awe at the ragged men who greeted them, and indeed, they initially took every word these men said as gospel truth – frequently to their cost.

There was a more serious side to the problem of new units coming into line that went beyond the looting of possessions and practical jokes. There is very little evidence of useful communication and exchange of information between different organizations. There is, for instance, nothing to suggest that experienced Marine scouts were assigned to introduce the new Army troops to the patrol routes and key terrain outside the perimeter. Indeed, a report of the 8th Marines complained that the regiment suffered unnecessary difficulties in adjusting to jungle warfare because they received no cooperation from the veteran units, which "resulted in many of the lessons being learned the hard way."[116] Against a decimated Japanese force in serious disarray and with all the advantages resting with the American forces, this ill-harmony had no serious consequences, but it was not a good sign for the future.

The relationships between units, and especially between men of different services, help illustrate the internal universe in which

114 Letter from Colonel Arthur to General Masters, dated 23 November 1943, RG 127/63A-2534/Box 6/file A112. The 2d Marines had been attached to the First Division at the time of the initial landings to compensate for the absence of the 7th Marines, which was on Samoa.

115 Leckie, *Helmet for My Pillow*, 108.

116 8th Marine Regiment, "Report of Operations, Guadalcanal, for period 22 October 1942–9 February 1943," dated 15 March 1943, p. 9, RG 127/63A-2534/Box 6/file A24-1.

every soldier or marine lived. Stereotypes and indoctrination created obstacles to full cooperation even before different units made contact with each other. Nor was firsthand observation guaranteed to modify highly subjective or irrational preconceptions. Views of other organizations by marines of the First Division always affected their conduct, whether in the bars of Melbourne or in the planning and conduct of an operation. It is not possible to point to any single, unified, or monolithic body of ideas that was held by every man in the division, but there were generally held attitudes that seemed to predominate at various times. As these attitudes fueled the interservice rivalry with the Army, they came to have serious repercussions for the division in the Peleliu operation.

4

"DEVIL DOGS" AND "DOGFACES"
IMAGES OF THE "SELF" ON PELELIU

Guadalcanal provided the Joint Chiefs of Staff with clear evidence that the separate services could work together harmoniously to maximize the limited resources that the United States could direct against the Japanese. Indeed, the history of the whole Pacific War is to a considerable extent the story of how the Army, Navy, Marine Corps, and their semi-autonomous air forces ironed out their disagreements and concentrated on the defeat of Japan. The decisiveness of the American victory is at least partly attributable to the success of various joint staffs in resolving their differences over strategic objectives and the best means for attaining them.[1] Nor were the American achievements insignificant when compared to the interservice rivalries that plagued Germany and Japan.[2] Nevertheless, interservice conflicts affected many American operations in the Pacific, and the Peleliu campaign in the fall of 1944 stands as a noteworthy example among them.

The planning and conduct of military operations revolved around the distinctive, often contradictory military rationales of the separate services. The Army and Navy professional school systems developed doctrine and trained staff officers to resolve problems arising from actual field operations, but the very universe in which they worked was itself the product of images by which this process evolved. Military planning involved the prejudices and idiosyncrasies of important leaders and institutional self-images as well as "rational" decision making. A profound narcissism fueled interservice conflicts, whether at the level of the service chiefs, theater commanders and their staffs, or between rank and file. Operations

---

1 Two of the best histories that emphasize the importance of the joint command structure are Samuel Eliot Morison, *Strategy and Compromise* (Boston: Little, Brown, 1958), and the Official Army History, vol. 2, pt. 10, *Strategy and Command: The First Two Years*, by Louis Morton (1962).
2 See relevant sections in Alvin D. Coox, "The Effectiveness of the Japanese Military Establishment in the Second World War," and Jürgen E. Förster, "The Dynamics of *Volksgemeinschaft*: The Effectiveness of the German Military in the Second World War," in Millett and Murray, eds., *Military Effectiveness*, vol. 3, *The Second World War*, 11–25, 191–204.

provided a mirror reflecting the planners' self-images and a means by which the different services could highlight their strengths and exaggerate their contribution to the war effort. The distortions introduced by these competing interests resulted in strategic and operational compromises that allowed the war to be conducted with reasonable speed but with nothing like the unified, single-minded rationality of Clausewitzian theory.[3]

The division of the Pacific War into two main theaters and the allocation of resources between them laid bare the jealousies that were often ill-concealed beneath the patina of interservice cooperation. The "Army" theater of the Southwest Pacific Area under General Douglas MacArthur and the "Navy" theater, Admiral Chester W. Nimitz's Pacific Ocean Areas (subdivided into the North, Central, and South Pacific areas), were technically joint commands, but each reflected the very different emphases of the dominant service in their respective areas. Indeed, the failure to appoint a single commander in the Pacific arose much more for reasons of public relations than any strategic calculus. MacArthur's popular appeal could not be ignored, but the bureaucratic skill and influence of Admiral Ernest J. King and the Navy made it equally impossible to place Nimitz in a subordinate position either.[4] At the time of Guadalcanal American resources were too meager to be divided in immediate pursuit of more than one strategic objective, but beginning in late 1943 the growth of American military power allowed two distinct axes of advance simultaneously, which should have led to definite goals and objectives. Instead, it resulted in a slippery arrangement more evocative of the smoke-filled room of politics than the spirit of cooperation conveyed to the public.

By the fall of 1944 both of the American drives against Japan were making good headway. In the Central Pacific, Army and Marine troops had captured Saipan, Tinian, and Guam; in the battle of the Philippine Sea, the "Great Marianas Turkey Shoot," American naval forces had destroyed the last of Japan's naval aviation; and heavy bombers were now able to strike directly at the Japanese

---

3 This was an acknowledged problem that led to the creation of the Joint Chiefs of Staff in 1941 and two years after the war to the "unification controversy." The literature on the general subject is vast, but Samuel P. Huntington, *The Common Defense: Strategic Programs in National Politics* (New York: Columbia University Press, 1966), and Paul Y. Hammond, *Organizing for Defense: The American Military Establishment in the Twentieth Century* (Princeton: Princeton University Press, 1961), offer the basic, if somewhat dated, arguments.

4 Spector makes this argument effectively in tracing the evolution of American grand strategic designs in the Pacific from Cartwheel (the isolation of Rabaul) through the Octagon conference in Quebec (*Eagle against the Sun*, 220–26, 252–57, 417–20).

home islands from their new bases in the Marianas. Likewise, MacArthur had successfully concluded the New Guinea campaign, completely isolated the Japanese bastion at Rabaul, and was poised for his return to the Philippine Islands. Before his invasion of Leyte was to take place, however, the Joint Chiefs of Staff agreed to an operation securing his eastern flank in the Caroline Islands: specifically, Operation Stalemate aimed at neutralizing the Palaus by capturing the two southernmost islands of Peleliu and Angaur.

Under command of Marine Major General Roy S. Geiger, the III Amphibious Corps, comprising the First Marine Division and the 81st Infantry Division, was to concentrate on Peleliu. The planners, dominated by Marine and Navy officers, decided to use the Marine division to seize the beachhead, keeping the Army division ready to reinforce the Peleliu assault or proceed with its own attack on Angaur. One Army regimental combat team was also to be used to seize Ulithi atoll, an important fleet anchorage.[5] The marines of the First Division, only recently freed from MacArthur's strategic control, were determined to make the seizure of Peleliu a showcase for their Army counterparts of how an amphibious assault should be conducted.

Although the operation was the shortest of the war for the First Marine Division and resulted in the seizure of all primary objectives, the Peleliu campaign was also one of the division's most intense and costly, both in casualties and in strained relations among the three services. When the marines made their run in to the beach on 15 September, following an extensive naval bombardment, they were fiercely opposed at the water's edge. Entrenched in the most elaborate cave defenses seen up to that time, the Japanese troops lacked the command coordination necessary to push the invaders back into the sea, but they made the marines' advance slow and costly. With the capture of the airfield on the second day and the elimination of organized resistance on Ngarmoked Island in the south by the end of the fourth day, the marines gradually pressed up against the elaborate Japanese defenses in the Umurbrogol ridges running through the center of the island north of the airfield

5 Strategic designs behind Stalemate and the brief overview that follows here are covered well in the Marine Corps Official History, vol. 4, *Western Pacific Operations*, by George W. Garand and Truman R. Strobridge (1971), 51–76; its Army counterpart, vol. 2, pt. 3, *Approach to the Philippines*, by Robert Ross Smith (1953), 450–56; and Morison, *U.S. Naval Operations*, vol. 12, *Leyte* (1958), 3–18. Two shorter monographs also cover the campaign in detail: the official Marine Corps monograph *The Assault on Peleliu*, by Frank O. Hough (Washington: Historical Branch, G-3, HQMC, 1950), and Harry A. Gailey, *Peleliu, 1944* (Annapolis: Nautical and Aviation Publishing, 1983). An RCT is an infantry regiment with armor, artillery, engineers, and other supporting units attached to allow for independent action.

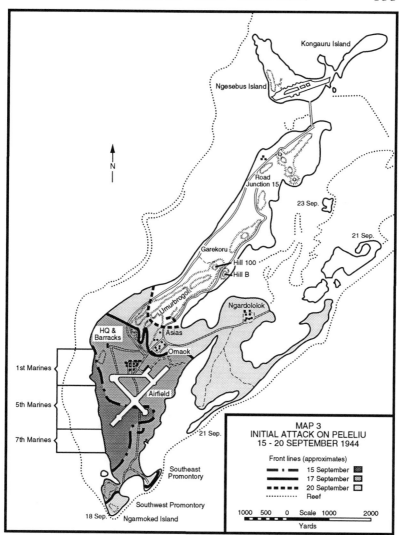

MAP 3
INITIAL ATTACK ON PELELIU
15 - 20 SEPTEMBER 1944

Front lines (approximates)

━ ∙ ━ 15 September
━━━ 17 September
■ ■ ■ ■ 20 September
∙∙∙∙∙∙∙ Reef

1000 500 0 Scale 1000 2000
Yards

(see Map 3). Despite heavy losses, the marines' progress had been sufficient for Geiger to release the 81st Infantry Division for the Angaur landings on the sixteenth.

By the second week of the campaign, the situation had not unfolded as anticipated. On 22 September, after days of relentless frontal assaults against formidable Japanese defenses, the First Marine Division had one of its infantry regiments virtually shattered and the other two significantly weakened. Over the division commander's vigorous protests, Geiger ordered one RCT from the 81st Division to land in support of the marines on Peleliu; the other would finish mopping up the Angaur garrison; and the corps reserve would proceed with the occupation of Ulithi. Operation Stalemate, an unfortunately apt name, became a protracted battle to reduce further the Japanese defensive perimeter and eliminate the last pocket of resistance.

The Navy declared Peleliu officially secure on 27 September. The assault phase ended on 12 October, and control of the island passed from the First Division to the Army on the twentieth. But not until 27 November could the island commander announce the end to organized Japanese resistance. By the time the First Marine Division was withdrawn on 20 October, all three infantry regiments had been wrecked as effective units, and practically every man capable of carrying a rifle had at some time been pressed into frontline duty.[6] There were roughly 12,000 Japanese soldiers and laborers on Peleliu, against whom the Americans eventually employed 40,000 men: 28,000 from the initial forces earmarked for the operation and later another 12,000 from the Army to complete the mission.

Although some marines expressed wonder in later years at the obscurity surrounding Peleliu as compared to other Marine Corps landings in the war, the reasons are not hard to understand. The standard explanation is that the division commander thought the operation would be over so quickly that few correspondents gave it much attention.[7] More to the point, however, was that the optimistic prediction itself placed the Marines' reputation on the line; when the list of excessive casualties graphically revealed how badly the Marine leadership had initially misjudged and subsequently ignored the situation ashore, it was natural that the campaign should be relegated to obscurity. There followed mutual recriminations with the Navy surrounding the quality of the preinvasion bombardment, and with the Army over old grievances from the Saipan operation, wounds that the Joint Chiefs were certainly unwilling to see reopened. Peleliu was an embarrassing and contentious success for the Marine Corps, and it was perhaps fortunate, from the institutional standpoint, that the spotlight shifted, predictably, to MacArthur's landing at Leyte shortly after the marines had reassembled on Pavuvu.

6 All three regiments had "fought themselves to impotency" according to M. H. Silverthorn (then chief of staff, III Amphibious Corps), letter to CMC dated 17 March 1950, RG 127/14051/Box 2/Comment File – Peleliu (hereafter Peleliu Comment File).
7 E. B. Sledge, "Peleliu: A Neglected Battle," 3 pts., *Marine Corps Gazette* 63 (November 1979): 88–95; 63 (December 1979): 28–41; and 64 (January 1980): 32–42; also Bill D. Ross, *Peleliu: Tragic Triumph* (New York: Random House, 1991), xi–xiv.

If interservice conflict could affect the presumably rational staff planners, it ran rampant at the lower levels. As with their senior leaders, the individual and collective identity of soldiers, sailors, marines, and airmen stressed their distinctiveness from one another – especially where two services performed identical functions. The acrimony, for instance, surrounding debates between Marine and Navy pilots over their relative effectiveness in flying ground-support missions arose because they each brought competing institutionally defined assumptions and skills to an identical mission. The largest and most serious interservice conflict developed between the Army and Marine Corps over their different approaches to the conduct of ground operations in the Pacific theater. These invidious comparisons have continued to this day and remain, at best, thinly disguised.

Arguments for the putative distinctions between soldiers and marines in ground combat fell into two basic categories. The first was that Army troops, as a result of their basic organization and indoctrination, were generally less well suited to the Pacific War than the marines, especially in the hard-hitting assaults of the Central Pacific drive. The Army's orientation toward fighting an extended, attritional type of warfare as was necessary in Europe and the larger landmasses of New Guinea, the Philippine archipelago, and the China–Burma–India theater required an emphasis on conserving manpower and unit effectiveness that was inimical to the type of combat necessary to seize small, heavily fortified islands. Army troops, in the opinion of many Navy and Marine officers, moved with too much deliberation, which endangered the overall success of operations by leaving naval support forces vulnerable to counterattack.[8] In contrast, the Marine Corps was specifically structured and trained for quick, decisive assaults. The heavy casualties they might suffer in the initial assault were justified, they argued, because the speed of conquest would reduce losses in the long run. This was a view heartily endorsed by naval commanders.[9]

Related to this basic organizational distinction, the second argument maintained that the marines were more effective than their Army counterparts on an individual level because they possessed an aggressiveness and spirit lacking in the soldiers. It was not simply that the Marine Corps provided its men with better training, the argument ran, but that the Marines recruited from men who were

8 Official History, vol. 3, *Central Pacific Drive*, by Henry I. Shaw, Jr., Bernard C. Nalty, and Edwin T. Turnbladh (1966), 8–13; Morison, *U.S. Naval Operations*, vol. 7, *Aleutians, Gilberts, and Marshalls* (1951), 79–84.
9 Speed of conquest was a "cardinal principle" of amphibious warfare (Isely and Crowl, *Amphibious War*, 11–12).

better than the soldiers in every respect.[10] This attitude was carefully cultivated by the Marine Corps through recruit indoctrination,
promotions, and public relations. Operationally, Marine formations
tended to be wielded more aggressively than Army units because
the officers and troops had a higher level of confidence and determination. Aside from an absence of empirical data to support
it, this argument failed to address how élan could carry operational
decisions beyond the limits of sound tactical doctrine. It was the
same lesson learned by the French in 1914 and witnessed by the
Japanese throughout the Guadalcanal campaign: human spirit
alone is not enough to overcome firepower in modern ground
combat.[11] There were occasions when the Army's more time-
consuming methods of massing overwhelming firepower or looking
for an open flank were ultimately quicker and more cost-effective
solutions than the marines' headlong frontal assaults. Besides, as
the marines frequently acknowledged, many well-led Army troops
could put their heads down and charge with the best of the marines
when the situation warranted.[12]

Although interservice conflicts were nothing new to the First
Marine Division, their influence on the everyday conduct of the
Peleliu campaign was greater than anything experienced in previous operations on Guadalcanal or New Britain. Superficially, the
capture of Peleliu might appear to have been a textbook example
of Marine Corps amphibious warfare doctrine: the First Marine
Division launched its assault on 15 September, sustained it until
the assault phase was declared over on 12 October, and formally
turned control over to the 81st Infantry Division one week later.
Or, as a marine might more bluntly have stated, they seized the
beachhead, did the heavy fighting necessary to secure the objective,
and left the mopping up to the Army troops. This was exactly the
role the marines had envisioned for the corps, and its hierarchical
assumptions were obvious. The concluding stanza to a satire of the
Army entitled "Our Fighting Men" reflected the marines' attitude:

10 Ayling, *Semper Fidelis*, 3–13 passim.
11 Three essays establish strong parallels to the French case: Michael Howard,
     "Men against Fire: Expectations of War in 1914," Stephen Van Evera, "The
     Cult of the Offensive and the Origins of the First World War," and Jack Snyder,
     "Civil–Military Relations and the Cult of the Offensive, 1914 and 1984," in
     Steven E. Miller, ed., *Military Strategy and the First World War* (Princeton: Prince-
     ton University Press, 1985). On the Japanese, see Chapter 3, above.
12 The Army put considerable effort into studying the low-level dynamics of bat-
     tlefield performance, and one of the official histories, *Small Unit Actions* (1946),
     offers a comparative look at three actions from the Pacific, Italian, and Western
     European theaters. The findings from Kwajalein in part confirmed some of the
     marines' stereotypes, but they also led to Army reforms that corrected many of
     the problems in subsequent campaigns.

"We can take it," said the Raider, "It won't be long,
Till the Admiral bellers, and we'll have to shove on.
And a little while later we'll be landing again,
To make Bouganville [sic] safe, for – "OUR FIGHTING MEN."[13]

Only in the Okinawa campaign would the First Division play an active role from beginning to end, which was itself to provoke a harsh reaction from the staff and ranks alike. The marines on Peleliu did not always express their contempt for the Army openly, but the conduct of operations ashore provides ample testimony to how some Marine officers reinforced their elitist self-image at the expense of the Army and even their own troops' welfare.

As measured by most standard military yardsticks, the marines did not outperform the Army troops to nearly the extent they might have wished. For example, it is clear from the casualty statistics that Army units accounted for almost one-quarter of the Japanese killed or captured on Peleliu and that they suffered proportionally fewer casualties in the process.[14] Army units lost fewer men than the Marines primarily because they were not part of the initial assault or first week of fighting ashore, but the combat seen by the 321st RCT in its first week ashore and following the marines' withdrawal was not simply low-intensity mopping up. When Geiger attached the 321st to the First Marine Division on 22 September, it was not for service as second string to the Marine varsity but rather to bolster the rapidly diminishing combat strength of the division. It should also be noted that this was the first time the 81st Infantry Division had been in combat, and the soldiers suffered some of the same adaptive difficulties as the First Marine Division had on Guadalcanal.[15] There were also significant differences in the way regimental and battalion commanders of each service employed their

13 "Our Fighting Men," no date or author, typed copy in the Archibald Hanna Papers, PPC, MCHC.
14 The First Marine Division claimed an estimated 10,695 Japanese killed and 301 captured; First Marine Division, Special Action report, Annex A, Personnel, n.d. (III Amphibious Corps endorsement dated 8 January 1945), p. 20, RG 127/74-93/Box 1/file A5-1 (hereafter 1stMarDiv SAR). The division lost 6,786 men on Peleliu, cited in Official History, 4:797, for a ratio of 1 marine per 1.62 Japanese casualties. The 81st Infantry Division killed an estimated 3,249 men and captured 180 at a loss of 1,290 men, for a ratio of 1:2.66; 81st Infantry Division, Operation on Peleliu Island, 23 September–27 November 1944, n.d., pp. 101, 109, RG 407/Entry 427/Box 12255 (hereafter 81st Operation Report). The errors that are rife in enemy casualty estimates are likely to be greater for the Marines than the Army, perhaps for subjective reasons of prestige but also for objective considerations regarding the pace of operations and the inability to take more accurate counts.
15 For useful insights into the difficulties faced in organizing and training the draftee divisions in the middle and later years of the war, see John Sloan Brown, *Draftee Division* (Lexington: University of Kentucky Press, 1986).

men, with the Marines demonstrating considerably less concern for the conservation of manpower and unit effectiveness, and Army leaders moving at a slower tempo.

Although statistics offer one measure of the high cost exacted for Marine aggressiveness, the real loss was more difficult to measure and impossible to replace. Of 6,786 total casualties in the First Marine Division, approximately 4,600 came from the three infantry regiments. The 1st Marines were hardest hit, losing 56 percent of their overall strength, and the 1st Battalion gained the dubious distinction of suffering the heaviest losses in the division, amounting to 71 percent of its initial strength.[16] In losing the cream of its veteran infantry, the division also lost its essential distinctiveness from the Army. A flood of replacements fleshed out the depleted regiments long before the Okinawa landings, but there was to be in that campaign little to distinguish the division from the veteran Army divisions alongside which it fought. The new men did not have the same attitudes that had animated the division earlier in the war, and although they claimed for themselves the same qualities that had distinguished their predecessors, their performance never fully bore them out. This is a recurrent phenomenon, as John Keegan points out when he concludes that the spirit of the Kitchener armies died, at least symbolically, on the Somme in 1916. An even more striking example emerges from the German experience on the Eastern Front, where the barbarization of warfare arose from precisely such a metamorphosis within the German army divisions that fought there from Operation Barbarossa until their final disintegration four years later. As a result of the conditions of combat, the environment, and the constant losses incurred, the structure, motivation, and cohesion within these divisions lost their initial forms, which were replaced by a ruthless instrumental and indoctrinational rationale tailored, and contributing further, to the harsh frontline realities. In a similar, if less apocalyptic, way the old spirit of the First Division died on the blasted coral slopes of the Umurbrogol.[17]

On the basis of close contacts with Army troops on Guadalcanal and under General Douglas MacArthur's command in the Southwest Pacific, marines of the First Division formulated opinions regarding their Army counterparts' courage, aggressiveness, and

16 Regimental losses numbered 4,527 as of 1200 14 October; III Marine Amphibious Corps, Operation Report, Enclosure E, Personnel, p. 1, RG 127/65A-5188/Box 39/file A4-6; 1st Marine Regiment, "Regimental Narratives," p. 12, RG 127/74-93/Box 1/unnumbered file (hereafter 1st Marines Narrative).

17 Keegan, The Face of Battle, 280–84; Bartov, Hitler's Army, 12–28.

leadership as compared to their own. Combining their firsthand experiences with what they had heard and read about Army units in other operations, especially on Saipan, most marines on Peleliu came to hold these units in low regard. This prejudice was not confined to the enlisted ranks and junior officers alone but extended to the highest levels within the division as well, including the commanding general, Major General William H. Rupertus. He envisioned the Peleliu operation as a showcase for his marines' spirit and aggressiveness, untainted by the presence of laggard soldiers claiming a share of the glory won by better men. Just as racial images formed a barrier between the marines and Japanese, so too did interservice prejudices create a wall between the First Marine Division and the Army.

Although the exhausted marines had welcomed the assistance of fresh troops on Guadalcanal, their impressions of the soldiers had been mixed. The Army troops clearly had suffered at least as much as the marines from lack of experience and inadequate preparation, but the marines were quick to pass judgment on the soldiers' failings. Men of the American Division were as "trigger-happy" and overawed by images of Japanese "supermen" as the marines initially had been. A Marine battalion commander who had an Army company attached to his command described the soldiers, including their captain, as being "scared to death" and "in a terrible state of mind" as a result of such rumors. Problems of small-unit leadership also proved to be as vexing for senior Army officers as they had for Major General Vandegrift. The commander of the 164th Regiment in the American Division considered shortage of good leaders to be his greatest problem, and he eventually relieved twenty-five officers "because they just weren't leaders!"[18] The new men learned to adjust to the environment and to the realities of combat against the Japanese, but they could never shake all of the initial suspicions with which the marines viewed them.

Although the marines generally recognized these problems, they reacted to them in different ways. Some saw these shortcomings in an identical light as their own: something common to all units first entering combat that would be ironed out with experience. Others, however, saw in the problems confirmation of their stereotyped preconceptions of Army ineptitude: something inherent and insurmountable. A Marine general later recalled the Army troops to

18 Lt. Col. N. H. Hanneken, Maj. Benjamin J. Northridge, and Col. B. E. Moore, in War Department, General Staff, "Fighting on Guadalcanal," 45, 51, 59–60. Moore's forceful leadership and the subsequent improved performance earned the 164th Infantry Regiment a degree of acceptance and even respect from the First Division marines that did not extend to other Army units on Guadalcanal.

be good when fighting from prepared defensive positions but poor in fast-moving offensive operations.[19] A former soldier turned Marine platoon sergeant compiled a list of important differences he found upon switching services: the Marine officers were closer to their men than Army officers; there was more comradeship in the corps; the Marine enlisted men were more "Spartan-like"; and he opined that "we baby our soldiers too much in peace-time."[20] Ideas like these, particularly when given the cloak of authority, were quickly and widely disseminated. Marines started to fit their observations of soldiers to these conceptualizations, and thus they created an independent truth of their own.

Sixteen months spent by the First Marine Division under MacArthur's command did nothing to improve the marines' attitudes toward the Army. MacArthur was personally despised by the marines for a number of reasons. During the defense of the Philippines in early 1942, the 4th Marines received no mention in any of MacArthur's communiqués, and they were excluded from his recommendation that the Corregidor garrison receive a Presidential Unit Citation.[21] Vandegrift blamed the lack of adequate maps for the Guadalcanal operation on MacArthur's intelligence chief, and some of the troops thought MacArthur to blame for not providing Army reinforcements in their support.[22] Worse, when the marines first arrived in Australia from Guadalcanal they were billeted near Brisbane, thirty-five miles from any recreational facilities, in incomplete cantonments, and in an area containing one of the highest concentrations of anopheles mosquitoes in Australia. As the hospital wards filled with reinfected malaria patients, MacArthur initially turned a deaf ear to urgent requests that the division be relocated. Finally consenting to the idea in principle, MacArthur then claimed he had no means to transport the marines. Vandegrift eventually got assistance from Admiral Halsey, who, as a personal favor, provided shipping to carry the division down to Melbourne, but it was an episode that permanently poisoned relations between the division and "the Great White Father."[23]

19 Brig. Gen. G. O. Thomas interview by John L. Zimmerman, 4 June 1947, RG 127/63A-2534/Box 9/unnumbered file.

20 "Fighting on Guadalcanal," 6.

21 Marine William Manchester explains this omission with MacArthur's blunt, unsubstantiated comment that "the marines had enough glory in World War I"; *American Caesar* (Boston: Little, Brown, 1978), 230. Better documented is the general resentment toward MacArthur in the 4th Marines and the strained relations between him and the Navy high command (Admiral Hart in particular); James, *The Years of MacArthur*, 2:22–23, 89–90.

22 James, *The Years of MacArthur*, 2:222, n. 18.

23 Vandegrift's correspondence is full of details of this disastrous beginning; see letters to Generals Vogel and Holcomb dated 20 December 1942; report to

The marines also had other concerns about being transferred to the Southwest Pacific Area command. MacArthur was conducting the fighting on New Guinea, and several Marine and Navy officers feared that he would commit one of the only veteran amphibious assault divisions to further jungle warfare, where this expertise would be wasted.[24] After almost a full year of rehabilitation and training, the First Marine Division was finally used in an amphibious assault role on 26 December 1943 against Cape Gloucester on western New Britain, but only after a series of confrontations with MacArthur's staff over the planning of the operation.[25] The division's second campaign developed into another protracted struggle, in which the debilitating effects of dense rain forests and the execrable weather took a heavier toll than the Japanese. Upon relief by fresh Army units in April 1944, the division finally reverted to the Pacific Ocean Areas command under Admiral Nimitz: the marines were back in a "Navy" command.[26]

In one sense MacArthur had been very useful to the marines because he acted as a lightning rod for all their criticisms. His actions were easily lampooned by contemptuous marines,[27] and MacArthur's megalomania might have been calculated to foster Marine antagonism toward the Army. In his reluctance to relinquish his control of the First Marine Division, he reportedly told

CinCSWPA (MacArthur) dated 23 December 1942; and letters to Holcomb dated 26 December 1942 and 15 January 1943; the final reference to MacArthur was used by Vandegrift – then commandant – in a personal letter to W. H. Rupertus dated 7 January 1944, A. A. Vandegrift Papers, PPC, MCHC. See also James, *The Years of MacArthur*, 2:225, 258–60.

24 Secret memorandum for Admiral King dated 28 November 1942, RG 127/63A-2534/Box 9/unnumbered file. On a letter from Rupertus dated 4 February 1944 detailing plans for the future employment of the division on New Britain, Vandegrift noted in the margin, "Six mos. there and it will no longer be a well-trained Amphib. Div." (Vandegrift Papers, PPC, MCHC).

25 McMillan, *Old Breed*, 168–70; as James points out, MacArthur gave full approval to the marine plan once their objections were brought to his attention (*The Years of MacArthur*, 2:343). Edwin A. Pollock, the division operations officer, who forcefully raised the Marine concerns to MacArthur, later admitted that MacArthur was very good at selling himself, and Pollock expressed his own admiration of the man (Edwin A. Pollock interview by Thomas E. Donnelly, 11–14 May 1971, 14 April 1973, 178, OHC, MCHC).

26 Details of the Cape Gloucester campaign are covered in the official monograph, *The Campaign on New Britain*, by Frank O. Hough and John A. Crown (1952); and Official History, vol. 2, *Isolation of Rabaul*, by Henry I. Shaw, Jr. and Douglas T. Kane (1963).

27 One example in Manchester, *American Caesar* (360), was their parody of the "Battle Hymn of the Republic," which began: "Mine eyes have seen MacArthur with a Bible on his knee / He is pounding out communiques for guys like you and me," and concluded: "And while possibly a rumor now, / Some day 'twill be a fact / That the Lord will hear a deep voice say, / 'Move over, God, it's Mac.'"

the division commander, Major General Rupertus, "you know in the Central Pacific the 1st Marine Division will just be another one of six Marine divisions, [but] if it stayed here it would be *my* Marine Division."[28] MacArthur's flamboyant style was in many ways akin to that of the Marines. In 1950 they would both be able to share the spotlight, but given the strains between the Army and Navy, there was room for only one prima donna in the Southwest theater. Back under Nimitz's control, the Marines prepared for their next campaign, arguably the most unnecessary of the Pacific War, which was supposed to secure MacArthur's flank for his imminent return to the Philippines.[29]

If their experiences under MacArthur's command had provided the men of the First Marine Division with firsthand insights into the manifold weaknesses of the Army, news of campaigns elsewhere, especially on Saipan, only reinforced their opinions. Open debates about the relative contributions of the soldiers and marines began to heat up in the American press in the wake of the Gilberts campaign in November 1943. When the Second Marine Division lost 20 percent of its initial strength seizing the Tarawa atoll, violently pro-MacArthur Hearst papers compared the assault to the Charge of the Light Brigade as both reckless and excessively costly.[30] This, in turn, prompted Marine Corps partisans, especially the Luce publications, to focus embarrassing public scrutiny on the 27th Infantry Division's performance in capturing Makin atoll. The corps commander, Marine Lieutenant General Holland M. Smith, had considered the operation "infuriatingly slow" at the time, and even the official Army history written after the war agreed that such a judgment appeared justified.[31] The Navy lost more men than the Army in the Makin operation after a supporting escort carrier, the *Liscome Bay*, was sunk by a Japanese submarine. As Navy officers had argued before the war, the importance of speed in such assault operations was crucial: had the atoll been captured more quickly, the naval forces would have long been safely out of the area.[32]

28 Cited in James, *The Years of MacArthur*, 2:345.
29 The postwar debate over whether the invasion of Peleliu should even have taken place has been as inconclusive as other such ahistorical questions, but it is worth noting that before the assault took place Admiral Halsey expressed strongly his opinion that the operation against the Palaus was unnecessary. Third Fleet, Action Report, Palau, Ulithi, Morotai, dated 14 November 1944, RG 127/65A-5188/Box 39/file A1-1; Gailey, *Peleliu, 1944*, 188–91.
30 San Francisco *Examiner*, 7 December 1943.
31 Official Army History, vol. 2, pt. 6, *Seizure of the Gilberts and Marshalls*, by Philip A. Crowl and Edmund G. Love (1955), 126.
32 Army forces suffered 218 casualties, and the Navy lost 644; Official History,

The most serious breach in Army–Marine Corps relations of the war occurred in the summer of 1944 during the Saipan operation. The landing force was corps-sized, again under Lieutenant General Holland M. Smith, again including the 27th Division, and this time featuring two Marine divisions, the Second and Fourth. Unlike the Gilberts campaign, however, all three divisions had to fight side by side. Problems arose in mid-campaign when the 27th Division, fighting in the middle of the American lines, failed to keep pace with the Marine divisions on either side. The crisis was precipitated when Holland Smith relieved its commander, Major General Ralph C. Smith, for poor performance. The Marine general wrote to Vandergrift on 15 July 1944 that "R. Smith is a weak officer, incapable of handling men in battle, lacks offensive spirit, and tears would come into his eyes on the slightest provocation."[33] Holland Smith acted entirely within his rights as corps commander in relieving Ralph Smith, and some Army officers, particularly Major General Sanderford Jarman, the senior Army officer on the island, acknowledged that the 27th Division suffered significant shortcomings. Nevertheless, Holland Smith's real purpose – to shock the 27th Division into more aggressive action – clearly was not achieved.[34]

The difficulties experienced by the 27th Division did not disappear with Ralph Smith's relief. Additional senior leaders up to regimental level were gradually removed as they failed to push their men, and there were frequent lapses that were magnified by the mutual animosity between the soldiers and marines. Nevertheless, the friction had started to ease toward the end of the campaign when a second crisis permanently poisoned relations between the New York National Guardsmen and the marines. Just before dawn on 7 July the largest banzai charge of the war erupted in front of the Army troops. Taking advantage of an almost inexplicable 500-yard gap in the lines, the Japanese surged forward, quickly surrounding two battalions of the 105th Infantry and overrunning an

3:97. Cooper gives a good summary of the divergent service philosophies toward amphibious assaults in *A Fighting General*, 118–19.

33 Cooper, *A Fighting General*, 180.

34 For official Army version of the operations and circumstances surrounding the relief see Official Army History, vol. 2, pt. 9, *Campaign in the Marianas*, by Philip A. Crowl (1960), 191–96. The most thorough and convincing summary in defense of Holland Smith is Cooper, *A Fighting General*, 166–81. Significant animosity afterward centered on correspondent Robert Sherrod, who defended the Marines in his articles and the book *On to Westward* (New York: Duell, Sloan and Pearce, 1945), and on Edmund G. Love's efforts to clear the 27th Division's reputation; the correspondence between Charles Nast and Henry R. Luce during this period supplements the official versions (Charles C. Nast Papers, U.S. Army Military History Institute, Carlisle Barracks).

exposed and surprised Marine artillery battalion. The attack was halted by midday, but the fresh Army troops made no effort to reach their trapped compatriots even though resistance had grown weak by late afternoon. Holland M. Smith's reaction was to blame not just the 27th Division but the soldiers themselves: "They're yellow. They are not aggressive. They've just held up the battle and caused my Marines casualties." Smith modified his tone somewhat afterward, but his intemperate response, echoed in many of the Marine commands, combined with the relief of Ralph Smith, made it impossible to heal the rift in the Central Pacific joint command or use Holland Smith in any future combined Army–Marine operation.[35]

Whatever the judgment leveled at Smith's action, news of the relief and the 27th Division's performance spread quickly throughout the Pacific theater and, in the case of the First Marine Division, clearly prejudiced many marines' attitudes toward the Army even further. Richard C. Kennard, a young lieutenant in the 11th Marines, followed closely the press reports in the summer of 1944 and recorded his reactions to them in letters home. "Spirit," he wrote at the time of the Saipan campaign, "counts about as much as fighting ability in this war[,] and that is why the marines never fail to take any position, stronghold, or island they invade." Soldiers, in his opinion, lacked the spirit and, by extension, the manhood, necessary for this sort of fighting. In a swipe at the dismal performance of the 27th Division as measured by an abstract Marine standard, Kennard added his wish that any "doggies" employed alongside the First Marine Division in future operations "have a little more courage and fighting spirit than the other outfits which have engaged the Japs."[36] This was just over two months before the 321st RCT came ashore to relieve the battered 1st Marines on Peleliu.

The opinions of lower- and middle-ranking marines, however prejudiced and intolerant, were less important for the conduct of operations on Peleliu than those of the division commander, whose resentment and animosity toward the Army were deeply ingrained. Rupertus's experiences as a division commander under Mac-

35 Cooper, *A Fighting General*, 184–91 (quoted portion, 188); *Campaign in the Marianas*, 255–66. Holland Smith served as corps commander on Iwo Jima, but he was never allowed to command Army troops again. Aside from the personalities involved – Smith, Admiral Turner, and General Richardson were unlikely ever to get along well – the intemperance of the press coverage exacerbated an already bad situation (Cooper, *A Fighting General*, 202–19).

36 Kennard, letter to parents, dated 14 July 1944, Richard C. Kennard Papers, PPC, MCHC.

Arthur's Southwest Pacific command had left him quite bitter,[37] and from the outset of the planning, he wanted the capture of Peleliu to be solely a Marine venture. Despite lacking decisive numerical superiority over the Japanese garrison, particularly in infantry, he wanted no support from the 81st Infantry Division. One member of the corps staff offered his opinion on the possible reasons for this attitude after the war:

> Whether it was a distrust of a Division new to combat, Army troops in general, or simply a pride in his Division which prompted his attitude was never clear. It is probable that he felt, like most Marines, that he and his troops could and would handle any task assigned to them without asking for outside help.[38]

Rupertus also had a definite idea of the shape the operation would assume. It would be, he told a group of officers, like Tarawa: "a short one, a quickie. Rough but fast. We'll be through in three days. It might take only two."[39]

In hindsight, it is difficult to understand the grounds for this confidence. Intelligence reports had quite accurately estimated the number of defenders, and from the number of positions pinpointed in aerial photographs, it was apparent that the Japanese had made elaborate defensive preparations. Planners decided that landing the division on the southwestern beaches would allow the troops to take advantage of the flat terrain on this part of the island, quickly seizing the airfield and cutting off the southern positions from support from the north. Rupertus did not anticipate several problems when he made his sanguine prediction for a speedy conquest: the massive preinvasion bombardment was actually far less effective than naval officers had expected; the terrain, covered by dense vegetation, was much more rugged than revealed in the photographs, especially in the hills of the Umurbrogol north of the

---

37 Rupertus's personal correspondence with Vandegrift during the New Britain campaign especially conveys his resentment and frustration clearly; letters to A. A. Vandegrift dated 7 December 1943, 4 February 1944, 18 February 1944, and 24 March 1944, Vandegrift Papers, PPC, MCHC.

38 Brig. Gen. W. A. Wachtler letter to CMC, dated 1 March 1950, Peleliu Comment File. Rupertus had also stated his reluctance to have Army troops assist the division in the Cape Gloucester campaign; letter to Vandegrift dated 18 February 1944, Vandegrift Papers, PPC, MCHC.

39 Quoted in McMillan, *Old Breed*, 269. Rupertus imparted the same message to the correspondent pool, convincing many that the operation was not going to be worth covering, which explains the dearth of press coverage common to other Marine operations; Oliver P. Smith interview by Benis M. Frank, June 1969, 133, OHC, MCHC.

146 AMERICAN SAMURAI

airfield; and the Japanese defenses and tactics were more formidable than any previously encountered by the division.[40]

From the moment they came ashore, the men of the First Division discovered that the confidence Rupertus had in their abilities was not sufficient to make his prediction come true. The shocking losses and tenacious Japanese resistance were comparable to the Tarawa assault, but the desperate fighting did not result in the quick capture of the island; on the contrary, the assault was occasionally in danger of bogging down. On the first day Rupertus even worried that the landing might collapse altogether. Throughout the tense early days, the division commander displayed symptoms of great stress, and despite the stiffening Japanese opposition, he steadfastly refused to call on the corps commander for any reinforcements.[41] Instead, Rupertus responded by spurring his subordinates to be more aggressive. The commanding officer of the 5th Marines later came under such great pressure from Rupertus to maintain an unrealistic schedule for securing the island that, in his opinion, only the eventual intervention of the III Amphibious Corps commander, Major General Geiger, kept him from being relieved.[42] The commanding officers of both the 5th and 7th Marines tried to protect their men so far as possible from the excesses of Rupertus's prodding, but the 1st Marine Regiment was under the command of a man who drove his men forward with little prompting from division headquarters and without argument about tactical difficulties.

Rupertus knew the character of his regimental commanders and had intentionally chosen Colonel Lewis B. Puller to command the dangerous left flank. Anticipating that the beachhead would be most seriously threatened from this side, and noting that it was closest to the critical high ground overlooking the entire southern portion of the island, Rupertus wanted his most aggressive leader on the spot. "Chesty" Puller was one of the most colorful figures in a service that boasts many, but like MacArthur, he seemed to excite extreme reactions in those who met him. To this day he is

40 The corps after-action report refers bluntly to the shortcomings in planning; see especially III AC Operation Report – Palaus, Enclosure B, Operations, RG 127/65A-5188/Box 39/file A4-3; Enclosure D, Supply, file A4-5; and Enclosure G, Naval Gunfire, file A4-8.
41 Rupertus appeared to some staff members around him at the time to be excessively nervous and felt himself not in sufficient control of events. See J. T. Selden letter to CMC, dated 26 October 1949, and L. J. Fields letter to CMC, dated 17 March 1950, in Peleliu Comment File. At one point Rupertus admitted, " 'This thing has just about got me licked.' " Harold O. Deakin, interview by Benis M. Frank, March 1968, 55, OHC, MCHC.
42 Transcript of interview of H. D. Harris, dated 28–31 October 1949; D. A. Peppard letter to CMC, dated 7 March 1950, also mentions excessive pressure exerted on the 5th Marines by division; both in Peleliu Comment File.

still held up to neophyte officers as a paragon of Marine leadership. On the other hand, he also had critics who characterized him as overzealous, unimaginative, and callous, and in a service that boasts of its highly aggressive leadership, his image as "an extremist" in the assault was one that remains very hard to acquire in the Marine Corps.[43]

Puller possessed all the traits that Rupertus idealized in his marines. When faced with a critical threat the first day ashore on Peleliu, Puller did not call for assistance from the division but made adjustments within his command to compensate. The division operations officer recalled that "this was typical of C[olonel] Puller. ... it is doubted whether he would have asked for other than more 'bullets' – never would he have asked for another unit. He was a fearless fighter, was tenacious and stubborn, would never admit defeat and above all hated the Japanese."[44] These traits made Puller an archetypal Marine warrior. Puller was not a man who would question Rupertus's wisdom in pressing costly frontal attacks or spare either himself or his men in carrying out his orders.[45]

As anticipated, the 1st Marines encountered grave difficulties ashore. A low, theretofore undetected ridge held up the advance; important Japanese positions enfilading the landing beaches were left untouched by the preliminary bombardment; and unexpectedly tenacious and disciplined resistance forced Puller to commit most of the reserve battalion to maintain his precarious position at an estimated cost of 500 casualties on that first day. In hard fighting the second day, the marines consolidated their positions, sealed the gaps in their line, and reoriented the regiment for its next advance. Although they had gained as much as 1,500 yards in one sector, heat and heavy fighting had raised the 1st Marines' losses to over 1,000 in two days – one-third of their original strength – forcing Puller to use all three battalions in line and rely on 2/7 for support. On 17 September, the third day, a general assault made appreciable gains all along the line, and units had seized Hill 200 on the southern end of the Umurbrogol. To Puller and his staff, results of that

43 Henry Berry, *Semper Fi, Mac* (New York: Arbor House, 1982), 287. One junior officer on Samoa wrote in his diary, "[He] has proven himself a great lunkhead in my, as well as many others['], estimation. He seems completely uninformed & powerless. I'm afraid I dislike him intensely." Entry for 2 June 1942, Joseph H. Griffith Papers, PPC, MCHC.
44 Fields letter, Peleliu Comment File; Fields interview, 122, 125. Puller expressed his virulent hatred of the Japanese in several ways: one man remembered that he had large signs posted in the 1st Marines mess halls on Pavuvu, "Kill Japs, Kill Japs, Kill Japs" (Gailey, *Peleliu, 1944*, 90).
45 Although biased, the best published portrait of Puller's warrior personality remains the Burke Davis biography, *Marine!*

day "were viewed with optimism." But in the line units the situation was grim: almost half of the 476 effectives in 3/1 were headquarters personnel, and the other two battalions were in no better shape.[46]

At this point, after three days of basically satisfactory progress, albeit at terrible cost, Puller threw his troops into a series of frontal attacks under execrable conditions that quickly bled away the remaining strength of the regiment. It may have been that Puller, like Rupertus, thought a Japanese collapse imminent, that if he forcefully drove his men ahead the battle would be brought to a quicker decision. As a battalion commander on Guadalcanal Puller had seen less aggressive leaders relieved, and he had never believed in sparing either himself or his men.[47] He rejected the opportunity to press around the flanks of the Umurbrogol where the Japanese resistance was weaker because of the strain he thought this would have imposed on the division to maintain a continuous line. Besides, part of Puller's philosophy was that you must attack the enemy's strength. In the words of O. P. Smith, the assistant division commander, Puller "believed in momentum; he believed in coming ashore and hitting and just keep on hitting and trying to keep up the momentum." Later, in walking over the ground taken by the 1st Marines, Smith was deeply impressed: "there was no finesse about it, but there was gallantry and there was determination."[48] The course of the fighting began increasingly to take on the appearance of a test of wills between the implacable Japanese in their caves and Puller's regiment. On Guadalcanal it had been a test of wills between warrior representatives; on Peleliu, Puller made it more personal. It was, moreover, a test of endurance in which the Japanese did not play fully human roles but were instead faceless elements in the landscape, deadly, but to be conquered along with the heat and blasted coral ridges. He had strong and well-founded faith in his men, and they always responded to his repeated calls to attack.

The 1st Marines showed astonishing cohesion in their prolonged and costly fight on Peleliu, even when companies had been reduced to platoon strength and casualties had riddled the officer ranks. Because of the mounting losses, on 19 September the staff consid-

---

46 1st Marines Narrative, 1–7. All statistics should be taken as approximations and are intended to be illustrative; precise figures were impossible to compile in the turmoil of battle.

47 Smith recounts, "They tell a story about Honsowetz . . . telling him to attack, and he said he only had 13 men or something like that. And Lewie said, 'You got yourself, haven't you?' " (Smith interview, 141).

48 Ibid. Harold O. Deakin doubted whether Puller had "a total grasp" of "the use of naval gunfire, artillery and supporting arms in general" (Deakin interview, 56).

ered amalgamating the decimated 1st and 2d Battalions but decided against handing the men of 1/1 over to the control of another battalion commander. As it is recorded in the unit history, the reaction of the men in 1/1 is illuminating:

> There was an immediate increase of morale as the natural pride of the men in their own unit exhibited itself when they learned that their own C.O. would direct them. Their sensations were not aroused at the thought of whether he were a sounder [tactician] or a better soldier. They would have followed Judas if he had been C.O., 1st. Battalion, 1st. Marines.[49]

This strong sense of unit identity and the dedication of the survivors to maintaining its standards were what was remembered by veterans of the campaign. How they fought became the ultimate measure to Puller and these men. The 1st Marines who burned and blasted a foothold on the Umurbrogol were an American counterpart to the German *Kämpfer* spirit of the Eastern Front that

> made a virtue of technological achievement and at the same time stressed not only the old Prussian ethos but also the mythical Germanic ideals; it saw battle as an embodiment of the natural struggle for existence, and yet presented the warrior as a medieval knight; it mixed chivalry and barbarism, nihilism and construction, strength and weakness.... [50]

None of the Marine infantrymen who survived Peleliu expressed any sentiment of "cause" or operational necessity, only the primacy of their ability in this costly battlefield triumph.

On 21 September, Geiger visited Puller's command post to see the situation for himself. After six days of incessant fighting with heavy losses there was still no end in sight to Rupertus's short, sharp fight. All of the island south of the Umurbrogol had been secured, including the airfield, but only scant gains had been made to the north. Moreover, these gains had been registered at a cost of over half the 1st Marines' strength alone. Colonel Coleman, one of Geiger's staff officers, described the scene at Puller's command post:

> At the regimental CP it became rapidly apparent that the regimental commander was very tired, he was unable to give a very clear picture of what his situation was and when asked by

49 1st Battalion, 1st Marines, Unit History, dated 23 November 1944, RG 127/74-93/Box 1/file A5.6-1.
50 Bartov, "Indoctrination and Motivation," 33.

Barrel-chested Colonel Puller greets Admiral Cochrane outside his regimental command post shortly before Major General Geiger ordered the 1st Marines relieved. *(USMC, National Archives)*

the Corps Commander what he needed in the way of help he stated that he was doing all right with what he had.[51]

Shocked by what he had seen, Geiger met with Rupertus, told him that he considered the 1st Marines to be ineffective as a fighting unit, and suggested that Puller's men be replaced with an Army regiment. "At this," Coleman observed, "General Rupertus became greatly alarmed and requested that no such action be taken, stating that he was sure he could secure the island in another day or two."[52] Geiger finally overruled Rupertus, and by the afternoon of the twenty-third, elements of the 321st RCT were already relieving units of the 1st Marines.

The introduction of Army troops marked an important turning point in the operation. For Rupertus it meant the personally galling acceptance of outside help thrust upon his marines; for Puller it meant the end of the campaign and an early return to Pavuvu to

51 W. F. Coleman letter to CMC, n.d., Peleliu Comment File.
52 Ibid.

reconstruct his battered command. It also marked a change in tactics from the unrelenting frontal attacks on the southern hills of the Umurbrogol to an effort aimed at bypassing this center of resistance. The change represented, in part, Rupertus's belated acknowledgment of the obvious futility in trying to force a quick decision by means of frontal assault and his inability to sustain the concomitant manpower losses. But it had also to do with his lingering doubts about the tactical abilities of the Army troops and their cohesion. Rupertus seemed to fear a debacle of greater proportions than had befallen the 105th Infantry on Saipan, and certainly some such thoughts influenced his employment of the 321st RCT for the remainder of the campaign.[53]

The change in tactics showed on the divisional operations maps in quick and dramatic fashion. Beginning on the morning of 24 September, men of the 321st RCT pushed up the coastal flat on the west side of the island as far as the village of Garekoru without encountering any determined opposition, and by the end of the day, patrols had reconnoitered as far as road junction 15 (see Map 4). Encouraged by this success, Rupertus began shifting his forces the next day to exploit the opportunities opened on the twenty-fourth. The 321st RCT turned east along the trail connecting Garekoru to the other side of the island, and the 5th Marines passed behind the soldiers to take up positions north of the road junction. By 27 September the 321st RCT had isolated the main pocket of Japanese resistance in the hills of the Umurbrogol, while the 5th Marines had sealed off another strong pocket at the northern end of the island and placed themselves in position for a shore-to-shore attack on Ngesebus Island.[54]

Although the soldiers of the 321st RCT had done much to make these dramatic gains possible, their performance in specific situations confirmed in the minds of those so predisposed, like Rupertus, their fears of Army incompetence and cravenness. On the twenty-fourth, 3/7, given the job of maintaining contact with the Army troops, saw a gap develop when 3/321 withdrew from the ridge paralleling the coastal road. The official Army history explains this as arising from the troops' inability to maintain contact with the

53 The change from the 1st Marines to the Army was driven home symbolically for Rupertus and other skeptical marines when Colonel Dark, commander of the 321st RCT, immediately moved his command post back about 1,000 yards behind the lines; Puller, who insisted on leading from the front, had placed his CP as close as 150 yards from the lines, often under heavy sniper fire (Smith interview, 142).
54 The details are well covered in Official History, 4:195–210. See also Eighty-first Wildcat Division Historical Committee, *The 81st Infantry Wildcat Division in World War II* (Washington: Infantry Journal Press, 1948).

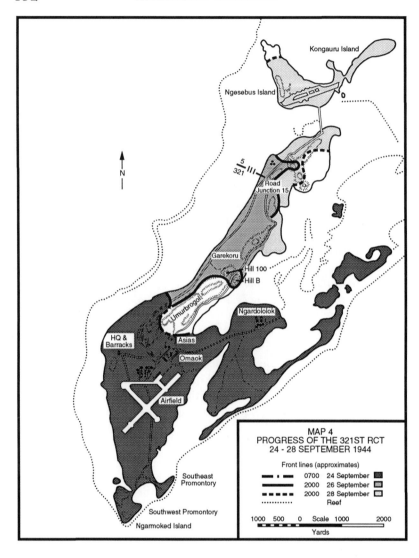

MAP 4
PROGRESS OF THE 321ST RCT
24 - 28 SEPTEMBER 1944

Front lines (approximates)

0700   24 September
2000   26 September
2000   28 September
Reef

1000 500   0   Scale 1000   2000
Yards

fast-moving men ahead because of the rugged terrain; the official
Marine Corps history implies that the troops simply ran away to
avoid heavy fire.[55] The commanding officer of 3/7 requested of his
counterpart in 3/321 that the Army troops advance back in to fill
the gap before Japanese troops could seize the ground and effectively cut off the troops advancing to the north. As he recalled, "I
watched several abortive efforts to do so before finally becoming

55 *The Approach to the Philippines*, 537; Official History, 4:197.

convinced that if friendly troops were going to control the ridge that night it would have to be our I Company."[56] The marines attacked the ridge and held it, but they lost several men, including their company commander. The marines had suffered, in their opinion, because the men of 3/321 had not fought their own battle.

Another trait that aggravated the marines and aroused feelings of contempt was the propensity for Army troops to pull back from exposed positions and regroup. Marines were extremely reluctant to relinquish any ground they seized, and throughout the campaign they did so only in the face of annihilating fire or when attrition had so reduced their forces that they could no longer defend their frontage. Soldiers of the 321st, however, seldom hesitated to pull back in the face of heavy fire if the situation allowed. Near dusk on 23 September, after their first few hours in the line, 2/321 was ordered to make an advance, which it began with two companies abreast, but when one of these companies received flanking fire while moving across open ground, both units dropped back to their starting point and dug in. The same battalion on the following afternoon withdrew 200 yards in the face of a Japanese counter-attack near Garekoru before pushing forward and retaking the lost ground.[57] If the tactical situation did not allow for a withdrawal, the soldiers would often resort to "unseemly," if effective, field expedients, such as the one seen on the afternoon of 23 October when a group of men from 1/321, advancing across open ground, used poles and broomsticks to shove sandbags in front of them for protection – with good success.[58] The greater tactical elasticity on the part of Army troops never sat well with Marine observers, and likewise, the tendency of Army assaults to slow or halt altogether in the face of desultory small-arms fire was a source of friction throughout the Pacific fighting.[59]

Notwithstanding any faults observed by the marines, the 321st RCT achieved some remarkable results in its first several days ashore. On the twenty-fourth and twenty-fifth, 2/321 had seized Hill 100 and Hill B, two strongpoints that marked the northern limit of the Japanese main positions. Moreover, the soldiers had held these positions in the face of determined Japanese counter-attacks and despite terrible difficulties in moving supplies and evac-

56 E. H. Hurst letter to CMC, dated 15 March 1950, Peleliu Comment File.
57 *The Approach to the Philippines*, 536–38.
58 321st Infantry Regiment, Operations Report, Stalemate II, 23 September–7 November 1944, dated 29 December 1944, p. 38, RG 407/Entry 427/Box 12324.
59 Cited in the investigation of the Smith controversy and by Robert Sherrod in his dispatches on the Saipan campaign (*Campaign in the Marianas*, 194–96); for several examples from the fighting around Nafutan Point see Cooper, *A Fighting General*, 167–70.

uating their wounded over the almost inaccessible terrain. Beginning on the twenty-eighth, however, Rupertus pulled the Army formations out of the line around the Umurbrogol ridges and used them over the next eighteen days to hold areas already seized in previous fighting. Certainly units had to continue mopping-up operations and protect against the possibility of the Japanese reinforcing Peleliu from islands held to the north, but to assign the single strongest regiment under First Division control to over two weeks of this comparatively minor duty showed that Rupertus still wanted to keep the capture of Peleliu as nearly an all-Marine operation as possible.[60] The soldiers did not file back into the front lines until 15 October, by which time the two remaining Marine regiments had to be withdrawn preparatory to shipment back to Pavuvu for rebuilding. On the twentieth, Rupertus handed formal command over to his counterpart in the 81st Infantry Division, his short, sharp assault still unfinished.

The intensity of combat and the devastating losses experienced by the marines on Peleliu caused that campaign to be remembered in terms quite distinct from anything the division had experienced previously. As the men looked at the empty cots in their tents back at the rest area on Pavuvu, the process of interpretation and justification that accompanied the camp visitations began the first stage of their rehabilitation:

> Release could only come when all the disjointed pieces of emotion had been fitted together again. One of the ways the Peleliu veterans went about this task was to go calling, to check up on their buddies, to see how many were wounded, how many killed, not only out of the motives of comradeship but also as if to measure the disaster they had just been through.[61]

Individually or in small groups, marines would go to the tents where friends had been billeted to learn from their tent-mates what had happened to them on Peleliu. These "wakes" in the evenings and on Sunday afternoons became an important way for men to gauge their experiences and establish a broader context in which to interpret them.[62] From what they heard and from their personal experiences, the marines came to view Peleliu as primarily a test

---

60 At full strength the Marine regiments numbered about 300 more men than the Army regiments, but after a week of fighting both the 5th and 7th Marines were weaker than the 321st Infantry.

61 McMillan, *Old Breed*, 345–46.

62 The importance of these visits comes through in Davis, *Marine at War*, 132–33; and Sledge, *With the Old Breed*, 165–69.

of their manhood and spirit. The jungle campaigns on Guadalcanal and Cape Gloucester had tested endurance and pitted the marines' personal skills against those of the Japanese, but neither of these campaigns had winnowed the marines' ranks as had Peleliu. The Japanese became more of an abstraction than had been the case before; the marines regarded survival almost as a matter of having beaten disembodied mathematical odds. It was in the way they faced these odds and maintained their spirit and cohesion that marines remembered Peleliu.

Peleliu became a celebration of what it meant to be a marine. The soldiers may have done adequately – although this was subject to much dispute – but the marines believed that no other service could have fielded units to rival their own. Kennard expressed this feeling with characteristic bluntness:

> My only answer as to why the Marines get the toughest jobs is because the average leatherneck is a much better fighter. He has far more guts, courage and better officers. . . . I'm not saying that the Army men are cowards. They are older men as a rule however and not nearly as tough and brave as any single average Marine. These boys out here have a pride in the Marine Corps and will fight to the end no matter what the cost.[63]

In his postwar memoir one former infantryman becomes almost rhapsodic in his effort to capture this attitude. At one point he describes how a motley group of men under Puller's command, "a fighting outfit only in the minds of a few officers in the First Regiment and in the First Division," formed up to attack again one of the hills of the southern Umurbrogol: "I have never understood why. Not one of them refused. They were the hard core – men who couldn't or wouldn't quit. They would go up a thousand blazing hills and through a hundred blasted valleys, as long as their legs would carry them. They were Marine riflemen."[64] That the author depicted every one of these men as a hollow wreck reinforced the idea that the individuals had been entirely subsumed into the larger spirit of the Marine Corps. In contrast, the soldiers were seen as clinging to amateurish or even civilian attitudes.[65] The sense of celebrating the Marine Corps spirit was also conveyed by Eugene Sledge, who basked in the curt praise extended to the

63 Kennard, letter dated 21 February 1945, Kennard Papers, PPC, MCHC.
64 Davis, *Marine at War*, 114.
65 This is reflected in one soldier's memoir of his service with the Army 454th Amphibious Truck Company, which was attached to the First Division for the Peleliu and Okinawa campaigns; LeRoy B. Bronemann, *Once upon a Tide* (Bryn Mawr: Dorrance, 1982).

survivors of his company by the first sergeant, "You people have proved you are good Marines." Another "old salt" from the Gloucester campaign added later that he had been unsure how Sledge would perform, "your ole man bein' a doctor and you havin' been to college and bein' sort of a rich kid," but in the end Sledge, by God, "did OK."[66]

Because their identity was closely tied to notions of personal strength and spirit, marines looked to these attributes as the measure of what truly distinguished them from Army troops. All of the shortcomings perceived in Army units that were based on institutional peculiarities meant far less to the individual marine than his sense of greater personal worth. Kennard wrote to his parents a long, ultimately mystical explanation of why he considered the marines better than soldiers:

> We are all American boys of the same breeding in general.... But between the two services there is a difference in training and spirit. Out here it is our belief, from seeing the Army that has worked with the Marines, that their chain of command is poor and their junior officers of an inferior grade.... The [marine] enlisted man will...hold much praise for his immediate superior officer and never flinch at an order no matter how hazardess [sic] the job is. This *fact* and the Marine Corps "spirit" which I cannot explain (one feels it in his body only and acts accordingly) is the reason why our's is the greatest fighting organization in the world!!![67]

Although Kennard, like most of the men of the First Division, had no direct contact with the Army troops on Peleliu, the mere presence of the soldiers close by and the small but steady stream of rumor were sufficient to make any marine so inclined an expert commentator.

As the Peleliu veterans knew, the toll exacted by the marines' brutal, head-on combat methods carried a price that went beyond the large numbers of killed and wounded. *Life* artist Tom Lea, who landed with the 7th Marines on the first day, probably captured this best. His previous work, in the words of James Jones, "could be pretty well classified as excellently done but high-grade pro-

66 Sledge, *With the Old Breed*, 165–67. The social consciousness in the ranks (working class, white, and predominantly Protestant) deserves more study as this civilian background was often seen as linked to performing in combat up to Marine standards. The most popular mustangs often came from such backgrounds. Conversely, soldiers were seen as older, often married, and from "softer" backgrounds.
67 Kennard, letter to parents, dated 20 October 1944, Kennard Papers, PPC, MCHC.

paganda. There was very little American blood, very little tension, very little horror." This sanitized approach disappeared with Lea's Peleliu paintings, like *Going In, Marines Call It That Two-Thousand Yard Stare*, and especially *The Price*. The flood of crimson in *The Price* creates "a painting at once so bitter and so unreal that it tends to turn into an abstraction, a fantasy.... It is as if Lea, with one sudden un-thought-out spastic gesture, recorded in one swiftly done canvas a distillation of all the death and horror he had seen and been bitterly unable to digest."[68] Although he spent only thirty-two hours on the island, Lea grasped the sense of utter isolation sometimes felt by men under heavy fire and found himself pushed to the very threshold of human experience. "A deep and numb kind of weariness," he wrote, "both of body and of mind made the trench and the battle, the anxiety and the uncertainty unreal, without the power of fact. I did not give a damn." He saw men literally blown to pieces: "With terrible clarity I saw the head and one leg sail into the air." And he described another type of casualty as well: "I noticed a tattered marine standing quietly by a corpsman, staring stiffly at nothing. His mind had crumbled in battle, his jaw hung, and his eyes were like two black empty holes in his head." Lea, in his written observations and in his dramatic sketches, captured one of the larger and more important effects of battle that remained virtually unrecognized in the Marine Corps: its neuropsychiatric costs.[69]

Of all the American military services, the Marine Corps was least responsive to the diagnosis and treatment of neuropsychiatric casualties. The problem, known under such blanket terms as "psychoneurosis" or "combat fatigue," was not a new phenomenon, but simply gaining official recognition of its seriousness was difficult. The different approaches of the Army and Marine Corps to these casualties as they affected combat effectiveness in ground units offer a startling contrast in basic philosophies. The Army was at the forefront of the services in recognizing the problem, establishing screening programs to reduce its incidence and formulating procedures to deal with its victims in a humane but militarily sound way. The Marine Corps tended to ignore the problem and often attempted in some way to camouflage it.

68 Jones, *WWII*, 113, 116–18. Although in his initial pencil sketch of *The Price*, there was no indication of the gore he would put in the painting, Lea writes this about the scene: "His face was half bloody pulp and the mangled shreds of what was left of an arm hung down like a stick, as he bent over in his stumbling, shock-crazy walk. The half of his face that was still human had the most terrifying look of abject patience I have ever seen. He fell behind me, in a red puddle on the white sand" (Tom Lea, *Peleliu Landing* [El Paso: Carl Herzog, 1945], 7).
69 Lea, *Peleliu Landing*, 7, 17, 34.

Both Kerr Eby (above) and Tom Lea (right) recognized the neuropsy-chiatric costs of Marine combat. *(Kerr Eby drawing courtesy of the Naval Art Collection, NHC; Tom Lea painting courtesy of the Army Art Activity, U.S. Army Center for Military History)*

Not only action in combat but military service itself often pre-cipitated a number of various disabling psychiatric disorders. Be-sides fear of death or wounds, many other things – perhaps initial separation from family or the hostile environment of basic training – produced in some men somatic symptoms that made them unfit for service. The Army had taken a particularly active role in trying to screen men upon induction and at overseas processing centers to find signs of emotional instability that would indicate those more likely to develop future problems. Under this policy the monthly discharge rate for neuropsychiatric disorders soared as high as 40,000, more men than the Army was shipping to the Pacific.[70] Not only was the discharge rate unacceptably high, but these early ef-forts also fell short of the goals set for the combat theaters. The worst case was in the Southwest Pacific theater, where Army units suffered a neuropsychiatric casualty rate that was more than five times that for all battle casualties in 1943.[71] To stave off this hem-

70 Edward A. Strecker and Kenneth E. Appel, *Psychiatry in Modern Warfare* (New York: Macmillan, 1945), 12.
71 Total neuropsychiatric disorders for 1943 were 10,061, which amounted to a rate of 53.0 per 1,000 admissions per year; battle losses numbered 1,998, for a

orrhage of personnel, Army Chief of Staff General George C. Marshall sent Brigadier General E. D. Cooke of the inspector general's office to investigate what was happening in the Mediterranean theater. His findings were illuminating.

Cooke discovered that many soldiers, especially line officers, assumed that in the absence of any visible wound all "combat fatigue" cases arose not from debilitating psychiatric dysfunctions but from cowardice. This quasi-official attitude was later stated quite bluntly by Major General Patton after the first of his two famous "slapping incidents" on Sicily:

> It has come to my attention that a very small number of soldiers are going to the hospital on the pretext that they are nervously incapable of combat. Such men are cowards and bring discredit on the army and disgrace to their comrades, whom they heart-

rate of 10.5 (*Neuropsychiatry*, 2:1020). Within the Department of the Navy, one-third of all men invalided from the individual services suffered from some sort of mental disease; half of these, 51,903, suffered from some kind of neuropsychiatric illness (*History of the Medical Department of the United States Navy*, 3:18).

lessly leave to endure the dangers of battle while they, themselves, use the hospital as a means of escape.[72]

In addition, the influence of their commanding officers and ignorance of psychiatry led many unit surgeons to share this medi-
cally unconstructive attitude.[73] The contrast in language used to
describe various psychiatric breakdowns by two doctors, one Navy
and the other Army, suggests the broad range of official attitudes.
In an article published in the *Marine Corps Gazette*, a Navy medical
officer discussed "combat hysteria" as more of a Marine leadership
problem than a medical concern:

> It must be recognized that under great stress men will some-
> times turn in as readily as you will let them. It is just such times
> that the officer must exert his utmost to resist weakness both
> in himself and in his men.... This is the time for the officer
> to get tough if need be. No man can be spared. Better to risk
> a few serious crack-ups than to risk the mass demoralization
> that invites disaster. The line officer may be assured that the
> medical department will back him up one hundred percent.[74]

Some men had a history of emotional problems that were exacerbated by combat service; others simply gave way under the strains
of battle. Generally it was the duration of battlefield stress, not its
intensity, that brought on neuropsychiatric breakdown. In neither
case, cautioned the chief Army psychiatrist on Okinawa, was the
generally accepted view justified:

> The soldier who breaks down usually does so *not* because
> he is a coward, quite the contrary, it is because he attempts
> to continue in the face of a biological situation that, at
> times, becomes overwhelming. The natural instinct for self-
> preservation must be put into the background. This conflict
> finally is resolved by the clinical manifestation "combat fa-
> tigue." It is caused by the soldier's desire to fight and not to
> run away.[75]

This was by no means an isolated or purely Army problem, but by
the time of Okinawa the Army Medical Corps had made some great
advances in educating line officers about the nature of psychiatric
casualties and in treating these men, while no comparable changes

72 7th Army memo dated 5 August 1943, in Martin Blumenson, ed., *The Patton
   Papers* (Boston: Houghton Mifflin, 1974), 333.
73 Cooke, *All but Me and Thee*, 17–18, 57.
74 Philip Solomon, "Military Aspects of Mental Disease," *Marine Corps Gazette* 30
   (January 1946): 51–55 (quoted portion, 54).
75 Lt. Col. M. Ralph Kaufman, report dated 16 May 1945, in *Neuropsychiatry*, 2:667.

were wrought in the Navy Medical Corps or among combat marines.

Although they received little attention in the press or the surviving official documents, neuropsychiatric casualties were not uncommon within the First Marine Division throughout the war. On Guadalcanal Marine neuropsychiatric casualties had been placed in an area called the "birdcage" to await evacuation from the island.[76] Although one doctor admitted that many of these men constituted the most severe psychiatric cases he had ever treated, for the Medical Corps as a whole that first campaign served as a valuable test bed for theories regarding the etiology, diagnosis, and treatment of various types of breakdowns that continued to evolve over every subsequent operation.[77] Of more immediate relevance were the comparisons made between Army and Marine psychiatric patients on Okinawa. One impression among the doctors of the 82d (Army) Field Hospital – the first purely psychiatric field hospital of the war – was that although fewer neuropsychiatric casualties seemed to be admitted from the Marine divisions than from the Army divisions, those who did enter the hospital, "perhaps because of the difference in basic philosophy between the Army and the Marine Corps," were generally more difficult to treat and less likely ever to return to their units:

> Some marines seemed to have a combat hardness which grew to be rather brittle so that, once their defenses had broken, some degree of personality disintegration occurred. Also, having been prepared by Marine indoctrination for quick and decisive beachhead action, they found themselves psychologically baffled by long, slogging operations. . . . Finally, . . . some marines showed an extraordinary amount of guilt which was found related to such ego factors as a feeling of complete loss of the idealized ego of the Marine Corps.[78]

This "idealized ego" of the Marine Corps, the "spirit" described by Kennard, Averill, and other memoirists, had produced some remarkably tough fighters, as was demonstrated on Peleliu and elsewhere. Yet although it was a source of great strength, the marines' reliance on this disembodied spirit, sometimes to the point of merging their personal identities with it, stripped them in effect of any

---

76 Clark, *Unlikely Arena*, 47.
77 Major Theodore Lidz of the 18th General Hospital in the Fijis, *Neuropsychiatry*, 2:773; James L. Sagebiel and Lee C. Bird, "A Study of Psychiatric Casualties Received at the U.S. Naval Base Hospital —— from the Solomon Islands Battle Area," *U.S. Naval Medical Bulletin* 41 (November 1943): 1627–37.
78 *Neuropsychiatry*, 2:663–64.

psychological "safety net" upon which they could rely. This is what Lea had seen in the eyes of the marine with the "2,000 yard stare."

The quasi-official attitude toward the problem was further reflected in the manner by which neuropsychiatric casualties were diagnosed within the division. On Peleliu, for instance, where temperatures almost daily climbed over 100° and water resupply was often inadequate, a large number of men were evacuated for heat-related illnesses. These men, most of whom also displayed at least some symptoms of concussion syndrome, hysteria, or anxiety reactions as well, were treated for severe dehydration and exhaustion aboard ships, whereupon their behavioral and emotional symptoms often subsided as well. This became a face-saving means for medical personnel to tag a man for evacuation from the beach without actually diagnosing any psychiatric illness. Most of these casualties returned to their units after a few days aboard ship and were able to adjust again to the nightmarish realities of the line. There were others, however, whose psychiatric problems were left untreated, indeed undiagnosed, who could not make the adjustment. Some of these other men were later rediagnosed and sent to base hospitals for further treatment, but a few simply slipped by medical authorities. Returning to Pavuvu, those who were unable to cope took the only option they felt left to them: suicide.[79]

Although this unofficial policy spared many marines from the stigma attached to "psycho" cases, it also, in another sense, victimized the more severe cases. Comparable naval medical practices at the time of Okinawa came in for some caustic criticism from one Army psychiatrist stationed at a base hospital on Saipan who had to treat these men. Labeling neuropsychiatric evacuees as "blast concussion" victims, he wrote, may have reduced the embarrassing figures for total Marine psychiatric casualties at the cost of inflating the figures for battle losses, but it also seemed a regression to "that abhorrent diagnosis, 'shell-shock.' "[80] This term, generally used in the First World War, inappropriately focused on external causal agents while denying the fundamental importance of the patient's

79 McMillan recounts how one marine on Pavuvu after the Cape Gloucester campaign killed himself on sentry duty; noteworthy in McMillan's eyes were the "self-conscious callousness" of the man who told of the incident and the "forced irreverence" of one of the observers (*Old Breed*, 231). In another example that followed Peleliu a marine remembered rowing with a friend far from shore and coming upon a swimmer who was struggling but refused assistance. In effect, the swimmer seemed to be deciding whether to head back to shore or simply let himself sink; the other two considered it natural to leave the choice to him and returned to the island (345).

80 Captain William Rottersman in a letter dated 5 June 1945, in *Neuropsychiatry*, 2:669–70.

personal psychiatric history. The practice also aroused the resentment of those in line outfits who thought many of these patients
received undeserved Purple Hearts.[81] Moreover, few of those marines sent back to base hospitals ever returned to useful service in
forward combat areas: the Marine Corps was, in effect, conceding
the loss of such men in exchange for burying the unpalatable truth
that even marines could reach their psychological breaking point
in intense combat.

Notwithstanding the virtual denial of the existence of psychiatric
casualties by men like Rupertus and Puller in the upper echelons
of the division command, there was much greater informal acceptance and sympathy for the problem in the enlisted and junior
officer ranks. Most men displayed at least mild psychopathic traits
under the stress of combat, and many held on to these mechanisms
after their return to Pavuvu. Being "island happy" or "Asiatic" was
the norm within the division, and a certain amount of eccentricity
was actually encouraged as being a healthy outlet for stress. Every
marine's memoir, the division history, and, in more subdued terms,
even the official histories, acknowledge these behavioral peculiarities as a plain reality of the war. Traits that were unacceptable in
stateside garrisons or in the civilian community – as many discovered upon their return – were accepted as personal idiosyncrasies
in line units. This behavior might take the simple form of a man
pounding on a coconut tree with his fist in fury and frustration to
the shouted encouragements of bystanders who understood his
feelings. In another instance a first sergeant roved the company
street on Pavuvu at reveille yelling to his men, " 'All right, let's hear
ya beat 'em. Let's hear you people chip 'em.' "[82] Some memoirists
also recounted the rumors that circulated throughout the division
of the "Mad Ghoul," allegedly a marine who had gone over the
edge and now attacked men in their sleep with a long knife. Like
the New England witches, the Ghoul received credence through
several spontaneous sightings following the first "attack," and the
rumor was only laid to rest when the division shipped out for its
next operation.[83] But whatever their precise forms, no man – private, senior NCO, or officer – was immune from the behavioral
idiosyncrasies that developed among combat veterans.[84]

81 7th Marine Regiment, Special Action Report, Okinawa, dated 11 July 1945, RG
    127/65A-5188/Box 24/file A47–1, recommendations.
82 McMillan, *Old Breed*, 231.
83 Davis, *Marine at War*, 168–69; McMillan, *Old Breed*, 231–32.
84 In their study of Army aircrews, Grinker and Spiegel noted that neurotic re-
    actions "are efforts on the part of the ego to prevent a break with reality on a
    larger scale characteristic of the psychoses. They are reactions to negate the

Various primary groups established their own parameters of acceptable behavior. Russell Davis noted when and to what degree the veterans displayed symptoms of their fear. He learned that others in the group, because of their own self-doubts, even after having passed the test of combat themselves, never branded a man as a coward. He also discovered that everyone had nightmares and superstitions, especially when fresh from combat, but they could not be too openly displayed:

> Still no one would admit, aloud, that he was nervous in the night. Then he might become suspect by the others, and no one wanted to be cut off from the rest.... This was the time when men sometimes told tales of their own bravery to remind themselves and their comrades that they were all good men.[85]

So long as a marine did not stray too far from the unspoken norms established among his comrades, he was free to rely on a number of mechanisms to deal with the various anxieties and fears he confronted before, during, and following an operation.

If comparisons are to be made between services with overlapping missions, their respective self-images must serve as the main point of comparison. Scholars have pointed out that soldiers and marines often fought in the Pacific War side by side with good results if not always complete harmony. Personality conflicts among general officers, bureaucratic politics, and genuinely felt partisanship all took a toll on interservice relations, but on the level of strategic planning there was no great distinction between the Army and Marine divisions. By the time of Peleliu, even the viability of Marine Corps claims to a monopoly on amphibious warfare expertise had disappeared. And yet the arguments over operational issues have continued up to the present time, and at this level distinctions between Army and Marine Corps seem to acquire greater substance. Surely the caution shown by the green 2d Battalion, 321st RCT, in action against the Japanese for the first time revealed fundamentally different philosophical foundations from those underlying the 2d Battalion, 1st Marines, as it stormed the jagged hills of the Umurbrogol. At this level, images of the Self do not simply highlight comparisons between services, they foster a reality in which historical events must be placed to be fully comprehended.

The institutional differences between Army and Marine Corps in solving complex problems of organizing and leading men in

external trauma or to isolate the anxiety thereby stimulated" (Roy R. Grinker and John P. Spiegel, *Men under Stress* [Philadelphia: Blakiston, 1945], 327).
85 Davis, *Marine at War*, 7, 171.

large-scale violence are very real and basic to any understanding of how this violence was controlled and directed. Kennard, in wondering why men from the same communities with similar social and cultural backgrounds acted so differently in combat, hit upon an important element when he singled out the marines' indoctrination. The nature of their psychological conditioning was the starting point for their successes and for the disparities noted by Kennard and others between how some soldiers and marines acted under fire. There was nothing mystical in the Marine Corps approach, and certainly if measured in terms of battle casualties and neuropsychiatric victims there was a high human cost to be associated with such methods. But it was a rational institutional tool and wielded with remarkable effectiveness to result in such pervasive self-confidence among officers and enlisted men alike.

Esprit de corps and dedication were not, however, unique to the Marine Corps. Moreover, combat experience sparked a metamorphosis of such ideas, changing them from the forms in which they were first instilled in the raw recruit and novice officer. By the time of Okinawa there was no significant difference between most of the veteran Army infantry regiments and their Marine counterparts. Marine units continued to be wielded more aggressively, led and manned by young men who still appeared to have the same unique values that had distinguished marine from soldier at Guadalcanal, but the marines did not, in the final tally, perform any better than the soldiers. Where the soldiers were as capably led in a type of fighting that had become dominated by technological imperatives, they were as tactically effective in the protracted warfare in the Okinawan countryside as the marines. The spirit of the Marine Corps could not survive four years of bitter fighting unchanged, and with this change the institution itself lost a part of its former identity.

5

OKINAWA

TECHNOLOGY EMPOWERS IDEOLOGY

Although marines' images of the Japanese helped to polarize the battlefield and their self-images served to sustain the ferocity thus engendered, it was only in the waning months of the Pacific War that the marines actually achieved a level of technological domination to realize fully their ideological goals. By the time of the Okinawa campaign, marines had become servants of a large, complex American military machine that had not existed on Guadalcanal. One explanation for the growing barbarization of the Pacific War after mid-1944 is that the great industrial and managerial power set in motion after Pearl Harbor, combined with Japanese fanaticism and intransigence, had simply outstripped the Americans' capacity to act within older, traditionally accepted ethical and moral guidelines. More plausible is the argument that the American people, and their political and military leaders, had consciously jettisoned such guidelines in the name of "military necessity." Virtually any policy that their technical and productive capabilities could sustain became militarily justifiable. American willingness to exploit to their fullest potential technologies of mass destruction was driven by a dehumanizing, racist ideology.[1] Even before the final ground campaign of the war, what Michael Sherry has labeled "the triumphs of technological fanaticism" fully controlled the American war effort.[2]

There was no longer any doubt about the ultimate outcome of the war; the only questions remaining were when and at what cost final victory would come. Symbolic gestures had given way to the

1 Dower, *War without Mercy*, 294.
2 Michael Sherry defines the term in his chapter entitled "The Sources of Technological Fanaticism" (*Rise of American Air Power*, 219–55, especially 234ff.); he then develops his model with the chapter "The Triumphs of Technological Fanaticism" (256–300), in which he presents a dynamic at work throughout American society, the political leadership, the media, and the military establishment in the final months of the war that abstracted and dehumanized the destruction of the strategic bombing campaign. The connections he establishes between broader cultural and institutional attitudes and actual strategic decisions apply in substance if not precise form to land warfare in 1945.

166

widespread, systematic, and highly mechanistic destruction of Japan's homeland and isolation of its overseas garrisons. At sea Japan had lost roughly 8.3 million tons of shipping to the aggressive American submarine campaign alone, and as mass starvation loomed ever larger over the home islands, little remained of the merchant marine besides small steamers plying the Inland Sea. The excitement that had surrounded Lieutenant Colonel James H. Doolittle's pinprick attack on Tokyo in April 1942 was overshadowed by far more devastating raids. Less than a month before the Okinawa landings, on the night of 9–10 March 1945, the single most destructive incendiary raid of the war created a fire storm that completely razed sixteen square miles in the heart of the Japanese capital, killing 83,000 and injuring a further 41,000 civilians. To the American public, Major General Curtis E. LeMay, the architect of this bombing strategy, had wreaked satisfying revenge on a faceless, nonhuman enemy: that he also redefined the boundaries of mass destruction made no apparent impression. The escalation of destruction generated among Americans feelings of "relief at the prospect of quicker victory; celebration of American technical genius, courage, strategic superiority, and warborne potential for world mastery; and denial or silence about destructive and vengeful instincts."[3] In land warfare the marines on Okinawa established a close reciprocal relationship whereby they harnessed their warrior image to the military machine, and in return that technology empowered their own specific exterminationist ideology.

Wherever one looked in 1945, United States military power in the western Pacific was colossal and still growing while Japanese resources dwindled rapidly in inverse proportion. Despite these material disparities, however, Japanese resistance continued. As conveyed in the press at home or by the veterans of Saipan, Peleliu, and Iwo Jima, the war seemed increasingly to require the utter annihilation of an unreasoning, fanatical enemy. Even before these campaigns, Richard C. Kennard wrote to his father, "We all believe that they must be exterminated out here."[4] Propagandists and others so inclined had amassed ample evidence to support the assumption that the primacy of defending national honor had become literally all-consuming for the Japanese. The fanatical re-

3 Ibid., 292; Morison, *The Two Ocean War*, 511–12; and Spector, *Eagle against the Sun*, 486–87, 504–6.
4 Richard C. Kennard, letter dated 20 February 1944, Kennard Papers, PPC, MCHC. Dower has a valuable discussion about the "linguistic softening of the killing process" through "the metaphors of the hunt and of exterminating vermin," especially after mid-1944 (*War without Mercy*, 89–93).

sistance of doomed garrisons, hopeless "banzai charges," newsreel films showing Japanese civilians hurling themselves off the cliffs on Saipan, and the appearance of kamikaze attacks in late 1944 all pointed to such a conclusion. Otto Tolischus, among the more virulent racist ideologues, wrote in this vein, "Beneath the trappings of modernity the Japanese people have remained what they always were – barbarians. Japanese conduct is the result of savage, warlike racial traits shaped to a code of barbarism now being employed in a program of conquest and world rule."[5] In the minds of many, such barbarous conduct could justify virtually any U.S. response.

In conception and execution, the Okinawa campaign epitomized the overwhelming attritional warfare that was the guiding principle in American operational thought.[6] To seize the island, which was approximately sixty miles long and up to eighteen across, the Fifth Fleet, numbering over 1,200 vessels, was assembled to support the Tenth Army, numbering over 180,000 men organized into the XXIV Corps and III Amphibious Corps (III AC), comprising altogether four Army and three Marine divisions. After the first troops came ashore on 1 April 1945 amidst an eerie calm, the Japanese ferociously hurled their carefully husbanded air and naval units at the fleet while the garrison ashore sought to inflict the greatest possible loss and delay on the invaders before being overwhelmed (see Map 5). Formidable as it was, this Japanese resistance, embodied in dramatic form by massive kamikaze attacks and the doomed sortie by the battleship *Yamato*, accomplished nothing to shift the balance of forces in their favor. Although 20 percent of U.S. Navy personnel losses in the entire Pacific War came in this one campaign – almost equal to all naval manpower casualties in the Atlantic during the war[7] – the Japanese neither loosened the U.S. stranglehold on the home islands nor endangered the landings scheduled for later that year.

5 Otto Tolischus, "False Gods – False Ideals," *Marine Corps Gazette* 28 (November 1944): 14–21.
6 This is the tenor of Weigley's general argument in *American Way of War*, 307–11; also Spector, *Eagle against the Sun*, 532–45. For more detailed analyses of the campaign see the Marine Corps Official History, vol. 5; its Army counterpart, vol. 2, pt. 1, *Okinawa: The Last Battle*, by Roy E. Appleman, James M. Burns, Russell A. Gugeler, and John Stevens (1948); the Marine Corps monographs *The First Marine Division on Okinawa*, by James R. Stockman (1946), and *Okinawa: Victory in the Pacific*, by Charles S. Nichols and Henry I. Shaw, Jr. (1955); Morison, *History of United States Naval Operations*, vol. 14, *Victory in the Pacific* (Boston: Little, Brown, 1961); and James Belote and William Belote, *Typhoon of Steel* (New York: Harper and Row, 1970).
7 Of 54,863 Navy casualties in the Pacific, 10,007 were suffered at Okinawa, almost equaling the 10,185 lost in the Atlantic (*History of the Medical Department of the United States Navy*, 3:84).

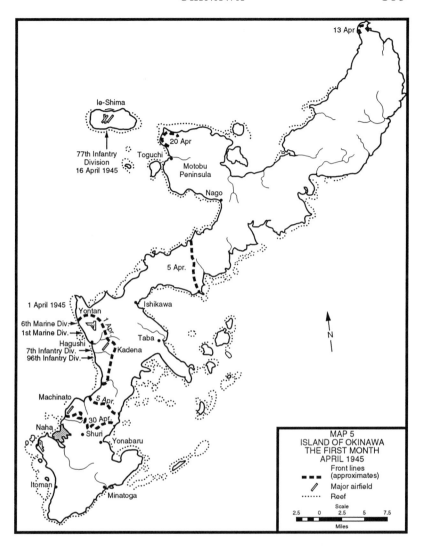

The Okinawa campaign was the costliest American victory of the Pacific War. In bloody, slogging ground combat more typical of the trench warfare of 1918 than previous operations in the Central Pacific, the Tenth Army lost over 65,000 men killed or wounded, which, when added to the Navy losses, left leaders feeling anxiety and dread at the prospects of the planned invasions of Kyushu and Honshu.[8] Despite close cooperation within the Tenth Army command, some old interservice wounds were reopened as well: Navy

8 Spector, *Eagle against the Sun*, 540.

admirals were furious about losing so many ships and men while the generals fought a long, slow campaign ashore, and the Army felt victimized by a public relations campaign suggesting that the Marine Corps's proposed second landing on southern Okinawa might have brought the operation to a quick end.[9] If the Americans had been shaken by the campaign, the same was also true for the Japanese. Many inside the military had begun to realize the hopelessness of their resistance and seek alternatives to senseless self-destruction. For the first time in the war, the remnants of a large Japanese army virtually disintegrated near the end of the campaign. Not only did the Americans take relatively large numbers of prisoners, including officers, but there were even cases of officers surrendering their entire units.[10]

Changes on the battlefield were the product of new images and improved weapons and methods. With three years' combat experience had come refinements in tactics and organization, from the scientific community arose new technological capabilities, and from the factories streamed a wealth of material, all of which the marines could hardly have dreamed of at the time of Guadalcanal. Defining problems in technical, instrumental terms allowed for concrete solutions that could ignore ethical or behavioral repercussions in the name of military necessity. The decisions to employ unrestricted submarine warfare, indiscriminate strategic bombing, and ultimately atomic weapons were the most striking examples of exploiting technological capabilities with little reference to those ideals espoused by Allied propaganda. There were also myriad smaller changes at the level of ground troops that were comparable in substance and intent if not in form or scale.

Compared to the sentiments and perceptions that affected the nature of combat on Guadalcanal, the attitudes of the marines on Okinawa seemed almost to belong to a different war. The theatrical quality of that first confrontation, symbolized by the jungle stalking,

---

9 Admiral Spruance wished operations ashore had " 'Holland Smith's drive' " (ibid., 539). Proponents of the second amphibious assault included the commandant of the Marine Corps, the commanding general, III AC, as well as vocal support from some Army leaders, in particular Maj. Gen. Bruce, commanding general, 77th Infantry Division (United States Army, *Okinawa*, 260–64; Belote and Belote, *Typhoon*, 212–14).

10 Headquarters, III Amphibious Corps, G-2, "A Study of the Use of Psychological Warfare in the III Amphibious Corps Sector during the Okinawa Operation," dated 5 July 1945, RG 127/65A-5188/Box 19/file A17-8 (hereafter cited as III AC, Psychological Warfare). First Marine Division, Special Action Report, Okinawa, dated 10 July 1945, Chapter 8, Intelligence, pp. 27–28, RG 127/65A-5188/Box 19/file A28-1 (hereafter cited as First Marine Division SAR). American figures on Japanese losses include 10,755 captured, which represents over 10% of the total combatants (Official History, 5:369).

had disappeared. Gone too was the immediacy of the Japanese threat, which had generated such naïve excitement at home and animated the young men three years before. Instead of a war that tested the individual characters of the warring countries' samurai, the subjugation of the Japanese Empire had become increasingly impersonal, mechanistic, and brutish. The marines of the First Division had discovered on Peleliu that personal ability had meaning only in the very narrowly defined sense that it increased one's chances of survival. Endurance and preserving unit traditions had become the new measures of personal success. Eugene Sledge wrote that

> the veterans of Peleliu knew they had accomplished something special. That these Marines had been able to survive the intense physical exertion of weeks of combat . . . gave ample evidence of their physical toughness. That we had survived emotionally – at least for the moment – was, and is, ample evidence to me that our training and discipline were the best.[11]

Given the perceived racial and technological disparities between the two sides, there was no longer anything to be proved in the extermination of Japanese troops, and heroic sacrifice meant little if final victory was already assured. For precisely this reason the storm battalion mentality familiar in the German fascist heritage, and culminating with the *Waffen-SS*,[12] suffused the Marine Corps as well. The symbols and metaphors used to describe the range of human experiences in combat are virtually identical among German and American memoirists, whether describing the Eastern Front or the Pacific. Eugene Sledge, in recounting his experiences with the First Marine Division on Peleliu and Okinawa, describes the pride and proficiency of highly trained and motivated men, the esprit and loyalty generated within an elite division, and the brutalization and dehumanization of frontline service in terms identical to those found in *The Forgotten Soldier* by Alsatian Guy Sajer, who fought on the Eastern Front in the *Großdeutschland* Division from 1942 onward.[13]

11 Note Sledge's switch from third person when discussing physical exertion to the collective "we" in dealing with emotional survival (*With the Old Breed*, 164).
12 "The new élitist ethos of war, combining ancient notions of chivalry with modern technology, methodical planning with irrational aspirations, outright nihilism with sensual passion, may be said to have found its most typical expression in European fascism"; Omer Bartov, "Man and Mass: Reality and the Heroic Image in War," *History and Memory* 1 (Fall–Winter 1989): 115.
13 There is a transcendence to many aspects of combat on a personal level, but the degree of similarity regarding the *Kämpfer* mentality in the two divisions and the degree of barbarization witnessed in the respective theaters make this

What distinguished the First Marine Division's campaign on Okinawa from its previous operations was the close reciprocal relationship between the integration of weapons developments and
tactical doctrine on the one hand and the ideological fanaticism
cultivated as part of the institutional self-image on the other. The
tremendous dedication inculcated in new recruits and demonstrated in action in previous campaigns was now subordinated to
a rationalized, systematized application of violence. On Peleliu the
First Division had encountered difficulties not simply as a result of
the Japanese' tenacity and the execrable topography of the Umurbrogol but also because their tactical training and indoctrination
had not prepared them for these conditions. They had clawed their
way ashore against fierce opposition in keeping with the best traditions of the Marine Corps but had then bled themselves white in
a series of frontal assaults. The division staff were determined that
their men would be better prepared for this sort of fighting in the
future, and as the marines on Pavuvu and Guadalcanal practiced
the tank-infantry tactics and close-assault techniques with flamethrowers and demolition charges that would be required on Okinawa, they harnessed their warrior ethos to that technology and
merged with it their identity as Marines. The jungle stalking on
Guadalcanal and the struggle to live up to abstract unit traditions
on Peleliu had saved the marines from serving as mere minions of
a machine designed for the impersonal slaughter of the Japanese.
On the eve of Okinawa the marines of the First Division eagerly
embraced this technocratic role as the only way they could preserve
the old ideals and sustain unit cohesion under the unremitting
pressures of intense attritional combat. By willingly surrendering
the highly individualistic warrior ethos of the jungle hunter for the
collective identification with a uniquely "Marine" war machine, they
created an organization of great destructive force that could, like
Sajer's *Großdeutschland*, be sustained through an almost mechanical
interchange of human and machine parts.[14]

Even before the Okinawa landings, the marines' self-image as
crack shock troops had been shaken. The situation was exacerbated,
however, when the marines found themselves tied down in the

comparison especially compelling. Sledge, *With the Old Breed*; Guy Sajer, *The
Forgotten Soldier*, translated by Lily Emmet (New York: Ballantine, 1967).
14 In a roughly nineteen-month period for which there are reliable figures, Sajer's
     division suffered 34,700 casualties, including 973 officers (this excludes any
     estimate of casualties from late 1943 through all of 1944). Such losses dwarfed
     those of the First Marine Division, but the processes of indoctrination and
     training shared important similarities; Omer Bartov, "Daily Life and Motivation
     in War: The *Wehrmacht* in the Soviet Union," *Journal of Strategic Studies* 12 (June
     1989): 201–2.

Training on Pavuvu after the Peleliu campaign, First Division marines harnessed technology and idelogy in preparation for the assault on Okinawa. *(USMC, National Archives)*

kind of protracted ground campaign that they associated with Army operations.[15] In actual practice, the men in the First Marine Division played no special role on Okinawa that could distinguish them from the other Marine division or even the three first-line Army divisions. They served the weapons needed to destroy the Japanese, and as individuals were killed or incapacitated they were replaced from a pool of men waiting to fill their vacated spot. Psychological toughness and individual endurance were more crucial than ever in order to sustain the offensive, but battlefield conditions rendered the traditional sources of cohesion of marginal value.

The men of the First Division on Okinawa gave it a collective identity different from what it had been before. There were still many veterans of Peleliu and even Cape Gloucester. Shortages, particularly in specialized fields, had prevented these men from

15 The 7th Marines report noted that "extended land operations," such as Okinawa, had in the past been Army, not Marine Corps, missions, and that structural changes were needed if similar campaigns were planned for the future; 7th Marines, Special Action Report, Okinawa, dated 11 July 1945, RG 127/65A-5188/Box 24/file A47-1.

rotating home earlier. By the end of the campaign approximately 200 officers and 3,200 men had two years or more in the field, and of these nearly 800 had thirty months. There were also some Guadalcanal veterans rotating back from Stateside duty or returning from convalescence among the 215 officers and 8,800 men absorbed by the division as replacements in the months following Peleliu. For the most part, however, the replacements were new men.[16] There were more draftees than ever, and a large number of the new men who now carried rifles had been too young to serve at the time of Guadalcanal. Tired veterans shorn of any illusions about battle and green youngsters, some of uncertain dedication to the corps and its ideals, filled the ranks of the division on the eve of a costly campaign in a war sure to end in an American victory: the spirit and attitudes of 1942 could not remain unchanged.

The marines' growing insecurity concerning their elite status was reflected in the continued animosity directed toward the Army. It was impossible to avoid comparisons of Army and Marine Corps performance on Okinawa, and the marines continued to pad their pride at the expense of the Army. First Division forward observers (FOs) served with Army units in April when their artillery battalions were sent south to support the fighting there, and the reports of the FOs from 3/11 who served with the 27th Infantry Division – of Makin and Saipan fame – were universally negative. Based on their close association with the soldiers in the line, the FOs found them to be both technically and temperamentally deficient: officers did not understand the limitations of artillery versus mortars; Army FOs called fire down in adjacent zones without ascertaining where the front lines actually lay; infantrymen drew heavy fire on themselves through inappropriate use of white phosphorous grenades; their medics were craven; they abandoned their dead and left them uncovered; and they were generally defeatist.[17] Richard C. Kennard was one of these FOs, and as usual, he quite frankly expressed the marines' opinion of the soldiers in a letter to his parents:

> Well in our opinion they are still no good and not nearly as good fighters as marines. The fact remains that again it is the Marine Corps which has to do the job of fighting the Japs. Right now our division is suffering heavy casualties but we have made more ground in two weeks than the Army did once they hit the Nip's line of defense. If there is no opposition the

16 First Marine Division SAR, Chapter 3, Personnel Annex, 3–4.
17 3d Battalion, 11th Marines, Forward Observer Reports, RG 127/65A-5188/Box 25/file A59-2.

soldiers make out all right but the minute they bump into something tough they scream to be relieved by the Marines.[18]

If Kennard's self-congratulatory observations concerning the Army were not entirely mistaken, neither could they conceal entirely the fact that the Marine divisions were, at best, improved versions of the same thing rather than something completely distinct and superior.[19] Actually many of the problems noted in the Army units plagued the marines as well: attacks would often jump off before supporting tanks had arrived; the strength and physical condition of units were too often ignored; big units were used where smaller ones would suffice and with fewer casualties; individual training in the use of cover and concealment was often deficient; and, in general, too much emphasis was placed on the number of yards seized rather than the destruction of the enemy. All of this pointed to the need, in the words of one report, to discard "some of our world war theories still prevalent as general dicta."[20]

It came as a psychological blow to the marines when they discovered the very conventional role they were to play on Okinawa. One veteran, as his unit staged for the move up to the lines at the end of April, vented the frustration and resentment he felt about assuming a role theretofore filled by the Army:

We were amphibious men. In the truck convoy there was none of that inspired momentum that comes when a line of boats wheels and drives in on a defended beach. We were commuting to work from the suburbs of the war, and the job ahead would be a dangerous, slogging grind, as dull as office routine. We thought we had escaped when our beach turned out to be soft and easy; we no longer had any enthusiasm for the campaign. They were placing us in double jeopardy.[21]

The Marine Corps tried to preserve something of its former role by calling for another landing behind Japanese lines as the campaign pushed through its first month and XXIV Corps bogged down before stiffening resistance. The refusal of the Tenth Army

---

18 Richard C. Kennard, letter dated 18 May 1945, Kennard Papers, PPC, MCHC.
19 The 27th Division was part of Island Command and had been intended for garrison duty rather than intensive frontline fighting; the 7th, 77th, and 96th Divisions, however, all fought as ably as the two Marine divisions. It is also worth noting that the two Marine divisions had substantially larger numbers of combat troops than called for in the Army tables of organization.
20 2d Battalion, 7th Marines, Special Action Report, dated 2 July 1945, RG 127/65A-5188/Box 24/file A49-1. 1st Battalion, 5th Marines, Special Action Report, dated 9 July 1945, RG 127/65A-5188/Box 23/file A44-1 (hereafter cited as 1/5 SAR). Every battalion SAR contained similar notes.
21 Davis, *Marine at War*, 209–10.

176   AMERICAN SAMURAI

commander, Lieutenant General Simon B. Buckner, Jr., to implement this plan consigned the Marines to a role indistinguishable from the Army divisions.[22]

The marines' discontent at having their elite status misused, the idea of the bloody fighting being dull office routine, and the image of men being part of a larger industrial machine were all captured in the term they used to describe combat: "processing." As recorded in unit diaries, message logs, and personal accounts, this single word became a linguistic convention that defined the realities of the battlefield, expressed the marines' reliance upon and identity with the tools of war necessary for the painstaking and costly reduction of Japanese cave systems, and served as a code word to express the collective experience shared by the individual riflemen, flamethrower operators, and engineers.[23] The refinements in technological means and tactical doctrine necessary to reduce the extensive, interlocking defensive positions produced what was, from a staff officer's perspective, a highly rationalized form of ground combat. "Processing" required no special abilities possessed solely by the marines, nor did it require any special relationship in juxtaposition to the enemy. It required lots of men, massive amounts of firepower, and vast logistical support. Like the attitudes expressed among the *Waffen-SS*, this sort of slogging grind was appropriate for common Army formations, not special assault troops.

The reduction of the Wana position over the last three weeks of May presents a record of almost daily attacks that were typical of the most bitter combat that raged throughout the campaign. The Japanese had constructed cave positions along Wana Ridge, facing north toward the American lines, on the reverse slope from where the village of Wana was situated, and covering the draw just south of Wana Ridge, which ended in an almost sheer 200-foot slope (see Map 6). The flanks were protected by Hill 55 to the southwest and 100 Meter Hill to the east, from where the Japanese were able to enfilade any advance on Wana itself. The defenders had zeroed in their supporting weapons to cover the open approach up the draw and to hit the reverse slope of Wana Ridge should the Americans seize the north side. The caves in this area were usually quite deep, often multitiered, and might have a dozen carefully camouflaged entrances or firing ports linked by tunnels. They were often equipped with flame baffles and were frequently blasted into the

22 For details see Official History, 5:195–96.
23 The 1st Tank Battalion used the term most frequently; see Daily Reports and S-2 Reports for examples, RG 127/65A-5188/Box 28/files A89-1 and A89-2; the infantry regiments also made free use of the term in field orders, unit reports, and SARs.

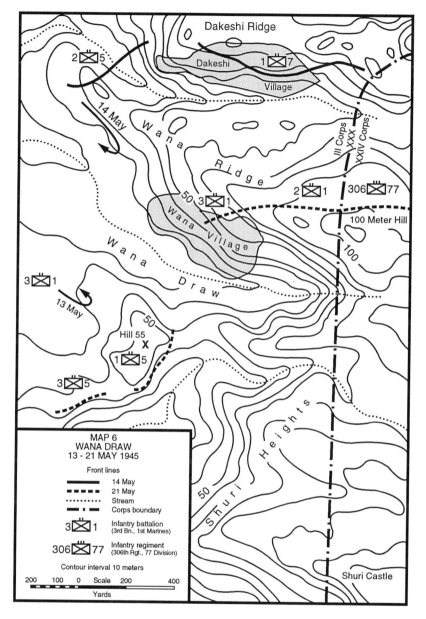

MAP 6
WANA DRAW
13 - 21 MAY 1945

Front lines

——— 14 May
- - - - - 21 May
·········· Stream
— · — Corps boundary

3⊠1 Infantry battalion
(3rd Bn., 1st Marines)

306⊠77 Infantry regiment
(306th Rgt., 77 Division)

Contour interval 10 meters

200 100 0 Scale 200 400
Yards

sides of cliffs or ravines inaccessible to tanks or armored flamethrowers. Because they were always covered by fire from other
positions, as many as twenty or thirty positions had to be screened
simultaneously by smoke or suppressed by highly accurate direct
fire in order to give riflemen and engineers a chance to isolate a

Wana Ridge, looking south from Dakeshi. *(USMC, National Archives)*

cave and destroy it. Even then, however, great vigilance was needed because survivors frequently remained inside, deep within the hillside, who would dig themselves out, sometimes days later, and inflict heavy casualties on unsuspecting marines nearby.[24]

The central technological innovation deemed essential for the reduction of defensive positions like those around Wana – and to which tactical doctrine and troop attitudes had to mold themselves – was the flame weapon. Flamethrowers were not new to ground combat: modern versions had been used in the First World War, and every major combatant in the Second World War equipped specialized assault troops with them. Firing streams of gelatinized gasoline and diesel oil, flamethrowers could often destroy – "reduce" in the parlance of training manuals – bunkers or cave positions that were impervious to small-arms fire or defiladed beyond the reach of naval gunfire or other heavy support weapons. The occupants would not necessarily die from burns; marines found many bodies, untouched by the flames, that were asphyxiated as

---

24 Headquarters, Army Ground Forces, "Information on Japanese Defensive Installations and Tactics," dated 3 August 1945, RG 127/65A-5188/Box 36/file C14-1.

the intense fires consumed all the oxygen in a confined position.[25] The jungle warfare of the early campaigns had provided limited opportunities for units like the First Marine Division to use the rather unreliable models they carried initially, but as the island campaigns shifted increasingly to rooting the Japanese out of elaborately constructed defensive fortifications, reliance on these weapons grew. The division's allowance of man-packed flamethrowers grew from 72 at the time of Guadalcanal to 243 by the time of Okinawa. Larger, longer-range flamethrowers had been mounted on amphibious tractors in the Peleliu campaign, and by the time of Okinawa a battalion of flame tanks available to the Tenth Army routinely attached one company to the First Division for daily operations.[26]

The Americans quickly discovered that the particular results achieved with flamethrowers depended upon who occupied the fortifications. The official Army history of flamethrower operations noted in its comparison that whereas "prisoners were the normal results of most flame actions in Europe, few, if any, prisoners were taken in the Pacific[,] and a position was not neutralized until its occupants were annihilated."[27] Not only were flamethrowers used less frequently in Europe than in the Pacific, but the history cites many instances in which German troops surrendered after the first burst of flame scorched the outside of their bunker.[28] In contrast, what the soldiers and marines encountered on Okinawa and in previous battles was the resolve on the part of most Japanese to continue their resistance in the face of the most terrifying prospects of death. Nor was this grim determination confined to combatants only: on Saipan and in the later stages of the Okinawa campaign, hundreds of civilians were immolated in their cave hideaways, either refusing to surrender on their own, prevented from doing so by soldiers among them, or denied the opportunity by American forces. Whether the Americans would have been so quick to kill equal numbers of German civilians in this way cannot be answered, but the intermixing of civilians and soldiers, the intense pressures

25 Sledge, *With the Old Breed*, 119.
26 United States Army, Office of the Chief, Chemical Corps, *Portable Flame Thrower Operations in World War II* (Washington: Government Printing Office, 1949), 39, 163. According to the companion history, *Mechanized Flame Thrower Operations in World War II* (1951), the 713th Tank Battalion (flame tanks) claimed an estimated 4,788 enemy killed and 49 captured; the figures for those killed by supporting infantry in these encounters were many times higher (370–74).
27 *Portable Flame Thrower Operations*, 223–24.
28 Ibid., 196–99, 202–4. The history explains the relatively limited use of flamethrowers in the European theater of operations in purely operational terms as arising from deficiencies in the weapons themselves and the dearth of suitable targets rather than ascribing it to any cultural scruples (190, 206).

of battlefield conditions, and the logic of tactical doctrine centered on the use of flame weapons provided convenient justifications for wholesale killing of civilians whatever the original intent.

To exploit the destructive potential of flame weapons, soldiers and marines on Okinawa tailored their tactical doctrine to fit the circumstances. Eliminating a single cave position required some form of what was dubbed the "blowtorch and corkscrew" technique: suppressing or killing the occupants with flame and sealing the entrances with demolitions. As discovered in the Wana fighting, however, this proved to be an exceptionally difficult task because the Japanese constructed their main defensive positions along ridges and deep draws that cut through the southern Okinawa landscape. These positions provided mutual support, making it difficult to attack any single cave without suppressing many others; they were often shielded from the indirect fire of ships and supporting artillery; and the American offensive deployment, which was based on strictly drawn boundaries between units, made it virtually impossible for a unit to swing outside its own zone of action to approach a draw or ridge position from a flank or rear.[29] As is the case with the other four first-line divisions, the First Marine Division history is a list of such positions that had to be systematically reduced in turn: Awacha, Dakeshi, and the final position before Shuri itself, Wana.

The marines' initial advances on Wana met with little success. Attempts by the 1st Marines to approach Wana Ridge from the northwest on 10 and 11 May exposed the troops to such heavy fire from Hill 55 and Shuri Heights that their attacks achieved nothing. On 13 May, 3/1 launched an attack against Hill 55 after a circuitous approach through the Sixth Marine Division's zone to the west, but the marines did not have sufficient firepower to suppress the enemy positions. One company commander, finding the open ground swept by extremely heavy and accurate fire and without the means to suppress it, refused to lead an attack through the area and was relieved of command; upon being led forward under a different officer, the company suffered heavy losses and came under such heavy, accurate fire from three directions at once that tanks had to be used to evacuate the casualties.[30] Nor did the 7th Marines

---

29 "There was too rigid adherence to fixed boundaries...and disregardance of local terrain forms that formed proper avenues of approach to designated objectives." This opinion was shared by most units in the division; 2d Battalion, 7th Marines, Special Action Report, Okinawa, dated 2 July 1945, RG 127/65A-5188/Box 24/file A49-1.

30 Upon his relief from command of L Company, 3/1, Captain Alton C. Bennett was replaced by 1st Lieutenant James J. Haggerty; 3d Battalion, 1st Marines,

fare any better attacking Wana Ridge directly south from Dakeshi, although they inflicted heavy losses on the Japanese. The division periodic reports convey a small measure of the intensity of the fighting: after two platoons from F Company, 2/7, were almost wiped out on the twelfth, the reports describe the survivors going on "a rampage" the following day, supported by a company of tanks and killing an estimated 250 Japanese in an hour's time.[31]

The Wana position was finally isolated when, after several costly repulses, the 5th Marines finally managed to seize Hill 55 on 20 May. It took an additional ten days to eliminate the pocket. Success derived from harnessing all arms in blowtorch and corkscrew attacks, but such "processing" proved far more difficult than the term conveys. In attacks on 16 and 17 May, Japanese mortar fire forced the Marine infantry to ground, leaving the gun and flame tanks vulnerable to well-concealed antitank guns that knocked out several of them and forced the others to retire. But as the marines pinpointed Japanese positions in the ruins of Wana, on the crest and slopes of Hill 55, and further up the draw, they were able to use supporting fires and smoke to isolate positions, systematically blasting and burning them by direct fire and close assault.

The use of flamethrowers to burn out positions, a central feature of "processing," was a grim and ugly prospect for both sides. The large, heavy weapons were difficult to manage and highly dangerous. With their large silhouette, operators made inviting targets to the Japanese, who quickly learned to concentrate their fire on such figures, and even if he survived the Japanese' efforts, a flamethrower operator was still in danger from faults in the weapon itself. At least one marine operator on Peleliu died when fuel leaking from the hose ignited and engulfed him in a ball of fire.[32] Moreover, the extremely short range of a man-packed flamethrower forced the operator to advance quite near the target, sometimes even to the point of being able to insert the nozzle of the weapon into a tiny firing slit.[33] Frequently the Japanese endured inside their caves and bunkers until overcome by smoke or even flame; at other times they were forced to flee their positions, running into the small-arms fire of tense, waiting infantrymen ringing the exits outside.

Special Action Report, Okinawa, dated 10 July 1945, p. 23, RG 127/65A-5188/Box 23/file A40-1 (hereafter cited as 3/1 SAR).
31 First Marine Division, G-2, Periodic Reports, no. 41, dated 13 May 1945, and no. 42, dated 14 May 1945, RG 127/65A-5188/Box 20/file A28-4 (hereafter cited as G-2 Periodic Reports).
32 Military Intelligence Division, Report No. 919, dated 18 December 1944; cited in *Portable Flame Thrower Operations*, 157.
33 HQMC, "Basic Tactics for the Portable Flamethrower," April 1944, reproduced in ibid., 297.

"Processing" on Okinawa involved the intense, costly destruction of extensive Japanese defensive positions one by one. *(USMC, National Archives)*

On the first day at Peleliu, Japanese troops in one bunker on the left flank of the 1st Marines fled only after their uniforms caught fire and started to ignite the ammunition they carried around their waists.[34] The widespread use of such weapons further polarized the battlefield, eliminating any sense of proportional response. The effect was to make combat even more of an "all-or-nothing" contest of increased desperation, brutality, and ferocity on both sides.

Returning to the lines north of Wana on 19 May, following four days in division reserve to rest and absorb badly needed replacements, the 1st Marines seized the crest of Wana Ridge on 20 May in an attack coordinated with the capture of Hill 55 by the 5th Marines. Although they repulsed Japanese counterattacks to throw them off the ridge, the marines found resistance on the reverse slope and in the draw just as fierce as what they had encountered in their approach from the front on the twelfth and thirteenth. In a desperate effort to reduce some of the protected positions below them, the marines rolled drums of napalm into the draw and set them alight with white phosphorous grenades, but with indifferent

34 Hunt, *Coral Comes High*, 65.

success. A few days later, using a pumping unit from the engineers, the marines resorted to spraying streams of napalm downslope with hoses and then used white phosphorous grenades to ignite it, this time with greater effect.[35] Nature then intervened to prevent the marines from making a speedy end of the remaining Japanese in the pocket.

The period 22–29 May saw virtually no progress in the lines as a week of torrential rains thoroughly nullified the Americans' technological superiority. The entire Okinawan countryside turned into a quagmire; tanks could not move; artillery pieces sank from sight if they fired too much; and supplies could only be moved forward on the backs of men struggling hip-deep in mud. Not surprisingly, the hospitals soon began to fill with a wide array of nonbattle casualties. By the twenty-ninth the 1st Marines reported unit effectiveness down to 30 percent, and every line company was seriously understrength.[36] Stripped of the coordinated support of tanks, artillery, and air strikes, the marines were unable to "process" the remaining pocket at the head of the draw, and the situation remained temporarily stalemated.

Although the rains demonstrated the marines' dependence on the close, synergetic fusion of all their mechanical tools in order to fight at peak efficiency and destructiveness, such a degree of cooperation was never easy to achieve. Examples abound throughout the campaign of attacks that stalled or suffered heavy losses when some critical element lagged behind. Even when tanks failed to show up or artillery fire was misdirected, the Marine infantry generally went forward anyway, but usually with little success and always with high casualties. Many historians have credited the marines' successes to the effective coordination and direction of supporting fires, but what often goes unaddressed is the demoralizing incidence of friendly casualties from buttoned-up tankers firing blind, short rounds from artillery and mortars, and misplaced bombing runs.[37] Air strikes in particular were often distrusted by the infantry, and notwithstanding frequent reports in upper command echelons about the efficacy of close air support,[38]

---

35 2d Battalion, 1st Marines, Special Action Report, Okinawa, n.d., RG 127/65A-5188/Box 23/file A39-1. 3/1 SAR, p. 27. 1st Marine Regiment, S-3 Periodic Reports, no. 52, 24 May 1945, RG 127/65A-5188/Box 22/file A37-5.
36 1st Marines, S-3 Periodic Reports, no. 57, 29 May 1945.
37 Typical of the histories that present the edited overview are Isely and Crowl, *Amphibious War*, and the official histories; for the other side see Sledge, *With the Old Breed*, 299; and Davis, *Marine at War*, 247.
38 III Amphibious Corps, "Report on Air–Ground Support Study, Okinawa," dated 1 June 1946, Enclosure B, "Report of First Marine Division (Rein) – Air Support," RG 126/65A-5188/Box 36/file C4-3.

many men hated the sight of attack aircraft flying anywhere near the front lines. The report of the 1st Marines went so far as to identify "the existence of stupidity, if not criminal negligence," among the pilots providing ground support, and Kennard expressed the opinion of many when he complained to his parents that battle decorations were handed out to these men with too free a hand even though they experienced none of the misery and fear that should have won greater recognition for those in the lines.[39] The suspicion was widespread that the pilots felt themselves to be figuratively as well as literally "above" the muck and horror of the infantrymen's world and cared little about where their bombs fell. "[O]ur own soldiers," confessed one Marine pilot long after the war, "were not much more real to us than the enemy.... Even our own Marine infantrymen were of a different species, called Gravel-crunchers or Crunchies – remote allies, at best."[40] Moreover, bombs and rockets were far less effective than artillery or naval gunfire, more difficult to control, and much less dependable.[41]

The blowtorch and corkscrew tactics essential in the Wana fighting and throughout the campaign were symptomatic of how the war had changed in both an instrumental and a motivational sense. When the marines' machine guns and mortars had scythed through the Japanese ranks at the Tenaru it was with a dual sense of desperation born of the unknown and satisfaction at seeing the results so graphically. Since the Peleliu campaign the marines had seldom seen similar piles of Japanese corpses to offset the all-too-visible evidence of their own losses. " 'I like to see them stacked up like cordwood,' " said a machine gunner on Peleliu. " 'Then you get the feeling you've done something.' "[42] Like the scene Tregaskis described as marines on Guadalcanal gleefully shot at the bobbing heads of the enemy swimming for safety, Sledge felt exultation as groups of Japanese were cut down fleeing their bunker on Ngesebus.[43] Similar scenes recurred on Okinawa as well, but in general the cave fighting provided little satisfying evidence of the individual marine's power; he was simply part of a large, complex machine

---

39 1st Marine Regiment, Special Action Report, Okinawa, dated 25 July 1945, p. 35, RG 127/65A-5188/Box 22/file A37-1 (hereafter cited as 1st Marines SAR). Kennard, letter dated 3 June 1945, Kennard Papers, PPC, MCHC.

40 Samuel Hynes, *Flights of Passage* (Annapolis: Naval Institute Press, 1988), 209. In contrast, aviators on Guadalcanal were much more easily accepted by men of the division in part because they shared the miseries of life inside the perimeter; John Howard McEniry, *A Dive-Bomber Pilot at Guadalcanal* (Tuscaloosa: University of Alabama Press, 1987).

41 1st Marines SAR, 35.

42 Davis, *Marine at War*, 58.

43 Sledge, *With the Old Breed*, 118.

engineered for wholesale, impersonal destruction. On Guadalcanal the marines had been untested, their weapons and tactics sound but unsophisticated, and the Japanese themselves were still shrouded in myth and rumor, but by the time they had reached Wana Draw, the processes of rationalization and refinement of weapons and tactics had produced a system of applying violence in carefully prescribed ways. And although this system broke down sometimes – through Clausewitzian "friction," acts of nature, or, as in the case of the infantrymen's view of close air support, because of lingering, divisive images of the Self – there was none of the ad hoc improvisation seen in 1942, as for instance with Whaling's scout–snipers. Even the examples of great bravery on Okinawa were of a different sort. Half of the Medals of Honor were awarded not for single-handed killing sprees against the Japanese or for gallant and inspirational leadership but for self-sacrifice in smothering enemy grenades.[44] Combat had meanings and dynamics in 1945 that had not existed three years earlier.

A major contribution to the shifting realities of the battlefield came from across the lines, where the behavior of the Japanese and the circumstances of the Okinawans changed the nature of the fighting in ways the marines had not anticipated. In what represented as profound a reform as any experienced within the American military, by the end of the war the Japanese had begun to shift away from the purely intangible, spiritual aspects of soldiering and to move toward a more instrumental approach.[45] An intelligence report of the time noted how "the Japanese soldier" was placing far greater reliance on firepower than previously. It explained: "Such a concept, if he entertains it . . . represents a reversal, or at least, a modification, of his highly publicized philosophy of war which would place the greatest stress on the power of the willingness to kill and gives only secondary consideration to the weapons necessary."[46] After having been badly mauled by the technologically superior Red Army at Nomonhan in 1939, the Imperial Japanese Army (IJA) leaders had made the conscious decision to emphasize the spiritual aspects of the Japanese soldier rather than modernizing and retraining the army according to Western military doctrine.[47] The problem was not simply that the Japanese were

44 Three of the six Medals of Honor awarded to men of the division were for smothering enemy grenades; McMillan, *Old Breed*, 452–58.
45 FMF Pac, Intelligence Memos, nos. 39–45, dated 13–18 June 1945, Japanese 32d Army Battle Instructions, RG 127/65A- 5188/Box 36/file C13-1 (hereafter cited as Intelligence Memos).
46 First Marine Division, G-2, Periodic Report no. 49, dated 19 May 1945, RG 127/65A-5188/Box 20/file A28-2.
47 The battle of Nomonhan was especially important in polarizing the Army reac-

comparatively poorly armed but that their doctrine was predicated on images and patterns of behavior projected onto their enemies that often bore no resemblance to what they actually encountered. As viewed from the American perspective, one marine saw only two alternative explanations: "Perhaps he is fanatic; perhaps he is merely stupid in underestimating us."[48] The battlefield was seen, in large measure, as a showcase for the sorts of intangibles and tactics that had resulted in victory in 1905 but were hopelessly anachronistic in the Pacific War.

Having had this lesson constantly repeated at the hands of the heavily armed Americans since August of 1942, the Japanese finally, informally, began to respond in kind. The familiar exhortations continued, calling for unshaking resolve and spiritual strength from every soldier, but they were accompanied by extensive instructions regarding technical and situational problems arising from the defensive strategy.[49] The Americans on Okinawa found themselves coming under heavier artillery fire than ever before, and the Japanese went to great lengths to protect their support weapons on the line. After years of fighting, martial spirit in the IJA was at last beginning to recognize and respond to the technological imperative imposed by the nature of the Pacific battlefields.

As the Japanese moved fractionally closer to the Americans' view of military rationality and the interrelation among technology, organization, and spirit, there began a barely perceptible shift in the views of soldiers on both sides of the lines toward each other. For one marine the change came as a revelation when he found some personal papers while searching a corpse: "At that moment, for the first time in the war, I felt pity for the enemy.... On Okinawa I had seen hundreds of dead, but I felt nothing toward them until we searched that Japanese in the gully and found the pictures of his wife and child."[50] For others, physical exhaustion and the foregone conclusion of the campaign and the war forced on them a

tionaries, further entrenching the emphasis on spiritual strength over material and doctrinal modernization. See Edward J. Drea, "Nomonhan: Japanese–Soviet Tactical Combat, 1939," *Leavenworth Papers* 2 (January 1981): 86–90; and Alvin D. Coox, *Nomonhan: Japan against Russia, 1939*, 2 vols. (Stanford: Stanford University Press, 1985).

48 Hunt, *Coral Comes High*, 92.
49 Intelligence Memos, in particular the "TAMA Staff Training/Memo/#128," dated 17 March 1945. 10th Army, G-2, Weekly Reports, no. 3, 11 June 1945, RG 127/65A-5188/Box 18/file A13-7. Also many of the translations that accompanied the G-2 Periodic Reports, for example, no. 62, 2 June 1945.
50 Davis, *Marine at War*, 244.

resignation that meliorated their attitudes toward the enemy. This was particularly true of the Japanese, who saw with increasing clarity the hopelessness of their resistance. Fear of American atrocities still prevented many from surrendering, but those who did so felt much less shame at the fact than had prisoners taken in previous campaigns.[51] The main danger lay in finding appropriate circumstances under which to approach the American lines.

In addition to the presence of the Japanese soldiers across the lines, there were an estimated 440,000 Okinawans on the island prior to April. Ethnically distinct, the Okinawans were disdained and discriminated against by the Japanese, but they nevertheless showed fair loyalty if little enthusiasm for the Japanese war effort. Approximately 39,000 men had been impressed in Home Guard units and labor battalions, and women were also pressed into duty, some as nurses and reportedly at least 600 as "comfort girls" in the official brothels.[52] Poorly armed, some with nothing more than sharpened bamboo spears, and virtually untrained, these men were victimized in much the same way the "termites" had been on Guadalcanal.[53] Unable to escape the battlefield or find safe shelter, Okinawans of all ages were caught up in the maelstrom around them. Tasked with hauling ammunition, water, food, and casualties to and from forward cave positions, they were exposed to the heavy American fire and suffered accordingly.[54]

The presence of civilians in the battle zone created additional problems for the marines of the First Division that they had not previously encountered. Predictably, civilian deaths were high. At night or in broken ground, the marines were not always able to distinguish uniformed combatants from civilians. In addition, Japanese soldiers frequently slipped kimonos over their uniforms in efforts to infiltrate the American lines. There were also many reports early in the campaign of civilians spying on American positions.[55] Civilians and soldiers often shared cave hideaways, and although the soldiers frequently acted to prevent the others from surrendering, especially in the early stages of the campaign, they later took advantage of the civilians' presence to aid their own escape or surrender.[56] Life for the civilians was inescapably harsh,

---

51 III AC, Psychological Warfare, 8.
52 G-2 Periodic Reports, no. 89, 29 June 1945.
53 Ibid., no. 63, 2 June 1945, and no. 76, 15 June 1945.
54 Interviews with Okinawa survivors, William and James Belote Collection, U.S. Army Military History Institute, Carlisle Barracks. Much of this was incorporated in their book *Typhoon of Steel*.
55 First Marine Division SAR, Chapter 8, Intelligence, 6–7.
56 III AC, Psychological Warfare, 8, notes that the presence of civilian refugees

and many of those captured complained of the abusive treatment by the soldiers and lived in fear of them.[57] Sickness, exposure, and famine took many lives, including many interned in American camps behind the lines.

The marines found their encounters with Okinawan civilians troubling and at odds with their previous sense of battlefield boundaries. In the collective imagination of the marines, blasting and burning fanatical, subhuman soldiers out of caves was simply what fighting had come down to at this stage of the war, but civilians, the marines thought, should have been sheltered or evacuated from the area before the battle. The old men and women who shuffled by the marines' columns in the first few days of the campaign were the first civilians they had seen in a combat area: "They were pathetic. The most pitiful things about the Okinawan civilians were that they were totally bewildered by the shock of our invasion, and they were scared to death of us. Countless times they passed us on the way to the rear with fear, dismay, and confusion on their faces." Even more striking were the children with their "round faces and dark eyes." "Cute and bright-faced," they more easily won the hearts of the marines because of their obvious innocence and friendly openness.[58]

The marines had created the necessary attitudes and conditions to wage an exterminationist campaign, and the presence of these civilians posed a dilemma: they must either be reduced to comparable status as the soldiers and slaughtered, or the exterminationist machine must falter in the face of shared humanity across the lines. Estimates of civilian casualties range from 80,000 to over 160,000, one-third of the population.[59] The scale of the civilian losses indicates that American soldiers and marines were largely successful at sustaining the polarized killer instinct, actively aided by the Japanese troops' brutal exploitation of the Okinawans. Nevertheless, just as Japanese surrenders revealed cracks in the foundation of their warrior code, there were enough exceptions to the depersonalized destruction of civilians since the Saipan campaign to show that the marine indoctrination was also not entirely successful. In an article published in the *Marine Corps Gazette*, a Marine lieutenant who served on Saipan noted how badly shaken

induced military surrenders and provided the soldiers with the opportunity to disguise themselves as civilians; 34.4% of the prisoners taken in the corps sector were dressed as civilians.

57 G-2 Periodic Reports, passim.
58 Sledge, *With the Old Breed*, 197.
59 Belote and Belote (*Typhoon*, 310–11) offer the lower figure; Dower (*War without Mercy*, 45–46, 298) gives the total as 150,000, 55,000 of whom were "civilians attached to the military"; the high figure comes from Ienaga, *Pacific War*, 199.

Marines found that Okinawan civilians, especially the children, introduced profoundly disturbing complications into the conduct of combat operations. *(USMC, National Archives)*

many marines were at killing babies or pregnant women who sheltered with the Japanese troops. He also warned his readers that the problem would become worse as Americans neared the home islands. It is noteworthy that although the author describes Japanese children as "war victims" of the intense fighting, he does not place responsibility for the victimization on the marines; indeed, he sees the marines themselves as circumstantial "victims" of the fanatical cruelty of the Japanese troops.[60]

The countryside itself contributed to the difficulties many marines experienced in maintaining sharply distinct physical boundaries around their destructiveness. The mild climate, cultivated fields, and quaint villages fostered an atmosphere more evocative of home, or at least normalcy, than previous battlefields.[61] In one sense the stench of rotting jungles or the nightmarish moonscape of the Umurbrogol may have helped the marines psychologically

60 Lewis Meyers, "Japanese Civilians in Combat Zones," *Marine Corps Gazette* 29 (February 1945): 11–16.
61 Sledge comments several times on the beauty of the countryside; for examples, see *With the Old Breed*, 199, 294, 297, and 313.

by providing an appropriate convergence of the emotional liminality of intense, exterminationist combat with the physical liminality of environment: everything and everybody outside the group was a target for destruction.[62] The discordance between the two on Okinawa, ferocious, primitive combat in the lines, pastoral beauty in the rear, was a factor behind ambivalent American attitudes in the campaign.[63] In making the same point Sledge draws an unusual analogy:

> From my experience at Peleliu I had unconsciously come to associate combat with stifling hot, fire-swept beaches, steaming mangrove-choked swamps, and harsh, jagged coral ridges. But there on Okinawa the disease was disrupting a place as pretty as a pastoral painting. I understood then what my grandmother had really meant when she told me as a boy that a blight had descended on the land when the South was invaded during the Civil War.[64]

Another memoirist recounts what happened on the third day of the campaign when the charm of the landscape clashed with the brutal warrior code as a Marine patrol sought to flush out a Japanese sniper who had taken refuge in a quaint village:

> In any group there are sadists, men who delight in doing damage and inflicting pain. As soon as we had blown up the first house, a group began systematically to fire the other houses in the village. Before the lieutenant and I could stop them, most of the houses were afire, and the lovely village on the hill was levelled.[65]

The destructive, killer mentality was not the cause of this man's concern; what he found so jarring were the circumstances and the particular setting in which this indoctrination was played out. A "lovely village" had provided the enemy with shelter or concealment, and thus its destruction was justifiable, but what made the observer so angry was that the enemy's desecration of this beauty for marginal military benefit had violated an unspoken boundary around what was to be protected and preserved. The enemy's ac-

---

62 This is one of the contributing factors Bartov identifies in the barbarization of the Eastern Front (*Hitler's Army*, 28).
63 Fussell's brief section "A Ridiculous Proximity" considers the more glaring example of the British experience on the Western Front, where the normalcy of London was only a few hours distant (*The Great War*, 64–69). This sense of disjunction, if not the actual circumstances, was in some respects comparable on Okinawa.
64 Sledge, *With the Old Breed*, 200.
65 Davis, *Marine at War*, 195.

tions had triggered the marines' "sadistic" response, and by firing the village they had restored some measure of the former balance, reducing the landscape to a form appropriate to the purpose behind their presence in it. The marines who fired and pillaged the Okinawan countryside were not sadists; they had been trained and indoctrinated to exactly that sort of behavior. They gloried in their total domination of the enemy and even the landscape itself, and they looted the countryside for trophies or rewards of this power. All kinds of colorful and exotic possessions found their way into the hands of the liberators, and had they been free to do so, the soldiers and marines might well have stripped the island for souvenirs to take home and razed what little remained standing at the end of the campaign.

The centrality of blowtorch and corkscrew tactics to the structure and operational conduct of the marines created a predicament that was never satisfactorily resolved. On the small-unit level, this type of warfare placed tremendous emphasis on trust and mutual cooperation within squads and platoons and between infantrymen and their supporting arms. In some cases coordination lapsed, either from accidents, poor staff work, or as a result of acting out inappropriate and exclusionary self-images that continued to interfere with close cooperation outside the immediate group.[66] In the absence of such cooperation units that attempted to close with the Japanese positions suffered appalling casualties. Nor, in areas like Wana Draw, where extensive Japanese defenses provided mutual support, was there much room for error. The problem that plagued every frontline unit on Okinawa was irreducible: the tempo of operations precluded the full integration of replacements into hard-hit rifle companies, and this in turn interfered with the close cooperation between individuals and units, leading to higher casualties and the need for yet more replacements. Yet even with as much as 100 percent turnover in the line companies during the course of the campaign, units managed to maintain some semblance of cohesion.

To understand better how groups of men function together both in and out of combat and to improve methods of organization and control, a specialized field of study in military sociology was established during the Second World War. As with neuropsychiatry, the Army led the way, collecting huge amounts of data and selectively

---

66 For example, the causes underlying the friction that arose between the two Marine divisions were often quite humorous, but also potentially damaging; see Pedro A. del Valle interview by Benis M. Frank, November–December 1966, 195–196, OHC, MCHC; O. P. Smith interview, 166.

publishing some of the results in the wartime series entitled *What the Soldier Thinks*. The Army promoted these studies to investigate a central paradox of its existence: that its formal command authority and the threat of disciplinary sanction, the glue that holds armies together, began to break down in the very situation for which they were created – combat.[67]

For years the source of unit cohesion in combat has generally been identified as the "primary group." The best-known study on the subject is the two-volume work *The American Soldier*. Part of an unofficial, multivolume series published after the war, it was derived from the Army's extensive wartime data but free from any official censorship or constraints. Its authors summarized the importance of the primary group succinctly: "The group in its informal character, with its close interpersonal ties, served two principal functions in combat motivation: it *set and enforced group standards* of behavior, and it *supported and sustained the individual* in stresses he would otherwise not have been able to withstand."[68] The informal group provided the controls that governed men's behavior when the established institutional apparatus for that purpose temporarily broke down in combat. It provided the physical and psychological support to keep men in battle, and it served to encapsulate the individual's moral universe during that period of time when his environment bore no readily discernable resemblance to the civilian world in which his values had originally been shaped.

Informal groups based on close interpersonal ties were indeed formed within units of the First Marine Division, especially through the first two years of the war. Thrown together for months, from final shakedown training in North Carolina in early 1942, through the long movement to New Zealand, and then the landings themselves in August, men were able to form strong friendships based on shared experiences in training and on liberty and the amount of time spent together without any real privacy. During the Guadalcanal campaign, because the division suffered few battle casualties, remained isolated without relief, and was unable to send any but the most seriously ill to the overcrowded division hospitals, infantry companies and the network of friendships remained remarkably stable. Likewise, the full year spent in Australia or staging before the Cape Gloucester landings, the again relatively small number of battle casualties in that campaign, and the limited num-

---

67 United States War Department, Army Service Forces, Research Branch, Information and Education Division, *What the Soldier Thinks*, especially January–September 1945.
68 Stouffer et al., *American Soldier*, 2:130–31. Emphasis in the original.

In this picture labeled "My Buddy," Pfc. Sam J. Bushemi of the division photo section tried to illustrate the importance of the primary group at the front. *(USMC, National Archives)*

ber of men rotated home afterward maintained a degree of security unusual for a combat unit.[69]

In the later stages of the war, however, and especially on Okinawa, this model of group cohesion collapsed as the primary groups themselves crumbled under the unremitting pressures of costly attritional warfare. The old conventional theory cannot explain the dynamics that kept infantry units together through the kind of fighting encountered on the slopes of the Umurbrogol or Wana Draw.[70] Aside from any doubts related to methodological problems in gathering and evaluating their data,[71] sociologists and interested observers like S. L. A. Marshall covered only a small portion of

69 Aside from the Eastern Front, which represents the highest sustained turnover of the Second World War, American Army units in the European theater of operations, even those serving in relatively low intensity sectors of the front lines, suffered higher rates of turnover.
70 Sledge writes that his company landed with 235 officers and men, joined an additional 250 as replacements, and finished with only 50, 26 of whom had landed with the original company (*With the Old Breed*, 268).
71 See Robert K. Merton and Paul F. Lazarsfeld, eds., *Studies in the Scope and Method of "The American Soldier"* (Glencoe: Free Press, 1950).

group dynamics. Unresolved were questions of how the group may have functioned in the different institutional environments of the Army and Marine Corps, or even what exactly constitutes the primary group.[72] By most definitions the primary group corresponds closely to formal unit organizations, making it difficult to identify where institutional boundaries end and the informal group begins. Whatever the size of this primary group, however, there is general agreement that the primary group, in its idealized form, is remarkably insular and sufficiently stable to fulfill the various supportive roles ascribed to it.

The real importance of the primary group is as a mythic ideal. Omer Bartov's argument applied to the *Ostheer* as aptly describes the Marine case:

> [W]hile the primary groups do not explain combat motivation due to their unfortunate tendency to disintegrate just when they are most needed, the *idea* of attachment to an *ideal* "primary group," composed of a certain *category* of human beings, clearly does have a powerful integrating potential. This kind of "primary group," however, is in some respects the precise opposite of the one presented in the original theory, for it is very much the product not merely of social ties, but of ideological internalization.[73]

The ideological categorization and internal idealization of the group sustained polarized relations as already suggested in Marine attitudes toward perceived sexual inferiors (women), racial inferiors (Japanese), or warrior inferiors (soldiers).

After mid-1944 the instability of personnel assignments within the First Division makes it difficult to apply the primary-group model to the Marine Corps. Men were often shuffled in and out of units with such great frequency, especially in combat, that they had little opportunity to establish the kind of strong, intimate, lasting relationships as portrayed, for instance, between Paul Bäumer and his comrades in *All Quiet on the Western Front*. As replacements became available, men were rotated back to the United States in increasing numbers. In addition, intradivisional reorganizations

---

72 Among the Germans interrogated by Edward A. Shils and Morris Janowitz the reference group extended to the company level, 150–200 men; on the other hand, S. L. A. Marshall found that American soldiers tended to think in terms of the squad, 10–12 men. See Edward A. Shils and Morris Janowitz, "Cohesion and Disintegration in the Wehrmacht in World War II," *Public Opinion Quarterly* 12 (Summer 1948): 280–315; S. L. A. Marshall, *Island Victory* (Washington: Infantry Journal Press, 1945); and the later synthesis of his observations, *Men against Fire* (1947).

73 Bartov, *Hitler's Army*, 6.

and the need for cadre personnel to create new divisions frequently undermined the sense of stability conveyed in most descriptions of the primary group.

Memoirs and personal papers make clear that individuals found the support necessary to sustain them in combat and in their relationship to authority partly from friendships based on strong interpersonal ties but also from chance encounters occurring within institutionally structured relationships. Donald A. Seibert, turned down by Marine recruiters when he tried to enlist right after Pearl Harbor, took a commission in the Army and eventually fought beside the marines with the 96th Infantry Division on Okinawa. Explaining why "military service is a powerful catalyst in the formation of close friendships," he perceptively noted, "The time spent together is apparently not important, but the circumstances, the experiences shared, the conditions under which one meets an individual exert influences which quickly cement warm relationships."[74] Boot camp, for instance, did not foster lasting friendships. Unlike the system of recruit training in most European armies, where men were kept together from the time of their induction onward, the Americans emphasized administrative and managerial efficiency at the expense of personnel stability. The transience of boot camp, the knowledge that the platoon would be broken up at the end of training, and the lack of freedom for real camaraderie all precluded the development of any intimacy.[75] On the other hand, sometimes men who knew each other only by sight found themselves thrown together for only a short time but were able to form a bond that served to support one or both through the hardships of battle. One marine from a rifle platoon on Okinawa sought comfort and support from an acquaintance, Eugene Sledge, who served with the company mortars, giving voice to all his fears and doubts; the next day he received his "million dollar wound" and dropped from sight. Sledge had himself found reassurance from an officer outside his chain of command nicknamed "Hillbilly" when they had fought together on Peleliu. That occasion had not been the result of, nor the precursor to, a lasting, informal friendship; it was a chance encounter of war.[76] What then was the source of cohesion under these conditions?

Although primary-group theory is of limited value in explaining unit cohesion, its functions of providing emotional support and standards of behavior were, nevertheless, clearly served somehow.

74 Donald A. Seibert, "The Regulars," Typed manuscript, 1988, 15, in Donald A. Seibert Papers, U.S. Army Military History Institute, Carlisle Barracks.
75 Leckie, *Helmet for My Pillow*, 12.
76 Sledge, *With the Old Breed*, 92–93, 219–20.

One explanation was the marines' sense of servicewide homogeneity, which helped reduce barriers to broad interaction between
individuals from widely separated backgrounds or units, but it was
no Shakespearean "band of brothers" that held Marine units together. The kind of interpersonal ties that had sustained units in
the lower-intensity campaigns on Guadalcanal and New Britain
could not continue to do so in the Okinawa campaign, where casualties were so high. Replacements who continually filled out units
weakened in the fighting had no personal ties to those they joined;
indeed, most of the combat casualties listed for the replacement
drafts were the result of men being hit before their new first sergeants were even able to carry them on the company rolls.[77] Instead
these men shared an institutionally defined relationship based on
the subordination of the Marine spirit to, or its identification with,
the technocratic functionalism of the larger American war machine.
In other words, the extensive organization of violence embodied
in "processing" produced precise functional relationships that held
units together, at least under the pressures of combat, even in the
absence of interpersonal ties.

Although the interpersonal and the functionalist models of
group cohesion operated side by side throughout the war, they also
tended to pull in opposite directions. This tension can be seen
perhaps most clearly between officers and enlisted men where the
institutionally defined relationship stressed appropriate detachment but where the force of circumstances and the personalities
involved tended to break such distinctions down. In recognizing
the importance of the officers' role, the authors of *The American
Soldier* noted, "The officer who commanded the personal respect
and loyalty of his men could mobilize the full support of a willing
followership; he therefore had at his disposal the resources of both
the formal coercive system and the system of informal group controls."[78] What the authors fail to add is that the two elements define
different relationships. The institutionally grounded relationship
allows for free and even arbitrary reliance on coercion, but winning
the use of "informal group controls" could only be done on an
interpersonal level. There were many marines who expressed powerful loyalty or love for particular officers and took their loss quite
hard.[79] This posed a dilemma, however, for many officers who

---

77 There were instances of trying to feed replacements to units while still in line,
   but administrative headaches, enormous losses among the new men, and reduced overall effectiveness put a stop to this practice; 5th Marine Regiment,
   Special Action Report, Okinawa, n.d., RG 127/65A-5188/Box 23/file A43-1
   (hereafter cited as 5th Marines SAR).
78 Stouffer et al., *American Soldier*, 2:118.
79 The most effective tribute is that of Sledge and the other men of his company

could not strike a workable balance in this relationship to their men. One lieutenant with the 7th Marines on Samoa discovered that his coercive authority meant little in the isolation of garrison duty on the eve of combat: "The men just don't give a particular damn about anything. Courts, fines & disciplining don't bother them."[80] In general terms, officers tended to become more formal and flaunt their perquisites the farther away from the battlefield they went, relying on the formal institutional authority of their rank to define their relationship with the men.[81]

Leadership on the battlefield was much more problematic and the role of the officer much less well defined. Describing how an attack on the Umurbrogol was led shortly before the exhausted 1st Marines were withdrawn from Peleliu, one marine wrote: "Rank meant nothing. Privates, who had something left, led sergeants who didn't have it any more, but who would follow, even if they wouldn't order other men to."[82] This was echoed in more general terms by Kennard when he was still on New Caledonia awaiting assignment to a line unit: "What with the confusion in battle when the Marines are fighting on the islands out here, it is the men with initiative who defeat the Jap strongholds. Regardless of rank, he who feels he can lead will take control during battle." In the same letter, Kennard also wrote about the undisciplined young lieutenants around him: "I'll bet that more than one gets shot in the back in combat by his own man. It takes only one serious mistake on the part of an officer for an enlisted man to think he isn't worth a damn."[83]

Although there is no evidence of officers being shot by their own men in combat, Kennard was quite correct about the speed with which an officer could destroy his own credibility. Sledge described his lieutenant on Okinawa as a "decent, clean-cut man but one of those who apparently felt no restraints under the brutalizing influence of war." Among his many shortcomings, this officer possessed the "ghoulish, obscene" habit of deliberately urinating in the mouths of Japanese corpses.[84] Officers such as this one could behave stupidly or shamefully and the discipline instilled in his men

to Captain Andrew A. Haldane, commanding officer of K/3/5 on Peleliu (*With the Old Breed*, 139–40).
80 Joseph H. Griffith, diary entry dated 15 July 1942, Griffith Papers, PPC, MCHC.
81 Leckie commented on officer privileges coming off of Guadalcanal (*Helmet for My Pillow*, 139); Sledge and a buddy experienced the same thing immediately after Okinawa had been secured (*With the Old Breed*, 314).
82 Davis, *Marine at War*, 114.
83 Kennard, letter dated 20 February 1944, Kennard Papers, PPC, MCHC.
84 Sledge, *With the Old Breed*, 202. Sledge also describes how this man carefully lined up the sights of his carbine and shot the head off the penis on a Japanese corpse (201–2).

would protect him from any overt rebellion or retaliation, but those men would never follow his guidance or respond beyond the letter of his commands. If a leader was actually dangerous, common sense and self-preservation tended to prevail. When an incompetent lieutenant nicknamed "Ivy League" placed his machine gun in an exposed position, Robert Leckie took it upon himself to move it to a tenable position; likewise, Sledge's mortar platoon went ahead and fired an important mission upon the order of an experienced NCO, while the lieutenant helplessly "ranted and raved."[85]

A serious problem facing primary-group theory is to explain the source of those moral standards of conduct that influenced all men whether in combat or on liberty. New men tended to look to one or two veterans to see how they reacted under fire and then molded their own behavior accordingly.[86] Certainly watching the actual conduct of other marines was far more crucial to the establishment of moral and behavioral limits on the battlefield than were any official mechanisms installed for that purpose. After his first battle, Robert Leckie followed the example of a man he knew nicknamed "Souvenirs" in seeking trophies from the dead. But unlike "Souvenirs," who went about on Guadalcanal with a bag around his neck filled with gold teeth taken from Japanese soldiers, Leckie sought only the equipment he was able to strip from the dead, in particular a pair of binoculars. Personal disgust and the ghoulishness of pawing the tumescent corpses prevented him from following the other's example.[87] In his own limited way, Leckie demonstrated how individual marines drew sharp personal distinctions between moral and immoral behavior that defied easy categorization by any informal-group theory. In a similar case, after describing how a marine extracted gold teeth from a wounded but still conscious Japanese soldier during the Peleliu campaign, Eugene Sledge confessed that such "incredible cruelty" represented a code of conduct that "differed drastically from that prevailing back at the division CP." But despite his feelings of revulsion, Sledge found himself soon thereafter bending over a Japanese corpse with a knife in his hand and was prevented from replaying the grisly scene he had witnessed earlier only by the vehement remonstrances of the unit corpsman. At the time dissuaded by warnings of the germs he might pick up, Sledge did not realize until reflecting on the episode after the war that "Doc Caswell didn't really have the germs in mind. He was a good friend and a fine, genuine person whose sensitivity

85 Leckie, *Helmet for My Pillow*, 110–11; Sledge, *With the Old Breed*, 235–36.
86 Davis, *Marine at War*, 14.
87 Leckie, *Helmet for My Pillow*, 86–89, 119–20.

hadn't been crushed out by the war. He was merely trying to help me retain some of mine."[88] Given such a gossamer web to rein in battlefield morality, the barbarization of the Pacific War becomes, perhaps, more comprehensible.

Practically every memoirist and correspondent recounts similar stories in which an individual's own actions imitated those of the men around him, whether in "bull session" discussions of home and women or shooting down Japanese soldiers attempting to flee a burning position. There are also cases of extreme censure when a man violated the moral code too blatantly. In one case, an elderly Okinawan woman, horribly wounded in the abdomen and suffering from gangrene, tried to persuade Sledge to kill her. He had refused and gone in search of a corpsman to help her, but before they could get back another marine had shot her. When this "quiet, neat, mild-mannered young man" explained that she was "'just an old gook woman who wanted me to put her out of her misery,'" Sledge and the corpsman exploded in anger with the expostulation, "'We're supposed to kill Nips, not *old women!*'" Whether "the executioner" received formal disciplinary action, Sledge never learned, but it was implicit that the fury of his comrades would likely strip the man of any future moral support.[89]

Although the two models of group cohesion coexisted with each other, the relative importance of the functionalist model increased during the war. At the time of Guadalcanal close interpersonal bonds seem to have been more important than was the case on Okinawa. The self-consciousness of the men going into battle for the first time as a unit and with very incomplete knowledge of the enemy or the realities of the battlefield forced a greater reliance on the few certitudes available, and that included placing great confidence in the men nearby. Robert Leckie was so familiar with every machine gunner in his regiment that during the fighting along the Tenaru he was able to identify the personal "signatures" from among all the noise and confusion of the battle.[90] On Okinawa, however, where new men constantly fleshed out depleted units just out of the lines, the turnover in personnel precluded the same sort of personal familiarity as had grown up over months prior to Guadalcanal. One veteran sadly noted that "the new men replaced the old men on the platoon rosters; they did not replace them in the minds and hearts of their friends."[91] What kept these reconstituted formations together despite the absence of close in-

88 Sledge, *With the Old Breed*, 122, 125–26.
89 Ibid., 289–91.
90 Leckie, *Helmet for My Pillow*, 80–83.
91 Davis, *Marine at War*, 222.

terpersonal ties was a common language and knowledge attendant to the technological rationale now superimposed on the nature of American ground combat. Veteran and replacement alike shared a technocratic identity that provided the bonds necessary to keep reconstituted units functioning in combat. Only in the absence of the kind of tactical improvisation seen on Guadalcanal with Whaling's scout-snipers could an engineered relationship evolve as an alternative source of unit cohesion to that offered by primary-group theory. Indeed, all of the complaints registered about the replacement system centered not on the individuals' deficiencies as emotional surrogates but on their incomplete knowledge of and preparation for the sort of warfare taking place.[92]

The replacement system worked, but at high cost to the troops. There was, for example, no mechanism for the indoctrination of replacements by the unit to which they would eventually be sent. There were efforts made to orient replacements as they joined their units, but there was seldom time to rectify any deficiencies in training. As a result, battle losses were often high among the replacements, and at least one battalion complained that additional veterans were lost trying to protect the new men.[93] The replacements for Sledge's company in front of Kunishi Ridge were not only frightened and "pitifully confused" but dangerously ignorant. One man had pulled grenade canisters from a packing crate and thrown them intact at the Japanese positions; the enemy had then unwrapped the individual canisters, removed the grenades, and thrown them back at the Americans with much deadlier effect.[94] For officers and NCOs coming into a new unit the problems could be even greater, and some battalions recommended that green lieutenants simply not be sent forward. Lacking experience or complete technical knowledge and having no interpersonal bonds with the strangers now under their command, new officers were prone either to make costly errors in judgment or to rely on experienced subordinates to such an extent that their presence was largely superfluous.[95]

To the losses incurred because of inadequate training had to be

92 Virtually every regimental and battalion SAR commented on the deficiencies of the replacements in terms of their overall numbers and their readiness for combat; a good example is 5th Marines SAR.

93 1/5 SAR, Comments and Recommendations, 1.

94 Sledge, *With the Old Breed*, 298–300. After being relieved on Kunishi, Sledge discovered his company had lost forty-nine men and one officer, half its strength, in a day: "Almost all the newly arrived replacements were among the casualties" (304).

95 2d Battalion, 5th Marines, Special Action Report, Okinawa, n.d., RG 127/65A-5188/Box 23/file A45-1. See also Sledge, *With the Old Breed*, 218–19.

added the nonbattle casualties of exhausted men who felt no personal ties to keep them from reporting sick. Units on Guadalcanal in the last two months of the campaign were full of men who should have been hospitalized. This was in part the result of overburdened medical facilities, but it also stemmed from the attitude among many men that they would be letting their friends down. It was part of the unspoken values system that a marine would not "crap out" if it would put a greater burden on the others. On Okinawa, however, a few weeks of intense battlefield attrition destroyed similar bonds in most infantry units; as personal friends disappeared, so did the obligation to endure hardship and sickness beyond a certain point. Rainy weather, poor diet, and fatigue stripped most men of their resistance, and with no overriding loyalties, sickness became as justifiable an excuse for leaving the lines as a wound.[96]

The functions ascribed by sociologists to the primary group in maintaining unit cohesion were served through two separate mechanisms, each having its own strengths and weaknesses. The actual sources of cohesion, as was the case with the general nature of combat itself, shifted from more informal, personal, and idiosyncratic bases to increasingly structured, impersonal, institutionally guided imperatives. The "old corps" mentality from the prewar years that had dominated the First Marine Division on Guadalcanal had largely disappeared on Okinawa. It was not so much that the division was without a collective soul, but rather that it had been thoroughly subsumed in serving the larger war machine that guaranteed ultimate victory and the survival of the unit if not the individual. In the absence of the material wealth seen later in the war, group cohesion on Guadalcanal was tailored to fit the limited capabilities of the division; but as a technologically grounded rationale gained primacy in the conduct of the fighting, the basis of human organization adapted to it through a structured functionalism. This change gave the division greater resilience and destructive power than it had ever had before, but subordination of the individual to the machine also built in greater dependence on Marine indoctrination than had been the case in 1942. Those marines in 1945 who failed to live up to the institutional self-image as elite assault troops descended to the level of the common herd. Harnessing the power required that indoctrination move in the direction of military fanaticism associated with the military elites of the Japanese Empire, the Third Reich, and the Soviet Union.[97]

96 On Guadalcanal see Leckie, *Helmet for My Pillow*, 99–100, 120–22; on Okinawa see Davis, *Marine at War*, 234–41, and Sledge, *With the Old Breed*, 295.
97 What Sledge labels the "meat-grinder" and what Davis describes as the business of war suggest descent into the largely undifferentiated mass of expendable

The Okinawa campaign marked the end of the fighting for the First Marine Division but not the end of the war. After the final sweep of the southern part of the island at the end of June, the men of the division discovered the rumors of being sent back to Hawaii were false; instead they were sent to the northern end of Okinawa to build cantonments, much as they had been forced to do on Pavuvu after Cape Gloucester. The expectation was that the division would again rest and rebuild prior to its participation in the landings on Honshu in November. Soon after getting settled in their new camps the marines heard the news of Japan's surrender, but this was accompanied by a big letdown when orders arrived sending the division to North China. The marines were poised to step into a new war, far different from the one just ending.

At the end, the fight against the Japanese had become dominated by a dispassionate, relentless military logic in which a technological imperative and martial spirit were harnessed together to force the enemy into complete subjugation. But just as the images and instrumentalities of 1945 had changed much from those of 1942, so too, as the marines were to discover, would the wars in China and later in Korea require new images and myths in order to accommodate vastly different dictates driving the violence forward and giving it form. The myths and legends of the Pacific War may never disappear, but their influence on the battlefield began to wane even before all of the dead had been buried on Okinawa.

infantrymen: the final step in Jones's "evolution of a soldier." In the face of this threat to individual and institutional distinctiveness, most marines emphasized even more – at the time, like Richard Kennard, or after the war, like Davis – the uniqueness of the corps. This edging toward ideological fanaticism supported Sherry's technological fanaticism to provide the focus for the division as it pushed south from Shuri in the final grueling weeks of the Okinawa campaign.

6

COLLAPSE OF THE PACIFIC WAR
IMAGES, 1945–1951

The four-year struggle against the Japanese Empire, which had
witnessed such important changes in how the marines perceived
and structured their universe, appeared to promise, by the sheer
scope and intensity of the images involved, some element of continuity that would endure far into the future, even amidst a rapidly
changing world. In practice, however, except for a period of about
six months at the beginning of the Korean War, the myths and
images of the Second World War proved utterly inadequate as a
means of organizing and interpreting the military realities confronted by the Marine Corps after September 1945. Concepts of
the Other and the Self and the synergy of technology and ideology
continued to provide a framework for imaginary constructions, but
the precise forms of the images had to change drastically when the
pounding force and minimal constraints of "total war" were replaced by wars of national liberation and limited "police actions."[1]
The gap between the combatants' understanding of war and that
of the public continued to grow. As postwar boom times and myths
of a "good war" allowed Americans to turn their backs on the
Second World War, marines saw former distinctions and verities
dissolve in wars bearing only superficial resemblance to the supposed archetype. None of the wars marines had to fight after the
Japanese stepped down from center stage aimed at unconditional
surrender, which had set the tone of the Second World War. The
limited aims pursued in American wars since 1945 have required
limiting means well beyond the Pacific War standards, which left
the Marine Corps trying to apply the logic of the old standards to
changed conditions.

---

1 The overused, hyperbolic term "total war" is misleading since organized, "rational" violence must have certain limits or boundaries. Even countries regarded
as heinously criminal have fought within generally recognizable boundaries; "total
war" designates more accurately a radical expansion of previously accepted
boundaries. Michael Howard argues this point convincingly in his essay "Tem-
peramenta Belli: Can War Be Controlled?" in Michael Howard, ed., Restraints on
War (New York: Oxford University Press, 1979), 4.

The surrender ceremonies aboard the *Missouri* on 2 September 1945 marked the end of open hostilities between Japan and the Allied forces but not the cessation of all the fighting in East Asia and along the Pacific rim. The abruptness of Japan's collapse had left power vacuums throughout much of its former empire, and there was no prospect that the former European colonial administrations would immediately reassert their control. Fueled on the one hand by years of war, occupation, and resistance, and on the other hand by the lofty declarations in the Atlantic Charter and principles of self-determination and anti-imperialism, nationalist groups of many kinds sought to seize control of their own fortunes, and fighting sprang up in many areas atop the ashes of the war just ending. In the Philippines and Indochina, on the Indonesian archipelago and in Burma, the killing continued. In some cases it was hunting out former Japanese overlords and puppets; in others it was the continuation of old feuds and civil wars; and in yet other places it was the beginning of violent decolonization, the overthrow of the Western imperialists. The most momentous of these struggles triggered by the final defeat of Japan was the open civil war that erupted in China between Chiang Kai-shek's Kuomintang and the Chinese Communist Party under Mao Tse-tung. The war to decide the political and ideological future of this vast, populous country dominated U.S. Asian policy in the first years after 1945 and long delayed the homecoming of the First Marine Division.

Late 1945 was an uncertain and confusing time for U.S. foreign policy. Even in its moment of ultimate triumph, the great wartime coalition was in the midst of disintegration. The reach of the Soviet Union extended from the Elbe River to the East China Sea, and although it would take several months for relations to collapse altogether in mutual distrust, the seeds of doubt had already been planted. Even the staunch British had become violently opposed to many American policies both as related to the situation on the European continent and in regard to the future disposition of their imperial possessions. Professing the best of intentions, the United States maneuvered to throw support behind noncommunist nationalist movements in an effort to make over East Asia in its own image. This meant continued backing for the Chinese Nationalists in their struggle for power against the Communists.[2]

For the American public, the first order of business after the ceremonies in Tokyo Bay was to begin demobilization and the

---

2 Two of the most useful works on this transitional period are John Lewis Gaddis, *The United States and the Origins of the Cold War, 1941–1947* (New York: Columbia University Press, 1972); and Christopher Thorne, *Allies of a Kind* (New York: Oxford University Press, 1978).

return to peacetime pursuits. Since the time of Shays's Rebellion, the specter of a mass of trained soldiers poised to descend on the country and take by force whatever they thought owed to them has frightened politicians, businessmen, and common citizens alike. Memories of the problems that followed the First World War were still fresh in the minds of many, and now, with more than sixteen million men and women in uniform during the Second World War, the threat looked much greater. Many Americans feared the economy would slip back from wartime boom to depression level, and the prospect of reintegrating the veterans appeared daunting. This sort of apprehension proved useful, however, in spurring the establishment of programs to make the adjustment quick and effective. The Serviceman's Readjustment Act of 1944, the GI bill of rights, laid the groundwork for the reintegration of returning veterans. Among its many provisions the legislation provided for job-training programs, opportunities to return to school, low-cost housing loans, and the "52–20 club" to help tide over those who could not immediately find work. There was also expanded medical care for veterans. Although many Americans were hostile toward what they perceived as New Deal social legislation for soldiers, critics were largely silenced by the results. The GI bill became the means not simply to reintegrate millions of veterans but to expand and educate the burgeoning American middle class.[3] At the time, however, few envisioned such a successful resolution of the problem.

In the latter half of the war several books attempted to warn civilians about the dangers posed by returning veterans, educate the public about the soldiers' plight, and emphasize the need to fit them back into society. Among those who offered dire warnings about the returning veterans was Columbia University professor Willard Waller, who gave one chapter of his book *The Veteran Comes Back* the ominous title "Politically, The Veteran is a Damoclean Sword." He saw veterans as outsiders, immigrants: "He is like an immigrant because he has no sure and settled place in society and because he derives many, if not most, of his social satisfactions from the company of his own kind; partly because he prefers their society and partly because he does not fit in anywhere else."[4] Other authors reminded their readers that the Russian Revolution and the rise

---

3 Figures for assistance provided under Public Law 346 and subsequent legislation are available in Administration of Veteran Affairs, *Annual Report* (Washington: GPO); the 1947 report in particular provides some statistical measures of the scale of the effort and the speed with which the bulk of the veterans were reintegrated through these programs: total disbursements, $7.8 billion; one quarter of the entire population had at least one family member drawing benefits; 14.36 million of those eligible were participating in that year (1–3).

4 Willard Waller, *The Veteran Comes Back* (New York: Dryden Press, 1944), 180.

of fascist dictatorships in Italy, Spain, and Germany stemmed in part from soldiers' discontent. J. Gordon Chamberlin, in his book *The Church and Demobilization*, expressed the concern of many clergy that veterans would spread the plague of sinfulness among a comparatively uncontaminated public. The language of Waller, Chamberlin, and others articulated a polarized, detached view of "us" and a monolithic "them" such as had been used to describe the Japanese. American society, to these authors, was good and pure; the social and moral turmoil of the war were expunged or ignored. "The veteran" stood for all veterans; they were seen to think and act alike, and it was assumed that they would vote – or revolt – as a body. It was almost as if the dark and angry images created after the First World War in *What Price Glory*, *Through the Wheat*, and *Company K*, rather than the heroes in *One of Ours* or *A Son at the Front*, had become the accepted archetypes for veterans returning in 1945.[5]

One competing view of "the veteran" that differed sharply from Waller's adversarial image was that of Dixon Wechter. Waller over-romanticized the veteran, according to Wechter; the ordinary soldier, he argued, wanted only "his girl, his job and a little home." The veteran would return as he left: "Friendly, generous, easy-going, brave, the citizen-soldier of America."[6] Waller and others viewed the process of military resocialization as a complete makeover of the individual's personality, virtually displacing his civilian upbringing. Such exaggerated views, however, failed to recognize that the environmental and contextual elements that gave military resocialization its force were absent in the landscape of postwar American society. In the all-male atmosphere of training or the company mess overseas, the worrisome traits identified by Waller and Chamberlin had a place and often an institutionalized purpose, but the very nature of the society to which the veterans were returning would erode many of those habits of thought and behavior. The role played by former soldiers in the European political upheavals of the 1920s and 1930s had been possible in part because the societies to which they returned had resembled, or were made over to resemble in crucial ways, the frontline environment the soldiers had left behind. Unscarred by the war directly, American society neither resembled the active theaters of operations nor was

5 J. Gordon Chamberlin, *The Church and Demobilization* (New York: Whitmore and Stone, 1945), 12–14. For other examples see Jack Goodman, ed., *While You Were Gone* (New York: Da Capo Press, 1974); and George K. Pratt, *Soldier to Civilian* (New York: McGraw-Hill, 1944).
6 Dixon Wechter, *When Johnny Comes Marching Home* (1944; reprint, Westport: Greenwood Press, 1970), 558.

COLLAPSE OF THE PACIFIC WAR IMAGES   207

in any danger of being recast in such a way by the veterans coming home after the Second World War.[7]

Although demobilization began immediately with the end of the war, delays in the process posed several difficulties with which the military services had to contend. The end of the shooting war in August 1945 could not result in the immediate discharge of all military personnel over peacetime strength limits. Huge tasks remained that required tens of thousands of troops: the home islands had to be occupied and administered, the Japanese military forces disarmed, and millions of Japanese nationals, uniformed and civilian, repatriated from overseas. The situation was further complicated because most of those overseas were at the top of the list for discharge and thus had to be replaced by more recent inductees sent over from the United States. More was involved than the simple transfer of men, however, because units were being disbanded or deactivated to reduce overall manning levels. This, in turn, increased the institutional difficulties of maintaining an acceptable degree of stability and unit effectiveness.

Largely ignorant of military policies or the broader political machinations shaping their destiny, the men of the First Marine Division in the late summer of 1945 rested uneasily in cantonments on Okinawa and awaited their fate. The costly, draining campaign for the island was over if not forgotten, and men anxiously added up their "points," awarded for time spent overseas, campaigns, decorations, and so on, to see if they were entitled to rotate home. Many had already left for the United States, and fresh replacements had filled their places, as well as those left vacant from the recent fighting. Those who remained thought it logical, having been the first division sent overseas, that they should be the first to return, but this was not to be.[8] As had been the case when many marines fresh from the trenches in 1918 had sailed for Hispaniola, so the men of the First Division were thrust into the midst of another ongoing war. The enemy, the rules of engagement, and the measure of victory all differed from those of the war just over, and the marines found adjustment difficult when the images formerly relied upon and the conditions that fostered them no longer applied in the new circumstances.

7 The contrast is striking between the American experience in 1945 of returning to a putatively Capra-esque society and that of the *Freikorps* members, whose primal fears from the front were reproduced in the landscape they faced in revolution-torn Germany in 1919–21 (Theweleit, *Male Fantasies*, 2:3–26).

8 Many also felt the division should lead the victory parade down the streets of Tokyo and were disappointed when that honor went to the First Cavalry Division (McMillan, *Old Breed*, 427).

The transition in the First Division from war to peacetime footing fostered a sharp break in the continuity of individual and collective experience that was marked by frustration, confusion, and resentment. This was a period that subsequently dropped virtually out of public sight or recollection. The marines of the First Division on Okinawa could mark the end of the war with a collective sigh of relief but little celebration. Looking out at the world from their isolated camps on Motobu Peninsula, the men could feel glad to have survived, but many were also caught in the grip of a malaise. Apprehensive about their future, impatient to return home, and uneasy over the thoughts of others who had died or been seriously wounded, they chafed at the circumstances that kept them in this condition.[9] One marine, "just a boot with fifteen months over and two campaigns in," asked his family not to write him about all the parades and celebrations occurring at home because he was still stuck on Okinawa. As he looked around at men who had thirty months overseas or four stars to their Pacific campaign ribbon or a couple of Purple Hearts and were still stranded on Okinawa and virtually forgotten, the bitterness he felt for those who had stayed at home boiled over: "But no, let the people in the States do the celebrating. They had their chow rationed and that gas rationing was awful. They had to work extra long hours and didn't even get a vacation."[10] The return to normalcy enjoyed by so many was denied the marines still stationed in the western Pacific, and this was a cause for concern among the top leaders.

Institutionally, the changes required by peace were disruptive but handled with bureaucratic professionalism. Several units were reduced to virtually the same condition as at the time of Pearl Harbor. The third battalion in every Marine infantry regiment was disbanded in the spring of 1946, and each of the artillery battalions lost one of its gun batteries. Moreover, as in 1941, those who manned the remaining units numbered relatively few veterans among their ranks; the rest were recent recruits without experience. By the summer of 1946 units in the division were reporting military efficiency levels of 25–35 percent, generally lower than the worst levels reported during the Okinawa campaign.[11] The logistical and administrative problems that attended in-place individual replacement, the deactivation or disbanding of units, and the reshuffling of unit designations and command structures were straightened

9 Ibid. McMillan quotes one man as saying that marines went through the motions of celebration because it was expected, but it also " 'seemed irreverent' " under the circumstances.
10 Charles A. Linhart, letter dated 28 August 1945, Linhart Papers, PPC, MCHC.
11 Official History, 5:615.

out with relative ease by competent, experienced staffs, but at an individual or small-unit level, the difficulties grew. Efforts to train the men together as units were hampered by continued personnel turnover, the constant need to emphasize fundamentals for new replacements, and the scattered deployment of the men in small formations. The division was able to function along the lines of its narrowly defined garrison duties, but it was in no condition, one year after the war, to fight in a pitched campaign.

On a personal level, the return to garrison life required a significant adjustment that many marines could not make. Discontent grew among reservist "old-timers" impatient for discharge: their recent memories of wartime permissiveness fostered resentment at the reimposition of more stringent discipline, and the growing numbers of new men coming into line units destroyed most of the remaining personal ties to a particular unit or commander. At the same time, senior Marine officers worried about quelling the growing unrest among the veterans and restoring a tough peacetime regimen. A memorandum circulated to all officers within the Second Marine Division while stationed in Kyushu and southern Honshu included a message from Major General Geiger, the commanding general, Fleet Marine Force, Pacific, in which he admitted that marines stationed on Oahu "were infected to a small degree on 8 January by the insidious bug that has bitten the Army and caused Army personnel to stage mass meetings protesting their demobilization program."[12] Geiger cautioned all marines in the Pacific against repeating such demonstrations and backed his warning with action as necessary.[13] The commandant, General Vandegrift, although recognizing "the great letdown that comes to a fighting force when they are sitting around seemingly doing nothing," warned that any reports in the press of demonstrations or protest meetings could damage the reputation of the Marine Corps and possibly threaten its very existence. With the unification controversy looming over the horizon, Vandegrift was correct in assuming that, should discipline fail, the Marine Corps might well not survive efforts in the Senate to consolidate the military services.[14] No marines were allowed to gather for any unauthorized

12 Headquarters Battalion (HQBN), 2d Marine Division, FMF, in the field, Memorandum to all officers, dated 8 February 1946 (quoting division-wide memorandum dated 31 January), Eugene W. Gleason Papers, PPC, MCHC.
13 According to O. P. Smith, Geiger "had a sergeant and a corporal who went bad, and boy, he got them up and convened a board, and they reduced those noncoms to privates just like that for inefficiency, and that was the end of any trouble in the Marine Corps." In contrast, the Army commander, Richardson, was ineffective in quelling the soldiers' unrest. See O. P. Smith interview, 152.
14 The unification controversy leading to the National Security Act of 1947 and

purpose, and officers tried to explain to their men that the demobilization was proceeding as quickly as possible. The relationship between officers and enlisted men, which had become less rigid as a result of shared combat experience and the somewhat informal conditions of camp life, grew stiffer and more impersonal. When officers of the Second Marine Division proved too lenient in curbing breaches of regulations occurring on occupation duty, the division commander warned that all judicial proceedings would be reviewed to stop such laxness.[15] The close wartime loyalties between officers and their men thus began to disappear, by the reimposition of tighter discipline from above and through the effects of demobilization. The extent to which such problems plagued the First Division remains unclear, but the North China mission may have mitigated some of the worst influences of idle overseas garrison duty.

For those marines with a strong sense of tradition, and in some cases with actual prewar ties, the landings in North China represented a kind of homecoming. With a presence extending back a hundred years to the time of the first landings in the area, "China duty" had been a hallmark of the interwar Marine Corps. The exotic atmosphere of Tientsin and Peiping, the foreign settlements, and the Chinese themselves had been legendary in the 1930s when the Pacific War was first brewing. Much of the attraction remained in 1945, based in part on the yarns of old "China hands," but also because almost any setting was more appealing than that of Pavuvu or Motobu Peninsula. Circumstances, however, had changed drastically from what they had been before the war. The marines' mission required them to intervene in a civil war of massive dimensions. Agreements between the United States and Chinese Nationalist governments called for the marines to be dispatched to Hopeh and Shantung provinces to disarm and repatriate the Japanese occupation troops and free Allied prisoners still held in the area. Most important, although not stated as such in their orders, the marines were to ensure that the Chinese Communists did not take complete control of the region once the Japanese and their puppets were

---

the "revolt of the admirals" in 1949 were both high-water marks of the greatest bureaucratic reorganization in American military history. Adjusting to new structural and political–military forces, the Marine Corps staved off amalgamation or dissolution, but this latest struggle reaffirmed the sense of beleaguerment and institutional radicalization that had affected service policy in the interwar period. Millett provides a good summary in *Semper Fidelis*, 456–64, 469–74.

15 HQBN, 2d Marine Division, memorandum.

removed from power.[16] In the initial chaos and mild sense of goodwill accompanying the end of the war, the marines were not in any inordinate danger, but it soon became clear that they were in the unenviable position of assisting a weak, corrupt, and manipulative dictator in a civil war in which the U.S. government was officially neutral.

The twenty-one months that the First Marine Division spent in North China served as a transition from war to postwar and from a sophisticated technocratically based combat expertise to the managerial considerations of peacetime regulars in garrison duties. Skills, values, and perceptions fostered by three full years of war against Japan were jumbled, made over, and reinstitutionalized with amazing rapidity. In the politically charged atmosphere of North China, Marine officers found their decisions closely scrutinized by senior commanders. This period marked the marines' first efforts to distill the meaning of events from the Pacific War as a way to understand better their role in the Chinese civil war, but the nature of battle had changed from straightforward annihilation of identifiable enemies to the strain of guerrilla warfare, having to endure raids, hit-and-run attacks, and ambushes at the hands of men not clearly marked as being Chinese Communists or bandits or something else entirely. The search for new understanding proved as elusive and frustrating as hunting down guerrillas.

To their added dismay, the marines soon discovered that they were no longer part of a great mobilized war machine. Americans at home wanted only the return to peace and normalcy that the Japanese surrender promised. People wanted to achieve the level of material prosperity, long deferred, that advertisers and politicians had been describing for years; weary of wartime demands and political issues, they showed no interest in the obscure North China mission or patience in postponing further the resumption of their peacetime routine.[17] This change in status required significant adjustments on the part of both the individual marines and the institution itself. Recent replacements had often been just finishing high school when the corps's exploits on Iwo Jima and Okinawa filled the newspaper headlines and newsreels. Marines' expectations for future combat, whether based on the veterans' hard experience or on a total-war fantasy of the postwar inductee, all revolved around some form of virtually unrestricted violence

16 This goal was made explicit in messages to General Wedemeyer; Forrest C. Pogue, *George C. Marshall*, 4 vols. (New York: Viking, 1963–87), 4:58.
17 Blum, *V Was for Victory*, 332.

harnessed to a polarized ideology like that witnessed on Okinawa, which no longer applied in the new situations. For the Marine Corps, demobilization required sharp cuts in manpower and the assumption of new duties. The new missions, however, were unsuited to the intellectual and organizational foundations that the service had laid down with the development of the amphibious warfare doctrine in the 1930s. Thoroughly ingrained during the Pacific War, images of total war would be carried inside the heads of at least another generation of marines and would affect the conduct of operations for the next thirty years.

While the Sixth Marine Division took up positions to the south in Shantung Province at the end of September, men of the First Marine Division landed in Tangku at the mouth of the Hai River in Hopeh Province. Although viewed primarily as an administrative move, the initial landings in North China were made by assault troops. Any apprehensions the marines may have had about what awaited them ashore were quickly allayed, however, when, on 30 September 1945, the first boatloads of marines heading for the wharves of Tangku received a warm welcome from thousands of Chinese who lined the river. Security was quickly established, and as the division assembled ashore, garrisons were installed in the cities of Tangku, Taku, and upriver in Tientsin.[18] From these main points the marines deployed to Peiping and its outlying airfields and to points along the strategic Peiping-Mukden railroad, which ran through Tientsin and Tangku and then north to the important port town of Chinwangtao at the boundary with Manchuria (see Map 7). The advance party had made arrangements with the local Japanese commanders to take over their facilities, barracks, airfields, warehouses, and so on. Property owned by the Japanese or Germans was seized, that of the French and British leased. The men of the First Division and the First Marine Air Wing settled into their new quarters with minimal difficulties and began learning their new duties and exploring their exotic surroundings.[19]

Within the limits of common sense and military security, the marines were encouraged to explore the Chinese culture and interact with the people among whom they were billeted. The "Marine's Guide to North China" put out by the First Division intelligence section in September 1945 provided both an indoctrinational briefing and a tour guide. The Americans had never in-

18 United States Marine Corps, *The United States Marines in North China, 1945–1949* (Washington: Historical Branch, G-3, HQMC, 1962), 1–3; Theodore H. Harbaugh, letter to Kay, dated 2 October 1945, Theodore H. Harbaugh Papers, PPC, MCHC.
19 Official History, 5:546–47; John B. Simms Papers, PPC, MCHC.

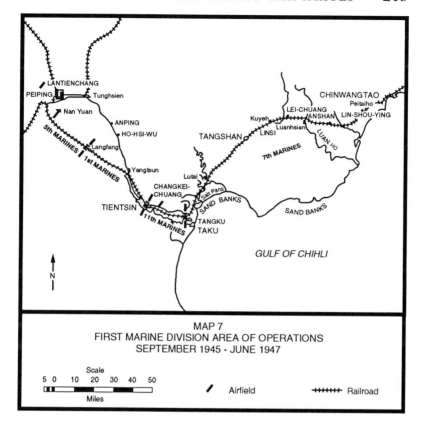

MAP 7
FIRST MARINE DIVISION AREA OF OPERATIONS
SEPTEMBER 1945 - JUNE 1947

vaded China, it emphasized, but marines in the past had frequently gone ashore to preserve order and to protect American lives and property. The North China expedition had largely the same purpose, although the presence of the Japanese and warring factions among the Chinese complicated the situation. At the same time that marines were warned to avoid security breaches and to guard against wandering about alone, they were encouraged to sample local customs, cuisine, and architecture: prompting few marines needed.[20] Soon marines could be seen wandering along the Great Wall and through the Tartar City in Peiping with their ubiquitous cameras.

Although it is difficult to get a clear understanding of the marines' personal attitudes toward their new surroundings and duties because the division was fragmented to provide widely dispersed

20 Copies of the pamphlet abound among the personal papers of marines stationed in North China, including the William F. Nolan Papers and the Ray Gallagher Papers, PPC, MCHC.

city garrisons, outposts, and patrols, there were positive and negative elements common to other Marine experiences when stationed in the midst of nonwhite societies. Many marines' scrapbooks contain pictures from North China, of buildings or statues, and a few of Chinese who were obviously acquaintances of some kind. Charles A. Linhart had several photographs of "Yuan" and his family; Linhart was a guest of theirs frequently, but how they met or what happened to the relationship later is not mentioned. On Okinawa and in North China Philip H. Bernstein took pictures of his friends trading with anonymous "gooks."[21] There seemed to be much goodwill, but there were also increasing frictions, caused by the tension and violence of guard duties, racial prejudices, or the eagerness of many to go home. Predictably, a separate economy sprang up around the Americans. Souvenir shops, restaurants catering to American tastes, and brothels all served the marines' wants. Or as one marine said, " '[W]ine, women and steaks were cheap. For the first time First Division men were able to pick up silks and jewelry as souvenirs instead of trinkets from the pockets of dead Japs.' " Marines also hired boys to do their washing, ironing, polishing, and sweeping out in the barracks. This economy operated at inflationary prices in American dollars, which generated rancor among the marines, who saw their purchasing power decline, and among other Chinese, who had to use the unstable Nationalist currency.[22]

Guard duties in teeming cities often proved especially difficult for the marines and exposed them to facets of Chinese society for which they were unprepared. Stationed in a provisional MP company in Taku, Robert Tuttrup was surrounded by squalor and abject poverty and appalled by what he saw:

The people were so poor, it just broke our heart. People would throw babies away. Somebody had thrown away a baby and there were some wild dogs. These dogs were eatin' up the baby. They called for some MPs and we got in a jeep and we go out – boom, boom, boom – shoot the dogs. That's what we didn't like.[23]

21 Charles A. Linhart Papers and Philip H. Bernstein Papers, PPC, MCHC. See also the photographs in the William C. Beall Papers, PPC, MCHC.
22 McMillan, *Old Breed*, 428–29. This parallel economy also proved an overwhelming temptation for some Americans in positions of authority. A Marine colonel was convicted of black-market operations after a long and complex court-martial; the other services apparently did little to bring major offenders to trial; Thomas interview, 698–99.
23 Terkel, *"The Good War,"* 174.

Too often marines shot more than just dogs. Guard assignments frequently required a handful of marines to keep out large numbers of Chinese refugees who, in desperation, risked their lives to steal anything salable on the black market. One officer's explanation reflected the opinion of many Americans: "They stole us blind, and we killed some of them, and that's when the Seventh Fleet commander would say 'the Marines are murdering the Chinese' and such nonsense. Well, a Marine on post with a rifle is told to protect his post, and when somebody busted in there and started to steal something, [he]'d shoot 'em."[24] The Chinese civilians were simultaneously objects of pity and of sanctioned violence, a combination that left many marines eager to leave.

Duty in North China also reordered the marines' images of the Japanese almost overnight. As the marines came into personal contact with Chinese Nationalist troops, they developed greater respect for the discipline and courage of the Japanese. Having taken over their billets and many of their duties, the marines understood what it must have meant to perform the thankless garrison duties for years on end. Escaping comment was how this attitude reflected a denial common to both the Japanese and the marines that their role could justly be regarded as an oppressive military occupation; they both viewed themselves as competent military professionals simply performing their duty as higher authority dictated. The venality and inefficiency of the Nationalist troops further accentuated the Japanese' military qualities. The Japanese cooperated to a remarkable extent with the Americans, helping them get materials in short supply, inventorying equipment stored in warehouses, and relieving the Americans of all internal administrative and logistical headaches associated with the organization and movement of soldiers and civilians to the coast for repatriation. The Japanese also showed their contempt for the Chinese and respect for the marines. The commanding general of the Sixth Division, Lemuel C. Shepherd, was presented a priceless samurai sword by a Japanese general " 'on behalf of all Japanese soldiers under my command who are moved by your open and honorable conduct toward them.' "[25] Military professionalism had provided at least a partial bridge over the wartime animosities, and it grew in impor-

24 Thomas interview, 697. Thomas's comment offers an interesting counterpoint to the familiar American stereotype that labels life cheap to Asians.
25 Official History, 5:581. The Japanese had good reason to be thankful for American supervision: when, in early 1946, the Chinese Nationalists were given control of Japanese repatriation, the process was marred by several incidents of unchecked mob violence, prompting the Marines to resume this duty again (597).

tance with time and distance as marines looked back on their experiences.

The military situation grew increasingly serious as the Communists and Nationalists maneuvered around the Americans for the advantage. In September 1945 the Communists could muster roughly 170,000 regulars in both Hopeh and Shantung, representing the only nonpuppet Chinese forces in the two provinces.[26] When Nationalist troops began to move up from the south, they made no effort to relieve the marines of their duties and instead massed their forces to move north into Manchuria. The Communists, being liberally supplied with Japanese weapons and provisions captured by the Soviets in Manchuria, stepped up their activities in Hopeh. They did not want to provoke an open alliance between the United States and the Kuomintang, but they used harassing tactics to establish their presence, disrupt rail traffic, and embarrass the Americans. Small groups exchanged fire with Marine train guards, shot at low-flying Marine aircraft, and raided exposed sections of track and vulnerable bridges, frequently breaking the line. To protect the vulnerable railroad linking Manchuria and the large KMA coal mines at Chinwangtao to the south, marines rode aboard trains and manned as many important points along the line as possible. Where the marines could not occupy many of the more remote areas contested by the Chinese Communists, their former enemy became an ally. Japanese soldiers, respected for their tight discipline and military prowess, assisted the marines in China, even to the point of standing guard with them over the railroads in Hopeh and continuing their counterguerrilla activities in much the same way as they had during the war.[27]

The marines found themselves in the impossible situation of having no effective ally among the Chinese and little public support at home. Press accounts of the so-called Anshan Incident of 4 December 1945, in which a marine was killed, demonstrated how unsympathetic many Americans were toward direct involvement in China's civil war. Marine efforts to intimidate villagers thought to be harboring the murderers of the marine prompted a writer on the *Washington Post* to compare their actions to Japanese or Nazi atrocities.[28] George Marshall negotiated a cease-fire that went into effect on 10 January 1946 and eased some of the marines' problems for almost six months, but meanwhile the Nationalists, rather than

26 Ibid., 543.
27 Ibid., 648–49.
28 Ibid., 589. The use of mortar fire, even if called down outside the village, was probably not the best approach, but whatever the truth about the marines' actions, the show of force proved ineffective: the murderers were not caught.

consolidating their hold on Hopeh, continued their attacks in Manchuria. The Communists gained from these activities the distinct impression that the marines in Hopeh were active allies of the Nationalists and their springboard into Manchuria. Accordingly, they stepped up their operations against the marines in the area in the summer of 1946.

Two events in July 1946 made clear to senior military commanders the hopelessness of the Marine Corps mission in North China. On the thirteenth, seven marines from a bridge guard, violating standing orders, entered a nearby village and were taken prisoner by Communist soldiers. The Communists, with their captives, succeeded in evading all efforts to locate them and forced the United States to negotiate for their release. These negotiations resulted in the United States apologizing for unlawfully violating a "liberated area" and giving assurances that no similar incidents would occur in the future, and prior to release, each of the seven men wrote a letter attesting to his good treatment by the Communists. It was, in the words of the official history, a "distasteful but necessary solution posed by the captured Marines."[29] It was also an intensely humiliating experience for the corps. At the end of the month, on 29 July, the Communists conducted a carefully planned ambush of an American convoy at Anping on the road to Peiping that left four marines dead and ten wounded. Marines were being singled out for direct action by the Communists without being granted the chance to retaliate as they had been trained and indoctrinated to do.

The First Division gradually reduced its responsibilities from July 1946 until the withdrawal of its last elements in June 1947. Even before Marshall's efforts were finally suspended in January 1947, the Marines had further reduced troop levels and withdrawn from their overstretched rail guard duties, but the entire experience in North China had been confusing and frustrating. Branded as war criminals in one extreme case at home and treated with suspicion by Marshall, who worried about overzealous marines undermining his delicate mission, the marines found themselves in a situation to which they could not apply familiar solutions.[30] The military and political dimensions of their mission circumscribed the relative freedom of action enjoyed during the Pacific War.

Psychological unpreparedness in many ways characterized the atmosphere in which the Marine Corps operated for the next thirty

29 Ibid., 610.
30 Marshall used the Marine presence as a lever in talks with Chiang, but he tried to ensure they did not exceed their orders (Pogue, *George C. Marshall*, 4:116, 122, 137).

years. Romanticized recollections of the Pacific War, held in juxtaposition to the aggravating and bewildering realities of the war
in China, provided a bond of mutual respect between the marines
and Japanese, but they also fostered a sense of disjunction that
could not be bridged as easily. Meanings ascribed to the organized
violence seen on Guadalcanal, Peleliu, or Okinawa allowed the warrior spirit to be revered in victory or defeat. Against guerrillas there
was no sense of any spiritual contest; such fighting allowed no
comparison of each side's relative moral strength.[31] The measure
of success or failure did not use the same yardstick. Traditional
military thought centers on the rationalization of instrumentalities
to achieve victory on the battlefield, but revolutionary war is concerned with maintaining a military and political presence that even
repeated battlefield defeats will not shake.[32] The marines had, as
measured by the traditional yardstick, been quite successful in their
mission: they had repatriated the Japanese quickly and efficiently,
and they had not overreacted to the Communists' tactics. But after
the combat experiences of the Pacific War, which revolved around
campaigns that had a definite beginning and end, the amorphous
nature of the mission along the Peiping-Mukden railroad was un-
satisfying. Upon securing Tarawa and Iwo Jima, surviving marines
had recorded their victories in yards of ground conquered or snapshots of piles of smoking corpses; North China offered no comparable, tangible measures of success or grisly testimony to
conquering warriors. The nature of the experience, and the speed
with which its lessons were dismissed, highlight the recasting of the
war-just-over into the "Good War" of today's memory. Revolutionary warfare as personal or national experience defied translation
into the traditional, conservative images and meanings by which
American society came to understand the Second World War. This
other type of warfare was, for as long as possible, ignored.

What permanently consigned the images of the Pacific War to a
mythic past was the decision made in the midst of another war six

31 This is a common reaction among regular military forces. The marines' views
here are essentially identical to those expressed by *Wehrmacht* units committed
to antipartisan operations, especially in the East; Headquarters, United States
Air Force, War Documentation Project, *The Soviet Partisan Movement in World
War II: Summary and Conclusions* (Maxwell AFB, Ala.: Human Resources Research Institute, 1954), 17–20; Bartov, *Hitler's Army*, 83–84, 92–93. There is in
this also a common element of the soldier as occupier and oppressor; not an
unfamiliar role in Marine Corps history, but one for which the latest generation
of recruits, raised on crusading propaganda of the Second World War, was
unprepared.
32 A detailed discussion of the subject is beyond the scope of this study, but the
nature of revolutionary warfare is central to what succeeds the Pacific War model
I present here. The best overview of the main ideas is John Shy and Thomas
W. Collier, "Revolutionary War," in *Makers of Modern Strategy*, 815–62.

years after Japan's unconditional surrender that the United Nations military forces would fight only to preserve the *status quo ante bellum* in Korea. The goal was to be stalemate and negotiated peace, not total victory. Ironically, the old nemesis of the First Marine Division in the Southwest Pacific, Douglas MacArthur – now commander in chief of the United Nations Command and heralded architect of the counteroffensive that triggered Chinese intervention – had become the primary spokesman for a style of war-fighting embodied in the Marine Corps campaigns against the Japanese. MacArthur's public pronouncements recognized the ultimate dynamic underlying the myths and images of the marines' Pacific War. "There is no substitute for victory," he wrote, and "War's very object is victory."[33] The final divorce of the old images from the process of creating new battlefield realities can be dated from the de facto demise by April 1951 of total war fought to unconditional victory. Operations, at least for the first months of the war, resembled those of the Second World War refought, or, as one historian of the Marine Corps colorfully writes, "For the Marine Corps the last five months of 1950 brought combat in Korea that for sheer drama, valor, and hardship matched the amphibious assaults of World War II – except, fortunately, in casualties." And like those who attempted to reconcile the meanings ascribed to Guadalcanal with events in Korea, the former marine adds, "Even stripped of Corps legend and media myth-making, the Korean campaigns of the 1st Marine Division in 1950 retain an epic quality."[34] The whole notion, however, of a series of Wana Draw–type battles in which tremendous carnage would be wrought to attain the complete overthrow of the enemy became subverted once that ultimate goal was changed. Because it was "limited," the Korean War carried the imaginary constructions of the past in new directions.

When war broke out on 25 June 1950, it appeared to be a smaller scale repetition of 1941, to be handled according to the lessons learned from that experience. The First Marine Division again began the war greatly understrength; on 30 June 1950, the aggregate strength of the division was only 7,789, a little more than one-third of its wartime complement.[35] Several commands, including the 7th Marines, had been disbanded, and other subordinate units were only weak cadres; the existing infantry battalions, for instance,

33 The "no substitute" statement was read aloud on the floor of the House of Representatives at the height of the Truman–MacArthur controversy, and the "War's object" was part of his address to the joint session of Congress after his relief (James, *The Years of MacArthur*, 3:590, 615).
34 Millett, *Semper Fidelis*, 481, 482.
35 Commander in Chief, U.S. Pacific Fleet, Interim Evaluation Report no. 1, 25 June–15 November 1950, vol. 5, Combat Operations Sections, Amphibious and Ground, pt. F, p. 868, RG 127/77-0048/Box 1 (hereafter cited as IER 1).

had only two undersized rifle companies each. By stripping much of the division as well as posts and stations throughout the country, the First Provisional Marine Brigade, numbering 6,600 men, was hastily assembled around the 5th Marines in less than two weeks. Sailing on 12 July for Pusan, the brigade numbered many Pacific War veterans among its officers and NCOs, and although it still suffered from shortcomings in equipment, training, and organization, the same kind of technocratic functionalism seen on Okinawa provided the glue to hold the unit together through the fighting ahead.

Having further weakened the First Division to assemble men for the First Brigade, the Marine Corps relied more heavily than in 1940 on the mobilization of the Reserves to bring units up to full strength. The initial activation notices went out on 20 and 23 July; by 4 August, all 33,527 members of the Organized Ground Reserve had their units called to active duty. Some men, especially those who were married or in college, resented the call-up; others wanted more time to settle their personal affairs; many were inadequately trained or out of condition for active duty; and a variety of other complaints also had to be resolved.[36] Despite the difficulties, reservists filled out cadres throughout the Marine Corps. Nearly 90 percent of the Organized Ground Reserve answered the call-up; half were judged combat-ready, and 2,891 assigned directly to the First Division. By the time the 7th Marine Regiment had formed in late August, 1,809 of its 3,836 men were reservists. Those who were not deemed combat-ready received refresher training and provided an important source of replacements later in the fall and winter.[37] The Volunteer Reserve of men not belonging to specific units provided an additional pool numbering almost 88,000 men; 99 percent of the officers and three-quarters of the enlisted men were veterans of the Second World War. Given the inability of reservists to train with their regular counterparts before going into combat, as had also been the case in 1940, the presence of these veterans in the training and support establishments proved crucial. By December 1950, 43,940 of these men had come on active duty.[38]

The experience of Buster W. Miller's reserve company from Charlottesville, Virginia, was typical of many during this period. Over a three-year period, the company had only a single one-day

36 Pacific Fleet Evaluation Group, Report, dated 7 November 1950, pt. 10, Personnel, pp. 2–5, RG 127/78-0049/Box 3/file 23.
37 *Marine Corps Reserve*, 165–68.
38 United States Marine Corps, *Mobilization of the Marine Corps Reserve in the Korean Conflict, 1950–1951* (Washington: Historical Branch, G-3, HQMC, 1951), 3:7–10.

field exercise; most training time was devoted to drill and rudimentary skills. Attendance tended to be quite low and discipline lax. Few men in the company, especially the younger ones, realized how serious was the call to active duty: "most of them felt that this was going to be a big picnic." Call-up was announced on 20 July, and although morale was generally good and enthusiasm high, there were several men who resented this untimely interruption in their lives and tried to back out of their commitment. When the company arrived at Camp Lejeune on 1 August, it was mustered into active service and then disbanded and its personnel distributed among the regulars of 2/6. Many men were shocked to be made riflemen even though they had not been specifically trained for that specialty. The whole battalion then entrained for the West Coast, arriving at Camp Pendleton on 18 August. Redesignated the 2d Battalion, 7th Marines, the men from Charlottesville embarked for the voyage to Korea, by way of Japan, on 28 August. Miller attempted to assign regular marines to key positions, especially with supporting weapons. Of his officers, Miller's company had six reservists and one regular; four of the reservists had combat experience, and all had enlisted time prior to commissioning. It was this thin leavening of experience from the Pacific War among the officers and many NCOs that allowed these newly reconstituted units to function.[39]

Several top leaders in the Marine Corps who expressed concern about the mobilization learned that purely operational requirements were secondary to sustaining the public image. Stationed at Camp Lejeune, the Second Marine Division began the war as attenuated as the First, but it was quickly reduced to nonoperational status as its trained men were siphoned off for deployment to Korea. The activation of the 7th Marines was accomplished largely through redesignation of the 6th Marines, brought up to strength with reservists; the 6th Marines were then reconstituted from cadre personnel, untrained reservists, and new recruits.[40] The director of Plans and Policies bluntly expressed his concerns in a memorandum to the commandant. The gross imbalance in the distribution of regulars and reservists between the two divisions was "extremely undesirable" since "great losses to the 1st Marine Division ... will be irreplaceable for some length of time in view of the concentration in that division of practically all available, ex-

---

39 Buster W. Miller interview, 1–46, one of eighteen interviews of Korean War veterans conducted by the 1st Provisional Historical Platoon (hereafter cited as KWV). Transcripts are in O. P. Smith Papers, PPC, MCHC.
40 By the end of 1950 there were 19,985 reservists in the Second Division, 80% from the Volunteer Reserves; *Marine Corps Reserve*, 168.

AMERICAN SAMURAI

controversy a different rationale proved overriding:

> The American public is expecting excellent results from the
> employment of Marines. Our reputation in the eyes of the
> public as well as the military is at stake. Successful employment
> of Marines during this emergency period will no doubt en-
> hance our stability, whereas a poor performance, regardless
> of excuses, might mean our decline and curtailment of further
> expansion.[41]

For the second time in eight years, slogans like "First to Fight" and
a reputation of readiness once again dictated thrusting the First
Division into combat without thorough preparation.

If the frenetic activity necessary to prepare a provisional force
for immediate deployment to Korea appeared, at least superficially,
to be a reenactment of the Pacific War, complete with large numbers
from the original cast, the character of the fighting between August
and early November 1950 lent further credence to such an illusion.
Landing at Pusan on 3 August, the First Marine Brigade began the
first of a monthlong series of ferocious small-unit actions only four
days later (see Map 8). During the period spent inside the Pusan
perimeter, the marines functioned as a "fire-brigade" "against a
numerically superior enemy," "a vicious, well-trained enemy."[42]
The brigade went into battle in the most seriously threatened sectors of the perimeter and inflicted, with Marine air support, an
estimated 10,000 casualties on the North Koreans at a cost of only
903 men killed, wounded, or missing.[43] Marines almost universally

41 Director, Division of Plans and Policies, Memorandum to CMC, dated 10 August
1950, RG 127/78-0049/Box 3/file 29.
42 Andrew Geer, *The New Breed* (New York: Harper, 1952), 10–11; T. R. Fehrenbach, *This Kind of War* (New York: Macmillan, 1963), 189–97. See also United
States Army, Office of Military History, *United States Army in the Korean War*, vol.
2, *South to the Naktong, North to the Yalu*, by Roy E. Appleman (Washington:
Historical Division, Department of the Army, 1961). The "fire-brigade" analogy
is identical to that used by the elite armored units of the *Waffen-SS* on the
Eastern Front, which was interwoven with their *Kämpfer* self-image; Bernd Weg-
ner, " 'My Honour Is Loyalty': The SS as a Military Factor in Hitler's Germany,"
in Wilhelm Deist, ed., *The German Military in the Age of Total War* (Dover, N.H.:
Berg, 1985), 220–39.
43 United States Marine Corps, *U.S. Marine Corps Operations in Korea, 1950–1953*
(hereafter Official History, Korea), vol. 1, *The Pusan Perimeter*, by Lynn Montross
and Nicholas A. Canzona (Washington: Historical Branch, G-3, HQMC, 1954),
239. Although the numbers seem to justify Marine methods, Fehrenbach's description of an attack on Obong-ni, or "No-Name" Ridge, on 17 August 1950
raises some questions. Company D lost 23 killed and 119 wounded out of 240
in a seven-hour period, mostly in futile charges taking the crest without being
able to hold it. The great bravery and determination do not explain why such
costly *Sturm* tactics were necessary where speed was not an overriding consid-

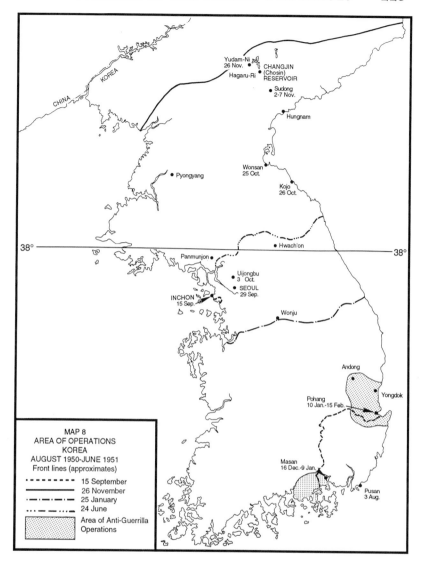

MAP 8
AREA OF OPERATIONS
KOREA
AUGUST 1950-JUNE 1951
Front lines (approximates)
- - - - - - - -   15 September
_____   26 November
·—·—·—·—·   25 January
··· — — ···_   24 June
[shaded]   Area of Anti-Guerrilla
Operations

credited their accomplishments foremost to outstanding small-unit leadership. In the words of the official report, the marines' early successes were the result of "aggressive subordinate leaders, possessing a common background of training and experience, and conditioned in the habitual exhibition of initiative and leadership." A veteran reserve officer tied leadership to the creation of an ap-

eration: there was no fleet to release or breakthrough imminent (Fehrenbach, *This Kind of War*, 192–95).

propriate psychological attitude: "The part of preparing the men mentally for combat, in my opinion, is building their confidence, and this again is done by an example of confidence, a spirit of optimism during all the training and in all the associations between these men and their unit leaders."[44] Vandegrift's lessons about Rogers' Rangers were still being passed along.

These early months confirmed in the minds of many the martial mythos of the Pacific War period. The official report maintained that "every marine was imbued with the determination and will to win." A young forward observer speaking in early 1951 sounded much like Richard Kennard seven years earlier when he emphasized that the "average rifleman" "was a volunteer, and well-trained, well-indoctrinated with Marine Corps spirit."[45] The Marines also relied upon tactics right out of the Pacific War manuals: tank–infantry teams, closely supported by artillery and aircraft, inflicted disproportionately heavy casualties on the enemy in virtually every encounter. But at least one officer sounded a note of caution about placing unquestioning reliance on the experienced Pacific War veterans:

> The most dangerous person in the Marine Corps today is the veteran who has had an awful lot of combat experience and comes back and says that isn't the way it's done. We didn't use bazookas at Guadalcanal, therefore we don't have to use bazookas in this operation. In other words, he likes to contradict the book.[46]

By maintaining the flexibility to adapt doctrine to the unique conditions of the Korean peninsula and by demonstrating highly aggressive leadership, the marines seemed to reach peak form in the early autumn of 1950 that had required four years of bloody experience in the Pacific War.

The capstone of the early part of the Korean War was the dramatic amphibious assault at Inchon, which led to the capture of Seoul and the rout of the North Korean People's Army (NKPA). MacArthur had been intent on the Inchon landings since July, and, indeed, his request to the Joint Chiefs of Staff for the First Marine Division had been for the purpose of forming the core of this

---

44 IER 1:Annex Z, Report of Activities, 25 June–to Inchon, Z:18–19; James F. McInteer, Jr., interview, 10–11, KWV; and William F. Goggin interview, 50, KWV.
45 IER 1:Annex Z, Report of Activities, 25 June–to Inchon, Z:18–19; Orlo C. Paciulli interview, 12, KWV. It is a truism that Paciulli defines "average" according to what he thinks it should be, not necessarily by objective observation.
46 Richard H. Sengewald interview, 56, KWV.

amphibious force. Only the precarious situation inside the Pusan perimeter had forced MacArthur to immediately commit the First Brigade in August. Major General O. P. Smith, commanding the division, and Lieutenant General Lemuel C. Shepherd, Jr., commanding general, Fleet Marine Force, Pacific, along with their naval counterparts, pointed out the immense risks involved. The port of Inchon might have served as a staff school example of what to avoid in selecting the objective of an amphibious assault. Relying on the force of his personality to sweep aside all objections, MacArthur transposed hyperbolic images of the Pacific War to the cold war to strengthen his case: "The prestige of the Western world hangs in the balance. Oriental millions are watching the outcome. It is plainly apparent that here in Asia is where the Communist conspirators have elected to make their play for global conquest." Winning the final approval of the Joint Chiefs on 8 September, MacArthur tried to assuage the misgivings of the Navy and Marine Corps commanders with visions of revisiting the glorious successes that they had witnessed a few years earlier.[47]

Vindicating MacArthur's most optimistic predictions, the landings at Inchon on 15 September 1950 and the subsequent exploitation that led to the capture of Seoul by 29 September seemed indeed to recapture the glory of the Pacific War. Not unlike the "easy lessons" learned in the early stages of Guadalcanal, the Inchon landings encountered only disorganized or isolated resistance, and the 7th Marines in particular, with the highest concentration of reservists among the three infantry regiments, benefited from the light combat between Inchon and Seoul. The commanding officer, Homer L. Litzenberg, even went so far as to suggest that the NKPA were useful primarily for honing combat techniques for future use against a tougher enemy: "Korea offers a fine training ground for officers and noncommissioned officers.... Korea, to my mind, is a training ground that we should use as fully as possible in the same way that the Germans and Russians used the Spanish Civil War for a training ground."[48] The difficulties encountered were largely ignored or dismissed as a part of the breaking-in process. Buster Miller's 3d platoon, all reservists, "had the misfortune to walk into

47 The problems posed by the Inchon operation and the clash of personalities are well covered elsewhere, in particular see Official History, Korea, vol. 2, The Inchon– Seoul Operation, by Lynn Montross and Nicholas A. Canzona (1955), 39–40; James, The Years of MacArthur, 3:464–74 (quoted portion, 470); and Robert D. Heinl, Jr., Victory at High Tide (Philadelphia: Lippincott, 1968), 18–38.
48 Homer L. Litzenberg interview, 19, KWV; on easy introduction to combat, ibid., 11–12; Sengewald interview, 15–16. The 7th Marines landed at Inchon on 21 September and was initially assigned a supporting role for the 1st Marines and 5th Marines driving on Seoul.

an ambush the first day in combat and at Seoul two or three days later." The half who survived these first three days of combat presumably became useful warriors.[49]

Whatever the technical problems and lessons, the division emerged from its first operation of the war to widespread acclaim. Public relations remained one of the corps's greatest strengths, and in contrast to what they felt in MacArthur's Southwest Pacific Area, the marines unquestionably received their full share of the credit for Inchon. As Michael C. Capraro, the division public information officer, pointed out, "In the initial phases of the Korean war, the 1st Marine Division was literally showered with the attention of all of the civilian correspondents in the area." With as many as twenty-three civilian correspondents following the division during this period, Capraro was understating the case when he noted that the division received "more than the usual amount of publicity commensurate with its size."[50] Throughout the first week of the campaign the marines achieved all of their objectives before the eyes of the proud MacArthur and a large, sometimes cumbrous audience of staff officers and correspondents who rhapsodized their exploits.[51]

Even as the marines basked in the glory of their victory, however, they also experienced difficulties that never surfaced in the glowing dispatches. One of the most serious involved friction between Smith and his immediate Army superior, Major General Edward M. Almond, the commander of X Corps. Smith complained of Almond's interference in the conduct of the battle, issuing orders directly to regimental and even battalion commanders without going through division headquarters. A more serious example of this friction arose on the evening of 25 September, when Almond ordered a night attack launched with little preparation after a day of hard fighting in the streets of Seoul. Almond wanted to capture the remainder of the city on that day so MacArthur could announce the capture

49 Miller interview, 48. Miller came down with malaria while in Japan and never made it to the war zone with the company he built, but he obviously kept track of its actions.

50 Michael C. Capraro interview, 3, KWV. With extensive service as an infantry company commander in the Pacific War and two years with the San Francisco *Chronicle*, Capraro made an unusually good choice for division public information officer; he had personal contacts in the press corps, a sympathetic understanding of their needs, and the institutional knowledge to make relations as smooth as ever seen in coverage of active combat operations.

51 During a complex crossing of the Han River, the command post of Colonel Murray was "overrun by correspondents and kibitzers" to the point that operational efficiency was impaired; but the senior Army generals seemed unconcerned about the effects of their "grandstanding" (O. P. Smith Papers, log entry, 19 September 1950, 37).

of the South Korean capital three months to the day after the invasion by the North. The city was declared secure that day, but three more days of bloody fighting followed. More to the point, the men of the 1st Marines were hit by a heavy counterattack before their night attack could begin, suffered heavy casualties, and yet received only impatient signals from X Corps about their lack of progress. "This episode," Smith laconically noted, "did not tend to restore my confidence in the judgment of the Corps Commander."[52]

With the collapse of the NKPA in early October and the opening of the pursuit phase of the UN campaign, the First Marine Division was already showing signs of wear. Three weeks of heavy fighting in Seoul and as far north as Uijongbu had reduced a few Marine rifle companies to platoon strength. Some men emerged from combat with a sense of elation in spite of such casualties, but others expressed growing concern. A company executive officer commented on the feeling of vulnerability felt among marines who saw no fresh replacements after six weeks of operations:

When he sees his organization gradually reduced in number, and he continues to make assault after assault, he is bound to begin to feel after a while that unless there are some replacements fed in to build his unit up to normal strength, his chances of getting hit are becoming progressively greater. When a man begins to feel that way, his morale and his will to close with the enemy and drive him out become progressively lower.[53]

The generally high spirits in the division after Inchon were the product of a successful campaign, but the defeated enemy had been badly disorganized and off-balance. In the aftermath of the operation, an "end-of-war atmosphere" developed at higher headquarters, which, when combined with a general letdown and overconfidence, was not conducive to peak military efficiency and sound planning. A poorly conceived and badly executed movement of X Corps to the east coast deposited the division at the port of Wonsan on 25 October, from where it deployed to hunt down large

52 Ibid., 45–46; Smith's subordinates refused to follow Almond's orders without approval from division (Smith interview, 203). See also Special Action Report, night of 25–26 September 1950, 3/1, dated 27 September 1950, RG 127/61A-2265/Box 80.
53 McInteer interview, 91. The incrementalism of the losses over an extended period of time seems to be more debilitating here than the case of catastrophic casualties suffered by the 1st Marines on Peleliu in a single week. The 1st Replacement Draft of 35 officers and 1,140 enlisted men reached the division "on or about" 7 November (Report of Pacific Fleet Evaluation Group, p. 4, RG 127/78-0049/Box 3).

bands of guerrillas and retreating NKPA troops returning north from positions around the Pusan perimeter. They also made preparations to pursue the retreating Koreans all the way up to the Yalu River, if required. They were now about to experience a harsher reality imposed by the nature of the country and different political and grand strategic designs.[54]

Given the success of the Inchon landings, it is interesting that present-day Marine Corps history and customs classes for officer candidates and recruits focus less attention on what MacArthur immodestly called a masterpiece of amphibious warfare and instead concentrate on the drama of the victory-in-defeat of the First Division at Chosin reservoir.[55] Unlike the saga of Wake Island, the Chosin retreat would not be overshadowed subsequently by strings of glowing American victories; this winter debacle was the highwater mark of the war for the Marine Corps. On 2 November, the 7th Marines came into contact with Chinese Communist Forces (CCF) units at Sudong and in a fierce, six-day fight destroyed the bulk of the 124th CCF Division. The strength and determination of this large, organized unit belied the hope expressed by Almond and others that growing reports of Chinese troops represented only piecemeal replacements of volunteers from across the border.[56] A division intelligence report dated a few days before the Sudong battle reflected confusion about CCF intentions and capabilities:

[U]ntil more definite information is obtained, it must be presumed that the CCF has not yet decided on full scale intervention. The advantage to be gained by all out intervention, at a time when the NK forces are on the verge of complete collapse, is not readily apparent. In view of the above, it is believed that the CCF units being presently engaged are only token forces not likely to prove a serious obstacle, at the present time, to our continued advance.[57]

54 On the administrative movement and the difficulties encountered see O. P. Smith, Aide-mémoire – Korea 1950–51, 161–67, Smith Papers, PPC, MCHC; the atmosphere at headquarters is recorded on p. 177. MacArthur had expressed wild optimism even before the Inchon landings, assuring Smith that everyone would be "home by Christmas" after Inchon; log entry for 22 August 1950, 6.
55 In yet another example of the lack of cultural awareness that figures so prominently in American military history, "Chosin" is the Japanese name, adopted because most U.S. maps were drawn from Japanese. The proper Korean name, Changjin, appears occasionally in the records (e.g., IER 2:1196), but since Chosin is the name most familiar from common usage, I use it here.
56 IER 2:1183.
57 First Marine Division, Period Intelligence Report, no. 6, dated 30 October 1950, RG 127/61A-2265/Box 39 (hereafter cited as PIR).

The staff of X Corps dismissed any pessimistic reports and ordered the marines to continue their advance. The division pushed northward, along a single, treacherous mountain road, away from their base of supply, with a growing sense of foreboding.[58]

By any military rationale, the overextension of the division defies logical explanation. Smith did a good job of keeping units within supporting distance of each other wherever possible and stockpiling supplies along the road back to the coast, but the unshakably sanguine faith and ignorance displayed by X Corps headquarters matched the optimism of MacArthur himself. The Eighth Army was 70 miles by air west of the First Division, but Smith was instructed to ignore that open flank and continue north; by 7 November, the northern- and southernmost battalions were more than 170 miles distant.[59] In a letter to the commandant, Smith expressed some of his ongoing concerns about Almond's leadership:

> I have little confidence in the tactical judgment of the Corps or in the realism of their planning. My confidence has not yet been restored. Planning is done on a 1:1,000,000 map. We execute on a 1:50,000 map. There is a continued splitting up of units and assignment of missions to small units which puts them out on a limb.[60]

On the Marine Corps birthday, 10 November, temperatures plunged to as low as $-10°$ to $-20°$ F on the high plateau leading to the reservoir. The commandant's birthday message echoed the words of the *Wehrmacht* high command nine years earlier as they attempted to press on to final victory before Moscow:

> In keeping with our long established and cherished traditions, all Marines make the solemn pledge that we through diligent self-application and devotion to duty will keep ourselves fit for the trying days that lie ahead. We must be ready to take our part in the relentless offensive which will terminate in final victory. Until that time I urge an all out effort. Train hard and fight with determination.[61]

The Chinese counteroffensive struck in force on the night of 27 November, attempting to isolate and overrun elements of the division scattered along forty-five miles of mountain road.

58 Almond tried to reassure Smith with the wishful thinking that has persisted to this day in some circles that the CCF forces were simply volunteers and that no significant Chinese intervention was likely; Smith Papers, 206, 223.
59 Ibid., 215, 223. The imagery that again crops up elsewhere is of an isolated expedition into "Indian country."
60 Letter to CMC dated 15 November 1950, Smith Papers, 233.
61 ALMAR 26, in Smith Papers, 222.

Like Guadalcanal, enough has been written on the legend of "frozen Chosin" that fact and fantasy have tended to merge.[62] The division suffered significant casualties and remained seriously over-extended after the first onslaught. Only on 30 November did the division receive permission to withdraw, which began, in O. P. Smith's words, not a retreat, but "an attack in a different direction." Like many examples of Germans extricating units cut off by Soviet forces on the Eastern Front in the winters of 1943 and 1944, the marines, over a ten-day period, inflicted enormous casualties on the enemy in pushing their way past exposed and isolated enemy blocking forces to reach the American perimeter outside the port of Hungnam, from where they were evacuated by sea.[63] The official Marine historians eulogize the campaign, quoting the tributes by Rear Admiral Doyle and O. P. Smith; they also invoke the parallel to the *Anabasis* and the Greek mercenaries who "cut their way to safety through Asiatic hordes." In a salute to the "individual and small-unit heroics" that matches Pat Frank's panegyric novel *Hold Back the Night*, another historian writes that the marines' exploits "matched Greek and Nordic legends – except that they really happened."[64] Nevertheless, although the Chosin retreat was a tactical victory, lauded in the American press, it came amidst a strategic catastrophe at the hands of the "Communist hordes."

Even before the Chosin debacle, the marines resurrected images of the Other that did not simply resemble those from the Pacific War but used them explicitly as benchmarks. An early report from the 5th Marines described the NKPA troops around Pusan as in-variably launching assaults at night "utilizing a Banzai type attack employed so widely by the Japanese Imperial Army in World War II."[65] The "stubborn defense of strong positions" utilizing log and

62 Aside from the official histories, campaign monographs include Roy E. Apple-man, *East of Chosin* (College Station: Texas A&M University Press, 1987); Anthony J. Campigno, *A Marine Division in Nightmare Alley* (New York: Comet Press, 1958); Eric Hammel, *Chosin* (New York: Vanguard, 1981); Robert Leckie, *The March to Glory* (New York: World, 1960); and Jim Wilson, *Retreat Hell!* (New York: William Morrow, 1988). It also inspired the novel by Pat Frank *Hold Back the Night* (New York: J. B. Lippincott, 1951).
63 Details of events are covered well in the Official History, Korea, vol. 3, *The Chosin Reservoir Campaign*, by Lynn Montross and Nicholas A. Canzona (1957). The division suffered far more cold-weather injuries than battle casualties during the operation: between 26 October and 15 December there were 4,418 battle casualties and 7,313 nonbattle casualties (one-third of whom returned to duty during battle). Estimates of CCF losses include 22,500 from ground action and 15,000 from air attacks (351). The Chinese suffered excessive losses also from their inability to provide basic logistical support; one army alone suffered over 10,000 nonbattle casualties, mostly frostbite (354).
64 Ibid., 357; Millett, *Semper Fidelis*, 493.
65 5th Marines, Report of Combat Lessons to CG, 1st Provisional Marine Brigade (Reinf), dated 1 September 1950, RG 127/61A-2265/Box 82.

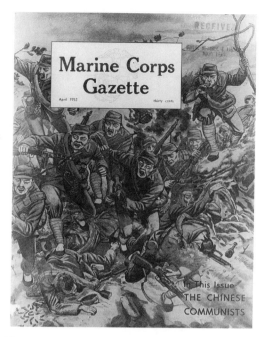

Even before this 1952 cover, the Pacific War imagery had been transferred easily from the Japanese to the Chinese Communist Forces. *(USMC, National Archives)*

earth bunkers "was similar to the tenacious tactics of the Japanese in World War II."[66] Another report claimed the Chinese forces "demonstrated little of a noteworthy nature," but the terms used to describe their characteristics are remarkably familiar:

> They are fair fighters, generally stolid and oblivious to danger, adroit at camouflage and excellent in night movement. They are able to operate on a very modest supply line but their offensive momentum and defensive staying power are adversely affected by logistical weakness. They do not match the Japanese in any major sense. It was frequently remarked that seizure of the high ground overlooking Hoensong, for example, would have been infinitely more difficult had the defenders been Japanese.[67]

Like the Japanese troops encountered by the marines in the Pacific War, the CCF units were seen as technologically backward com-

66 U.S. Pacific Fleet Operations, Third Evaluation Report, Chapter 15, p. 25, RG 127/77-0048/Box 4.
67 IER 2:Appendix 7, Report of Inspection Trip by CG FMFPac and Staff, 25 February–8 March 1951, 1249–50.

232   AMERICAN SAMURAI

pared to American forces, and whereas the suicidal resolve of the
Japanese provoked contempt and fear among marines on Guadalcanal, the absence of similar resolve on the part of the Chinese
was seen almost as a weakness. One officer stated that in his opinion
Chinese attacks were not as effective and that "the Japanese was
much more skilled, even in his fanatical banzai charges with his
coordination of fire and his definite objective." The Chinese, in
contrast, seemed better at organizing defensive positions.[68] Survivors of a company overrun in a night attack near Kojo on 27
October 1950 reported North Korean troops using American
phrases to trick them into giving away their positions, and they
even shouted "Banzai" as they overran the Marine positions.[69]
Whatever they may have shared in outward appearance and behavior or tactical tricks, the menace posed by the Asian enemies
encountered in Korea was viewed in a very different light from
that of the Japanese in the Pacific War.

Although racist assumptions about the Japanese were easily
transferred to the Koreans and Chinese, the ideological threat
against which marines defined their role in the Korean War was
quite distinct. From an American perspective, Japan's military oli-
garchy had driven the nation to imitate the Western countries and
flaunt its claims to equality among modern, industrialized nations.
In contrast, the Democratic Republic of Korea and the People's
Republic of China were portrayed as a primal threat that bore as
much in common with the German vision of the Eastern Front as
with the American Pacific War imagery. The comparatively larger
masses of troops actually seen in the open gave combat operations
much more the appearance of battling the "Yellow hordes" than
had been the case against the Japanese. In addition, the Red Scare
of communism was explicitly linked with the traditional Yellow Peril
imagery, producing a sense of desperation that was heightened by
fighting on the Asian mainland, especially after PRC intervention. These twin elements mirrored the fears and potency behind
Nazi ideological radicalization of the "Jewish/Bolshevik" menace.[70]
One of the more notable places where this ideological extremism

68 Martin J. Sexton interview, 108, KWV.
69 IER 1:Annex DD, 13. Given the large numbers of Koreans who served with the
    Japanese in the Pacific War, this is a plausible account, and reports of "banzai
    attacks" crop up elsewhere, such as 1st Marines, Type B Report, Historical Diary,
    dated 10 October 1950, p. 7; RG 127/61A-2265/Box 80. However well substan-
    tiated such reports were, many marines clearly were thinking in terms of the
    Pacific War experiences.
70 It is important to note how closely the United States adopted the Nazi imagery
    of the Asian/Bolshevik threat in support of the cold war (Keen, *Faces of the
    Enemy*, 19–24).

surfaced was at the truce talks over the issue of repatriation of prisoners. Charges and countercharges of "brainwashing," mistreatment, and misrepresentation rendered prisoners on both sides into pawns and transformed the POW camps into a tertiary military front. As the ideological war raged in the prisoner compounds, American training focused on better preparing men to resist or evade capture, or, if captured, to continue the struggle by other means.[71] Along with traditional rumors and documented evidence of atrocities on both sides, this ideological component gave the fear of surrender a different twist from the Pacific War.[72]

In operational terms, comparisons of the Korean and Pacific wars yield "lessons" of very limited value. Over roughly forty months, the First Division fought in four Pacific campaigns, making one opposed amphibious assault and spending approximately twelve months total in combat. The objectives had all been islands, and except for Okinawa, the division had never fought with more than one other full division. In contrast, the marines in Korea found themselves fighting like Army troops for almost thirty-six months, with never more than a month out of the line and without the logistical assets for extended ground operations. No matter how hard MacArthur pressed the UN air forces, the Korean peninsula could not be effectively isolated from the rest of the Asian mainland

71 A "what-went-wrong" literature sprang up in the wake of the Panmunjom discussions on POWs that contributed to the stridency and fear of the immediate post-McCarthy era; the most notable are the point–counterpoint books Eugene Kinkaid, *In Every War but One* (New York: W. W. Norton, 1959), and Albert D. Biderman, *March to Calumny* (New York: Macmillan, 1963). The issue appears in the official Army history as well: vol. 3, *Truce Tent and Fighting Front*, by Walter G. Hermes (1966). Marine prisoners earned praise for withstanding the difficulties of captivity better than the other American servicemen; for full details see United States Marine Corps, "The Problems of U.S. Marine Corps Prisoners of War in Korea" (Washington: Marine Corps Historical Division, HQMC, 1988, Typed manuscript). See also the novel by Duane Thorin, *A Ride to Panmunjom* (Chicago: Henry Regnery, 1956).
72 As with the Pacific War, the Korean War raises questions about American mistreatment of prisoners. In the First Division the gravest concern surrounds the slaughter of 200 Chinese prisoners "gunned down in a mass escape attempt" during the evacuation from Chosin reservoir. "[T]he marines didn't have any second thoughts about what to do – they started shooting" (Smith interview, 277). In more general terms, what constituted a guerrilla in the frequent sweeps conducted south of the front lines was often subjected to broad interpretation. On the Chinese side, there were several reports of generally humane treatment, especially by captors in the frontline units; see Report from 1st Marines to G-2, n.d.; and Enclosure (1) to PIR no. 44, "Interrogation of CCF-Held Marine." On the other hand, one man, heading a graves registration team, mentioned mutilation of Marine corpses, whether prisoners or found in the field is unclear; Robert B. Gault interview, 47, KWV. The North Koreans were often regarded as much more vicious, although less so against Americans than against South Koreans; see Special Action Report, 441st CIC Team, dated 1 November 1950, RG 127/61A-2265/Box 39; and PIR no. 23, dated 16 November 1950, 3.

– with operational implications the marines had never had to confront in the Pacific campaigns. The war was confined to a limited area in which amphibious warfare was necessarily circumscribed, and soon after Inchon, Marine leaders expressed concern that their amphibious warfare expertise was quickly eroding. In all, the Korean War was a costlier, more frustrating experience for the division than the Pacific War.[73]

Another major difference between the Pacific and Korean wars was the conduct of operations in and around heavy concentrations of civilians. In many respects, Korean civilians were virtually invisible, or at least not fully human, in the eyes of Americans. On Okinawa, the large civilian population was exclusively "enemy"; and so, other than the usual strictures against random or indiscriminate violence, the marines felt themselves under no special legal or moral obligation to protect them. In Korea, however, the marines were supposed to be safeguarding their Korean allies – from Korean enemies. They remained, however, unprepared to deal with huge numbers of civilians and the problems associated with the conduct of operations around large population centers. Only one week before the Inchon landings the division legal officer was given the additional duty of civil affairs officer. Assurances from higher headquarters that civil affairs would be handled by trained teams accompanying the division proved wrong, and so these operations were handled on an ad hoc small-unit level, with some disastrous results.[74]

The most common observations in Marine reports were on the disruptive influence of civilian refugees on operations. Many described civilians as victims caught in the middle. The enemy was frequently accused of deliberately driving civilians forward into American positions and either infiltrating soldiers with civilian robes over their uniforms or following behind, using the civilians as living shields. Army troops "hesitated to slaughter the helpless civilians while the enemy took advantage of the tragic situation."[75]

73 The First Division suffered roughly 20,500 battle casualties in the Pacific War; with much more time spent in the lines, losses in Korea were over 27,000. On equipment shortages, especially trucks, see IER 1:Part F, 870–71. On erosion of amphibious abilities once the stalemate had been settled in 1951, the Third Evaluation Report, pt. 1:12, minced no words: "Prolonged employment of Fleet Marine ground units in their collateral functions of supporting and supplementing the Army has resulted in serious deterioration of the Marines' skills in the air–ground amphibious attack."
74 IER 1:817.
75 Secretary of Defense, Report from the Secretary of Defense to the President of the United States on Operations in Korea during the Period 25 June 1950 to 8 July 1951, n.d., III:32, copy in RG 127/77-0048/Box 5. Similar problems arose with air interdiction efforts as NKPA units and refugees intermixed.

The First Marine Brigade reported on the problems posed by refugees during operations inside the Pusan perimeter:

The Communists will round up thousands of refugees and drive them headlong into a defended position. Among the refugees is a ration of as many as one to five Communist soldiers, with disassembled arms and ammunition in the usual refugee bundle. At times the mere overwhelming number of people will force a commander to abandon his position. If he doesn't abandon his position, the Communist troops will assemble in his rear, create a road block, and man positions from which this road block can be covered by fire.[76]

Marines falling back on 9 December at Koto-ri were so concerned about being overwhelmed by an estimated 3,500 refugees that they opened fire on them to drive them off. Even so, the next day marines abandoned seven tanks when overrun by CCF troops dressed as civilians and intermingled with the Koreans.[77] One marine recorded how rumors of enemy troops in civilian clothes could be exaggerated and lead to potential tragedy. When reports filtered back that enemy soldiers in civilian clothes were pouring gasoline on rooftops in Seoul to spread fire, marines wanted to kill these men. After capturing a few of them, however, they quickly discovered that these men were indeed civilians who were pouring water on the roofs in an effort to protect their own homes.[78]

Compounding difficult relations between Americans and Korean civilians was the widespread guerrilla activity. Several times during its first year in Korea the First Marine Division found itself conducting sweeps while out of the line.[79] The hard-bitten Homer L. Litzenberg welcomed the opportunity to acclimate new replacements with such live-fire training around Pohang after the Chosin campaign, but where the enemy were indistinguishable from the

---

76 Headquarters Marine Corps, "Information concerning Tactics and Techniques used by North Korean Forces Furnished by the 1st Provisional Marine Brigade," dated 29 September 1950, p. 1, RG 127/78-0049/Box 3.

77 1st Marines, Historical Diary, 16–17.

78 McInteer interview, 82–83. The use of civilian clothes had been seen on Okinawa, and the marines were not averse to taking advantage in an emergency. In the Seoul fighting a Marine corporal received the Bronze Star after escaping capture dressed in Korean robes; Lynn Montross, "The Capture of Seoul: Battle of the Barricades," *Marine Corps Gazette* 35 (August 1951): 26–37; several *Gazette* Korean War reprints are collected in *Our First Year in Korea* (Washington: Historical Branch).

79 See, e.g., Lynn Montross, "The Pohang Guerrilla Hunt: 1600 Square Miles of Trouble," *Marine Corps Gazette* 36 (January 1952): 18–27. Because of the difficulties of identification, this sort of "hunt" carried very different connotations from the use of the term on Guadalcanal.

BEST DAMN SOOVENIER IN KOREA !

Cartoon humor reflects some long-standing marine attitudes toward Asians and women whose imagery has disturbing implications for marine behavior toward Asians and women back in American society. *(USMC, National Archives)*

common peasants the UN forces were defending, misidentification often carried fatal results for innocent people.[80] The marines became occupiers, and their relations with the people they were protecting were often impersonal, exploitative, and destructive.

Images of the Self drew even more heavily upon contrasting images of the Army than had been the case in 1944. The abysmal relations between the Marine Corps and Almond were an incessant source of friction until General Ridgway finally ensured the marines would not be placed in X Corps after early 1951.[81] There were also the usual stories about Army incompetence and cowardice in the early months inside the Pusan perimeter, when the First Provisional Marine Brigade helped save this last enclave, and again in the face of the CCF counteroffensive in November. In particular, many stories spread of soldiers' cowardice or weakness during the retreat from Chosin reservoir. One sergeant offered his opinion that had

80 Operations around Pohang in October 1950 and Masan in early 1951 were the most important for antiguerrilla duties (Litzenberg interview, 76–77, KWV).
81 In Smith's version, he told Ridgway, " 'After all, there has been a loss of confidence in this Division and it goes down to the Pfc's.' And he said, 'Well, that's a question of leadership.' I said, 'General, these boys read *Newsweek* and other periodicals; that's where they get their impressions.' He didn't put us back in the X Corps again" (Smith interview, 204).

"the Army stayed on their flank, like they were supposed to, a lot of good Marine officers, . . . a lot of good Marines, would have been alive today." Smith later complained that "those Army people – they had no spirit." The marines would give them weapons and they would throw them away; they would not help put up warming tents and would fake injuries to get scarce space on evacuation flights out of the encirclement.[82]

A final element in changing self-images within the Marine Corps relates to a major change in all the American services that accompanied desegregation. The Marine Corps had been among the more backward and reluctant about using blacks in the Second World War, even in segregated units. When the Korean War started there were only 1,075 blacks in the corps, 427 assigned as stewards.[83] In Korea, even those white officers who praised the change gave indications of ongoing problems. Smith's racism appeared in his comments about Army divisions serving in the Eighth Army at the time of the CCF counteroffensive: the Third Division was "a bunch of tramps. They had one regiment of Puerto Ricans, they had black battalions in each of the other regiments – oh, it was a mess! . . . [the Third Division commander] said he wasn't worried about casualties among his Negroes; he said they never stayed around long enough to get wounded." Within his own division, Smith denied any racial troubles: "if Negroes are with good people they'll be good Negroes. It's the example."[84] Under the exigencies of combat, integration was made to work, and by the time of the armistice there were 15,000 blacks in the Marines, or about 6 percent, roughly six times the proportion in 1950. Moreover, blacks were being assigned to all specialties. But out of the lines and back in the United States many problems remained, and this internal turmoil contributed to the general institutional sense of slipping anchor as compared to the Pacific War experience.[85]

Events in early 1951 quickly overtook the First Marine Division

82 Gault interview, 32; Smith interview, 227–28. S. L. A. Marshall chronicles the difficulties of the Second Infantry Division in the face of the CCF counteroffensive in *The River and the Gauntlet* (1953; reprint, New York: William Morrow, 1964).
83 Bernard Nalty, *Strength for the Fight* (New York: Free Press, 1986), 262.
84 Smith interview, 293–94.
85 Nalty, *Strength for the Fight*, 255–69. North Korean and Chinese propagandists distributed well-written leaflets that tried to exploit black resentment surrounding desegregation, quoting Truman's 1947 Civil Rights Committee: " 'The Marine Corps has 7,798 officers not one of whom is Negro. . . . the records show that the members of several minorities, fighting and dying for the nation in which they meet bitter prejudice, found that there was discrimination against them even as they fell in battle' " (Leaflet, "Negro Soldiers! There's a Letter for You Inside. Read It!" in Robert F. Kelly Papers, PPC, MCHC).

and any possibility of duplicating the achievements or the methods of 1945. Even after their withdrawal from Hungnam and a period of rebuilding, when the division returned to the frontline fighting in February 1951 there remained for a few months an overall sense that the ebb and flow of Communist offensive and UN counter-offensive was building toward some final showdown from which the Americans would emerge clear victors. When Operation Killer began on 21 February, the division pushed forward almost twenty miles in less than two weeks. The continuation of the general UN offensive, Operation Ripper, made similar gains until the fifth major Chinese offensive began on 22 April. By the time of Mac-Arthur's relief in April, the marines were still inflicting heavy casualties on CCF and NKPA forces, but without achieving any military decision. One year after the Inchon landings had held out the hope of a decisive victory, the war had settled into an organized and acknowledged stalemate without any chance of a military victory as measured by the Pacific War standards.[86]

As it became obvious that the division would remain in the lines indefinitely, policies and attitudes began to shift. Army troops were rotated out of the lines to take leave in Japan, but the Marines took a different approach. In somewhat wishful words one official report maintained, "As the Korean war continued to drag on and the Marines' role in it became the same as any other UN infantry division fighting the land campaign, their aggressive spirit was nourished by maintaining a fairly regular system of replacement drafts." From May through December 1951, 747 officers and 19,640 enlisted men from replacement drafts 8 through 15 joined the division, well above the 7,116 battle casualties. This allowed reservists to be returned to the United States and mustered out, and it meant that most men would have to spend no more than twelve months in Korea.[87] As would become common in Vietnam with the individual rotation system, the idea of doing your time and getting out supplanted the close unit cohesion emphasized in the First Division during the Pacific War. Among those who wrote of their experiences in the division after mid-1951, there remained expressions of great loyalty to a small group, but the group's transience was clearly acknowledged. In 1944, Sledge or Leckie or Davis

86 Chapters 4 and 5 of Official History, Korea, vol. 4, *The East-Central Front*, by Lynn Montross, Hubard D. Kuokka, and Norman W. Hicks (1961), give full details on the two operations, and 20 September 1951 is the date seen as the turning point in the shift from "warfare of movement" to "warfare of position" (200–201).
87 Casualty figures from Commander in Chief, Pacific Fleet, Interim Report, Chapter 1:31, RG 127/77-0048/Box 4. Replacement draft figures are from Third Evaluation Report, 15:26–27.

could see several Marine divisions and discern particular attributes of the First Division, however chimerical; such fine distinctions had largely disappeared in 1951.[88]

In a sense, the demise of the Pacific War images as instrumentalities came months before the stalemate and the routinization of combat with individual rotation. The "Great Debate" prompted by Chinese intervention in the waning days of 1950 combined racism, political antipathy, and ideological extremism to raise the specter that the Korean War might explode into a conflagration that would dwarf the Pacific War in scale and barbarism. As MacArthur's mood swung abruptly from euphoria to despondence he held out only two options after the Chinese initial offensive, what biographer D. Clayton James labeled the "false dilemma": complete withdrawal from the peninsula or massive escalation. This simplistic dualism, which "marked the beginning of the end of his military career," reflected the warrior ethos of total war or no war. The marines' Pacific War imagery required such an approach, and only total war could produce the necessary preconditions to sustain that imagery: the goal of unconditional surrender, the domination of a technologically grounded rationality, and an exterminationist ideology. When neither of MacArthur's extreme alternatives was selected by President Truman and the Joint Chiefs, a different set of assumptions and expectations left the Pacific myths and images unsuited to the operational conditions at the front.[89]

In the oft-quoted words of Joint Chiefs of Staffs chairman Omar Bradley, Korea was "the wrong war, at the wrong place, at the wrong time, and with the wrong enemy."[90] War had become routinized in ways that destroyed the old forms of unit cohesion, redefined a new rationale behind the application of violence, and set different standards to regulate the marines' images of themselves, the enemy, and technology. Although only a portion of those who served in the division in the Pacific had to deal with the new battlefield realities of the post-1945 world, nobody who survived the war could escape his own recollections. Veterans, their families,

88 The papers of A. Andy Andow, PPC, MCHC, convey his close sense of community with other Hispanics, but less with the First Marine Division as a whole. Likewise, Martin Russ's Korean memoir *The Last Parallel* (New York: Rinehart, 1957) reads much more like a Vietnam memoir than a Second World War memoir, with its descriptions of tedious, indecisive patrolling actions and turbulent personnel situation.

89 On the "false dilemma" and the "Great Debate" see James, *The Years of MacArthur*, 3:540–59 (quoted portion, 559); and John W. Spanier, *The Truman–MacArthur Controversy and the Korean War* (Cambridge: Harvard University Press, 1959), 134–51.

90 Cited in James, *The Years of MacArthur*, 3:633.

and the American public examined and reexamined events of the Pacific War, focusing on some to the exclusion of others, and these events were given labels and meanings like "decisive" or "tragic" or "heroic." Had there been a dramatic, visible break between the images of the Second World War and the altered circumstances of Korea, the Marines and the American public could more readily have adjusted. In words and pictures the Pacific War was relived and refought in many places and many ways, and its images have been distilled into a national history of the war. Scrapbook photos and bundles of letters have become historical artifacts whose content is measured against assumptions about the war that are more the products of postwar America than events on remote battlefields. Hollywood, best-seller lists, and pedestals serve as the last stages upon which the Pacific War images can play. In films, books, and monuments, some of them remain with us to this day.

7

REWRITING THE WAR

Although the myths and images spawned by the Pacific War ultimately proved unsuitable for molding the realities of the Korean battlefields, the ways by which veterans, the Marine Corps as an institution, and the American public have remembered them and invested them with meaning are a final measure of their importance and endurance. Removed from their original context and reduced again to abstractions, specific myths and images have been appropriated to create a historical narrative of the Pacific War that has in turn served a variety of uses in cold war American society. Individuals and groups have highlighted and embellished traditional wartime memories of heroism, sacrifice, and higher cause to serve their own specific needs. As already seen, the myths surrounding the Japanese, which had been so useful to the First Marine Division as it headed into Guadalcanal, were easily displaced onto new enemies once Japan was needed as a political and economic ally to oppose communist expansion in Asia. It is difficult not to be impressed, as John Dower writes, with "[t]he abrupt transition from a merciless racist war to an amicable postwar relationship." As their application to the rise of Red China illustrates, such images and stereotypes proved extremely malleable:

> The war hates and race hates of World War Two . . . proved very adaptable to the cold war. Traits which the Americans and English had associated with the Japanese . . . were suddenly perceived to be really more relevant to the Communists (deviousness and cunning, bestial and atrocious behavior, homogeneity and monolithic control, fanaticism divorced from any legitimate goals or realistic perception of the world, megalomania bent on world conquest).[1]

Americans have always stored a large collection of invidious images of the Other, whoever it might be, available for resurrection and reuse in new situations; but although the racist stereotyping in

1 Dower, *War without Mercy*, 302, 309.

society at large might be quickly forgotten once peace returned, the war and race hates were slower to dissipate among some of the participants. By the late Vietnam period, increasingly strong voices were questioning earlier assumptions about American involvement in Southeast Asia and by extension challenging the conventional understanding of the Pacific War and its place in the American past.

Examining the structure and forms of the personal and public histories of the war raises complex questions about which myths and images were preserved, who made the selections, the ways they were represented, and how they were interpreted. In simplified terms, two elements can provide useful perspectives on these issues. First, inherent limitations on the communicability of human experience suggest some answers as to why certain myths recur more frequently than others and how particular images have been set before us. Second, the fundamentally revelatory nature of battlefield violence and its changing value in the American cultural landscape defined a sliding ideological scale by which historical events were measured. In the crucible of war, simple, abstract assumptions about the nature of good and evil or humanity and barbarism were burned away once combatants were forced to act upon deliberate and irrevocable choices. Personal and collective exegesis was therefore informed by and commonly used not solely to justify choices made but also to mediate shifting American ambivalences regarding the forms and uses of violence. As revealed in the writings of Hawthorne and Melville or in numerous contemporary films, Americans have characteristically believed in human goodness and perfectibility while simultaneously fearing "people's innate and irredeemable wickedness." The irreconcilability of the two establishes the essential tension against which the Pacific War images and the postwar realignment are played.[2] Restated, how the war was remembered and structured was largely a product of the easily communicable; how those recollections were interpreted was a factor of changing social attitudes toward war as both a cultural and a political tool.

Given the inevitable disjunction between the combatants' firsthand experience of war and how it is usually understood by the public, who shapes the memories of war can become not simply an emotionally charged issue but in the minds of some veterans actually "another sort of battlefield."[3] Reflecting on all the horror of

2 John Fraser, *Violence in the Arts* (New York: Cambridge University Press, 1974), 145–46.
3 Paul Fussell, *Thank God for the Atom Bomb and Other Essays* (New York: Summit Books, 1988), 9. On this battlefield "the enemy consists of habitual euphemizers,

the Second World War in light of his own traumatic experiences as a rifle platoon commander in Europe, Paul Fussell, in his book *Wartime*, rails against those who can never fully understand his trials: "optimistic publicity and euphemism had rendered [the troops'] experience so falsely that it would never be readily communicable. They knew that in its representation to the laity what was happening to them was systematically sanitized and Norman Rockwellized, not to mention Disneyfied." Although rather extreme, and overall unconvincing, Fussell's argument nevertheless sheds light on the perceived stakes involved in who selects the myths and images to be preserved. In Fussell's sharply divided view there are on one side "the sentimental, the loony patriotic, the ignorant, and the bloodthirsty" as represented by government publicists, journalists, advertisers, and Hollywood screenwriters – none of whom, Fussell falsely assumes, shared his experience of the war.[4] On the other side are those, to draw out Fussell's choice of words, who stand separate from the public "laity" as graduates of the battlefield seminary, and who perforce join a clergy whose religion is only revealed in war. To Fussell's further indictment that history cannot accurately record the war as understood by participants like himself, one keen critic responds,

> But the charge of ignorance against "historiography later," besides being anachronistic and wrong, is symptomatic of a mind too certain that we cannot understand the reality it knows, however books, film, or art may present it, a mind that enjoys thinking that only the experience itself confers accurate knowledge.... How is one to answer the charge of not understanding, while suspecting that one is being told that significant understanding is not possible because one was not there?[5]

Aside from the emotional and philosophical stakes involved, tremendous political and social power have habitually devolved upon those who narrate the histories of war. Fussell's opinion, that one must have experienced war to understand and record it accurately,

professional dissimulators, inadequately educated administrators, censors, artistically pretentious third-rate novelists, sexual puritans," and so on until Fussell culminates with the president.

4 Fussell, *Wartime*, "loony patriotic," ix; "Disneyfied," 268.
5 For a model critique of this book see Jonathan Marwil, "Paul Fussell's Wars," *Michigan Quarterly Review* (Summer 1990): 431–52 (quoted portion, 435). In other works Fussell is quite forceful and adamant in criticizing authors of military histories who did not experience the infantryman's terror of the front lines; Fussell, "Thank God for the Atom Bomb," in *Thank God for the Atom Bomb and Other Essays*, 18–20.

has been shared by many veterans and served to sustain a historical divide along gender lines.

The Pacific War offers no exception to the American tradition of excluding women from writing the histories of war, which have, in turn, consistently marooned them on the distant periphery of events. To the extent this separatism reflects the idea that conventional tropes of life-givers and life-takers define gender roles, then the history of war is in one very important sense about defining maleness. It is designed primarily for the consumption of males and is freighted with far too much social power for men to relinquish easily their positions as narrators and allow women to participate actively in its writing.[6] The Clausewitzian maxim that war is a continuation of international politics by other means may be transferred to the arena of gender relations and applied as readily to the sexual struggle.

In considering the landscape of gender relations for the fifteen years following the Pacific War, some feminist scholars have argued that the myths and images to which it gave rise were employed as successfully against women as against the Japanese. The entrenchment of the feminine mystique in the fifties would seem to represent in one respect as crowning an achievement as the flag raising on Mount Suribachi: as though "uncommon valor" on Iwo Jima earned for the warriors the redomestication of women. The stereotyped, homogenized attributes of this mystique as listed by Betty Friedan read like a fantasy list of a common soldier: "young and frivolous, almost childlike; fluffy and feminine; passive; gaily content in a world of bedroom and kitchen, sex, babies, and home."[7] Yet just as the flag raising becomes far more ambiguous with closer scrutiny, so too does the issue of postwar gendering become increasingly complex upon detailed inspection. As several historians have recognized, women were far from passive victims either in the return to the realms of home and motherhood or in the continued idealization of those roles.[8] Nevertheless, the language of the early war

6 Elshtain makes this point clearly in a number of places in *Women and War*, e.g., 3–13, 92–94; in citing Michel Foucault she suggests the matter is put "rather starkly" but accurately in linking "the fact of killing and the fact of writing, the deeds done and the things narrated" (92).
7 Betty Friedan, *The Feminine Mystique* (New York: W. W. Norton, 1963), 36.
8 Fussell's argument would seem to carry over to this issue as well: that the same men who Disneyfied his war also pushed women into unwelcome roles. However, Leila Rupp in her comparative study *Mobilizing Women for War* and D'Ann Campbell in *Women at War with America* both suggest that many women throughout American society viewed their wartime roles as aberrations of the natural social order and contributed actively to the postwar realignment. The extent to which this eagerness can itself be brushed off as the product of male manipulation raises

narratives contributed to this restoration of the traditional gender tropes.

With traces of the heroic tradition pervading the early postmodernist literature, a romanticized language of war offered the best means by which combatants could communicate to the uninitiated in their audience some kernel of their actual experiences. Aside from its commonality among both groups, reliance on a neoromantic view of the war was virtually dictated by the social and political climate in the United States after 1945.[9] It fitted the idea of a just crusade against the Third Reich and Imperial Japan, sanctioned all sacrifice, high and low, and gained popularity as the cold war cast its shadow over the postwar international and domestic order. Another factor in defining the language of historical discourse was the struggle between the sexes over defining roles. According to two authors who examine the dynamics of this process through the twentieth century, postmodernist writers in the 1940s and 1950s "reimagined masculine victory" in reaction to the feminist successes – and masculine Depression-era failures – of the preceding twenty years.[10] One way to resurrect mid-Victorian images of male domination was to return to traditional war narratives. Few combat veterans wanted to observe the realist orthodoxy defined by Fussell and remain cloistered from the rest of society, or worse, from wives or parents, and they quickly discovered that the best bridge linking them to the secular public was one built on romanticized myth and imagination, a subject humorously lampooned in some literature.[11]

an important issue that unfortunately is beyond the scope of this chapter and the immediate implications of wartime myth and imagination.

9 One literary scholar sees American World War II novels wrestling with the conflict between "native pragmatism" and the "heroic tradition." Norman Mailer and James Jones viewed the war as the product of irrepressible human instinct; Herman Wouk and William Styron saw it as an aberration of human behavior and death as inherently unheroic: the fundamental conflict noted by Fraser above. The difficulty in reconciling the two sides pushed the literary movement toward the absurd that appeared around the end of the fifties (Aichinger, *American Soldier in Fiction*, 61–65). It is worth noting that the "heroic tradition" is most strongly sustained in the early war memoirs.

10 Gilbert and Gubar, *No Man's Land*, 1:4–5. The authors consciously emphasize militarized images of this cyclical process: "The Battle of the Sexes: The Men's Case" and "Fighting for Life: The Women's Cause." I consider the word "struggle" more appropriate here than such terms as "battle" or "war" given their linguistic associations with the male tropes; a point supported in Enloe's more general remarks (*Does Khaki Become You?*) concerning the militarization of women's lives.

11 The best example is the story "Passion," in which a conscientious doctor, in his capacity as a mail censor, discovers that salacious and purely fictive embellishments of others' letters make them not only fascinating reading but also seem

However galling such imagery may be to Fussell and others, what Eric J. Leed labels the liberal experience of war, with its emphasis on death, suffering, stupidity, and futility, has never been readily communicable to society. It has traditionally been preserved in quiet ways without much public recognition in scrapbooks and personal memories, and it has existed simultaneously and unreconciled beside the more public conservative experiences centering on comradeship, personal strength, release, and higher cause. Only after the political and social upheaval of the Vietnam War – in many ways the product of American political and military hubris of the Pacific War period inappropriately applied to the cold war – could later memoirists like Eugene Sledge, Samuel Hynes, and Fussell find a truly receptive audience and discover a new grammar and syntax by which they could reevaluate their experiences and communicate more effectively certain aspects of that liberal experience of war.[12]

The Americans who served in the Second World War entered the service, if not with a firm grasp of war's realities, then at least armored with a cynicism bred in the chaos of the post-Versailles world and the suffering of the Great Depression. Yet, whether despite, or precisely because of, the same kinds of institutional "chickenshit" that Dos Passos described after the First World War and all the horrendous experiences of the combat veterans in Europe and the Pacific, Americans returned to the traditions of the romantic age and remade the wartime experience into something unified, uplifting, and purposeful.[13] Not only have such "Disneyfied" versions of war always existed, but quite often it is the combat veterans who lead the way in sanitizing and reinterpreting their experiences. Emerging from the Civil War shaken by the terrors, pain, and hardships he had suffered, in later years Oliver Wendell Holmes became a powerful and eloquent advocate of war's moral and spiritual values. Similarly, many participants in the Second World War returned physically and psychically battered, and yet they too began to sanitize their experiences in ways that seem so foreign to Fussell's sensibilities. Reflecting on his Pacific service in the Army long afterward, James Jones wrote:

to tie the men closer to their correspondents; James A. Michener, *Tales of the South Pacific* (1948; reprint, New York: Henry Holt, 1976), 190–205
12 The same could be said for other modes of communication, such as with memorials or film. See, for example, the discussion of Edward Kienholz's 1968 sculpture *The Portable War Memorial* in James M. Mayo, *War Memorials as Political Landscape* (New York: Praeger, 1988), 264–65.
13 Fussell devotes a full chapter to the subject entitled "Chickenshit, An Anatomy" (*Wartime*, 79–95).

It would seem the internal Universe as well as the external is built on the principle of letting the dead past bury its dead.

Thus we old men can in all good conscience sit over our beers at the American Legion on Friday nights and recall with affection moments of terror thirty years before. Thus we are able to tell the youngsters that it wasn't all really so bad. Perhaps fortunately for us all, there appears to be a psychic process one might label THE DE-EVOLUTION OF A SOLDIER, as well as the process I called THE EVOLUTION OF A SOLDIER.

And perhaps because of it, perhaps the hardest thing is to try to recreate it as it really was.[14]

Evidence of this sanitizing process has already been seen with the marines who remained in the Reserves after 1945 and returned to active duty in Korea, and it appears also in the literary accounts left by veterans since V-J Day.

The earliest postwar memoirs and histories of the marines set the tone of the next thirty years. George P. Hunt's 1946 account of his experiences as an infantry company commander on Peleliu became a minor classic. One of "Chesty" Puller's leaders, Hunt recounts the protracted and bitter struggle for the small point that enfiladed the left flank of the landing beaches. With an introduction by Vandegrift that emphasizes the courage, resourcefulness, and self-respect of the individual marines, Hunt's gripping and heroic account accentuates the role of the common man, his "cold professionalism" and "tough-minded aggressiveness":

[U]nifying them into one driving spirit was an unshakable loyalty to each other, a unity far deeper than mere comradeship, and governed by a stern, silent code of mutual respect which could not be broken by a man in battle without his incurring the humiliating contempt of former friends. This was a force that would never allow them to let each other down and that would impel them to perform acts of bravery which, in the normal circumstances of peace, would seem incredible.[15]

14 James Jones, WWII, 16.
15 Hunt, Coral Comes High, ix–x, 12, 17, 20–21. Even Fussell could harbor no reservations that Hunt, a reserve officer with combat experience on both Guadalcanal and New Britain, was eminently qualified to speak of the frontline perspective. An even more striking contrast between the mild tone of his memoir and bitter wartime experience as a prisoner of the Japanese and victim of U.S. unpreparedness appears in the account of James P. S. Devereux, The Story of Wake Island (New York: Lippincott, 1947).

Hunt's stress on the unifying loyalty, incredible bravery, and the primacy of personal honor is consistent with the conservative experience of war noted by Leed and American traditions of war narrative. In another example to come out one year later, Frank O. Hough's book, *The Island War*, provided a historical overview of Marine exploits that reflected still the bitterness and wartime hatred of the Japanese. Hough, who had served as the First Division public relations officer at Peleliu and witnessed fierce combat firsthand, continued to portray the Japanese in highly racist, objectified terms that in some ways convey a very accurate picture of the emotional struggle although concealing the barbarization to which it gave rise.[16] The first of the official Marine Corps campaign monographs, John L. Zimmerman's *The Guadalcanal Campaign*, was published in 1949, following on the heels of the unification crisis and in the same year as China was "lost." Superseded by later scholarship, this is nevertheless a useful study because it reflects the strong concern for selectively highlighting events in corps history so as to help preserve the corps and armor its reputation against future attacks.[17]

Along with conventional war memoirs and official histories, military autobiographies also conveyed only selected aspects of the war. Senior Marine officers A. A. Vandegrift and Holland M. Smith wrote autobiographies that covered their experiences in some of the bloodiest battles of this century without conveying any sense of what gave combat its actual form or character. Their circumspection in describing Pacific battlefield experiences cannot be explained, however, simply by their relative distance as senior commanders from such aspects or by years of institutional "brainwashing" or misplaced loyalties. Along with citizen-soldier reservists called to active duty like Hunt and Herbert C. Merillat, these men witnessed and understood the sorts of realities that Fussell finds lacking in most memoirs. There was no "cover-up" that sometimes plagues Vietnam-era memoirs; instead these men consciously chose to emphasize the positive, uplifting aspects rather than dwell on that "other" reality. This is partly human nature balking at the

16 The examples are rife in this book where the Japanese are labeled as stupid, vicious, savage, devoid of imagination or scruples, etc. (Hough, *Island War*). Notably, Hough became a prominent member of the historical section and was author or co-author of several books in the series, including the official monograph on Peleliu.
17 United States Marine Corps, *The Guadalcanal Campaign*, by John L. Zimmerman (1949). Other, unofficial, histories of the Marine Corps and collected anecdotes served the same ends, such as Fletcher Pratt, *The Marines' War* (New York: Sloane, 1948), and Patrick O'Sheel and Gene Cook, eds., *Semper Fidelis* (New York: William Sloan, 1947).

unpleasant and trying to heal painful wounds; it stems also in part from the realization that the mundane, everyday aggravations of service life that are of personally consuming interest at the time make for very poor stories.[18] Iconoclast Bill Mauldin poked fun at this phenomenon in the first cartoon appearing in his book *Up Front*, where Willie, his spade-wielding dogface, mutters, " 'You'll get over it, Joe. Oncet I wuz gonna write a book exposin' the army after th' war myself.' "[19] Besides simply avoiding painful or banal truths, the contents of all war memoirs are the product of what veterans were able to remember and express and what their audiences could understand.

Memoirists are subject to complex psychological limits to recollection and recall over which they have limited conscious control. In a unique study of memory and oral history that began in 1978, Alice M. Hoffman conducted two series of interviews, four years apart, with her husband, Howard, concerning his service in the Army from 1943 to 1945. They discovered that memories of certain events were so firmly encoded that particular stories were recounted in virtually identical words. These were memories the authors labeled "archival," consisting of "recollections that are rehearsed, readily available for recall, and selected for preservation over the lifetime of the individual. They are memories selected much as one makes a scrapbook of photographs, pasting in some, discarding others; they define the self and constitute the persona one retains, the sense of identity over time." Other memories could not be voluntarily recalled but could be triggered by association with a particular word or photograph. Finally, some events in which an individual had clearly taken part could not be remembered at all. Although particularly emotional or visually spectacular events were often remembered with great clarity, it proved impossible to identify clear criteria for inclusion or rejection of specific events.[20] After constant exposure to danger, for example, some men forget specific instances of being under fire unless they are somehow especially noteworthy: to take one case, although other experiences of being under fire sometimes went unrecorded, none of the memoirists who suffered through the night battleship bombardment of the airfield on Guadalcanal forgot the terror of it. Fussell's expe-

18 Vandegrift and Asprey, *Once a Marine*; Holland M. Smith and Percy Finch, *Coral and Brass* (New York: Scribner, 1949); besides his wartime account *The Island*, Herbert C. Merillat also wrote a retrospective almost forty years later, *Guadalcanal Remembered* (1982).
19 Bill Mauldin, *Up Front* (New York: Henry Holt, 1944), 2.
20 Alice M. Hoffman and Howard S. Hoffman, *Archives of Memory* (Lexington: University Press of Kentucky, 1990), 145 (quoted portion), 146.

rience of being wounded and of failing to save the life of his sergeant or prevent other young men in his platoon from being "so
cruelly killed and wounded" affected his selection of memories
differently from those of Hunt or Vandegrift, who certainly faced
many similar situations, but all provided reasonably honest testimony of reality as they remember it.[21]

Just as the preceding transitions from civilian to soldier to
blooded veteran were important for shaping battlefield behavior,
so too did the transition back to civilian life affect the subsequent
narratives of the war. Fussell's sense of disjunction and the language
adopted by veterans like Hunt and Vandegrift were equally products of this final transformation. Except for the full autobiographies
of a few senior career officers, most memoirists begin their stories
only upon joining the service and fall silent again with the moment
of their departure from the Pacific. With the telescoping of events
common to all memories, the entire wartime experience tended to
be viewed as something separate or detached from what preceded
or followed.[22] Both governmental and public attitudes toward veterans encouraged this idea by emphasizing that the citizen-soldier
was in uniform simply "for the duration." The perception of military service as somehow exceptional compared to the rest of their
lives allowed many veterans to distance themselves from events and
attempt to insulate themselves from their actions of the time. The
culling of memories and ascription of meanings in this process were
also served by the nature of memory itself: in effect, memories of
service in an active theater were stored at a much higher density
than events preceding or especially events following intense combat
experience. Recollections of events immediately after the war
ended tended to be more vague and difficult to recall.[23] The transition to civilian life, combined with a reaction to the privations of
active duty, contributed to the sense of exceptionalism and often
pushed wartime events into the background.

For those who mustered out of the Marine Corps shortly after
the war, their main concerns centered on establishing themselves
in the civilian community and enjoying the pleasures denied by

21 Quote from Fussell, *Thank God for the Atom Bomb*, 32. These psychological factors
    are profoundly influential, but relatively little is known about the processes
    involved; and the particularity of specific cases, as with Fussell and Hunt, make
    them difficult to pursue. Added to this is the second, very conscious screening
    of recollections for purposes of publication.
22 Writing to his parents from Okinawa, one Sixth Division marine remarked that
    his high school experiences of two years earlier "just kinda seems like a life time
    away" (Joseph Kohn, letter to parents, dated 13 May 1945, Joseph Kohn Papers,
    PPC, MCHC).
23 Hoffman and Hoffman, *Archives of Memory*, 142, 147–48.

overseas service. Mostly men in their early twenties, these former marines sought to join the flood of veterans in distancing themselves from their recent experiences. Heavily polarized images central to the entire military resocialization process, whether in depicting the enemy, fostering distinct institutional identities, or defining gender roles, were carried over into the civilian community, where they contributed to changing business ethics, politics, and even marital relations in the postwar era. In his 1948 study of American social character, *The Lonely Crowd*, David Riesman suggested that a society of "other-directed" people had emerged as predominant among what he labeled the "new" middle class in the United States. Other-directed people were attuned, in Riesman's words, "to receive signals from far and near.... What can be internalized, then, is not a code of behavior but the elaborate equipment needed to attend to such messages and occasionally to participate in their circulation."[24] Although Riesman was talking about patterns of consumption and the adoption of popular social attitudes, his description can also serve as a functional definition of military discipline as instilled in basic training. Other-directed people emerged primarily as a product of changing economic conditions, but given the large proportion of the new middle class who were veterans of the war, this national character shift was also encouraged by the nature of that military service: a reaction to its elements of compulsion and an affirmation of its discipline, camaraderie, and empowerment.[25] Although much remains obscure in this transition, some of the ideas shared among the marines upon their return to mainstream American society are revealed in the iconography to arise after the war.

As witnessed in public ceremonies, sculpture, cinema, and literature, the conservative experience remained the dominant mode of interpretation through the Vietnam period. In an excellent study of the enshrinement and reinterpretation of a specific wartime event, Karal Ann Marling and John Wetenhall spin out the complex story surrounding the flag raising atop Mount Suribachi, its immortalization as a memorial, and the personal stories linked to it. Joe Rosenthal's spontaneous photograph captured the triumph and heroism of six men in combat. The two marines and one corpsman

---

24 David Riesman, *The Lonely Crowd* (New Haven: Yale University Press, 1961), 20, 25.
25 According to official VA statistics for 1947, 25% of the population had at least one immediate family member who was a World War II veteran: since 97.8% were males and 60% were married, the majority were officially "heads of households"; United States Administration of Veterans Affairs, *Annual Report* (Washington: GPO, 1947), 2–3.

The dedication of the Marine Corps War Memorial helped to reconcile the combatants' and the public's views of the Pacific War. *(USMC, National Archives)*

to survive the campaign became overnight heroes, touring the country together in the tumultuous Seventh War Loan drive. Because it came to represent America at the height of its military power, triumphant over all, and because it could be easily commercialized, the Suribachi icon became the most famous and instantly recognizable of the war. With the dedication of the Marine Corps War Memorial on 10 November 1954, the Marine Corps birthday, the enormous Felix de Weldon sculpture, with figures approaching the height of a three-story building, paid daunting tribute to that moment.

Yet this story of American triumph and heroism is not nearly so straightforward as was first portrayed. The famous flag raising was actually the second, to replace the smaller initial flag with a larger, more visible one. The men who had first fought their way to the top of the volcano and whose actions were preserved in a photo-

graphic record by Lou Lowery were quickly lost in obscurity that
Marine Corps publicists actively fostered so as not to confuse the
desired symbolism of the second raising. The identities of all six
men in the Rosenthal photograph were never even firmly fixed.
In particular, the identity of one man, killed during the campaign,
became the subject of a congressional investigation that is still discussed.[26] Even the biographies of the known men, especially the
three who returned to the States, became the subject of intense
public scrutiny and grave institutional concern. Marine publicists
insisted that collectively, the flag raisers were typical American boys:
the son of Czech parents from the Pennsylvania Alleghenies, the
Pima Indian from Arizona, "a student from the dairylands of Wisconsin," the others from Kentucky, New Hampshire, and south
Texas. Although faceless and anonymous in the photograph, they
were subsequently spotlighted. The three survivors, an undertaker,
a tragic alcoholic, and one who could not seem to hold a job, were
transformed by the media and the Marine Corps into living symbols
of something in which they had been caught by the purest chance.[27]

The choice of the sculpture itself for the memorial was a source
of bitter controversy. Called upon to make an appearance at the
dedication, President Eisenhower, who had risen to fame based on
his exploits in Europe, seemed uncomfortable with the enormous
size of the memorial, its literal depiction of a minor, militarily
insignificant event, and the glorification of the Marine Corps. The
selection of de Weldon, an outsider to the art community, to receive
the lucrative contract drew heavy criticism from established artists,
who attacked the aesthetics of the monument and the character of
the sculptor in virulent terms. At the dedication ceremony, de
Weldon defended the monument by offering his own interpretations of how the sculpture spoke to the American character:

> The outstretched hands of his figures, he said, stood for Amer-
> ica's help to the suffering peoples of the world, a striving after
> the blessings of a higher power, the strength of a nation united

26 Marling and Wetenhall, *Iwo Jima: Monuments, Memories, and the American Hero*,
84–89. Sergeant Henry O. Hansen, who took part in the first flag raising, was
initially listed as a participant in the second as well until a congressional investigation put Harlon Block in his place. A recent example of the continuing
debate on this subject was a paper presented by Parker B. Albee, Jr., "Sergeant
Henry O. Hansen and the Flag-Raising on Iwo Jima," at the American Military
Institute meeting in Durham, North Carolina, 22 March 1991.
27 John Bradley was the undertaker; Rene Gagnon, the sometime contractor and
thwarted actor, airline pilot, and state trooper; Ira Hayes, the sullen alcoholic.
Michael Strank, Franklin Sousley, and Harlon Block were identified as the other
three flag raisers; all died on Iwo Jima (Marling and Wetenhall, *Iwo Jima*, 3–4,
9–10, 169).

in the pursuit of a single goal. The three dead Marines in his group of six recalled the sacrifice of all who fell in battle; the three survivors, the gallantry of all who served.[28]

Notwithstanding de Weldon's efforts to expand on its symbolic meaning, the massive hundred-ton bronze sculpture was bluntly documentary and self-consciously populist art that eschewed all subtlety. Weighing in again with a pithy critique of the "heroic realism" of the monument, Fussell comments, "Change the flag to red and you have 'Soviet Art.' Strip the men and you have Italian fascist sculpture."[29] The memorialization of the flag raising became itself an ideological and political battleground. The actual dedication of the monument fell to Vice-President Richard M. Nixon, to whom "the historical background of the bronze tableau – the Rosenthal photo, the identity of the raisers, who got there first, Iwo Jima itself – was far less important than its message for the perilous world of 1954. The image *was* America, vast and powerful; America, heroic and strong."[30] With the dedication of the Iwo Jima memorial, the Pacific War images had, in a sense, come full circle: themselves the product of myth and imagination reified on the field of battle, they were once again rendered into abstractions effectively divorced from events.

The active process of reinterpreting and sanitizing the war that took place in the publishing houses and movie studios can be divided into two waves. The first stretched thirty years from the end of the war up through the mid-seventies, from the early works of Hunt and Hough through the bulk of the published Marine memoirs like those of Davis, Gallant, and Leckie. Their recollections affirmed various conservative beliefs and showed more pride than misgivings about personal and national decisions regarding wartime attitudes and behavior. The second wave, not very large, began to emerge around the time of the American evacuation of Saigon as the Pacific War generation started to thin more rapidly. Age, troubling memories, and different public attitudes had carried some authors beyond the need to uphold the romanticized accounts of events thirty or forty years in the past. They also had a more literal language of war arising from Vietnam that ascribed new meanings to old symbols and metaphors and conformed better to

28 On Eisenhower, see Marling and Wetenhall, *Iwo Jima*, 13–16; artists' reactions, 153–57; paraphrasing of de Weldon's comments, 16.
29 Paul Fussell, *The Boy Scout Handbook and Other Observations* (New York: Oxford University Press, 1982), 232.
30 Marling and Wetenhall, *Iwo Jima*, 17.

the new sensitivities of their audience. American society had become more attuned to the liberal experience of war in ways that
had never been so widely demonstrated before.

Quoting Walt Whitman, Fussell seconds his opinion that "the
real war will never get in the books." To the extent that he means
this in an all-inclusive sense, he is of course correct. No single book
or even handful of books can encompass all aspects of the war. Yet
the charge that all the individual pieces are therefore invalid cannot
stand.[31] Whitman himself, in poems like "The Wound Dresser,"
offered some of the most emotive views of the Civil War put down
on paper. Even more problematic is Fussell's self-appointed role
in selecting what constitutes the valid reality of the war. The memoirs of participants cannot be so easily discounted as unfaithful to
events, especially as defined by Fussell's own limited experiences.
In the wake of Vietnam it became both more popular and cathartic
to reevaluate some of the attitudes and policies of the Pacific War
period. A booming historical literature grew up around the relo-
cation policies directed at Japanese-Americans, and old liberal arguments were dusted off in reconsidering the decision to use atomic
weapons. These shifts were accompanied by more graphic accounts
of events on the Pacific battlefields and uncensored attitudes on
the home front.

Whatever the literary shortcomings of some, Pacific War memoirs
are historically useful and intriguing both for the occasionally intimate glimpses they give of life in uniform and combat against the
Japanese and also for the contrast they offer to the public's understanding of the war. Jones's "DE-EVOLUTION OF A SOLDIER"
was about slipping into new patterns of thought. The concern of
civilian observers that veterans tended to mingle with each other
was overdrawn, but there were in such associations benefits that
former combatants could not find elsewhere. With a private audience that could understand the totality of the battlefield experiences, veterans could soften their own memories and distill out
elements for more public discourse. Jones was astonished by his
recollections of Guadalcanal:

> It is scarcely believable that I can remember it with pleasure,
> and affection, and a sense of beauty. But such are the vagaries
> of the human head. One can hardly credit that a place so full
> of personal misery and terror, which was perfectly capable of
> taking your life and on a couple of occasions very nearly did,
> could be remembered with such kind feelings, but I do. The

31 Fussell, *Wartime*, 290.

pervasive mud, and jungle gloom and tropical sun, when they are not all around you smothering you, can have a haunting beauty at far remove. When you are not straining and gasping to save your life, the act of doing so can seem adventurous and exciting from a distance. The greater the distance, the greater the adventure.[32]

Fussell sees parallels between the "real" war, as extrapolated from his experience of battle, and another author's view of the Holocaust: "[it is] not that it's 'unknowable,' but 'that its full dimensions are inaccessible to the ideological frameworks that we have inherited from the liberal era.' "[33] The central difficulty returns to the fact that war and warriors operate in a social and psychic sphere distinct from society at large. All recollections and interpretations of wars necessarily revolve around the primordial violence of Clausewitz's trinity.

Because violence is literally and metaphorically the cutting edge of ideas and ideologies,[34] the narrative of the Pacific War serves as part of a larger cultural self-portrait. For Hunt and Hough the perceived threat of unbridled Japanese militarism and the unquestioning acceptance of an American-styled world order were sufficient to justify all Allied actions in the war. Written over thirty years after Hough's *Island War*, Eugene B. Sledge's memoir, which even Fussell considers "one of the finest memoirs to emerge from any war,"[35] seeks only personal understanding without attempting to explain or even address decisions and attitudes beyond his own horizons. His stark recollection of the precise moment, years ago, when his "rage and hatred for the Japanese" crystallized and "the least pity or compassion" for the enemy instantly evaporated[36] testifies not only to the intensity of his memories of those experiences but also separates his transformation from the ideological agenda that is by definition a central component of the conservative narratives of war.

Although for many marines the intense feelings of war hatred have faded with time, memories of the hatreds have often remained vivid. This trick of memory is analogous to the human mind's inability to re-create the intense physical pains felt when wounded while recalling with excruciating clarity having suffered such pain.

---

32 James Jones, *WWII*, 48.
33 Barbara Foley cited in Fussell, *Wartime*, 290.
34 Fraser, *Violence in the Arts*, 162.
35 Fussell, *Wartime*, 292.
36 Sledge had just stumbled across three horribly mutilated marines, decapitated heads on their chests with the penis stuck in the mouth, hands severed at the wrist (*With the Old Breed*, 148).

William Manchester, who fought on Okinawa with the Sixth Marine Division, can still neither forget nor forgive the Japanese after over forty years: "There are too many graves between us, too much gore, too many memories of too many atrocities. . . . The fact is that some wounds never heal."[37] On the occasion of the fortieth anniversary reunion held by both sides on Iwo Jima, many American veterans simply stayed away:

> Men who lived in the past could not cross that last yard of beach to clasp the hand of a "Jap." Yet even those who had decided to forgive but not forget – to forgive one another while refusing to forget the heroism of the honored dead and the tragedy of all war – found it hard to take the first step forward, to grasp the first gnarled and wizened hand. "They were the enemy!" cried Greg Emery, a former Navy corpsman haunted by the memory of the carnage he had seen.[38]

Some were better able to put the wartime hatreds behind them, but frequently only after many years. Twenty-six years after he left the island, the Marine chairman of the Guadalcanal veterans association wrote to his former enemies, "Oddly, we find much more *in common*, than we ever had differences. A soldier is a soldier – I guess."[39] Sledge's memoir conveys no sense that the fervid wartime hatreds linger today, even though it expresses clearly his total immersion in the fury of the Peleliu and Okinawa battlefields.

For those caught inside war, whether on the battlefields themselves or in their backwash, the violence reveals aspects of human suffering and sacrifice found nowhere else.[40] Wartime violence also conveys to combatants the distance separating those caught in the actual behaviors and morals of the battlefield from those who sit in judgment apart from the conflict as self-appointed guardians of society's values or more often simply as voyeurs fascinated by the spectacle unfolded before them. The combatants return having been forced to take action, their beliefs crystallized, though often only retrospectively interpreted; those at home remain insulated

---

37 William Manchester, "Feelings Are at War over Okinawa," *New York Times Magazine*, 7 June 1987.
38 Marling and Wetenhall, *Iwo Jima*, 230–31.
39 Harry R. Horsman, letter to Yoya Kawamura, Chargé d'Affaires, Japanese Embassy, Solomon Islands, dated 26 December 1958, Harry R. Horsman Papers, PPC, MCHC.
40 The concept of being "inside" rather than simply "on" a battlefield reflects the linguistic difficulties veterans encounter in trying to relate their experiences; Gray's opening chapter, "Remembering War and Forgetfulness," captures well the effects of being immersed in a world of numbing violence, and his chapter on confronting death goes into several paradigms regarding sacrifice (*The Warriors*, 3–24, 97–129).

from facing such tests of their own beliefs, free to sit in detached judgment, and often uncomfortable lest they be forced to test as severely their own beliefs.[41] Unless the poetic fantasies of angry veterans – like that of Briton Siegfried Sassoon bayoneting "Yellow-Pressmen" and clearing "those Junkers out of Parliament" – are actually brought to pass, veterans have to learn to reconcile their thoughts with those of the vast majority who remained behind.[42] The pain of those memories and the confusion of conflicting values usually silence the vast majority; those who actually record their thoughts and share their suffering with a public audience are very few indeed. Most take the view expressed by one Iwo Jima veteran, " 'you don't want to remember the bad stuff.' "[43]

The actualities of that primordial violence tend to be rendered mystical or abstract. Sassoon's fantasy, for example, dissipates the very real rage he and other line officers felt toward the spectators of their misery by giving his image a darkly humorous and ironic cast. Those who are victims of the violence are often made invisible or converted into something horrible themselves. As racial enemies, the Japanese virtually disappear as humans from American accounts and re-creations of the war.[44] Even Americans, if horribly mutilated, were usually rendered invisible or, if recognized at all, were stripped of their human qualities and reduced to objects of pity.[45] The structural and linguistic limitations faced by Marine

41 Fraser's brief summary of the revelatory aspects of violence in general is extremely thought-provoking (*Violence in the Arts*, 157–62). Drawing on the movie *Le sang des bêtes*, about the butchering industry, he also illustrates the ease with which people insulate themselves from unpleasant truths about the violence around them, to which, in this case, they actually give rise (139–40). Gray emphasizes the voyeuristic aspect of war as spectacle (*The Warriors*, 29–31).

42 Siegfried Sassoon, "Fight to a Finish," *Collected Poems, 1908–1956* (Boston: Faber and Faber, 1961), 77. Sassoon in particular reveals many of the transcendent aspects of the British experience in the Great War that apply to the United States in 1945; indeed, ideas expressed in a poem like "Glory of Women" (79) find great resonance in the fiction of Jones and Mailer.

43 Larry Ryan cited in Marling and Wetenhall, *Iwo Jima*, 235.

44 Two cinematic exceptions that failed commercially were *None but the Brave* (1965), in which a planeload of marines who crash-landed on an isolated island come to a temporary truce and even spirit of cooperation with the small Japanese garrison before wiping them out at the end, and *Hell in the Pacific* (1968), in which Lee Marvin and Toshiro Mifune reduce the war to a gladiatorial contest.

45 One of the best examples of this in American literature is from the Great War in the character of Donald Mahon, in William Faulkner, *Soldier's Pay* (New York: Liveright, 1926). The wartime biography *Al Schmid, Marine*, and the Hollywood screen version, *Pride of the Marines* (1945), tell the story of Al Schmid, the Marine machine gunner blinded in the battle of the Tenaru on Guadalcanal, making his loss of sight his red badge of courage; this was only possible, however, because blindness was a publicly acceptable injury. Men who suffered major scarring from burns or mutilating wounds were never publicized. The most effective film treatments that pushed the boundaries of public sensibilities at the time

combat veterans were analogous to the even greater barriers faced by certain others. Concentration camp inmates, for example, have often testified to their feeling of "the impossibility of conveying to outsiders what the experience was like, and related to this, almost certainly, was the implicit recognition that by endeavoring to do so they were in fact estranging themselves from their listeners and converting themselves into a species of freaks or monsters." *Concentrationaires* are frequently seen as passive victims of violence, but even active victims – those who consciously risk death or dismemberment – do not automatically foster empathic feelings from detached observers.[46] Several war films, for example, have more easily elicited from audiences a sense of anguish for the victimization of a unit mascot than for the men themselves.

The coalescence of broad social consensus regarding the war's meaning and the enshrinement of its symbolic representations received its greatest boost from the movie industry. Hollywood producers, in cooperation with the Office of War Information, had, in the interest of wartime harmony, promoted particular views of the world:

> Wartime movies fused two powerful myths that had deep roots in American popular culture and political discourse. One was the division of the world into slave and free. They divided a world of total peril into forces of either ultimate evil or righteousness.... The other myth was a newly universalized version of the idea of regeneration through war.... "the different races and classes that divided American society might restore their 'harmony,' through a sanctified and regenerative act of violence."[47]

Popular wartime movies had been reassuring and escapist, two ingredients that helped ensure the revival of the genre in the late forties.[48] By that time the cold war climate of the country helped

---

were *The Best Years of Our Lives* (1946), with its use of actual veterans coping with their physical and emotional injuries, and *The Men* (1950), in which Marlon Brando plays an infantry officer who suffers a paralyzing wound. Even here, however, the sailor's loss of his hands was an emotive but acceptable injury to air before the public in the former case, and the paralytic Brando was hardly disfigured.

46 Fraser, *Violence in the Arts*, 60. The entire chapter entitled "Victims" (51–82) thoughtfully explores viewer relations toward literary and cinematic depictions of different kinds of victims and various forms of violence.

47 Clayton R. Koppes and Gregory D. Black, *Hollywood Goes to War* (New York: Free Press, 1987), 325.

48 After accounting for almost one-third of the film industry's product in 1943, war films went through a hiatus immediately after the war because the studios predicted Americans would be tired of the war, but as the cold war began to

260 AMERICAN SAMURAI

to ensure that films would conform to the conservative, romantic view of war.

The single most important and lasting movie for the Marines' image was *Sands of Iwo Jima* (1949), with John Wayne playing the lead character, Sergeant Stryker. He had been known for his cowboy roles before the war, but it was this movie that made John Wayne's name synonymous with the popular image of the American warrior. The embodiment of this ideal, the John Wayne persona has exercised an extraordinary influence over generations of young men.[49] As one movie critic writes, Wayne "has become just as much a military hero, a frontier hero, and a supporter of God, country, and motherhood as the Andrew Jacksons, Davy Crocketts, Buffalo Bills, and Teddy Roosevelts of the past."[50] Republic Pictures chose the flag raising as a topic "[b]ecause it was the clearest expression of that make-believe version of recent history" symbolic of a valorous and victorious America when it was still free of the shadow of the communist menace. Wayne and this movie inspired a stream of Hollywood imitators, but none have matched its impact.[51]

Although the picture received unprecedented help from the Marine Corps, with wartime heroes as advisors and a third of the 7th Marines as extras and labor, the gap between the public's understanding of battle and the combatants' actual experiences remained as wide in 1949 as it had been four years earlier. David Shoup, Medal of Honor winner at Tarawa and advisor for the extensive battle scenes set around the seawall, admitted that the picture was "sort of a screwed up thing, really," but he also felt that it captured the battlefield as effectively as any Hollywood film had ever done. Reviewers were impressed with the "savage realism" of the battle scenes, which was heightened by interspersing newsreel footage with the staged elements.[52] In ways reminiscent of the flawed hero Captain Flagg, Stryker is the quintessential "doer" who acts instinctually and whose commitment to the Marine Corps and his men

take shape and the House Un-American Activities Committee began inquiries of communist influence in the industry in 1947, the genre was quickly revived; Russell Earl Shain, *An Analysis of Motion Pictures about War Released by the American Film Industry, 1930–1970* (New York: Arno, 1976), 31; Ivan Butler, *The War Film* (South Brunswick, N.J.: A. S. Barnes, 1974), 79–83.

49 The actor or the term "John Wayne" – meaning an act of bravado – was featured prominently in so many Vietnam memoirs that the term has since become a common part of the vernacular.
50 Suid, *Guts and Glory*, 102.
51 Marling and Wetenhall, *Iwo Jima*, 127. Similar Marine films include *Halls of Montezuma* (1950), *Flying Leathernecks* with Wayne (1951), *Tarawa Beachhead* (1958), and *Marines Let's Go* (1961).
52 Ibid., 128–33.

John Wayne's portrayal of Sergeant Stryker in *The Sands of Iwo Jima* created a Hollywood image of the Marine Corps that lured men into the service more than a generation later. *(Courtesy of* Leatherneck)

lends him a father/teacher image that is the central facet of his character. After a manner Fussell finds predictable, Stryker meets an easy death in the film – instantaneous, neat, bloodless. And although Stryker's is not in itself a meaningful death, it is a moment of fulfillment when his once-rebellious protégé steps forward to fill his spot and continue the fight.

Symbolically, Stryker fills several useful roles. A precondition for official Marine Corps support was that the character exemplify the institution's warrior image, and to the extent that Stryker is wholly occupied with his martial profession to the virtual exclusion of the pressures, passions, and politics of civilian life, he certainly fitted the ideal touted in the newly organized Department of Defense. The Stryker character also represented the suppression of the kinds of overt hero making that had discredited many wartime movies. Consistent with other films released in 1949, in particular *Battleground* and *Twelve O'Clock High, Sands of Iwo Jima* avoided overglamorizing war while simultaneously finding it a useful milieu in which men successfully confront and overcome their personal demons. For both the cold career sergeant, whose professional commitment is only reinforced after an interlude with his wife and baby, and for the formerly sheltered young boy who comes into full manhood, the war exposed character weaknesses and resolved them. Finally, the film conformed with the social changes noted by Riesman:

> Wayne's hardboiled, blood-and-guts sergeant provided an imaginative antidote to the placid – even boring – course of life in the peacetime suburbs. Marriage and a mortgage, for such a man, could only put a stop to his adventuring. Perhaps the Strykers of the world were better off dead, if the alternative was crabgrass. Only the fortunate moviegoer could enjoy homelife and a wild, vicarious freedom from its strictures simultaneously.[53]

For all these reasons, the icon persists to the present day with separate meanings for different audiences.

With their colorful characters, dramatic visual images, and stirring soundtracks, Hollywood war movies have played an important role in cleansing wartime events and lending them at least some superficial meaning. The movie *Battle Cry* (1955), for example, based on Leon Uris's novel of the same name, appealed to many Marine veterans as capturing more effectively the totality of their wartime experience than *Sands of Iwo Jima*.[54] The marines in the movie were not pinned down as definitely belonging to a particular division or fighting in specific campaigns, and the film captured more of the marines' off-duty experiences of masculine camaraderie – drinking, chasing women, and dodging the Shore Patrol. It captured the emotions of teenaged warriors seeking friendship and dealing with loss and rejection. But it also ruthlessly subordinated many of the unattractive or complicated aspects of the story to simplistic entertainment, and many found the combat scenes overdrawn and unrealistic.[55]

The film industry operated under several constraints that shaped how the war was portrayed. Foremost, the studios were interested in profit, and Fussell's view of the war was not considered even remotely marketable until antiwar sentiment became more pervasive after 1970.[56] Those who had been severely traumatized by

---

53 This general discussion of the symbolism of the Stryker character proceeds from that of Marling and Wetenhall, ibid., 134–38 (portion quoted, 138).
54 *Battle Cry* featured a cross section of stock American characters, but the specific choices fitted much more closely the composition of the real flag raisers than was common to many war films.
55 Suid, *Guts and Glory*, 101; James Robert Parish, *The Great Combat Pictures* (Metuchen, N.J.: Scarecrow, 1990), 36–38.
56 Even after a six-year hiatus following three big 1970 war film releases, there were very mixed messages from Hollywood: a nostalgic hunger for the somehow better times before Vietnam, a growing interest in antiwar/antiestablishment

war were unlikely to find a vivid reminder of it therapeutic any more than broader audiences would have found an antiwar message inherent in exceptionally realistic and graphic film entertaining. Expressing in 1945 his horror of such realism as recorded in uncensored newsreel footage from the battlefield, film critic James Agee branded it the pornography of violence.[57] Another factor in the sanitizing process was the obligation most producers felt, at least before the early seventies, to continue to accentuate the positive, especially if they wanted to secure cooperation from the services. They often claimed to be against war and militarism, suggesting their films carried this message in a "war is hell" theme, but at the same time their films usually justified war and violence as acceptable tools to fulfill personal and national destiny.[58] Big box-office stars also helped this process by insisting on scripts that provided stories outside wartime events against which they were set – an essential feature if women were to have any significant presence. Finally, political and ideological pressures continually arose to conform to certain images of war. Whether under the threat of the Red Scare during the McCarthy witch hunts or constrained by a zealous Johnson administration in the early days of the intervention in Vietnam, the struggle – in an expression of the latter period – for the hearts and minds of the American viewing public was persistent and highly charged.

The political and ideological values imbedded in all war narratives have always been subject to subversion and appropriation by competing groups. Perhaps the most familiar and obvious case from the Second World War was that of the German military leaders who sought to distance themselves from the Nazi regime. Soldiers sought refuge in a supposedly transcendent profession of arms, portraying themselves as men of honor who only performed their duty, victimized and duped by a ruthless dictator. In their memoirs, such luminaries as Heinz Guderian, Erich von Manstein, and Hans-Ulrich Rudel attempted to deny their active support of National Socialist ideology or the direct linkage between their military service and the crimes committed in support of Hitler's racial and political agenda.[59] Under the threat of postwar international justice such

messages, and finally a lapse into pure fantasies of revenge and retribution. See Parish, *The Great Combat Pictures*, 295–304, 309–21; Brock Garland, *War Movies* (New York: Facts on File, 1987), 12–13.

57 Agee cited in Marling and Wetenhall, *Iwo Jima*, 133.
58 Suid, *Guts and Glory*, 7–8.
59 Bartov discusses in particular the Guderian and Rudel memoirs in "Indoctrination and Motivation in the *Wehrmacht*: The Importance of the Unquantifiable," 16–34. Manstein's *Lost Battles* has virtually identical passages intended to distance himself from the ideological roots of the Third Reich.

selective memory might be expected from these men, but they also received active support from sources on the "other side of the hill." For example, B. H. Liddell Hart gained notoriety for his forgiving attitude toward the Germans. Motivated by a number of factors, including sincere personal concern, professional curiosity, and self-justification, Liddell Hart suggested that the "victor's justice" at Nuremberg might be applied even more easily to the Allied military leaders than the Germans and sought to record a history of German military leadership divorced from its political and ideological roots, an outlook that was quickly embraced in Germany itself for the next twenty years.[60] There were few Americans who would offer any excuses or assistance for Tojo Hideki or Yamashita Tomoyuki, but the efforts to record a particular type of history are easily visible.

Although driven by different forces, there has arisen an American historiography of the Pacific War that shares similar exculpatory tones as seen in the German case. Emphasis on the aggression of the Axis powers has often been used to cloak the role of the United States and other Allied powers in destabilizing prewar international relations and as legitimation for wartime decisions.[61] The Pacific War presents a unique case because, unlike the liberation of Europe, Americans have considered the defeat of Japan entirely their own doing and viewed East Asia as an area of special U.S. responsibility by virtue of their military and economic dominance. Contributions of Australians, New Zealanders, Indians, Chinese, Filipinos, and others seldom receive much recognition in American histories of the war if they are mentioned at all. Conversely, many accounts of the U.S. services exaggerate their own contributions while glossing over issues embarrassing to the institutions themselves or the American public. Histories of the Marines, for instance, as with the German generals, have tended to focus narrowly on their role as warriors and to mute their ideological radicalization. The Japanese are blamed for the ferocity of the fighting and the measures adopted by the Americans to defeat them. Concentrating on virtues, like the "uncommon valor" of Iwo

---

60 Liddell Hart excuses the German generals as "essentially technicians, intent on their professional job, and with little idea of things outside it." They were "hoodwinked and handled," instruments of Hitler. B. H. Liddell Hart, *The German Generals Talk* (New York: William Morrow, 1948), x. For an evenhanded overview see Brian Bond, *Liddell Hart* (New Brunswick: Rutgers University Press, 1977), 180–89, 227–35.
61 For useful insights on the destabilizing roles, especially of the United States, see Paul Kennedy, *The Rise and Fall of the Great Powers* (New York: Random House, 1987), 333–43; Sherry's *Rise of American Air Power* is filled with examples of the self-justificatory rationales for indiscriminate strategic bombing used during and after the war.

Jima, has allowed the "Good War" to emerge stripped of the terrible truths recognized by Fussell and others that would make the public or the Marine Corps uncomfortable. This historical cleansing was carried over into Korea as well. In discussing the Chosin operation, for example, one partisan writes, "Viewed in emotional terms – focusing on the endurance and heroism of the 1st Division's Marines – the Chosin Reservoir withdrawal remains one of those military masterpieces that occur when skill and bravery fuse to defy rational explanation."[62] Placing the focus on "endurance and heroism" in this case reduces the narrative to a level of mystical romanticism in which events lie beyond "rational explanation." Rendering an emotionally reassuring and uplifting story becomes an end in itself. As with the German case, appealing to the heroic traditions of military narrative provides a shield to protect martial honor and conveniently buries questions about responsibility and consequences. Such accounts of the Chosin campaign, for example, not only deposit the First Division safely at the port of Hungnam but also leapfrog bothersome issues concerning the strategic debacle or American conduct during the campaign toward Korean refugees and Chinese prisoners of war.

The history of the Pacific War has been integrated into the American cultural consciousness. The cold war helped to make concrete the mythologized motivations of the United States and reduced to remote abstractions the violence and brutality to which they gave rise. Understandably, Fussell bemoans the strain this has placed on the truths about war as he knows them, but this history, aside from conforming to political and ideological demands of the postwar period, has also served a functional role in the recovery from the war of combatant and noncombatant alike. Humans deal with pain and trauma in different ways, but the ideological and social atmosphere in which Hunt and Hough edited the memories of their experiences contributed directly to the collective recovery from war's effects in ways that veterans since have come to envy and sometimes resent.

The First Marine Division has fought in two major wars since 1945. In both cases the division was unprepared and undermanned, but in each case it was hastily reconstituted with reservists or conscripts. On these later battlefields it created new legends and myths that were in part built upon myths arising from the Pacific War. The increasingly ill-defined and idealized old corps of those days remained a measuring stick long after the realities of ground combat

62 Millett, *Semper Fidelis*, 494.

had moved in different directions. The North Koreans, the Chinese, and later on the Vietnamese were often judged according to the spirit and ability shown by the Japanese at Iwo Jima and Okinawa even though these were very different wars and unfamiliar enemies. The society that supplied the Marine Corps with new recruits continuously changed to the point that the draftees who filled out the combat units of the division in the late sixties were those whom the political leaders deemed most expendable.[63] The institution itself had changed, and new battlefield situations required images and myths different from what had existed before. One final autobiography helps to illustrate the dynamic evolution of martial myth and imagination as well as its most enduring and universal features.

Lewis B. Puller, Jr., literally and metaphorically carried the Pacific War imagery of his legendary father into the Vietnam War of the succeeding generation. Conceived upon his father's long-delayed return to the States after the bloody Peleliu campaign, this "fortunate son" was immersed in the spirit of the Marines as few are. He vividly recalls at age six watching the parade given for his father when, for heroism in the Chosin campaign, he received his fifth Navy Cross: "on that now distant drill field beneath the glare of a California sun, I had first begun to grasp the concept of battlefield glory and with it sensed a commitment to a calling over which I would be powerless."[64] Surrounded by the military life until his father's forced retirement in late 1955, Puller learned intimately its unwritten cult of manhood, stoically suppressing tears of pain and embarrassment as a small child and developing a hunter mentality by shooting his first deer at age eleven. There was never any doubt what he would do after completing college.

Living constantly in the shadow of his father, Puller eagerly joined the Marine Corps in 1967 and volunteered for combat as an opportunity to become his own man rather than simply Chesty Puller's son. While Puller was still in the Basic School, the Tet offensive gave the immediacy of the Vietnam War a new edge that was reflected in the desktop graffiti he read: "What the fuck, drive a truck," became a motto for those who began to question their chances of survival, whereas someone more bellicose inscribed

63 The argument can be made, however, given the methods for assigning personnel in the Second World War, that those who filled the combat arms, especially in the Army Ground Forces, likewise represented the least educated and valued of the draftees.

64 His father, incidently, looked to the mythologized memory of his Civil War heroes, Robert E. Lee and Thomas J. Jackson; Lewis B. Puller, Jr., *Fortunate Son* (New York: Grove Weidenfeld, 1991), 5.

"War is our business, and business is good." The images of war
Puller carried off to Officer Candidate School, unshaken by Tet
or news of Marine casualties, were the Disneyfied version decried
by Fussell and common to all uninitiated civilians. Filled with the
stories overheard during his father's talks with streams of well-
wishers who visited his Saluda, Virginia, home after his retirement
and raised on a steady diet of Hemingway novels and John Wayne
movies, Puller joined the Marines confident of his ability to face
the challenges of combat. Amidst growing doubts and concerns as
the ultimate test drew closer, the John Wayne image occurred to
him again as he headed for Okinawa, feeling like "John Wayne in
a World War II movie."[65]

Arriving in Vietnam in the summer of 1968, Puller had not been
with his company long before he started to question his earlier
assumptions. Certain he did not want to make a career of the
Marine Corps, he quickly became uncomfortable making life-and-
death decisions about the men in his platoon. Puller experienced
Jones's evolutionary transformation:

> I began to develop mixed feelings toward the Marine Corps
> and my country, alternately loving and despising both, and I
> was confused by the ambivalence of my feelings toward both
> corps and country. A part of me had already begun to regard
> the enemy as some sort of inhuman cannon fodder. I realized
> that my reaction was a defense mechanism that allowed me to
> accept and dispense death and mutilation more readily, but I
> also knew that I was going to lose a part of my soul if the
> thinking progressed much further.

The traumas of frontline service had different settings and new
agents, but they were the same in broad outline as those confronted
by Jones, Sledge, and Fussell. Those men had returned from the
war with scars, physical and mental, but outwardly intact; Puller
did not. Whereas his father's career spanned thirty-seven years,
including twenty-six overseas, and five wars, Puller's ended just
short of three months in Vietnam when a booby-trapped howitzer
round blew off his right leg at the hip, left a six-inch stump of the
left, tore away much of his buttocks, most of the thumb and little
finger on his right hand, all but the thumb and half the forefinger
on his left hand, split his scrotum, dislocated his shoulder, and
ruptured his eardrum. He was in such wretched shape when he

65 The "John Wayne" image, ibid., 32, 63; graffiti, 47; more than Chesty's son,
67.

was brought into the hospital that the surgeon who attended him
seriously considered allowing him to die.[66]

The rest of Puller's life has been a struggle to resolve its conflicting legacies. He long felt a failure to live up to his father's
heroic record or the Hollywood versions with which he had grown
up. He felt extreme bitterness toward those who had not faced the
same dangers, like Coast Guard and naval officers he had met in
safe Stateside billets. In his 1978 run for the House of Representatives, he became especially resentful of his Republican political
opponent, Paul Trible, a jingoistic anticommunist who wrapped
himself in the American flag. A year younger than Puller, he "had
engineered a questionable deferment to avoid the war that had
killed a dozen of my friends. I despised him for having been spared
the most catastrophic episode of our generation." He also grew
increasingly disillusioned about the justness of the war itself and
American efforts to disengage from it. Official statements intended
to mask the abandonment of South Vietnam with assurances of
their ability to defend themselves angered Puller:

> It seemed incredible to me that the American people would
> swallow such claptrap or that our leaders, both military and
> civilian, had become so jaded by the war that they were willing
> to go on record with their hypocrisy. I also came to feel that
> I had given myself to a cause that, in addition to having robbed
> me of my youth and left me crippled and deformed, allowed
> me no pride for having been a participant.

Like Fussell, Puller was insistent that only those who had the firsthand experience were truly qualified to narrate its history or make
military policy, but in contrast to the post-1945 period, the shift in
American public opinion toward the war silenced veterans' voices
and left them outside the traditional process of collective healing.[67]

Confronting a variety of his own personal demons, Puller discovered that American cultural attitudes toward violence had
changed drastically since his father's time. Civil unrest was reaching
heights untested even by the Bonus Army of 1932 or the race riots

66 Ibid., long quotation, 137; description of injuries, 158–59. The doctor who
treated Puller later wrote in a letter: "Your survival had seemed to me a miracle
of dubious value which severely tested the moral imperative of my Hippocratic
oath.... Your running for the House of Representatives ten years after our
meeting in Vietnam reaffirmed the worth of my service there and is a source
of great personal satisfaction to me" (323).
67 Ibid., on those officers and men with safe jobs Puller thought "of the differing
degrees of sacrifice demanded of a pig and a chicken when forced to contribute
to a breakfast of ham and eggs," 54, 56, 62–63; on Trible, 293; on American
attitudes (long quotation), 233–34; veterans exclusion, 202–3.

in the summer of 1943; uniformed veterans were scorned and branded as criminal; the political and military leadership was largely discredited and with them the war in Southeast Asia. At the same time Fussell was ridiculing the lack of artistry in the Iwo Jima memorial, Puller was placing enormous hope in the construction of the Vietnam Memorial – another subject of bitter controversy. When the John Wayne image ceased to propel large numbers of young men into the military, Rambo appeared, seizing control of his own cinematic destiny. American political leaders have since insisted on popular consensus for military action and then taken liberties with the truth that would have made Office of War Information officials cringe. In cultural myth and imagination, the centrality of violence continues to underpin social organization. The forms, victims, and controls continue to evolve even as the structural aspects of victim and victimizer remain as recognizable today as they did when Chesty Puller signed on as a private.

The atomic age and the era of "limited" wars, the baby boom and the age of mass consumerism: these were the new realities underlying the instrumental thinking and the new imaginary constructs. Militaries do not always plan to fight the next war as they fought the last, but they necessarily interpret and evaluate their options according to existing standards. For the Marine Corps, which had reached the height of its power and prestige in the Pacific War, it was difficult not to compare everything to those days. In American society at large, with a booming economy, and filled with men who had done their duty and then wanted to enjoy the fruits of their labor, there seemed to be no place for the old Marine image. There were no more "banana wars" – at least for the time being – nor any more exotic legation duty in China. There seemed few who were interested in such things in a time of prosperity, only youngsters like Puller or Philip Caputo, raised on Hollywood war heroes, who, for a variety of reasons, sought manhood and validation in uniform. The Pacific War images, thoroughly abstracted, drew men to the service and continued to permeate operational planning until circumstances, like those encountered by Puller in the Riviera area near Da Nang, in physical therapy at the Philadelphia naval hospital, and as a recovering alcoholic in Washington, D.C., generated new ones. But that belongs to another story.

All military actions and decisions, in one way or another, might ultimately be characterized as outgrowths of myth and imagination. No modern army enters combat *tabula rasa*. It prepares for battle on an institutional level in how it organizes, equips, and trains its forces, and individuals steel themselves according to a wide array of customs and beliefs. By definition, preparation, whether by a staff planner or a common soldier, begins with the imagination – with the construction of expectations for what lies ahead. By projecting their assumptions onto people, events, and situations, combatants actively shape the landscape in which they must kill and destroy. The study of such imaginary constructions offers valuable insights in two respects. First, as cultural phenomena, these constructs supply the best means available for understanding national distinctions between armies. What is unique, for instance, about the American way of war arises from soldiers' reliance on their own culturally, socially, and institutionally defined ways of structuring, understanding, and reacting to their world. Second, the particular myths and images drawn upon to sanction and set boundaries on the use of violence also determine its relative brutalization. Americans behaved with far greater savagery in the Pacific War than they did in Europe precisely because their images of the Japanese directly fostered the escalation of barbarism in ways that images of the Germans did not justify.

Among the many broadly defined categories of imaginary constructions that are nearly universally shared, three categories in particular provide a useful framework for the study of the Marines in the Pacific War. First, images of the Other objectified and dehumanized the enemy. Second, images of the Self defined their own particularistic code of behavior and military rationality that affected directly the planning and conduct of operations. And third, by late in the war, the Marines had harnessed technology to empower their indoctrination.

The process of drawing boundaries and reconstructing the landscape began with recruit training and continued until discharge. The Marine Corps actively fostered the objectification of those who did not belong, but its precise forms often carried beyond the control of the service. Through the manipulation of gender roles recruits learned to look with suspicion on all "outsiders," be they women, who did not belong in the all-male atmosphere of training and war, members of the other services, who were denigrated for failing to meet the abstract standards set by the marines, or a national enemy perceived as racially inferior. In each case, marines focused specifically on traits that differed from their own as a means of emphasizing their distinctness and denying strong parallels. Images of Self were created and sustained by polarizing relations. The profound internalization of the institutional self-image gave the marines important advantages on the battlefield, but they also carried high costs for individuals and the group that often carried beyond the battlefield.

In general outline, the Marines did nothing especially unique from what all military institutions strive to achieve. To the extent that their indoctrination was more deeply ingrained than that of men belonging to the other services, this could be attributed to specific historical factors. The elitist image created and magnified after the First World War reflected both the unusual degree of selectivity enjoyed by the Marine Corps and its battlefield performance. Even despite the Marines' reliance on draftees, these images of selectivity continued through the Second World War. As the smallest and most homogeneous of the services, the Marine Corps imposed its indoctrination on members more easily than the others. Finally, operational considerations helped this process enormously. Assigned the role of amphibious shock troops, a specialty lost by 1945, the marines were able to cultivate their self-image as a military elite that intertwined doctrine and organization with their ideology and the warrior spirit.

By 1945, as a result of an evolving process of indoctrination and instrumental innovation, the Marines had created, in effect, a mechanism for perpetual war. Although the men who carried out the "processing" on Okinawa were part of a rationalized system of destruction, they still retained their imaginary construction of the battlefield. As a result, while the technological sophistication required of mechanized war subordinated the actions of individuals to machines, at the same time the destructive power of the machines was directed according to the basic fears and desires that had motivated the marines since the beginning of the war. The logical progression of staff operational thought had bridged the gap between the ideological indoctrination of the individual marine warrior and the means to achieve the annihilation of a putatively subhuman enemy.

This perpetual-war machine was never dismantled and has adversely affected U.S. policy ever since. Immediately after V-J Day the machine was put into neutral and subsequently found inadequate for dealing with the crises of the new cold war world, including the Chinese civil war. The ideological component of the perpetual-war machine flourished in the midst of a massive war against Asian communism, but the military force necessary to empower American ideology was never committed directly against Mao. It appeared for a time that both components offered a solution in the Korean War, until Chinese intervention forced a decision to back away from a protracted, expanded war on the Asian continent. Subsequent American leaders have wanted to utilize the destructive power of the machine without fully unleashing the apocalyptic, exterminationist imagery underpinning it. The Clausewitzian trinity requires both ideological and military mobilization that has not been possible in post-1945 American society on a scale commensurate with stated U.S. political goals.

The imagery of the Pacific War has been transformed. Whether commercialized, romanticized, or, in Fussell's words, Norman Rockwellized, the jagged knife edge that served the marines in their fight against the Japanese has been chipped and dulled, but it remains available to be honed anew. In the meantime, many of the differences exploited in conceptions of Self and Other continue to burst into the open in other ways, like the rattling lid on a boiling pot. After all, American wartime images have often provided external relief for ongoing internal pressures of race, gender, and identity. Collectively, the marines were neither dupes nor monsters. They were representatives of a society that draws upon its unique cultural heritage to prepare for and wage war. The forms such preparations and conduct take are often deplorable, but recognition of them must be the first step to correcting them. Solutions must move beyond instrumentalities to encompass as well new myths and images.

SELECT BIBLIOGRAPHY

PRIMARY SOURCES

Archival Materials

National Archives. Record Group (RG) 112. United States Army. Office of the Surgeon General.

National Archives. Record Group 407. United States Army. Adjutant General's Office (Operational records).

United States, Department of the Navy Records. Subject Files (administrative records pertaining to the Marine Corps held by the Department of the Navy).

United States Marine Corps Records. Record Group 127. United States Marine Corps. Geographic File, 1941–49. Accession Numbers 63A-2534 (Guadalcanal); 74-93 (Peleliu); 65A-5188 (Peleliu and Okinawa); 63A-2489 (Correspondence File, 1941–45); 14051 (Comment Files to the official histories); 77-0048, 78-0049, and 61A-2265 (Korea).

Published Documents

United States Administration of Veterans Affairs. *Annual Report*. Government Printing Office, 1944–48.

United States Marine Corps. *Annual Report of the Commandant of the United States Marine Corps to the Secretary of the Navy for the Fiscal Year 1939 [through 1951]*.

United States War Department. Army Service Forces. Research Branch. Information and Education Division. *What the Soldier Thinks* (December 1942-September 1945).

Personal Papers

United States Marine Corps Historical Center (MCHC), Washington Navy Yard:

E. D. Allen	Eugene P. Boardman	Werner Claussen
A. Andrew Andow	Kenneth Bogard	Jack Colegrove
William C. Beall	Wilburt S. Brown	Pedro A. del Valle
Philip H. Bernstein	Clifton B. Cates	Christopher S. Donner

George M. Dunn	Harold D. Harris	Nolan V. Marbrey
Harry G. Findlay	Robert E. Hogaboom	Herbert C. Merillat
Ray Gallagher	Harry R. Horsman	Sherwood F. Moran
Eugene W. Gleason	Robert F. Kelly	William F. Nolan
Robert Graff	Richard Kennard	John B. Simms
Joseph H. Griffith	William C. Koch, Jr.	Oliver P. Smith
Archibald Hanna	Joseph Kohn	Gerald C. Thomas
Theodore H.	Charles A. Linhart	A. A. Vandegrift
Harbaugh	Richard F. Lyons	William H. Whyte

Army Military History Institute, Carlisle Barracks:

> William and James Belote Collection
> Paul J. Mueller
> Charles C. Nast
> Donald A. Seibert

Oral Histories

United States Marine Corps Historical Center, Washington Navy Yard:

Eugene P. Boardman	Herman Hanneken	Edwin A. Pollock
Wilburt S. Brown	Korean War	Joseph Rosenthal
Harold Deakin	Interviews	Oliver P. Smith
Pedro A. del Valle	(23 separate	Gerald C. Thomas
Lewis J. Fields	interviews,	Merrill B. Twining
Samuel B. Griffith II	transcripts located	
	with the O. P.	
	Smith Personal	
	Papers collection)	

Periodicals and Paper Series

History and Memory	*Marine Recruiter*	*Royal United Service*
Journal of Strategic	*Michigan Quarterly*	*Institute Journal*
Studies	*Review*	*U.S. Naval Institute*
Leatherneck	*Pacific Historical Review*	*Naval History*
Leavenworth Papers	*Public Opinion Quarterly*	*U.S. Naval Institute*
Marine Corps Gazette		*Proceedings*
		U.S. Naval Medical
		Bulletin

Memoirs, Published Letters, and Contemporary Commentaries

Averill, Gerald P. *Mustang*. Novato: Presidio Press, 1987.
Ayling, Keith. *Semper Fidelis*. Boston: Houghton Mifflin, 1943.

Bailey, Gilbert P. *Boot*. New York: Macmillan, 1944.

Bayler, Walter L. J., and Cecil Carnes. *Last Man off Wake Island*. New York: Bobbs-Merrill, 1943.

Boswell, Rolfe. *Leatherneck*. New York: Thomas Y. Crowell, 1943.

Bronemann, LeRoy B. *Once upon a Tide*. Bryn Mawr: Dorrance, 1982.

Brown, David Tucker, Jr. *Marine from Virginia*. Chapel Hill: University of North Carolina Press, 1947.

Butterfield, Roger. *Al Schmid, Marine*. New York: Norton, 1944.

Campigno, Anthony J. *A Marine Division in Nightmare Alley*. New York: Comet Press, 1958.

Caputo, Philip. *A Rumor of War*. New York: Holt, Rinehart and Winston, 1977.

Chamberlin, J. Gordon. *The Church and Demobilization*. New York: Whitmore and Stone, 1945.

Clark, Lester W. *An Unlikely Arena*. New York: Vantage, 1989.

Collins, Clella Reeves. *When Your Son Goes to War*. New York: Harper and Brothers, 1943.

Cooke, Elliot D. *All but Me and Thee*. Washington: Infantry Journal Press, 1946.

Crane, Aimée. *Marines at War*. New York: Hyperion Press, 1943.

Davis, Russell. *Marine at War*. Boston: Little, Brown and Company, 1961.

Devereux, James P. S. *The Story of Wake Island*. New York: Lippincott, 1947.

Empey, Arthur Guy. *"Over the Top" by an American Soldier Who Went*. New York: G. P. Putnam and Sons, 1917.

Flagg, James Montgomery. *Roses and Buckshot*. New York: G. P. Putnam and Sons, 1946.

Flowers, Montaville. *The Japanese Conquest of American Opinion*. New York: George H. Doran, 1917.

Fukuzawa Yukichi. *An Outline of a Theory of Civilization*. Translated by David A. Dillworth and G. Cameron Hurst. Tokyo: Sophia University Press, 1973.

Gallant, T. Grady. *On Valor's Side*. Garden City: Doubleday, 1963.

Geer, Andrew. *The New Breed: The Story of the U.S. Marines in Korea*. New York: Harper, 1952.

Gibbons, Floyd. *"And They Thought We Wouldn't Fight."* New York: George H. Doran, 1918.

Goodman, Jack, ed. *While You Were Gone*. New York: Da Capo Press, 1974.

Gray, J. Glenn. *The Warriors*. New York: Harper and Row, 1970.

Hersey, John. *Into the Valley*. New York: Alfred A. Knopf, 1943.

Horan, James D., and Gerold Frank. *Out in the Boondocks*. New York: Putnam, 1943.

Hunt, George P. *Coral Comes High*. New York: Harper, 1946.

Hynes, Samuel. *Flights of Passage*. New York: Frederic C. Beil; Annapolis: Naval Institute Press, 1988.

Lea, Tom. *Peleliu Landing*. El Paso: Carl Herzog, 1945.

Leckie, Robert. *Helmet for My Pillow*. New York: Random House, 1957.

Liddell Hart, B. H. *The German Generals Talk.* New York: William Morrow, 1948.

Lucas, Jim. *Combat Correspondent.* New York: Reynal and Hitchcock, 1944.

McCahill, William P. *First to Fight.* Philadelphia: McKay, 1943.

McEniry, John Howard. *A Dive-Bomber Pilot at Guadalcanal.* Tuscaloosa: University of Alabama Press, 1987.

Manchester, William. *Goodbye, Darkness.* Boston: Little, Brown and Company, 1979.

Mauldin, Bill. *Up Front.* New York: Henry Holt, 1944.

Merillat, Herbert C. *The Island.* Boston: Houghton Mifflin, 1944.

Metcalf, Clyde H. *A History of the United States Marine Corps.* New York: G. P. Putnam and Sons, 1939.

The Marine Corps Reader. New York: G. P. Putnam and Sons, 1944.

Myers, Martin L. *Yardbird Myers.* Philadelphia: Dorrance, 1944.

O'Sheel, Patrick, and Gene Cook, eds. *Semper Fidelis.* New York: William Sloan, 1947.

Paige, Mitchell. *A Marine Named Mitch.* New York: Vantage Press, 1976.

Parry, Francis Fox. *Three-War Marine.* Pacifica: Pacifica Press, 1987.

Pratt, Fletcher. *The Marines' War.* New York: Sloane, 1948.

Pratt, George K. *Soldier to Civilian.* New York: McGraw-Hill, 1944.

Puller, Lewis B., Jr. *Fortunate Son.* New York: Grove Weidenfeld, 1991.

Pyle, Ernie. *Last Chapter.* New York: Henry Holt, 1945.

Russ, Martin. *The Last Parallel.* New York: Rinehart, 1957.

Sajer, Guy. *The Forgotten Soldier.* Translated by Lily Emmet. New York: Ballantine, 1967.

Shane, Ted. *Heroes of the Pacific.* New York: Messner, 1944.

Sherrod, Robert. *On to Westward.* New York: Duell, Sloan and Pearce, 1945.

Sledge, E. B. *With the Old Breed.* Novato: Presidio Press, 1981.

Smith, Holland M., and Percy Finch. *Coral and Brass.* New York: Scribner, 1949.

[Storey, Mansfield]. *Secretary Root's Record, "Marked Severities" in Philippine Warfare.* Boston: George W. Ellis, 1902.

Strecker, Edward A., and Kenneth E. Appel. *Psychiatry in Modern Warfare.* New York: Macmillan, 1945.

Terkel, Studs. *"The Good War."* New York: Pantheon Books, 1984.

Thomason, John W., Jr. *Fix Bayonets!* New York: Charles Scribner's Sons, 1926.

Tower, H. H. *Fighting the Devil with the Marines.* Philadelphia: Dorrance, 1945.

Tregaskis, Richard. *Guadalcanal Diary.* New York: Random House, 1943.

Tupper, Eleanor, and George E. McReynolds. *Japan in American Public Opinion.* New York: Macmillan, 1937.

Vance, Rowland. *They Made Me a Leatherneck.* New York: Norton, 1943.

Vandegrift, A. A., and Robert B. Asprey. *Once a Marine.* New York: Norton, 1964.

Waller, Willard. *The Veteran Comes Back.* New York: Dryden Press, 1944.

Wechter, Dixon. *When Johnny Comes Marching Home.* 1944. Reprint. Westport: Greenwood Press, 1970.

Willard, W. Wyeth. *The Leathernecks Come Through*. New York: Fleming H. Revell, 1944.

Wolfert, Ira. *Battle for the Solomons*. Boston: Houghton Mifflin, 1943.

Fiction

Anderson, Maxwell, and Laurence Stallings. *What Price Glory*. In *Three American Plays*. Edited by Kenneth MacGowan. New York: Harcourt, Brace, 1926.

Boyd, Thomas. *Through the Wheat*. New York: Charles Scribner's Sons, 1923.

[Campbell], William Edward March. *Company K*. 1933. Reprint. New York: Sagamore Press, 1957.

Dos Passos, John. *One Man's Initiation: 1917*. Ithaca: Cornell University Press, 1969.

Three Soldiers. Boston: Houghton Mifflin, 1921.

Faulkner, William. *Soldiers' Pay*. New York: Liveright, 1926.

Frank, Pat. *Hold Back the Night*. New York: J. B. Lippincott, 1951.

Jones, James. *The Thin Red Line*. New York: Charles Scribner's Sons, 1962.

Mailer, Norman. *The Naked and the Dead*. New York: Holt, Rinehart and Winston, 1948.

Michener, James A. *Tales of the South Pacific*. 1948. Reprint. New York: Henry Holt, 1976.

Sassoon, Siegfried. *Collected Poems, 1908–1956*. Boston: Faber and Faber, 1961.

Seeger, Alan. *Poems*. New York: Charles Scribner's Sons, 1917.

Thorin, Duane. *A Ride to Panmunjom*. Chicago: Henry Regnery, 1956.

Uris, Leon. *Battle Cry*. New York: Bantam, 1953.

SECONDARY SOURCES

Official Histories

United States Air Force. Historical Division. *The Army Air Forces in World War II*. Edited by Wesley Frank Craven and James Lea Cate. 7 vols. Chicago: University of Chicago Press, 1948–58. Vol. 4, *The Pacific: Guadalcanal to Saipan*. 1950. Vol. 5, *The Pacific: Matterhorn to Nagasaki*. 1953.

United States Air Force. War Documentation Project. *The Soviet Partisan Movement in World War II: Summary and Conclusions*. Maxwell AFB, Ala.: Human Resources Research Institute, 1954.

United States Army. Office of the Chief. Chemical Corps. *Mechanized Flame Thrower Operations in World War II*. Washington: Government Printing Office, 1951.

Portable Flame Thrower Operations in World War II. Washington: Government Printing Office, 1949.

United States Army. Medical Department. *Neuropsychiatry in World War II.*
Edited by Albert J. Glass. 2 vols. Washington: Office of the Surgeon
General, 1973.

Preventive Medicine in World War II. Vol. 5, *Communicable Diseases, Transmitted through Contact or by Unknown Means.* Edited by Ebbe Curtis Hoff.
Washington: Office of the Surgeon General, 1960.

United States Army. Office of Military History. *Small Unit Actions.* Washington: Historical Division, General Staff, 1946.

United States Army in the Korean War. 4 vols. Washington: Historical Division, Department of the Army, 1961–72.

United States Army in World War II. Vol. 1, *The Army Ground Forces.* Wash-
ington: Historical Division, Department of the Army, 1947–48. Pt. 1,
The Organization of Ground Combat Troops, by Kent Roberts Greenfield,
Robert R. Palmer, and Bell I. Wiley. 1947. Pt. 2, *The Procurement and
Training of Ground Combat Troops,* by Robert R. Palmer, Bell I. Wiley,
and William R. Keast. 1948.

United States Army in World War II. Vol. 2, *The War in the Pacific.* Wash-
ington: Historical Division, Department of the Army, 1948–62. Pt. 1,
Okinawa: The Last Battle, by Roy E. Appleman, James M. Burns, Russell
A. Gugeler, and John Stevens. 1948. Pt. 2, *Guadalcanal: The First Of-
fensive,* by John Miller, Jr. 1949. Pt. 3, *Approach to the Philippines,* by
Robert Ross Smith. 1953. Pt. 6, *Seizure of the Gilberts and Marshalls,* by
Philip A. Crowl and Edmund G. Love. 1955. Pt. 9, *Campaign in the
Marianas,* by Philip A. Crowl. 1960. Pt. 10, *Strategy and Command: The
First Two Years,* by Louis Morton. 1962.

United States Marine Corps. *A Brief History of U.S. Marine Corps Officer
Procurement, 1775–1969,* by Bernard C. Nalty and Ralph F. Moody.
Washington: Historical Branch, G-3 Division, Headquarters Marine
Corps, 1970.

History of U.S. Marine Corps Operations in World War II. 5 vols. Washington:
Historical Branch, G-3 Division, Headquarters Marine Corps, 1958-
71.

"Marine Corps Administrative History." Washington: Marine Corps Historical Division, 1946. Typed manuscript.

"Marine Corps Ground Training in World War II," by Kenneth W.
Condit, Gerald Diamond, and Edwin T. Turnbladh. Washington: His-
torical Branch, G-3 Division, Headquarters Marine Corps, 1956.
Typed manuscript.

Mobilization of the Marine Corps Reserve in the Korean Conflict, 1950–1951.
Washington: Historical Branch, G-3 Division, Headquarters Marine
Corps, 1951.

[Monograph Series, World War II]. Washington: Historical Branch, G-
3 Division, Headquarters Marine Corps, 1946–55. *The First Marine
Division on Okinawa,* by James R. Stockman. 1946. *The Guadalcanal
Campaign,* by John L. Zimmerman. 1949. *The Assault on Peleliu,* by
Frank O. Hough. 1950. *The Campaign on New Britain,* by Frank O.
Hough and John A. Crown. 1952. *Okinawa: Victory in the Pacific,* by
Charles S. Nichols and Henry I. Shaw, Jr. 1955.

"The Problems of U.S. Marine Corps Prisoners of War in Korea." Washington: Marine Corps Historical Division, Headquarters Marine Corps, 1988. Typed manuscript.

U.S. Marine Corps Operations in Korea, 1950–1953. 5 vols. Washington: Historical Branch, G-3 Division, Headquarters Marine Corps, 1954–72.

The United States Marines in North China, 1945–1949. Washington: Historical Branch, G-3 Division, Headquarters Marine Corps, 1962.

Division of the Reserve. *The Marine Corps Reserve: A History.* Washington: Division of the Reserve, Headquarters Marine Corps, 1966.

United States Navy Department. *Administration of the Navy Department in World War II,* by Julius Furer. Washington: Government Printing Office, 1959.

The History of the Medical Department of the United States Navy in World War II. 3 vols. Washington: Bureau of Medicine and Surgery, 1953.

Bureau of Naval Personnel. *The History of the Chaplain Corps, United States Navy.* 2 vols. Washington: Government Printing Office, n.d.

General Histories

Adams, Henry H. *1942: The Year That Doomed the Axis.* New York: McKay, 1967.

Adas, Michael. *Machines as the Measure of Men.* Ithaca: Cornell University Press, 1989.

Aichinger, Peter. *The American Soldier in Fiction, 1880–1963.* Ames: Iowa State University Press, 1975.

Appleman, Roy E. *East of Chosin.* College Station: Texas A&M University Press, 1987.

Barnhart, Michael. *Japan Prepares for Total War.* Ithaca: Cornell University Press, 1987.

Bartlett, Merrill L. *Lejeune.* Columbia: University of South Carolina Press, 1991.

Bartov, Omer. *The Eastern Front, 1941–45.* New York: St. Martin's Press, 1986.

Hitler's Army. New York: Oxford University Press, 1991.

Belote, James, and William Belote. *Typhoon of Steel.* New York: Harper and Row, 1970.

Berry, Henry. *Semper Fi, Mac.* New York: Arbor House, 1982.

Bérubé, Allan. *Coming out under Fire.* New York: Free Press, 1990.

Best, Geoffrey. *Humanity in Warfare.* New York: Columbia University Press, 1980.

Biderman, Albert D. *March to Calumny.* New York: Macmillan, 1963.

Blum, John Morton. *V Was for Victory.* New York: Harcourt Brace Jovanovich, 1976.

Blumenson, Martin, ed. *The Patton Papers.* Boston: Houghton Mifflin, 1974.

Bond, Brian. *Liddell Hart.* New Brunswick: Rutgers University Press, 1977.

Borg, Dorothy, and Shumpai Okamoto, eds. *Pearl Harbor as History: Jap-*

anese–American Relations, 1931–1941. New York: Columbia University Press, 1973.

Brown, John Sloan. *Draftee Division*. Lexington: University of Kentucky Press, 1986.

Butler, Ivan. *The War Film*. South Brunswick, N.J.: A. S. Barnes, 1974.

Campbell, D'Ann. *Women at War with America*. Cambridge: Harvard University Press, 1984.

Chenault, Libby. *Battlelines*. Chapel Hill: Rare Book Collection, Wilson Library, University of North Carolina Press, 1988.

Clausewitz, Carl von. *On War*. Edited and translated by Michael Howard and Peter Paret. Princeton: Princeton University Press, 1984.

Coffman, Edward M. *The War to End All Wars*. Madison: University of Wisconsin Press, 1986.

Cooper, Helen M., Adrienne Auslander Munich, and Susan Merrill Squier, eds. *Arms and the Woman*. Chapel Hill: University of North Carolina Press, 1989.

Cooper, Norman V. *A Fighting General*. Quantico: Marine Corps Association, 1987.

Coox, Alvin D. *Nomonhon: Japan against Russia, 1939*. 2 vols. Stanford: Stanford University Press, 1985.

Costello, John. *Love Sex and War*. London: Collins, 1985.

The Pacific War. New York: Rawson Wade, 1981.

Davis, Burke. *Marine!* Boston: Little, Brown and Company, 1962.

Deist, Wilhelm, ed. *The German Military in the Age of Total War*. Dover, N.H.: Berg, 1985.

D'Emilio, John. *Sexual Politics, Sexual Communities*. Chicago: University of Chicago Press, 1983.

Dower, John W. *War without Mercy*. New York: Pantheon Books, 1986.

Drinnon, Richard. *Facing West*. New York: New American Library, 1980.

Eighty-first Wildcat Division Historical Committee. *The 81st Infantry Wildcat Division in World War II*. Washington: Infantry Journal Press, 1948.

Ellis, John. *The Social History of the Machine Gun*. New York: Arno Press, 1981.

Elshtain, Jean Bethke. *Women and War*. New York: Basic Books, 1987.

Enloe, Cynthia. *Does Khaki Become You?* Boston: Pandora Press, 1988.

Fehrenbach, T. R. *This Kind of War*. New York: Macmillan, 1963.

Fleming, Keith. *The U.S. Marine Corps in Crisis*. Columbia: University of South Carolina Press, 1990.

Frank, Benis M. *Denig's Demons and How They Grew*. Washington: Marine Corps Combat Correspondents and Photographers Association, 1967.

Frank, Richard B. *Guadalcanal*. New York: Random House, 1990.

Fraser, John. *Violence in the Arts*. New York: Cambridge University Press, 1974.

Friedan, Betty. *The Feminine Mystique*. New York: W. W. Norton, 1963.

Fussell, Paul. *The Boy Scout Handbook and Other Observations*. New York: Oxford University Press, 1982.

The Great War and Modern Memory. New York: Oxford University Press, 1975.

Thank God for the Atom Bomb and Other Essays. New York: Summit Books, 1988.

Wartime. New York: Oxford University Press, 1989.

Gaddis, John Lewis. *The United States and the Origins of the Cold War, 1941– 1947.* New York: Columbia University Press, 1972.

Gailey, Harry A. *Peleliu, 1944.* Annapolis: Nautical and Aviation Publishing, 1983.

Garland, Brock. *War Movies.* New York: Facts on File, 1987.

Genthe, Charles V. *American War Narratives, 1917–1918.* New York: David Lewis, 1969.

Gilbert, Sandra M., and Susan Gubar. *No Man's Land.* 2 vols. New Haven: Yale University Press, 1988–89.

Ginzberg, Eli, James K. Anderson, Sol W. Ginsburg, and John L. Herma. *The Ineffective Soldier.* 3 vols. New York: Columbia University Press, 1959.

Goodstone, Tony, ed. *The Pulps: Fifty Years of American Pop Culture.* New York: Chelsea House, 1976.

Griffith, Samuel B., II. *The Battle for Guadalcanal.* Philadelphia: Lippincott, 1963.

Grinker, Roy R., and John P. Spiegel. *Men under Stress.* Philadelphia: Blakiston, 1945.

Hammel, Eric. *Chosin.* New York: Vanguard, 1981.

Guadalcanal. 3 vols. New York: Crown Publishers, 1987–88.

Hammond, Paul Y. *Organizing for Defense: The American Military Establishment in the Twentieth Century.* Princeton: Princeton University Press, 1961.

Hartman, Susan M. *The Home Front and Beyond.* Boston: Twayne, 1982.

Heinl, Robert D., Jr. *Victory at High Tide.* Philadelphia: Lippincott, 1968.

Hemingway, Albert. *Ira Hayes: Pima Marine.* Lanham, Md.: University Press of America, 1988.

Higonnet, Margaret Randolph, Jane Jenson, Sonya Michel, and Margaret Collins Weitz, eds. *Behind the Lines.* New Haven: Yale University Press, 1987.

Hobsbawm, Eric, and Terence Ranger, eds. *The Invention of Tradition.* New York: Cambridge University Press, 1983.

Hoffman, Alice M., and Howard S. Hoffman. *Archives of Memory.* Lexington: University Press of Kentucky, 1990.

Holmes, Richard. *Acts of War.* New York: Free Press, 1985.

Holt, Kermit. *Guadalcanal, 25 Years Later.* Chicago: Chicago Tribune, 1967.

Honey, Maureen. *Creating Rosie the Riveter.* Amherst: University of Massachusetts Press, 1984.

Hough, Frank O. *The Island War.* Philadelphia: J. B. Lippincott, 1947.

Howard, Michael, ed. *Restraints on War.* New York: Oxford University Press, 1979.

Hoyt, Edwin P. *Guadalcanal.* New York: Stein and Day, 1982.

Huie, William Bradford. *The Hero of Iwo Jima and Other Stories.* New York: Signet, 1962.

Huntington, Samuel P. *The Common Defense: Strategic Programs in National Politics*. New York: Columbia University Press, 1966.

Ienaga, Saburō. *The Pacific War, 1931–1945*. New York: Pantheon, 1978.

Iriye, Akira. *Power and Culture*. Cambridge: Harvard University Press, 1981.

     ed. *Mutual Images*. Cambridge: Harvard University Press, 1975.

Isaacs, Harold R. *Images of Asia: American Views of China and India*. New York: Harper, 1972.

Isely, Jeter A., and Philip A. Crowl. *The U.S. Marines and Amphibious War*. Princeton: Princeton University Press, 1951.

James, D. Clayton. *The Years of MacArthur*. 3 vols. Boston: Houghton Mifflin, 1970–85.

Jones, James. *WWII*. New York: Grosset and Dunlap, 1975.

Keegan, John. *The Face of Battle*. New York: Viking Press, 1976.

Keen, Sam. *Faces of the Enemy*. San Francisco: Harper and Row, 1986.

Kellett, Anthony. *Combat Motivation*. Boston: Kluwer-Nijhoff, 1982.

Kennedy, David M. *Over Here*. New York: Oxford University Press, 1980.

Kennedy, Paul. *The Rise and Fall of the Great Powers*. New York: Random House, 1987.

Kinkaid, Eugene. *In Every War but One*. New York: W. W. Norton, 1959.

Koppes, Clayton R., and Gregory D. Black. *Hollywood Goes to War*. New York: Free Press, 1987.

Langley, Lester D. *The Banana Wars*. Lexington: University of Kentucky Press, 1983.

Leckie, Robert. *Challenge for the Pacific: Guadalcanal, the Turning Point of the War*. Garden City: Doubleday, 1965.

     The March to Glory. New York: World, 1960.

Lee, Robert Edward. *Victory at Guadalcanal*. Novato: Presidio Press, 1981.

Leed, Eric J. *No Man's Land*. New York: Cambridge University Press, 1979.

Leonard, Thomas C. *Above the Battle*. New York: Oxford University Press, 1978.

Linderman, Gerald S. *Mirror of War*. Ann Arbor: University of Michigan Press, 1974.

Lindsay, Robert. *This High Name*. Madison: University of Wisconsin Press, 1956.

McMillan, George. *The Old Breed*. Washington: Infantry Journal Press, 1949.

Manchester, William. *American Caesar*. Boston: Little, Brown, 1978.

Marder, Arthur. *Old Friends, New Enemies*. New York: Oxford University Press, 1981.

Mares, William. *The Marine Machine*. Garden City: Doubleday, 1971.

Marine Corps Association. *Our First Year in Korea*. Quantico: Marine Corps Gazette, 1954.

Marling, Karal Ann, and John Wetenhall. *Iwo Jima: Monuments, Memories, and the American Hero*. Cambridge: Harvard University Press, 1991.

Marshall, S. L. A. *Island Victory*. Washington: Infantry Journal Press, 1945.

     Men Against Fire. 1947. Reprint. New York: William Morrow, 1964.

The River and the Gauntlet. 1953. Reprint. New York: William Morrow, 1964.

Mayo, James M. *War Memorials as Political Landscape.* New York: Praeger, 1988.

Merillat, Herbert C. *Guadalcanal Remembered.* New York: Dodd, Mead, 1982.

Merton, Robert K., and Paul F. Lazarsfeld, eds. *Studies in the Scope and Method of "The American Soldier."* Glencoe: Free Press, 1950.

Miller, Stephen E., ed. *Military Strategy and the First World War.* Princeton: Princeton University Press, 1985.

Miller, Thomas G. *The Cactus Air Force.* New York: Harper and Row, 1969.

Millett, Allan R. *Semper Fidelis.* 2d ed. New York: Macmillan, 1991.

Millett, Allan R., and Williamson Murray, eds. *Military Effectiveness.* 3 vols. Boston: Allen and Unwin, 1988.

Mitchell, W. J. T. *Iconology.* Chicago: University of Chicago Press, 1986.

Morison, Samuel Eliot. *History of United States Naval Operations in World War Two.* Boston: Little, Brown, 1947–62. Vol. 5, *The Struggle for Guadalcanal.* 1951. Vol. 6, *Breaking the Bismarcks Barrier.* 1950. Vol. 7, *Aleutians, Gilberts, and Marshalls.* 1951. Vol. 12, *Leyte.* 1958. Vol. 14, *Victory in the Pacific.* 1961.

Strategy and Compromise. Boston: Little, Brown, 1958.

Two Ocean War. Boston: Houghton Mifflin, 1963.

Musicant, Ivan. *The Banana Wars.* New York: Macmillan, 1990.

Nalty, Bernard. *Strength for the Fight.* New York: Free Press, 1986.

Paret, Peter. *Makers of Modern Strategy.* Princeton: Princeton University Press, 1986.

Parish, James Robert. *The Great Combat Pictures.* Metuchen, N.J.: Scarecrow, 1990.

Pogue, Forrest C. *George C. Marshall.* 4 vols. New York: Viking Press, 1963–87.

Polenberg, Richard. *War and Society.* New York: J. B. Lippincott, 1972.

Porch, Douglas. *The Conquest of Morocco.* New York: Alfred A. Knopf, 1983.

The Conquest of the Sahara. New York: Alfred A. Knopf, 1984.

The French Foreign Legion. New York: HarperCollins, 1991.

Pyle, Kenneth. *The New Generation in Meiji Japan.* Stanford: Stanford University Press, 1969.

Rawls, Walton. *Wake Up, America!* New York: Abbeville Press, 1988.

Riesman, David. *The Lonely Crowd.* New Haven: Yale University Press, 1961.

Ross, Bill D. *Peleliu, Tragic Triumph.* New York: Random House, 1991.

Rupp, Leila J. *Mobilizing Women for War.* Princeton: Princeton University Press, 1978.

Schmidt, Hans. *Maverick Marine.* Lexington: University of Kentucky Press, 1987.

Shain, Russell Earl. *An Analysis of Motion Pictures about War Released by the American Film Industry, 1930–1970.* New York: Arno, 1976.

Sherry, Michael S. *The Rise of American Air Power.* New Haven: Yale University Press, 1987.

Spanier, John W. *The Truman–MacArthur Controversy and the Korean War.* Cambridge: Harvard University Press, 1959.

Spector, Ronald H. *Eagle against the Sun.* New York: Free Press, 1985.

Stouffer, Samuel A., A. A. Lumsdaine, M. H. Lumsdaine, R. M. Williams, Jr., M. B. Smith, I. L. Janis, S. A. Star, and L. S. Cottrell, Jr. *The American Soldier.* Vol. 2, *Combat and Its Aftermath.* Princeton: Princeton University Press, 1949.

Stouffer, Samuel A., E. A. Suchman, L. C. De Vinney, S. A. Star, and R. M. Williams, Jr. *The American Soldier.* Vol. 1, *Adjustment during Army Life.* Princeton: Princeton University Press, 1949.

Suid, Lawrence H. *Guts and Glory.* Reading, Mass.: Addison-Wesley, 1978.

Theweleit, Klaus. *Male Fantasies.* 2 vols. Minneapolis: University of Minnesota Press, 1989.

Thorne, Christopher. *Allies of a Kind.* New York: Oxford University Press, 1978.

Tuchman, Barbara W. *Stilwell and the American Experience in China.* New York: Macmillan, 1971.

Van Creveld, Martin. *Fighting Power.* Westport: Greenwood Press, 1982.

Virilio, Paul. *War and Cinema.* Translated by Patrick Camiller. New York: Verso, 1989.

Weigley, Russell F. *The American Way of War.* Bloomington: Indiana University Press, 1973.

  History of the United States Army. Bloomington: Indiana University Press, 1984.

Werstein, Irving. *Guadalcanal.* New York: Crowell, 1963.

Wilson, Jim. *Retreat Hell!* New York: William Morrow, 1988.

Wires, Richard. *John P. Marquand and Mr. Moto.* Muncie: Ball State University, 1990.

Wu, William F. *The Yellow Peril.* Hamden: Archon Books, 1982.

INDEX

285

flamethrowers, 13, 172, 176–83
Flowers, Montaville, 90
Frank, Pat, 230
French and Indian War (1754–63), 117–18
Friedan, Betty, 82, 244
Fu Manchu, 91
Fussell, Paul, 256
    on Iwo Jima memorial, 254, 269
    on reality of war defined by experience, 245–46, 248–49, 255, 262, 265, 268–69
    on sanitization of war, 243, 261, 267, 272
    war experiences of, 249–50, 255–56, 267

Gallant, T. Grady, 71, 254
Gallipoli campaign (1915–16), 37
Gavutu–Tanambogo, battle of (1942), 108, 120, 125
Geiger, Roy S., 132–33, 137, 146, 149–50, 209
gendered myths and images
    female symbols, 65–66, 76–79
    love and war, 73–75, 81
    military service as defining gender roles, 28, 68–69, 244–45
    misogyny in Marine training, 49, 66
    natural order, 72–73
    sexual objectification, 69–71, 74–75
    tropes, 64–66
German military organizations and units, 230
    Waffen-SS, 171, 176
    Wehrmacht, 84, 229

Großdeutschland Division, 171–72
    28th Division, 23
German soldiers
    compared to Japanese, 114–15
    Kämpfer spirit, 149, 171
    primary group theory, 194
Gibbons, Floyd, 46
GI bill, 205
Gilbert Islands campaign (1943), 142–43
Goettge, Frank, 111
Gray, J. Glenn, 50–51, 73–74, 81
Guadalcanal campaign (1942–43), 166, 170–71, 174, 179, 219, 224–25, 230, 257
    Aola, 122
    defensive battles, 120
    deployment, 118–20
    documentation, 16
    Goettge patrol, 111–12, 113
    Henderson Field bombardment, 249
    Japanese combat tricks, 124
    Japanese misjudgments, 100, 101–2
    jungle warfare, 71, 115–18, 155, 255–56
    Kukum, 109
    leadership, 116–18, 148
    losses, 112–13, 120, 201
    Lunga Point, 109
    marine attitudes toward Army, 136, 138–39
    marine attitudes toward Japanese, *see* Japanese laborers; Japanese soldiers
    marine behavior in combat, 23, 31, 33, 126–27, 196
    marine group dynamics, 192, 201

Marine/Navy, 134–35, 169–
70
Iwo Jima, battle of (1945), 87,
167, 211, 218, 244, 257–
58, 260–61, 264–65
Iwo Jima memorial, *see* Marine
Corps War Memorial

James, D. Clayton, 239
Japanese Imperial Army, 84,
185
Ichiki detachment, 123
Sendai Division, 103
Japanese laborers, 107–9, 125,
187
Japanese soldiers
as animals, 95–96, 115, 121
attitude toward surrender,
112–14, 179, 187
brutality, 102n, 111, 125
endurance, 124, 179
as jungle warriors, 104–5,
114–15
myths held by, 101–3
in North China, 215–16
personal possessions of, 109–
10, 186
as suicidal, 101, 120–22, 125,
126, 232
as supermen, 104–5, 139
and technology, 185–87
treachery, 110–11, 125
as unimaginative, 121–23
Jarman, Sanderford, 143
Joint Chiefs of Staff, 130,
131n, 132, 134, 224–25,
239
Jones, James, 53, 81, 156, 246,
255, 267

kamikaze attacks, 168
Keegan, John, 6, 14, 138
Kennard, Richard C., 70, 76,
144, 155–56, 161, 165,

167, 174–75, 184, 197,
224
Kennedy, David, 47
King, Ernest J., 131
Kojo, battle of (1950), 232
Korean soldiers compared to
Japanese, 230–32, 266
Korean War (1950–53)
Chinese counteroffensive,
92, 219, 228–29, 236,
271
civilians, 234–36
Fifth Chinese offensive, 238
"Great Debate," 239
losses, 227
marine attitudes toward
Army, 226–29, 236–37
mobilization, 219–21
Operation Killer (1951), 238
Operation Ripper (1951),
238
peace negotiations, 233
protracted operations, 233
replacements, 238
rotation system, 238
Koto-ri, North Korea, 235
Kyushu, Japan, 209

Lamour, Dorothy, 70
Lea, Homer, 93
Lea, Tom, 156–58
painting, 159
Leckie, Robert, 67, 69, 71, 78,
198–99, 238, 254
Leed, Eric J., 9, 15, 47, 51, 73,
246, 248
Lejeune, John A., 27–29, 33
LeMay, Curtis E., 167
Leyendecker, Joe, 26
Leyte campaign (1944), 134
Liddell Hart, B.H., 264
Life, 156
Light Brigade, Charge of the
(1854), 142